————————————FIFTH EDIT

HOW TO BE A
WORKING
ACTOR

THE INSIDER'S GUIDE TO

FINDING JOBS IN

THEATER, FILM, AND TELEVISION

MARI LYN HENRY & LYNNE ROGERS

FOREWORD BY

JOE MANTEGNA

HOW TO BE A
WORKING
ACTOR

MARI LYN HENRY & LYNNE ROGERS

Back Stage Books
an imprint of Watson-Guptill Publications/New York

Copyright © 2008 by Mari Lyn Henry and Lynne Rogers

ISBN: (13) 978-0-8230-8895-9
ISBN: (10) 0-8230-8895-2

Printed in the United States

Back Stage Books, an imprint of Watson-Guptill Publications
Nielsen Business Media, a division of The Nielsen Company
770 Broadway, New York, NY 10003
www.watsonguptill.com

Library of Congress Control Number: 2007922227

All photographs are used with the kind permission of the actors and photographers.

Chapter 19: "The Theatre Audition: Creating Characters for a Monologue":
For information about John Whitney, author, *Flood,* contact Charles Sexton at the Walden
Theatre, csexton@waldentheatre.org

Excerpt from *Voices in the Dark* is published by Broadway Publishing, Inc., 56 E. 81st Street,
New York, NY 10028, www.broadwayplaypubl.com

Chapter 20: "The Soap Opera Audition: Creating Characters for Daytime Dramas":
Scenes in Seconds, permission granted by Jeanne Davis Glynn

Chapter 21, "The Prime Time Series Audition: Creating Characters for Episodic Television":
For information about Caitlin Willenbrink, author, *Let's Be Bricks,* contact Charles Sexton at
the Walden Theatre, csexton@waldentheatre.org.

Goober's Descent is from *Impassioned Embraces* by John Pielmeier, copyright © 1989
Courage Productions, John Pielmeier, President
CAUTION: *Goober's Descent* in this volume is reprinted by permission of the author and
Dramatists Play Service, Inc. 440 Park Avenue South, New York, NY 10016. No stock or
amateur production of the play may be given without obtaining, in advance, the written
permission of the author who can be contacted at john@highlands.com.

Excerpt from *Building 116* is given with the permission of the author Dan Ramm, writer/producer.

The use of scripted excerpts from *Joan of Arcadia* is courtesy of CBS Broadcasting Inc.

Chapter 22, "The Film Audition: Creating Characters for Movies": The use of the excerpt from
Sybil by John Pielmeier is courtesy © Warner Bros. Entertainment Inc. All rights reserved.

1 2 3 4 5 6 7 8 9 / 15 14 13 12 11 10 09 08

CONTENTS

This book is dedicated to the men in our lives.

This book could not have been written without the assistance and support we received from our many, many friends and industry professionals.

Actors • Agents • Artistic Directors • Casting Directors • Directors • Managers • Online Entrepreneurs • Photographers • Producers • Teachers • Union Representatives

And the members of professional organizations on both coasts, in regional markets, and throughout the world who were happy to be interviewed, who responded to our e-mails, and who provided insight and generously volunteered to share their expertise.

We are very grateful to Dan Ramm, John Pielmeier, and the young writers at the Walden Theatre for allowing us to use their work. We give special thanks to Jeanne Davis Glynn, who passed away in the summer of 2007, for her generosity in giving us a unique sample of her soap writing skill for our Script Analysis Section.

Special thanks also to the Apple Creative Team: Matty Gregg, Scott Peterman, Becky Morrow, and Edmund Choi.

We are extremely grateful to our best friend on the Internet, Google.

MARI LYN HENRY, partner, Henry Downey Talent Management LLC, has advised thousands of actors on how to have successful careers in film, television, and theater for more than thirty-five years.

Upon leaving her position as Director of Casting, East Coast, for ABC, which she held for more than thirteen years, she launched an image and career consultation business. For many years she has taught workshops and given seminars on on-camera techniques, script analysis, marketing strategies, and impression management in cities and universities across the country. Her seminars on The Business of Show Business are based on the best-selling book *How To Be A Working Actor.* For more information about Mari Lyn's seminars and workshops, visit www.howtobeaworkingactor.com.

LYNNE ROGERS has been "the voice" of a slew of nationally advertised products as well as a producer of instructional video series. Her first book, The Love of Their Lives, is a behind-the-scene look at the soap opera industry. She has since written about the theater for American Heritage magazine, and is the author of Working in Show Business: Behind-the-Scenes Careers in Theater, Films, and Television.

Lynne has served on the National and Local Boards of AFTRA and on the Board of Governors of the National Academy of Television Arts & Sciences (earning their medal for Distinguished Service).

She is currently Co-President of the League of Professional Theater Women.

Having been a working actor for almost forty years, it's little wonder I've been intrigued by a book containing that very phrase in its title: *How to Be a Working Actor*. When I think about it, that one word "working," appearing before the word "actor," speaks volumes about the art and the profession so many of us have chosen, which probably includes yourself if you're reading this foreword.

The word "actor" has been bandied about a lot over the centuries, and not always kindly. Whenever one deals with an art form, there's the risk of the inevitable scrutiny the outside world will subject it to. Call yourself a doctor, or a lawyer, or practically any other sort of profession, and you will at least be capable of conjuring up a degree of education and competence that you must have had in order to earn that title. It's when you get into the more abstract areas such as music, art, or acting that the conjuring becomes blurred, and it becomes totally a matter of perception as to what constitutes a musician, an artist, or an actor. Add the term "working" in front of those words and you have made an important leap into an area that separates the men from the boys (pardon the chauvinistic aspects of the statement). A lot of people call themselves actors, but not a lot are able to call themselves working ones. That's the beauty of this book. In an industry rife with impracticality, here is something that is chock-full of practicality. With its vast array of knowledgeable facts and numerous techniques and tips, the book gives readers invaluable information to help them achieve the jump that takes them from an inspired dream to a practical profession.

There's no getting around the fact that making a living in the acting profession is as hard as the jokes have made it out to be. But knowing that only increases the importance of having as many tools as possible to help guide and educate whoever pursues it. It's no wonder this book has had so many editions. Its value was evident when it first came out; its value is as cur-rent and pertinent today. Read it, take what you can and what you need from it, and most of all enjoy the ride. Being an actor is a noble dream; being a working actor is a noble profession. I wish you all the luck and twice the fun.

"If you're not afraid, if you take everything you are, everything worthwhile in you and direct it at one goal, one ultimate mark, you've got to get there."

—James Dean

You are about to enter a strange and wondrous land.

You are approaching that singular community of theater-TV-films that lies somewhere between the Twilight Zone and the Land of Oz and is known as "The Business." It is a world of bright lights and of frenzy, crowded with inhabitants who love what they do with a fervent passion that sustains them, often for years, and enables them to exist under primitive conditions, working frequently for no compensation other than the thrill of participating in each endeavor, and the shimmering prospect of future greatness.

That's how it has been for generations.

That's the way it *was*.

However, since the end of the twentieth century, two major occurrences have transformed that world, everybody's world: the shocking terrorist attacks on September 11, 2001, and the emergence of what has been termed the "Information Superhighway."

Who could have imagined, even so many years after the 9/11 attack on the World Trade Center, that the formerly bustling neighborhoods of lower Manhattan would still be hurting? And while the area is widely acknowledged to be the financial capital of the world, it is also home for a roster of revered Off-Broadway theater companies that for decades had presented stimulating works by emerging and established playwrights, with wonderful actors playing to standing-room-only crowds. However, after 9/11, the city was in shock after the sudden devastation and death. Understandably, New Yorkers as well as tourists were afraid to go anywhere near Ground Zero for a while. The downtown theaters would struggle to regain a portion of the clientele they lost as a result of that horrible day. Recovery would not happen overnight. According to the many theater owners and managers we've spoken to, only now are they beginning, very slowly, to count a few more friendly faces on the ticket buyers' line.

Within the same time period of the attacks of September 11, 2001, the entertainment business has also found itself catapulted into a turbulent new universe where theater-TV-films have been joined, or as some say, confronted by an aggressive new contender for their audiences' attention: digital technology.

Think of it: 1,000-plus channels, Movies on Demand, DVDs, interactive programming, TIVO, computer downloads of music, movies, soap opera episodes, and prime-time programs, CD-ROMs, e-mail, text messaging, personal and professional Web sites for anybody, anywhere, to view. Today's cell phones encourage us to take photos whenever we like, wherever we happen to be, and allow us to share them instantly with our friends, to send and receive e-mail, watch broadcast TV, or play video games. On screens the size of postage stamps we can even create programs of our own, and zap them to unknown viewers continents away, for viewing on a screen that could be eighty inches wide. This new entertainment is called *viewer created content*, a product form that emerged in 2006.

Welcome to Cyberspace, where there are no boundaries. Its technological capabilities continue to expand at a breakneck pace. The cumulative effect of these stunning advances has been to change the ways the world does business.

The future, particularly as imagined by Ray Bradbury in *Fahrenheit 451* and by George Orwell in *1984*, is here!

That said, The Business nonetheless remains a very accepting community. Whatever the ultimate means of production, distribution, communication, or display, whether it's meant to be viewed on a gigantic home-theater media center or the tiny screen of a cell phone, *something* will have to be transmitted along those digital-cellular-fiber-optic bands—some bit of material that will make viewers want to return to a channel, revisit a Web site, or possibly induce them to put aside their electronic toys and venture out to experience the singular pleasure of seeing real live performers working in a real live show. In this community there is always room, at least on the outskirts, for a newcomer—someone who thrives on the brightness and the energy and responds to the irresistible lure of personal satisfaction. The primary requisite is dedication. It is the devoted ones who eventually make their way toward the centers of recognition, money, and power.

It is this uniquely personal journey that concerns us now. We are going to provide you with a map, show you how to proceed from where you are now to where you want to be, enjoying a career as a working performer, being part of the delicious excitement that characterizes life in the magical cities of New York and Los Angeles. Along the way we may also open your eyes to opportunities in production centers blossoming across the country in places like Chicago, Miami, and Atlanta.

We have been living in this community for a long time. We know the way. And we have asked our friends—performers whose names or faces you know very well, casting directors, and talent agents, as well as other professionals whose names you will want to know—to share with us the benefit of their experiences in The Business. Their wisdom is here, too.

Some sobering facts before we begin: As we write this guidebook, there are some 200,000 professional performers, by which we mean members of Actors' Equity Association (AEA), Screen Actors Guild (SAG), and the American Federation of Television and Radio Artists (AFTRA) in New York and Los Angeles and their locals and branches around the country. You should be aware that unemployment for performers greatly exceeds the national average. According to the unions' own reports, only about 20 percent of their members earn more than $10,000 per year. Performers who earn more than $25,000 per year constitute about 8 percent of the membership. Only about 2,000 actors earn more than $100,000 per year. They are the ones you recognize working in commercials and in major roles in soap operas, the bankable names in feature films and starring on the Broadway stage.

Do these gloomy numbers mean that you should abandon the idea of trying to make your journey? Only if you are not serious about your commitment. If there is any other work that you can see yourself doing, that will bring you just as much happiness, that offers a higher ratio of success and a far more tranquil existence while demanding less application, then by all means involve yourself in those activities.

"Don't do it. Unless you're insane, unless you love it so much you cannot live without it, unless you're a masochist able to take rejection ninety percent of the time, and acceptance—if you're lucky—ten percent of the time, then you can be an actor."

—Ben Gazzara, award-winning actor

Such advice as that given by Mr. Gazzara shows how hard it is to succeed as a working actor. But you may have a longing that just cannot be denied:

"When I was five years old I told my parents I wanted to be an actress. I wanted to be in a Broadway musical. That's the only thing I wanted to do. And I did it."

—Amy Dolan Fletcher, Actors' Equity Outreach executive

If that is how you feel, if acting is what you know you absolutely must do, welcome to our world.

We believe that despite the numbers, there is always room for talent. Every day another "new" face "makes it." Consider these recent Tony-Award winners, all of them relatively new on Broadway: Idina Menzel in *Wicked*, John Lloyd Young in *Jersey Boys*, Norbert Leo Butz in *Dirty Rotten Scoundrels*, Sara Ramirez in *Monty Python's Spamalot*, Adriane Lenox in *Doubt*.

Meanwhile, TV brought about "overnight" success for actors such as Golden Globe winner Kyra Sedgwick in *The Closer*, and Emmy winners Tony Shalhoub in *Monk*, Brad Garrett in *Everybody Loves Raymond*, and Kiefer Sutherland in *24*.

No one was paying much attention to Adrian Brody before his Academy Award–winning performance in *The Pianist*, or Scarlett Johansson before *Lost in Translation*, Rachel Weisz before *The Constant Gardener*, Jamie Foxx before *Ray*, and Virginia Madsen and Paul Giametti before *Sideways*. Young Dakota Fanning's multifaceted performance in *I Am Sam* boosted her to the level of one of Hollywood's hottest properties.

Each season, Broadway, television, and films feature new showcases with new people, some of whom will endure if they have the necessary drive, persistence, discipline, focus, and smart self-promotion.

Keep in mind that the casting director (or the producer, or the network) and the actor share aspects of the same problem: one is constantly seeking to find new, interesting, arresting talent, and the other is talent hoping to be found. Whenever these two forces get together, the result is always jobs—and careers and recognition and, sometimes, fame and fortune.

Fame and fortune, however, are accidental and they are not the immediate goal of this journey. Too often they are the result of being in the right show in the right season, on the right day of the week, on the right channel, in the right time slot, or in the right commercials or some other outrageous, unpredictable bit of luck.

Julia Roberts is now one of the highest paid movie stars in history, but she was only a tall, thin actress with a very wide smile who had caught the eye of Hollywood in *Mystic Pizza* until she auditioned for and won a role in the movie that made her a star, playing opposite Richard Gere in *Pretty Woman*.

Hugh Jackman had received nice reviews for his work in films, but it was his stunning stage debut as a singing and dancing cyclone in the Broadway musical *The Boy From Oz* that vaulted him to the ranks of international stardom. For the first time in theatrical memory, the star of the show had neither a standby nor an understudy. When Mr. Jackman was due for his much-needed vacation, no actor would attempt to equal his performance. The show simply shut down, and everyone in the cast had a paid hiatus until he returned.

Before you can have a chance at fame and fortune you need to have a job. And to do that you must be a talented, determined performer who knows how to get your work seen by the people who can give you a job. That is what we call knowledgeable job-seeking, and that is what this book—this journey—is all about: getting to the centers of activity and knowing exactly how to function under the wackiest circumstances.

Asked to give a word of advice to students entering the Actors Studio's three-year graduate program, Academy Award winner Paul Newman did indeed deliver one word to the group: "Tenaciousness."

Jobs, careers, and recognition are what we hope you are after. Then you can try for fame and fortune. Are you ready?

PART ONE

NUTS AND BOLTS

CHAPTER 1

What You Will Need to Get Started

"Try to remember that wherever you are is where it's at. And don't think you have to be in a particular place. And don't ever give up and don't ever give in."

–Frank Langella, Tony Award–winning actor

If you were planning a career in dentistry, archeology, or accounting instead of performing, you would not be at all surprised to learn that establishing yourself requires the mastery of specific skills, as well as the investment of serious amounts of time and dollars. Yet show business, more than any other field of endeavor, is so loaded with legends of success achieved by accident, with tales of plucky but enthusiastic amateurs winning out over seasoned professionals, that it is frequently perceived as a fantasy playground even by those who make their living in it.

Every dramatic form has glorified the waif who gets off the bus in Los Angeles or New York with little more than a knapsack, a pair of tap shoes, and a load of moxie. She then collides with a powerful producer, celebrity, or agent who, struck by her artless quality, declares, "You're what this tired old town needs," makes a few phone calls and, in minutes, transforms her into a superstar. Doesn't that sound like the plot of a movie you've seen a couple of times? It's a wonderful story. Let's hope you can audition for the lead when they cast the next remake. In the meantime, let's not confuse that myth with reality.

This book is all about how to be a *working actor*. We do not aim to tell you how to enjoy being a struggling, unemployed actor. While we may acknowledge the magic and passion and the truly immeasurable satisfactions of performing, we have been careful to point out that there are thousands of dedicated professionals who earn very little money.

Auditioning for and winning an acting job is an accomplishment. Doing the job, once you get it, demands total concentration. Having to contend with the pressures of rehearsal, production, and performance while at the same time worrying about whether you'll have enough money to pay the rent is worse than foolish: It's suicidal and should not be attempted. Imagine for a moment that you are not a talented performer, but a computer programmer looking for a job. Would you pack your duffel bag, head for Silicon Valley, and simply hope for the best? Of course not. You'd make certain that you had sufficient resources to enable you to lead a relatively normal life until you found the position you were seeking. Aware that you'd be interviewed by a slew of personnel directors, you'd want nothing to interfere with your ability to impress them as the ideal candidate for their needs. The aspiring performer requires and deserves no less.

Now think of the times you've gone on vacation. Remember the hours of planning? Figuring out whether to fly or drive? Which clothes to pack? And, most important, how much was this trip going to cost? Could you afford it? That's the sort of pre-planning you need to do now.

Before you go anywhere, make a list of what it costs you to live where you are now. Every day, write down every penny you spend on food, clothes, magazines, movies, video rentals, your phone, your utilities, your car—on all the things that make up your current life style. Do this for at least a month. Like so many dieters who are told to keep a food diary and account for every morsel that goes into their mouths, and are aghast to realize how many pounds all those incidental sips and snacks add up to over a four-week period, you may be shocked to see how many dollars you spend on just plain, everyday stuff. If you're living at home, or in a dorm, or if you're sharing an apartment, find out how much it would cost for you to live on your own. This exercise will give you some idea of your current expenses and prepare you for the job you must master—that of being your own financial planner.

YOUR MONEY

In the pages that follow, we are going to explain both the start-up costs and the continuing costs of living sensibly, not lavishly, in New York or Los

Angeles for six months with *no squeeze*. By that we mean you should not need or expect to earn one cent during that starting-out period. We've offered current figures to help you plan, but remember that there is always going to be some inflation; at the rate the world is spinning, everything will surely cost a bit more in the future.

INITIAL COSTS

The first item to consider is what it costs to travel to Los Angeles or to New York City. This trip can be planned far enough in advance to allow you to take advantage of whatever bargain fares may be offered by the buses, trains, or airlines. This may be the time to use your airline frequent flyer miles, and you should search the various Internet travel search engines to find a flight for the price and date you say you want to travel.

Ideally, you should plan a preliminary scouting trip with your family and/or your potential roommate. High school seniors are encouraged to visit several campuses to acquaint themselves with a number of college communities before deciding where to apply for admission; newly hired or transferred corporate personnel are routinely escorted on a tour of their future location. If you've never been to the city before, it makes particularly good sense to do an exploratory trip.

New York and Los Angeles, while totally different in appearance and atmosphere, are both awesome places. Even the most sophisticated traveler needs time to absorb their impact. Yes, you will be dumbfounded by New York's tall buildings and the huge numbers of people hurrying along the streets at all hours of the night and day. Yes, in Los Angeles there is smog that you can see, and flotillas of cars perpetually zooming at ninety miles an hour along the endless freeway (or stalled in a mile-long traffic jam).

Devote ten days to two weeks to discovering the places that are, or will be, significant to your life as a performer. See as much as you can of the city in the daytime, beginning with a sightseeing tour. Listen to the spiel of the tour guides and feel free to ask questions; many guides are, or have been, actors: they enjoy the opportunity to personalize a tour with special details or bits of insider information, and they appreciate passengers who exhibit particular interest. Then, venture out on your own. Scout for your location, just as a production company would do when shooting sequences outside the studio. You are seeking the best background for you—and trying to effect a workable compromise between comfort and affordability.

It should not be necessary to squander thousands of dollars on this visit. This is not the time to indulge in the splendors of the Four Seasons or the Beverly Hills hotels (although you may wish to saunter through their lobbies). A growing number of refurbished small hotels near New York's theater district, and/or near the Hollywood power base, offer cleanliness and convenience at a reasonable price. You can find out about the ones in New York, and get information on cultural attractions, as well as maps of subway and bus routes, from NYC & Company (formerly the New York Convention and Visitors Bureau) at 810 Seventh Avenue, New York, NY 10019. Their Web site is www.nycvisit.com. Other Web sites, such as www.priceline.com, www.travelocity.com, www.hotels.com, and www. soyouwanna.com, can give you the cheapest prices for adequate accommodations on both coasts.

Bed-and-breakfast establishments frequently offer attractive accommodations at fairly reasonable rates, often in the residential areas where you may eventually want to look for an apartment. The number of bed-and-breakfast places increases daily. A good network to check out is www. bedandbreakfast.com. Or, you can write to the Bed and Breakfast League, Ltd., 2855 29th Street, NW, Washington, D.C. 20008, (800) GO-B-AND-B.

RENT

Here, of course, is where the major chunk of your capital will go. It should come as no surprise that apartments in New York and Los Angeles cost significantly more than they do in many other cities. In Los Angeles, studio apartments that are approximately 500 square feet will cost $750 a month with a roommate. (For $1,200 a month you might be able to find a two-bedroom apartment in the San Fernando Valley.) Try not to be shocked to learn that the same-size studio can cost $2,200 a month in Manhattan. Or more, or a little less, depending upon the neighborhood. Neighborhoods affect the price of everything, even tomatoes. You should only consider neighborhoods that are decent and safe and apartment buildings that either employ a 24-hour doorman or have a very good security system. It is essential for you to be able to come and go safely at all hours: rehearsals and theater will keep you out late, while calls for TV and film jobs are usually early.

Most actors share apartments. If you have friends or relatives already living in the city to which you're relocating, take advantage of their hospitality. Investigate your alumni network for referrals. If you are unable to find a roommate through these sources, you may want to take advantage of notices posted on the bulletin boards where you take classes, or at the unions, if you are a member. Tack your own "Roommate Wanted" notice up at your health club or dance studio. Besides getting more space for less money, you gain the valuable sense of support that comes from being with people who know and care about you.

It is customary in New York and Los Angeles to pay the first and last month's rent in advance; in Los Angeles you may also pay a security deposit and even a cleaning fee. You will not necessarily be asked to sign a long-term lease, but you will need to commit for a definite time period.

Finding a Place

To get a preview of the housing market in New York, Los Angeles, or any other city, glance through the apartment rental sections in the Sunday editions of their local newspapers, which you can access on the Internet, or find in the current periodicals section of your local library.

The Internet is probably the best place to look for affordable, safe housing. You can go to Google and type in "finding an apartment in New York City/Los Angeles." Visit www.soyouwanna.com for the local wisdom on which areas qualify as "nice" and which may be "less pleasant," as well as the questions to ask about neighborhood characteristics. On this site you can choose a neighborhood or city by zip code and access apartment listings based on how much you want to spend; it even links you to a site for tenants' rights. Other sites include www.villagevoice.com (New York), the apartment classifieds on www.latimes.com (Los Angeles), and www.craigslist.org.

Before you sign a lease do a thorough exploration of the territory. Check out distances to supermarkets, office supply stores, dry cleaners, banks, and any other places you'll patronize regularly.

Sublets and Shares

There are such things as leases for subtenants, but you and the person living in the apartment may simply make a private agreement on a month-to-month basis, which will allow you to move as soon as you've found a place of your own. But before you do business on the basis of a handshake, it's a good idea to specify each person's privileges and responsibilities on a written document, of which both of you will keep a copy.

Let us assume the rent for your one-bedroom apartment is $1,000. You may also be required to pay a broker's fee (which you should ascertain beforehand), and you'll surely have to pay the first and last months' rent, and/or a security deposit.

– Apartment rental, initial cost… $3,000, plus possible additional costs

In an Emergency

Try to find a friend, a classmate, a sorority sister, or a distant cousin who will let you sleep on the sofa for a couple of days.

Backpacking friends, for whom traveling across the country or through-out Europe on the slimmest of budgets is great fun, may suggest you take advantage of the bargain rates at a Youth Hostel or the Y until you can get settled. We say no. Roughing it may be fine for a change of pace, but it's no way to embark on a career. It's unrealistic to expect you'll find a suitable place by "tomorrow afternoon."

In all honesty, if you are so alone, and if your funds are so tight, per-haps the better, smarter plan would be to wait until you've saved the money for a decent place of your own or managed to get a referral to a possible apartment share. You are not embarking on an adventure *vacation*. This ad-venture happens to be your life, and your business. And for that you need a long-term plan.

In New York

The frantic scramble for space in New York has in large part to do with the gradual phasing out of rent stabilization. Often, when long-term ten-ants leave apartments that have been rent stabilized (meaning that rent increases are controlled), landlords are permitted to raise rents to the fair-market level and landlords are free to charge whatever they can get. The rent specified on the lease becomes the amount due each month for the duration of that contract. To add to the complexity of this situation, apart-ments in newer buildings may also be unregulated.

Though the ideal apartment would be in Manhattan, within walking distance of the studios, theaters, and offices, living there is certainly not a necessity. The subways and buses of New York's far-reaching, 24-hour mass transit system make travel uptown, downtown, and to the other bor-oughs—the Bronx, Brooklyn, Queens, and Staten Island—relatively quick, easy, and inexpensive. Upper Manhattan's Washington Heights is just a few subway stops from Midtown. Plenty of performers reside in Long Island City, Astoria, and Jackson Heights, which are convenient residential areas in Queens, and others rave about the attractive, affordable spaces they've found twenty-five minutes from Times Square in Park Slope, Carroll Gardens, Cobble Hill, and Fort Greene, all colorful neighborhoods in Brooklyn. Staten Island probably offers the greatest bargains, although the requisite half-hour ferry ride to and from Lower Manhattan every day may present a challenge, especially when the weather becomes really windy or cold. Wherever you choose to live in New York, you'll probably find that one of the city's appeals is the relative ease of getting around. As theater director John Znidarsic says,

> To me, New York is like the biggest college town. Nothing's more than forty-five minutes away. You can call anybody, get together in a few minutes. In Los Angeles, we'd have to make an appointment, and drive somewhere, and something would happen, so we'd have to reschedule. We'd never get around to what we were thinking about doing in the first place!

Possibly in response to the city's valiant efforts to recover after the devastating attack of 9/11, New York has lately become a magnet for young people in all professions. Only a few years ago, parts of Manhattan's Lower East Side were relatively grungy. Nowadays the neighborhood is thriving, but many of its refurbished apartment buildings are still comparatively affordable (remember, that's by New York standards). Best of all, some of the displaced Off- and Off-Off-Broadway theater companies have relocated to the neighborhood.

Many actors are venturing across the Hudson River to New Jersey to nearby Fort Lee, Weehawken, and Hoboken, which offer housing that is grander and far less costly than anything Manhattan has to offer—and sometimes even boast a spell-binding view of the city's stunning skyline. However, there may be a drawback to living according to a limiting train or bus schedule, for you can miss out on opportunities to spend time networking over coffee with other actors.

In Los Angeles

The housing situation in Los Angeles differs from that in New York to the extent that the entertainment industry plays such an enormous part in the local economy that real estate people are accustomed to serving a transient population—the performers, technicians, and production people who come and go according to TV and motion-picture industry shooting schedules. Furnished apartments can be rented on a monthly basis. Studio apartments may begin at $750. Again, prices will depend upon neighborhood, and in a city seventy miles wide, there are plenty of neighborhoods. The main centers for the motion picture and television industry are Hollywood, Universal City, Century City, Culver City, Beverly Hills, and Burbank.

L.A. actors find the best deals in Valley locations: Studio City, Sherman Oaks, Toluca Lake, Valley Village, Van Nuys, and Burbank, which is a small city-within-a-city. Given the expanse of the Los Angeles area, it is truly impossible to be near everything, which may be why your rent in California includes the cost of garage space for the car that you will definitely need.

A TALE OF TWO CITIES

Actors Kim and Ryan Shively decided that Los Angeles offered greater opportunities for both of them. They knew the move from New York had to be very well planned. Here are their observations:

Kim: *Your house has to be in order. Otherwise you will always be repairing and not preparing. A really good actor spends every day preparing for the future. The lazy actor is always repairing what they didn't get done. We were blessed to come out of our wedding already in a state of preparing.*

Ryan: *You have to be willing to be unemployed for at least a year when you make the transition from New York to Los Angeles. Don't look at unemployment as a curse, but as a blessing. If you are really serious you have to give it at least two years to get established in this business.*

Kim*: You really have to give it three to five.*

Ryan: *Acting in New York is a different game from acting in Los Angeles. After you go through a void period, you realize you have to define what you're doing. In New York, you might have more than one callback and not hear for a month; in Los Angeles, I could be booked as a guest star on an episodic show tomorrow. The trick out here is to enjoy each experience and enjoy meeting people. Less craft, more relationship building. That will take you where you want to go. I so enjoyed meeting a casting director this week, and the audition felt like a nonevent. I talked to her for twenty minutes and then the "Okay, let's* read it." And if you leave feeling like you have enjoyed it, that is the key. In New York, you walk in ready to work.

Kim: *You have to know what you are going to be doing here. A lot more is asked of you. In New York it is pretty basic. You are an actor, you do stage, etc., if a soap comes along, great. Here you have to be intentional about what you want your career to look like. On a personal level you have to be more aware of what you want as a performer. In New York, when you say you are an actor, they want you to prove it. In Los Angeles, everyone's an actor!*

I remember after I did a Toyota ad in New York, I would be sent on commercial auditions with the same twenty-five gals and we got to know each other. Out here there are literally hundreds of gals auditioning! If you come with expectations and only give yourself three months, you are not going to get a really good idea of what is here.

Ryan: *It's a myth that Los Angeles is cheaper than New York. The life style is easier, the weather's nice, and everybody's laid-back, but don't think life in Los Angeles is easier financially. What I paid for rent and travel and transportation in New York now goes into car insurance and payments on two cars.*

Kim: *Stay with four-cylinder cars, because insurance on them costs less and you'll get better gas mileage.*

Ryan: *Try Hollywood Auto and independent car dealers. Walk around, meet the guys, and don't offer the asking price. You can go to Carmax.com and check the bin number and its history to see if the proper maintenance has been done. You can negotiate. They want to move the car. We saw a car listed at five thousand nine hundred dollars, drove it around, saw it needed some new tires. We sat down with them and said we'd offer four thousand six hundred dollars. We demanded new tires, and they gave them to us. Give as much of a down payment as you can on a good used car, two thousand dollars if you can, so the monthly payments will be lower.*

Kim: *Get a printer/copy machine to keep records of everything. When tax time comes around you'd have kept every receipt for deductions.*

Ryan: *It was cheaper for us to hire a mover than to drive our stuff across country, given the price of gas. But these costs are constantly changing. If you are in New York and want to rent a truck, go to Connecticut or New Jersey and save yourself probably one thousand dollars.*

Kim: Give yourself a month to get settled. We had packed our air mattress, computer, headshots, papers, clothes for auditions, and the other items we'd need to live for a month in the back of the car. We packed everything else for the movers.

Ryan: You can come here and not have a clue where you are going to live. Walk around, drive up and down the blocks and you'll see hundreds of vacancies at all times of year and day. Pick up a phone, make an appointment, and look at a place. If you like it, get the credit, and it's a done deal.

Kim: You have to be prepared for the fact that sometimes landlords don't want out-of-state checks. Open a bank account as soon as you can. Find out how long it takes for the money to clear. Then begin to look for your apartment. Have all of your pay stubs, past employment records, tax returns, and references. Have all your credit info in a file. If you are young, you're going to need a parent to cosign with you.

Ryan: I would recommend starting out in the Valley. Everything is here. Studio City, Burbank, fifty percent of your auditions are here. You'll save a lot of gas mileage. Get a job. Starbucks is the best employer, with great health benefits, great hours, part-time shifts, insurance. They really take care of their people. They have hiring fairs. Ask the folks at your local Starbucks when the next one is. And there are temp agencies, like Appleone.com and Royal-jobs.com.

Kim: You have to have a credit card. It is a grown-up thing to function in the world. Ryan uses Microsoft Money software to watch where his money is going. Everything that we spend clicks on something and it shows a pie chart of where all the money goes.

UTILITIES

Heat and water are included in the rent for apartments in New York and Los Angeles. Gas and electricity are usually additional. In New York you are billed monthly for gas and electricity and in Los Angeles you are billed every sixty days. Of course, the more you use appliances, the higher your bill will be. Apartments in Los Angeles do not always come with refrigerators. You can either buy your own, or rent them from the building manager.

   – **Electricity/Gas... $90 to $150 per two-month period**

TRANSPORTATION

No matter where you decide to live, it is necessary to remember that money will be needed for transportation to auditions, interviews, rehearsals, and jobs.

Getting Around Los Angeles

Los Angeles has been described as a sprawl of suburbs in search of a city. The quintessential complaint, "There is no there there," has been variously credited to Lillian Hellman, Dorothy Parker, and Gertrude Stein. Whoever said it was right. You can drive for hours along crowded highways, passing through one small community after another, and never reach anything that looks like the center of town. Quartered in modern office towers or cozy bungalows, production houses, networks, studios, and casting people are scattered in all directions.

By Bus

Los Angeles does have a bus and rail system, the Metropolitan Transit Authority, serving greater Los Angeles from the San Fernando Valley to northern Orange County. The MTA's 2,500 buses and 54 light rail cars run twenty-four hours, seven days a week over 200 routes. There are also local city buses: Culver City Municipal Bus Line, the Glendale Bee Line, and the Santa Monica Bus Line. Check the local telephone directory (in Los Angeles each community has its own directory and area code) for the number to call for instructions on getting to your destination. You can request route maps from the Los Angeles Convention and Visitors Bureau. Buses supposedly run every twenty minutes, which suggests that you could memorize one or two of Hamlet's soliloquies while waiting for the right bus to come along. Excellent for seeing the town, buses are not for actors doing serious job hunting.

To lessen air pollution, the DASH shuttle service operates Monday through Saturday for short runs within heavily trafficked areas, using small buses or mini vans powered by propane/natural gas.

You can get information on some L.A. area bus and rail routes at www.mta.net.

By Taxi

Los Angeles, like New York, has plenty of taxis and you can hail them as they cruise by or phone the local cab company before you are ready to leave;

allow ten to twenty minutes pickup time. Cab companies serve specific areas: there's a Valley Cab Company, for example, to take you from wherever you are in the valley to downtown, but you may need to use another cab company, such as LA Checker, which serves the downtown area, to take you from that appointment back to the valley. For easy reference, keep a list of taxi company numbers in your address book or electronic organizer.

However, taxis in Los Angeles are so costly ($30 for a short ride is not uncommon) you should consider this mode of travel only for dire emergencies.

By Car

Driving your own car is the only sensible way to get around Los Angeles, and unless you drive to the city or plan to buy a car once there, you'll probably want to rent a car for your stay. Lower-cost options include Rent A Wreck (www.rentawreck.com), which offers vehicles that are far from decrepit and are just a few seasons away from being new. Drivers who prefer newer models can learn all about them on the Web sites of the many nationally and locally advertised rental outlets. The lowest monthly rates hover around $750, plus insurance.

Many people recommend leasing cars directly from local auto dealers. They say the costs are lower, and the cars and service are better. You can find out about the latest local rental or leasing charges on the Internet; to get started, simply type "car leasing in Los Angeles" into the Google search engine.

For security purposes, car rental and leasing establishments require a credit card for payment, and many companies require that renters be twenty-five or older; Rent A Wreck is the only company we know of that rents to drivers who are eighteen, and they must have their own car insurance.

If you know that you're going to stay in Los Angeles for at least a year, it might be sensible to buy a car. Do so before you arrive in California, where you will be required to pay an impact fee of $300, as well as a registration fee, and the car you buy will need to pass a smog check.

Membership in the Automobile Association of America (AAA) is a necessity. The annual fee of $40, plus the cost of the original application, buys access to an extensive database of travel routes, updates on driving conditions, and the assurance that on that rare occasion when you find yourself in unfamiliar territory with a car that won't start, help is just a phone call away.

- Car rental... from $150 per week; $500 to $700 per month
- Car insurance... $1,200 or more, per year
- Other protection (such as OnStar, GPS, The Club, Alarm, etc.)... price varies as needed

What about car repairs? Certainly you'll want to entrust your car to a shop with warranties that cover repairs. You want people who are reliable, know your car's eccentricities, and can get it back to you quickly.

To the cost of renting, or leasing, operating, and insuring your vehicle, you must add the daily expense of parking at or near each office you visit. Everyone tries to find parking on the street. But, in Los Angeles, as in New York, it seems the minute your time on the meter expires, a ticket appears on the windshield. The fine will be even heavier when you are parking in a residential area or a No Parking zone. To avoid the risk, figure you're going to have to wait for any audition and buy more time than you think you'll actually need. A lot of municipalities now have parking meters that allow you to use debit and credit cards, but many don't, so it's still useful to carry rolls of quarters to feed the meter.

On business calls, you may often park for free if you have your parking lot or garage ticket validated by a company receptionist. Always ask in advance about validated parking, since the cost for thirty minutes in a parking garage can be four dollars to eight dollars. Parking lots at shopping malls allow two hours' free parking. So, when their appointments are nearby, smart actresses wear comfortable shoes for driving and walking, carry their high heels, and walk to the audition. "Better to schlep and save money," is the motto.

Caveat: No matter where you park, be sure to take your belongings with you, even if you don't think anyone can see them. This means take anything portable, such as your cell phone, camera, and other electronic equipment, DVDs, and change of outfit. Car theft is epidemic in Los Angeles.

- Parking... $20 and up per week

Rules and Regulations

One of the stops on your exploratory trip to California should be at the Department of Motor Vehicles to acquire a copy of the *California Drivers' Handbook* and *The Registration Handbook*. If you own your car, find out about the state's regulations concerning private vehicles. There are requirements for smog certification, registration, service and vehicle license fees, and a use tax. Members of AAA can get this information from their local offices. Also check the bookstores and/or the Internet for Thomas street guides (www.thomasguidebooks.com). Long considered to be invaluable for getting around Los Angeles, a copy should be among the things you buy when you get to town and have in your car at all times. You'll also find www.mapquest.com, where you can punch in an address to get a route map and driving instructions, to be useful.

Getting Around New York

Unlike Los Angeles, New York is a walking city, and the ease of getting around is further enhanced by an elaborate subway system and dozens of bus lines. For the most part, theater, film, and television offices are clustered in or near the heart of Manhattan, which is about a mile wide at 42nd Street. The farthest outposts—the Kaufman Astoria (Queens) Film Studios, Chelsea Piers (Twelfth Avenue, Manhattan), and the Long Island City (Queens) Silvercup Studio—can all be reached by bus or subway.

By Bus and Subway

It's possible you'll find yourself having a commercial audition at an advertising agency on East 54th Street and Third Avenue, followed by an interview for a play reading on the west side at 42nd Street and Tenth Avenue on Theater Row, and then an acting class downtown on Bank Street in Greenwich Village.

You can take buses and subways to all of these appointments. The current fare is two dollars per ride. Exact change is required on buses; drivers do not make change, and the fare boxes on buses do not accept paper money.

Fortunately, MetroCards now make it easy to travel throughout the city without loading your pockets or purses full of tokens or heavy coins. Purchase a card, for any amount up to $80, at a subway station change booth or at the self-service MetroCard vending machines, which accept credit and debit cards. Then, whenever you go through a subway turnstile or board a bus, you swipe the card through a sensor; a small electronic screen shows the amount deducted for your fare and how much you have left on your card. Free transfers, within two hours, are permitted between bus and subway routes. When the balance on your card falls below the cost of a ride, simply present the card, with as much money as you wish to add, to the change booth attendant at any station, or use your credit card to refill it at a vending machine. If you travel by bus and subway frequently, you'll probably find that you'll save quite a bit of money with cards that allow you to make unlimited rides for $7 a day, $24 for seven days, and $76 for thirty days. However, unless you have a regular routine (such as a steady job) and don't use public transportation every day, you can waste money on time-sensitive cards, because you won't be utilizing the amount you spend for them.

– New York mass transit... $24 or less per week

By Taxi

You should come to think of taxis rides as rare luxuries. They start at $2.90, and each one-ninth of a mile costs 40 cents. After 8:00 P.M. there's an additional nighttime charge of one dollar. Rarely will a trip cost less than six or seven dollars, plus tip for the driver. Fares are subject to change (which means they will go up) with each negotiation of the taxi owners' and drivers' agreements.

By Bike

Bike riding in New York, despite the heavy street traffic, happens to be an efficient way to get about town. However, bike security—where you can safely park your wheels while you are at your audition—may be a problem. We've seen actors approach the receptionist's desk with one bike wheel in hand. Sometimes, actors walk their bikes right off the elevator and park them in the waiting area. Of course, if you're going to an office on the fourth floor of a walk-up, that may not be a practical approach, and you are not allowed to bring bikes into many buildings. A number of buildings do have bike-parkers near the entrance. When in doubt, inquire when you set up the appointment. You may have to leave your bike on the street and put your trust in heavy chains and locks.

YOUR BIZ PHONE

Most actors today depend solely on their cell phones for their professional and personal needs. The phone is your lifeline to jobs, appointments, news about what's happening in The Business and at home, and just plain gossip. Apartment sharers should have separate telephones.

Cell phone companies continually offer new calling plans for local and long-distance calls. Monthly charges can range from $50 or less to as much as $120. Investigate the services available in your calling area and decide which plan works best for you. Once you've made your choice, it's still a good idea to check with the phone company every few months; a new offer may be a better bargain than the one you originally selected.

No matter the phone or the plan you choose, always remember to keep the phone's battery fully charged. How many times have you missed a call because your phone was dead? Or you lost the person you were speaking to right in mid-sentence because you'd forgotten to check your battery? Make charging your phone a part of your daily routine.

You might want to invest in a voice-mail service. This way, agents, managers, casting directors, and other business-related callers can always reach you at the number you give them, even if you change your cell phone number, if your cell phone is lost or stolen, or if you move from one town to another. Fees for voice-mail providers range from four dollars to ten dollars a month. In New York, www.messagebureau.com offers voice mail for $7.95 per month, with up to 250 messages. Caller ID, date, time stamp, unlimited email and pager notification are included. Also check out www.weanswer.com, which is nationwide.

If you have a land line you can install a telephone answering machine or buy a phone with a built-in answering device; the one-time purchase price is the entire cost of your investment, and these machines provide a simple way to keep track of your personal and business calls. Be sure to select an answering machine that is highly rated, with a simple call-in system. Look for machines that let you change your out-going message while you're away, store messages, tell you what time calls came in, and even keep a record of the caller's phone number. Voice mail from Verizon or another carrier, in which voice mail is accessible by a call-in number, is also very handy and easy. Above all, get in the habit of checking your messages frequently. If you don't return calls right away, callers may fear that the machine isn't working or that you're not interested, and move on to the next person on the list. It's been known to happen.

You can also purchase an answering machine equipped with a fax, which can be a lifesaver when you're expecting to receive professional documents.

- Telephone answering machine... $20 to $200
- With fax... from $200

The outgoing message on your phone, answering machine, or voice-mail service should sound intelligent and cheerful. Always record a message with a smile. An example is, "Hello, you've reached Amanda Chapman. Sorry I'm unable to take your call. Please leave your name and number, and I will get back to you as soon as possible." Do not leave a laid-back greeting such as, "Hi, it's me. Leave a number and I'll get back to ya," or "You're there. I'm not here. You know what to do."

Avoid gimmicks and attitude. Speak slowly so the caller can understand your message. Conversely, when you're the one who leaves a message, speak clearly and slowly so the listener can understand your name and numbers.

BEEPERS AND PAGERS

As it becomes increasingly important to answer messages almost as soon as the calls are placed, you may want to consider easy-to-carry beepers or pagers that let you know instantly when there is a call for you. These devices make it possible for you to be on alert with everyone connected to your business at all times. You pay a few cents per minute of air time when you retrieve messages, and some services assign you a local voice mail phone number that you can keep even if you change your address. You can also get your own personal 800 number; this additional, relatively small investment makes it easy for people in other cities to contact you.

- Beeper and pagers... $20 and up per month

FOOD

New York and Los Angeles boast thousands of fantastic restaurants at all price levels—but dining out is one adventure you should treat yourself to only on special occasions. Let's be real: Eating in restaurants is never cheap. So, if you've not yet mastered the technique of boiling water, let alone an egg, consider this a marvelous opportunity to learn. In both Los Angeles and New York there are plenty of markets offering fine, fresh produce, as well as additive-free locally raised meats, fish, and poultry, in addition to all the canned and packaged stuff you grew to love at home.

What we cannot overemphasize is the need to nourish yourself adequately. No one can bear up under the rigors of a twelve-hour camera day while consuming a diet of junk food, soft drinks, and candy bars. Treating yourself poorly will show on your face, and this is a close-up business. Sharing meals with friends, roommates, or scene partners is a way to reinforce relationships while making certain that you take the time to eat well.

Start with Mark Bittman's excellent basic *How to Cook Everything*, or the equally useful *Cooking for Dummies*, written by former *New York Times* restaurant critic Bryan Miller. For comfort food with a theatrical background, treat yourself to esteemed actress Uta Hagen's classic *Love for Cooking*; it's loaded with tasty, actor-friendly recipes, plus a sprinkling of gossip. Learn a few tricks watching the roster of celebrity chefs on the Food Network.

Two proven ways to economize: Always make a list and never shop for food when you're hungry (you'll want to buy everything in sight).

 – Food... $120 and up per week (for two people)

Add to the cost of your food whatever beverages you're accustomed to drinking.

THE "SCHMOOZE" FACTOR

Give yourself a separate budget category called "Incidentals." This is for lunches, snacks, and just hanging out with friends at Starbucks. Swapping career advice, choosing audition scenes, running lines, critiquing each other's performance, and shooting the breeze are all part of maintaining a healthy, positive attitude. Managing the time and the cost of "hanging out" can be tricky. It all depends on what your lifestyle permits.

A New York actor who relocated to Los Angeles told us:

> One good thing about Los Angeles is that everybody wants to meet you for breakfast. Six o'clock in the morning I'm driving to Marina del Rey! But I must tell you it's a lot cheaper than going out to dinner. And nobody drinks. I mean, if I was out at night and I just might have had a couple of beers or whatever, and some cop happened to stop me, he could take my license. DWI. I lose that and I am out of business. Dead.

For nondriving New Yorkers, the ubiquitous chains of gourmet coffee bars are comfortable, convenient, relatively inexpensive, nonalcoholic meeting places. And if coffee makes you too hyper, most of them now offer a selection of teas, along with cakes, cookies, and simple sandwiches. So do cyber-cafes, where a limited menu of tasty food, but no alcohol, is served. No one pressures you to order anything. There's no risk of overindulging and no worry about how you're going to feel the next day, let alone what condition you'll be in as you drive home.

> – **Incidentals... $150 per month**

ENTERTAINMENT

Movies, theater, ballet, and concerts represent more than diversion for you: They are invaluable opportunities to learn more about your business. You should see as much as you can. Of course, with first-run movie tickets costing as much as $11, and Broadway orchestra seats going for more than $100, this can be a costly assignment. Fortunately, there are ways to pay less than the regular price for theater tickets.

In New York, there are several programs that promote live theater. Among them is the Theatre Development Fund (TDF), which operates TKTS booths that sell discount tickets for same-day performances and have been a boon to audiences and producers. There are two TKTS booths in Manhattan: the original one at West 47th Street and Broadway, in the heart of Times Square and the theater district, and a second booth, downtown at the South Street Seaport. The TKTS booths do not accept credit or debit cards or personal checks. You must pay cash or use travelers' checks. And be prepared to stand in line a while.

TDF also offers mail order and online sales of selected theater, cabaret, and dance tickets at cut-rate prices to members (membership costs $25 per year). In addition, TDF sells vouchers in sets of four for $36; these are open tickets that can be used at the discretion of the box office at some Broadway theaters, as well as at numerous showcase and Off-Off-Broadway productions of theater, music, and dance. The opportunity to see new, innovative works that you might otherwise have ignored is a great way to expand your own artistic and critical sense. Write to TDF, 1501 Broadway, New York, NY 10036, or go to www.tdf.org.

Reduced-price tickets to long-running Broadway shows, commonly called "twofers," are available through local merchants, or in person at the Hit Show Club, 630 Ninth Avenue, 8th floor, New York, NY 10036. Give them your name and address and they'll mail the vouchers to you each month. Other outfits offering reduced-price tickets include Audience Extras, Inc., with which a deposit of $115 entitles you to see any number of shows for three dollars per person. For further details go to www.audienceextras.com.

Some Broadway shows that are selling out make standing room available at very low cost; the line begins about two hours before curtain time. At some plays, such as *Rent* and *Spamalot*, a limited number of bargain-price student tickets are available for each performance.

At institutional (member subscription) theaters, such as Manhattan Theater Club, Playwrights Horizons, Second Stage, the Mint Theater, the Vineyard, and the Irish Repertory Company (to name just a few), you can volunteer to usher for free. Aside from seeing the show, you can introduce yourself to people who produce plays for which you might audition. You meet other actors or artists who are doing the same thing, thus involving yourself in a larger network. You can also occasionally enjoy free performances around the city. During the summer New Yorkers can see live performances by such stellar actors as Meryl Streep and Kevin Kline when the New York Shakespeare Festival performs at the open-air Delacorte Theater in Central Park. It costs nothing to attend the theater, music, and dance programs at the Bruno Walter Auditorium of the Library of Performing Arts in Lincoln Center, or at the Donnell Library on West 53rd Street, and in many branch libraries throughout the city.

Symphony Space, in a former movie palace on the Upper West Side, is one of several venues that offer a wide variety of performances at a lower cost. Check the arts and leisure sections of your Sunday papers, *Time Out New York*, and *New York* magazine for inexpensive programs around town. Plays at Off-Off-Broadway theaters are also often much less expensive than offerings on Broadway and Off-Broadway. Members of Actors' Equity Association frequently receive free passes to plays on Broadway and Off-Broadway. These are distributed at Equity headquarters (165 West 46th Street) on the day of performance.

Screen Actors Guild (SAG) members can join the union's Film Society. The $100 annual fee admits two people to screenings of more than twenty films each year, which averages out to less than three dollars per person, per showing.

DVD rentals provide some of the least expensive entertainment. These are excellent resources when you're researching a role, a script, a new adaptation of a classic, or the work of a director you're going to meet. Netflix and other online subscriber services offer an especially inexpensive way to see a lot of films for relatively little money. Don't forget the myriad opportunities to see great screen performances on the cable channels, including AMC, Bravo, IFC, Sundance, TCM, and TMC. Charges will, of course, depend upon your service provider.

— **Entertainment… only what you can afford**

PROFESSIONAL ORGANIZATIONS

Every profession has its particular clubs, associations, leagues, and coalitions, groups of people engaged in the same or related kinds of work, who get together regularly to discuss what's going on in their world. It should come as no surprise that within The Business there are many, many such societies, which are dues-paying organizations.

In most cases, the members are seasoned professionals, energetic in fulfilling their group's specific mission. With so much to do, they welcome new people. All of which translates into excellent opportunities for associating with colleagues on a congenial basis, and for learning about important aspects of The Business that aren't taught in schools.

The National Academy of Television Arts and Sciences (www. nyemmys.org) is the preeminent membership organization serving the television industry. Members come from all areas, from production to direction to managerial, and from all the major companies in the industry: networks, unions, guilds, and more. These organizations join to bestow the annual Emmy and Daytime Emmy Awards.

The Academy was founded in 1955, in New York, by newspaper-columnist-turned-variety-show-host Ed Sullivan, the originator and master of ceremonies of television's first variety program, *Your Show of Shows*. It has been said that more than half of America tuned in to CBS every Sunday at eight o'clock to watch Ed Sullivan. Over the years they saw him introduce America to the Beatles, Elvis Presley, Dame Margot Fonteyn of the Royal Ballet dancing with Rudolf Nureyev, and a tiny puppet named Topo Gigio, among many hundreds of other talented professionals. Catch the movie version of *Bye Bye Birdie* just to see Paul Lynde's show-stopping rendition of the song about his lifetime goal, to be on "Ed Sullivan."

New York Women in Film & TV (NYWIFT) and Women in Film (WIF) in Los Angeles, include performers as well as writers, directors, agents, casting directors, producers, programming executives, and technical people. They occasionally have screenplay readings every season, and cast from their files. Nonmembers may attend for a nominal fee. NYWIFT, 6 East 39th Street, New York, NY 10016, www.nywift.org; WIF, 8857 West

Olympic Boulevard, Beverly Hills, Suite 201, CA 90211, www.wif.org.

Women in Theater, based in Los Angeles, is a full-service organization where you can take classes; work on scenes; attend seminars; meet agents, casting directors and photographers; prepare staged readings; and network with colleagues. 11684 Ventura Boulevard, Suite 444, Studio City, CA 91604.

The Lambs, the oldest theatrical club in America, boasts a long list of musical and variety performers as active members. During the theater season their Friday night Low Jinks performances provide an informal opportunity to meet theater stalwarts, and to join them in a song or production. Members working on a project may reserve rehearsal space at no charge. Particularly pleasant for business appointments, it's centrally located, with a good kitchen and bar staff, and there's never a check to pay: The member simply signs the tab, and charges are billed monthly. 3 West 51st Street, New York, NY 10020.

The Episcopal Actors Guild, a generous charitable organization, makes its headquarters in the legendary Little Church Around the Corner, at 1 East 29th Street, New York, NY 10016. The Guild's monthly calendar of activities includes programs by actors, singers, musicians, comedians, poets, and writers, or a medley of all disciplines. Original program ideas are welcomed.

The Hispanic Organization of Latin Actors (HOLA) has since 1975 been the New York beacon for Spanish-speaking performers, the place where Latino performers get together, to help one another get meaningful work in the United States.

Executive Director, Manuel Alfaro, recalls:

> Opportunities were extremely limited because no Spanish language commercials were being produced, other than hiring an actor to dub the Spanish track on a regular English commercial. It hurt us as actors. The negative stereotypes—the criminal with the moustache, the cigar, and the heavy accent—limited us in the minds of casting directors, who kept saying, "Where are the actors?" And we said, "We're here!" Little by little, showing what we could do, we made them aware of us. I booked my first Spanish commercial when I was thirty-two. From then on I was able to make a living in this business.

HOLA is one of several artistic enterprises housed in a landmark building at 107 Suffolk Street, a huge 1898 marble-fronted former schoolhouse on Manhattan's Lower East Side. Artists from many countries perform here for the Spanish Language Repertory company of New York. Also on the premises is The Puerto Rican Traveling Theater, the only children's traveling theater company, which recently celebrated its twenty-first anniversary.

HOLA's Web site, www.hellohola.org, features a members' online talent directory that casting directors may access at any time, and then request a performer's photo and résumé. HOLA Pages lists Spanish-language theater companies in the United States, as well as their casting calls and auditions. There is now a playwright's unit as well.

These are merely a few of the dozens of organizations with which you might become affiliated. A database search, or simple networking, will lead you to others. *Time Out New York* carries information about places that aren't on the usual radar. Or, you might consider forming your own group. We've met actors who've done that. We discuss them in Chapter 13, "Finding a Vehicle to Showcase Your Talent."

CREATING YOUR NEST

The amount you spend for furniture, linens, utensils, and appliances will depend upon your bargain-hunting skills, your sense of style, and whether the apartment you find is already furnished or is a pristine, empty space waiting to be transformed into your personal environment. Some furnished apartments may be stocked with china and glass, flatware, and a slew of kitchen utensils, in addition to the requisite sofa, tables, and chairs. Others may provide only the barest essentials to qualify as "furnished."

Thanks to the growing number of big-box home furnishings chains, good design and good quality at sensible prices are easy to find. Best of all, stores such as IKEA; Home Depot; Bed, Bath and Beyond; Kmart; Staples; Office Depot; Office Max; Target; and Sears now employ capable salespeople, trained to offer space-saving and money-saving advice, should you need it. All of these stores have Web sites to help you locate the center nearest you.

Make sure the bed you'll be sleeping on provides proper support. There are few things more aging to your face or detrimental to your body and general health than inadequate sleep and bad sleeping posture. Even if space is tight in your apartment, look for a sofa bed or sleep sofa with a firm mattress and spring combination. They exist. Search for sales. Get the best you can afford.

　　– Sleep sofa or sofa bed... as much as $500

A traditional mattress and box spring may cost about $500. If you wish to purchase a platform-style bed, allow a bit more than half of that for the mattress alone.

– **Mattress and box spring... depends on size**

Smart shoppers know that taking advantage of white sales—held in January, May, and August—and patronizing discount outlets from coast to coast saves money on linens and towels. Buy at least two sets of linens, so you can use one while the other is being laundered.

– **Bed linens... $150 and up, per set**

– **Towels, bath mat, shower curtain... $120 and up**

Other necessities are a clock radio, a toaster oven, a coffeemaker, and a can opener—the foolproof, handheld kind—and without a doubt, a microwave oven.

– **Clock radio... $20 to $80**

– **Can opener... $12**

– **Toaster oven... $50**

– **Coffeemaker... $40 and up**

– **Microwave... about $100 (depends on size and features)**

Items you may not need to purchase but which you should have are grooming aids such as an electric razor, styling/blow-dryer, and hot rollers.

PROTECTION DEVICES

Nowadays it takes more than a lock on your door to keep your premises burglarproof. On the other hand, scenes (as in Neil Simon's uproarious The Sunshine Boys and The Prisoner of Second Avenue) where neurotic characters arrive home at the end of a day and meticulously close six or more complicated bolts, and then, just as laboriously, must open every one of them whenever someone comes to call, are best left for comedy. Sensible protection lies somewhere between these two extremes: foolproof deadbolt locks, such as a Medeco, and sturdy bars or gates on accessible windows, patio doors, and fire escapes.

Or, you may opt for an alarm system that alerts an outside security company in case of emergency. The community liaison at the local police precinct will be able to advise you. Remember, while you want to keep intruders out, you also want people to be able to get in, should you need assistance.

– **Protection devices... prices vary**

– **Alarm system... $1,000 installation; $350 annual maintenance**

YOUR HOME OFFICE

As the executive in charge of your life in show business, it's time to behave like a CEO and set up your home office, ASAP.

Check out The Business supplier Web sites, such as those for Staples, Office Depot, Office Max, and IKEA to find a desk and an ergonomic chair that fit your space. The chair should be adjustable, with a contoured seat and back support. It should move easily. Ideally, your desk should be at least three feet wide and two feet deep. Once you've seen what there is online, visit the stores to see if the furniture you liked in the catalogue actually works for you.

Make sure you have adequate outlets and phone jacks for all of your equipment, plus your Internet connection. You'll need a modular shelf system, or an enclosed cabinet with holes in the back for all the connecting cords. Your file cabinet can be freestanding or a part of your desk, and roomy enough to contain folders for all your business records, submission materials, correspondence, your photos and résumés, DVD reels, and promotional materials.

Your computer should be equipped with Adobe Acrobat, Microsoft Word, and high-speed Internet access.

Hewlett-Packard produces a printer-copier-scanner for about $100. A few dollars more will also get you a built-in fax machine. If you opt for a separate fax machine, get one with a phone—you'll want a phone at your desk, anyway.

> – Desk & chair, file cabinet, shelves… $500 and up
> – Computer, printer, fax, phone setup… about $1,000

You will need a supply of 9 x 12 manila envelopes, with clasps, as well as letter-size (number 10) envelopes, in which you can safely send your 4 x 6 picture-postcard. Stock your home office with ink cartridges/toner, notepads, a stapler and plenty of staples, paper clips, a ruler, postage, and a calendar or daily planner.

On your computer you can create a letterhead with "From the office of," or "A note from," or your name and contact number. You can also create mailing labels and labels with your return address.

Invest in bimonthly editions of major industry publications, such as *Ross Reports Television & Film*, for updated contact information.

> – Stationery supplies… about $350

From now on, you are responsible for overseeing your professional expenditures. The job can be made easy with ActorTrack, career management software for actors that is available at www.holdonlog. com. For a nominal annual fee, this user-friendly program helps you keep track of all appointments, audition-callback-booking details, income and expenses, and contacts. An overview feature makes it easy to track where your money has gone at the end of each year.

KEEPING THE PLACE AND YOURSELF LOOKING GOOD

Maintenance of your living space, which we assume you intend to do yourself, will require more time than money. You will have to purchase some basic supplies, such as a mop, a broom, and household products.

– **Cleaning Supplies... $90**

Invest also in a steam/dry iron, an ironing board, and handy items such as spot cleaners for the necessary daily touchups on your clothing. Laundry (there are usually laundry facilities in the building or nearby), dry cleaning, and shoe repair costs are additional expenses to work into your monthly budget.

– **Iron, ironing board, spot cleaner... $75 and up**
– **Laundry, dry cleaning, alterations, shoe repair... $75 and up a month**

ARRANGING FOR CREDIT

You now have some idea of the costs. To deal with them in a business like manner, you need to establish credit. You want to be able to buy things and pay for them on credit over time, and may deal with merchants who do not take cash or checks but require a credit card.

Because actors do not usually have permanent employment—looking for work is the "steady job" in The Business—actors more than most people have historically found it a problem to establish credit. You can avoid much of this difficulty by making your arrangements ahead of time, ideally during your preliminary visit. You can do so by opening a savings account, preferably at a bank located near your apartment. The simplest way is to have a certified check (or a cashier's check) drawn on your current account by your hometown bank for the amount you wish to deposit in your new bank. At many major banks these checks are treated as immediate cash or are cleared within a few days; personal checks drawn on out-of-town banks may take as long a few weeks to clear.

In some locales, new depositors need to show proof of residence—a copy of your lease, perhaps, or a bill or postcard sent to you at your new address. You will also usually have to show a government-issued ID, such as your driver's license or passport. Make copies of your ID materials and keep them in a safe place.

You will definitely need a personal checking account. You should pay by check or debit card whenever you can to avoid carrying large amounts of cash. A canceled check can serve as your proof of payment (helpful if you have a problem with an item you've purchased) and useful for income tax purposes.

Using a major credit card or debit card also provides a record of the purchase. Some credit cards also offer buyer's insurance, which replaces an item that you break or lose. If you don't already have a credit card, apply for one while you are still at home. Some companies permit family members to have separate cards in their individual names; the bill is sent to the original card holder.

Members of AEA (Actors' Equity Association), SAG (Screen Actors Guild), and AFTRA (the American Federation of Television and Radio Artists) have the option of joining the Actors Federal Credit Union, which offers regular banking services as well as a low-interest credit card, and all other banking features. You'll learn more about this in Chapter 9, "Understanding the Unions."

PROPER IDENTIFICATION

Some form of identification is usually necessary when paying by check, when cashing a check, or when purchasing an unusually expensive item. A valid driver's license usually suffices. A Social Security card is no longer considered acceptable identification.

Actors who may be shooting a film or a commercial in St. Maarten, Buenos Aires, Paris, or Tokyo, will need a passport and should obtain one before auditioning for an overseas job to make sure it's in hand when the job comes through. As this valuable article is easily lost, we suggest making copies of your passport (along with any other forms of ID).

BECOMING YOUR OWN ACCOUNTANT

You will need to keep receipts for all business-related expenses. Keep a daily diary of what you spend on trade papers, entertainment costs, transportation to and from auditions and jobs, and all other expenses related to your business. Performers usually have many different employers, and do their work in a number of locations over the course of a year (and different states have different tax codes). They incur business expenses that do not fit a customary employment profile. At income tax time, if the IRS computer hiccups when it reads your tax return and a representative from the IRS questions you, you will need to produce these records.

YOUR HEALTH

Young people accustomed to consistently good health may think that allowances for doctors' and dentists' bills and health insurance are optional. That would be a mistake. Accidents happen; emergencies arise. And they inevitably happen when you least expect them and cannot afford them. Not every emergency is life-threatening, but even a minor injury can be serious and painful and keep you out of work for weeks. The horrifying truth is that a hospital may refuse to admit even emergency patients who do not have health insurance coverage.

Until you have worked under union jurisdiction and earned enough money to become eligible for no-cost, or low-cost medical coverage, you must provide your own health insurance.

– Medical insurance and medical care... varies enormously

You should also have a complete physical checkup before you embark on your journey. Tell your regular physicians that you're moving—they may be able to recommend colleagues practicing in New York, California, or wherever you will be living. Friends, too, may know internists, dentists, gynecologists, chiropractors, or podiatrists whom they admire. Anyone with chronic medical conditions—and that includes allergies and skin problems—should ask for copies of all medical records. You should also obtain hard copies of the prescriptions for your lenses and/or medication.

WISE INVESTMENTS

Keeping yourself in good shape is essential to looking and feeling your best. Surely you've noticed how revealing the outfits worn in film and on television have become and how often the heroes and villains are seen shirtless. Sculpted is the "must have" physique. Membership in a health club, with swimming pool and lots of exercise classes, is a worthwhile expense. Yoga also enhances vitality.

– Health club... $800 and up per year; monthly plans available

– Yoga classes... $20 and up per class

While we're at it, massages, manicures, and pedicures help you look good and feel good, too.

– Massages... $60 and up

– Manicures, pedicures... $15 to $30 each

And after all the attention paid to your outer self, it's quite possible that you might want to visit an understanding therapist from time to time, or locate a support group, many of which can be attended on a walk-in basis.

– Therapist... fees on a sliding scale

THE GRAND TOTAL

As we indicated at the start of this chapter, the performer, like any other professional, needs to plan ahead for a successful career. The best way to proceed is to be able to devote yourself totally to the task of getting interviews and jobs without worrying about supporting yourself, at least for the first six months.

Once you've arrived and had a chance to unpack, you can pay attention to the real task, which is getting a job!

CHAPTER 2

Getting Your Act Together

"Every new girl who came in to RKO had to go through the plastic surgery, the teeth and all the cosmetic changes. And I wouldn't do it. I was not so gung ho that I was going to wreck my life to be a *movie star.*"

—Ruth Warrick, actress, Phoebe Tyler Wallingford, All My Children

Do you know that studies have proved that within seven seconds your appearance will indicate your financial stability, education, trustworthiness, social position, level of sophistication, marital status, success, moral character, occupation, and lifestyle?

Can you look at yourself objectively? When you look in the mirror, who do you see? When you look at your reflection, do you tend to magnify every slight deviation from perfection? Does your close scrutiny make you consider a new nose, a different chin, a stronger jaw line?

To venture out on interviews when you are unhappy about your teeth, your nose, your hair, or your weight is to burden yourself unnecessarily. Your concentration will be centered upon what is wrong with you and whether the interviewer will note your deficiency on the back of your photo ("bad teeth," "needs to lose weight") or will tell you to come back when you have lost the twenty pounds. A first impression is what people will ultimately remember. You may not get a second chance. Industry professionals want the look to be there when you make your entrance.

Never try to imitate someone else. But if your dissatisfaction is real and of long standing, have imperfections attended to before you start your professional career.

HISTORY

In the glory days of the huge Hollywood studios, production departments created stars' images.

In *The Power of Glamour*, an excellent overview of eleven of the greatest stars from that era (including Joan Crawford and Norma Shearer), Annette Tapert writes, "Would-be actresses escaped from generally drab backgrounds and arrived in Hollywood eager to become their fantasy selves. The studios did the rest. Teeth were straightened, jaws realigned. Doctors recommended by studios prescribed strict diets. Studio-approved beauticians reshaped eyebrows."

Columbia Pictures' top hairstylist Helen Hunt described how she made Rita Hayworth's hairline appear higher by creating a bleached streak across her forehead:

> One day I talked to Harry Cohn (head of the studio) about making Rita's hair red so we could do away with the streak. I worked with the electrolysist drawing lines on a still picture showing the line we wanted. Treatments were fifteen dollars each. This lasted a year until the work was finished. Achieving a new design for Rita's forehead entailed a long and very painful process. Each hair had to be removed individually. Then the follicle was deadened with a charge of electricity.

Rita's biographer John Kobal affirmed that Rita was acutely sensitive to pain but that her determination to succeed was stronger. Glenn Ford, who costarred with Rita Hayworth in a number of films that included *Gilda* and *Affair in Trinidad*, was a contract player at Columbia for nineteen years. Regarding how they tried to change his look, he recalled:

> When I first got there, they used to put what they call corrective makeup on me. My nose was crooked, one of my cheeks is a little bigger than the other, and my eyes are too close or something. I've still got the chart of my corrective makeup from the old days, which I framed. They shade here and they highlight there and they move this and that and it's terrible.

Talented designers under contract to the studio created clothes to enhance, and eventually to exemplify, the performers' images. Bette Davis was indebted to Oscar-winning designer Edith Head for understanding how the right costume helped her find her character. "Edith was my mirror. I could see the expression on her face and knew that she had made me look as good as I could for the part and that was what I wanted."

The exaggerated shoulders and smooth lustrous fabrics that Adrian, MGM's leading costume designer during the 1930s, used to create Joan Crawford's glamorous leading lady persona are quite different from the unstructured, lace-collared, short sleeved rayon frocks she wore as an ingenue. Ms. Crawford herself was heard to say, "Any actress who appears in public without being well groomed is digging her own grave."

Award-winning hairstylists, such as Sidney Guilaroff, created individualized coiffures. Makeup artists designed a special look. Claudette Colbert, Rosalind Russell, Myrna Loy, and Joan Crawford were all fair-skinned, dark-haired, sophisticated leading ladies but they all had different hairstyles, eye makeup, and mouth shapes created for them.

The image-making process operated for male performers as well. Think of some leading men of the period: James Stewart, Gary Cooper, Cary Grant, Fred Astaire, and Clark Gable. They had the finest tailors and couturier designers supplying them with their wardrobes in luxurious fabrics and individualized color palettes. The best hairpieces adorned those with early thinning problems and lifts were supplied in their shoes if it was necessary to add to their height.

The exquisite packaging that was the hallmark of the Hollywood glamour factory is now largely a memory, gone with the demise of the studio system in the 1950s. Today's actors must develop an image themselves or seek expert guidance in the creation of it.

Renie, the noted costume designer who clothed numerous superstars of the 1940s and 1950s gave concise advice on style that still seems as appropriate today as it did when her words were published in 1959. Here are a few of her tips:

- Color and line are the governing factors in everything you wear that shows.
- As you grow a bit older, an entire new color scheme can make you look more interesting than ever before.
- Line means the changing line of style, and your best line is probably one that doesn't hug you too tight. To be elegant, be conservative.
- A lot depends on the shape you're in.

- Watch your posture! Learn how to get up gracefully from a table. Never slouch. Make your movements leisurely and sure, and look years younger.
- Good shoes are not necessarily the most expensive. Heels can do wonders for the feminine leg.
- Before you purchase slacks, shorts, or other sports outfits, install a full-length mirror with a rear view.
- Buy clothes that match you and conform to good style in your community (New York versus Los Angeles).
- Best of all, take a good look at yourself. Everybody else does!

YOUR LOOK FROM HEAD TO TOE

The eye immediately focuses on your hair: its color, condition, and style. Skin care, meanwhile, is the most effective way to retard the aging process, to protect the skin from the elements and dangerous ultraviolet rays, and to stay youthful and vibrant. Properly applied makeup can enhance and define your features.

CROWNING GLORY: YOUR GLORIOUS HAIR

Your hair color should complement your complexion, while the style frames your face and enhances your image. Stylists and colorists are trained to look at performers in terms of recognizable types. Let them know how you seek to present yourself.

Alan Adler, a stylist, and Tom Frasca, a color specialist, are a team at New York City's very popular Gerard Bollei Salon. Their theatrical clients have included Jill Clayburgh, Kate Capshaw, Faye Dunaway, and Mary Steenburgen. They feel that "there is nothing matter-of-fact about a dramatic actor. Actors exude experience, and their hair color and style should compliment them, visually projecting individuality while transcending trends."

Adler and Frasca offer the following advice.

Hair Color

If the color isn't right, it will sometimes reflect off your skin and will cause you to look pale or washed out. If it is done correctly, it can make you look brilliant and stunning. The overall appearance will pop out on camera.

The best process is to use a mild lightener on fine strands of hair within aluminum foil packets that direct color where it is needed. Highlights will give a depth of color to dull brown hair and give the illusion of widening a narrow forehead. They will also create a dimension in the shadows or the way the wave falls. Matte lights will remove a concentration of gray, accent the low base tones, and flatter and rejuvenate without loss of texture or shine.

Very dark hair may have a healthy shine and be a breeze to manage, but it can contrast too greatly with pale skin. Even though you look sensational in real life, the sharp contrast will present problems for TV and film work. Have a colorist give you some well-placed highlights, so your hair can have a feeling of movement and dimension.

When brunettes have to use more makeup, they may actually need to warm up their hair color. A shade lift will bring back the color to the chestnut browns, maroons, burgundies, and mahoganies, whatever it takes to remove the ashiness. Hair that has highlights photographs better than hair that is one flat shade. When the contrast with your natural color becomes noticeable, it's time for a retouch—about every four to eight weeks.

Hairstyle

Once the color is accomplished, you are ready to work on the style. If you have great hair, show it off. A short cut is great for a statement but don't hide a diamond in the shadows. Long hair should start at the collar bone and graduate longer over the shoulders. A round face needs volume on top. Adding soft fringe near the cheekbones will give a narrowing illusion. The oblong or long face can handle shorter lengths to play down features, but if long is what you want, consider a wave to add volume on the sides, or a long bang to cut the length of the face.

A good stylist will take your positive features into consideration. Play up those exotic eyes, the nose, a cleft chin, pouty lips, and high cheekbones. The style should downplay weak features like an exaggerated bump on the nose, the weak chin, or extreme angles in a jaw line. Parting hair at the arch of the brow will accentuate the eyes. Waves at the nape of the neck will lift the hair out, causing it to look fuller and to give more foundation to straight hair.

Hair Care

When caring for your hair, think of it as fabric or your best cashmere sweater. You wouldn't expose it to harsh detergent shampoos or to excessive sun or heat from blow-dryers and expect it to retain its elasticity, shine, and color. Girls wearing rubber bands or men with tight baseball caps on backwards are damaging their hair. Fibers need to breathe or they will break. If you want your hair to look lustrous on camera, use humectants and conditioners that restore moisture every day. Use a small dab in the palm of your hand, work it first on the oldest hair (the ends) and then through to your scalp. Always brush your hair before shampooing to loosen and remove shedding skin and product buildup, which are often confused with dandruff, and to stimulate the oils. Limp hair will wake up with a little sculpting lotion. Add a body wave on top to avoid flatness.

Hair should be away from the face to show your expressions around the eyes and mouth. Avoid bangs that hug the eyebrows, hair that is too tightly pulled back, and a helmetlike look caused by too much styling gel. Low-maintenance, high-performance hairstyles are preferable for your photo shoot and on-camera appearance. It is recommended that you get your haircut and styled at least a week before the photo session so you have time to work with it.

Options for Versatility

Actors who start to lose their hair frequently rush to cover their baldness with a toupee or a permanent hair transplant. Toupee wearers should realize that nature has enabled them to have two looks: leading man and character actor. We know an actor whose postcard showed him with and without his hairpiece. The clever caption read: "Toupee or not toupee."

Similarly, women who feel their hair is the wrong length, texture, or fullness have the opportunity to use wigs, extensions, and hair weaving. Use whatever helps to connect you with your image, whatever works with your face shape.

Dr. Kathryn Duplantis, director of the Hair, Laser, and Liposuction Center of Dallas, has observed that "thinning hair is common among both men and women—even in their twenties and thirties. However, advances over the past few years have made it possible to shrink wide bald spots, add hair to sparse areas, and create new natural looking hairlines." For more information, go to www.drkathrynduplantis.com.

No matter how well you care for your hair, remember that humid or inclement weather can still cause those "hair days from hell." Carry your personal hair maintenance kit—a cordless curling iron or portable hot roller set, styling brush/comb, environmentally friendly hairspray (odor free), gel, clips, scrunchies, or headbands—and head for the nearest restroom to achieve the necessary repairs before the interview or the audition.

A HEALTHY COMPLEXION

Both men and women should cleanse, condition, and moisturize their skin regularly. Many dermatologists consider exfoliating, which rids the skin of dead cells and impurities, the single most beneficial thing we can do to maintain a healthy complexion.

When you walk into a store to buy skincare products, the salesperson may not be thoroughly educated in the product. Actress and skincare expert Kim Shively recommends Dr. Nicholas V. Perricone's books (www.nvperriconemd.com) to learn about your skin. "Your skin is the first thing that registers when others meet you. Visit a dermatologist when you have serious problems or erratic breakouts." She recommends regular, deep-cleansing facials. Among the inexpensive options are the well-trained students at the Manhattan-based Christine Valmy School, who charge a nominal fee for facials.

Know your skin type: sensitive, dry, oily, or a combination of these. If you have allergies or problems with acne, have your doctor prescribe a regimen for you. Otherwise, choose from the wide selection at any drugstore or cosmetic counter. Many products are allergy-and-fragrance free, but what's most important is finding what works best for you. Give each new product a fourteen-day trial. Buy small sizes to ensure freshness.

Cleanse your face at least twice daily, when you wake up and when you go to bed. Pat Riley, CEO/Founder of Clientele®, (www.clientelebeauty.com) emphasizes the need to cleanse to wash away impurities, excess oils, pollutants, makeup, and aged skin cells. Be sure you rinse away the cleanser or you will get that dry, tight, itchy feeling. Replace the moisture your skin tends to lose each day with a lotion or cream. For dry skin, use an emollient-rich night cream or moisturizer.

Regular use of exfoliants removes dead skin cells, diminishes blotchiness, and gives your skin a younger and healthier glow. Use exfoliants or facial scrubs only once or twice a week, and use a soft friction cream, usually an almond paste, that you dilute with water. Rub it gently all over your face and feel the tingling sensation. Your skin can also benefit from a weekly facial mask—many varieties are sold in drugstores as well as at cosmetic counters. Periodic collagen treatments can maintain the skin's elasticity and correct frown lines, acne scars, vertical lip lines, lip outline, worry lines, crow's-feet, and smile lines. The amount of collagen required for correction depends on your age, your skin condition, and the amount of sun damage you have incurred.

And finally, some general rules: Drink plenty of water, maintain a sensible diet, and get regular exercise. During the day always wear a moisturizer with an SPF (sun protection factor) of 25 if your skin is sensitive or very fair. Also wear tinted glasses to protect your eyes and to prevent the development of squint or frown lines.

Beware of the Sun

Just think: There may come a day, possibly by the year 2020, when researchers will have sufficiently developed gene therapy to retard and even reverse aging. Until that day comes, however, you should be aware that signs of aging are caused mainly by sun damage. Dermatologists are finding that exposure to the sun's rays is more harmful than originally suspected. A ninety-year-old Buddhist monk who never smiles, frowns, or exposes himself to the sun can probably appear at least forty years younger. But the rest of us have to rely on our common sense—and wide-brimmed hats.

There's another important professional advantage to sun protection: Actors should never show up on the set with a suntan. If color is necessary for purpose of plot or character, the makeup artist can always apply a dark base tone, but as a rule producers do not want the leads in their adaptation of Jane Austen's *Pride and Prejudice* to look like they just got back from a Caribbean vacation.

TATTOOS

Many young actors have adorned their bodies with one or more tattoos. Unless discreetly placed, a tattoo is an attention-getter. For certain edgy characters or street-smart roles, skin decorations may be appropriate. But there's no place for them in the classics—Molière, Shakespeare, Shaw, Ibsen, and Wilde, for instance—in which aristocratic complexions tend to be pale, delicate, and unadorned.

Jane Iredale's Disappear, a camouflage cream that completely conceals tattoos, is one of the numerous natural beauty products that can be found at www.dermstore.com.

MAKEUP TECHNIQUE

Knowing how to successfully apply makeup is essential for meeting agents and going to auditions and professional networking events. Judith Ann Graham, a Manhattan-based image consultant, makeup artist, and airbrush makeup expert, has prepared many actors and celebrities for photo sessions and television appearances. She recommends a user-friendly regimen. outlined below.

Basic Application

Always cleanse the skin and apply moisturizer before you begin applying makeup.

Eyes first: Expert makeup artists always start with eye makeup so the tiny grains from powders and shadows don't fall onto your foundation.

Eyeliner: Begin with eyeliner, following the natural curve of the upper lash line. Do not extend beyond the outer corner of the lid and do not apply liner to the lower lashes—the eyes will appear smaller. Use dark brown liner instead of black for a more natural look. Eyeliner helps define the eyes and allows them to stand out.

Eye shadow: Next apply eye shadow so the eyes pop. Use a color similar to your natural lid color and apply it from the lash line (brush over the eyeliner) up to the brow bone. Be careful with dark tones on the lid as the darker the shadow the smaller the eyes become. Lighter shades open up the eyes. Stick with neutral colors such as brown, grays, and taupes to accentuate eyes in the crease. Don't apply shimmer under the brow bone, because natural lighting supplies its own highlighter. Avoid blue, green, or violet shadows unless you are going to a fashion meeting. Even then, blend, blend, blend.

Concealer: Instead of using a light concealer under the eyes, which can cause a raccoon look, use a salmon-color concealer to diminish dark circles. Blend with your fingertip or a sponge.

Foundation: Match foundation to your skin tone and apply using a sponge for even coverage. For women of color, the base tone should be three shades lighter so it will neutralize and absorb naturally with your skin. Matching your skin tone will make you appear darker and weaken your features.

Powder: There should be no difference between the color of your face and neck, so adjust accordingly. A setting powder can be used over the foundation for longevity and softness. MAC (www.mac.com) is a popular line of makeup products that work well for all skin tones and look good on camera. Mac's Studio FX foundation combines base and powder in one compact that produces a matte finish to match your skin tone.

Brows: Keep your brows neatly groomed and tweezed in a shape that follows your natural arch. Use an eyebrow pencil to fill in sparse areas and even the shape. Eyebrows should never be more than two shades darker than your hair. Consider your face shape. Women with square faces can have a slight curve in the brow to help soften the angles of the face. Round faces can have a slightly more arched brow to give the face more definition. Women with oval faces look best with a slight arch. To determine where your brows should begin and end, hold your eyebrow pencil against your nostril in a straight line up to the brow. Your brow should start here. Next, angle the pencil from your nostril to the outer edges of your eyes. This is the point where your brows should end. Carefully fill in the area with your brow pencil. If your brows are unruly, or tend to grow downward, apply brow gel or clear mascara, or spritz some hairspray on an old mascara wand or thoroughly washed toothbrush and comb it through your brows to set them.

Blush: Blush, in cream or powder form, gives your face balance and helps to define the cheekbones. Start at the temples and blend forward to the apple of the cheek. Smile when applying blush so you can get the right placement. Blush must never overpower the face. Use a color that gives you a healthy glow and goes on sheer. Depending on your natural coloring, try soft peaches, pinks, or bronzes. Women of color look best in deep russet or mulberry colors.

Finishing Touches: Lips and Lashes

Make sure your lips are in good condition by using an exfoliant to get rid of dead, dry skin. Use a moisturizer like Vaseline to keep them from chapping. Your lipstick color should complement your skin tone and your wardrobe color. An orange dress and a fuchsia lipstick are not a happy pair. A lip liner pencil lets you create a perfectly defined mouth, and even allows you to extend your lips subtly, correcting or enlarging their shape and size. A neutral brownish liner, slightly deeper than your natural lip color, will work with virtually any lipstick color you own. Outline your mouth, fill in with your lipstick, and blot. If you want a bit more shine, add a dot of gloss to the center of both lips. When selecting lipsticks at a cosmetic counter, always be sure the sample is sanitary. At the MAC counter, if you bring back six empty shadow or foundation cases for recycling you will be rewarded with a free lipstick.

Finally, apply two coats of mascara to your lashes. To avoid a heavy, beaded look, allow your mascara to dry before applying the second coat. Replace your mascara every three months to avoid bacteria buildup on the wand. False lashes or lash extensions are an option to create fuller, longer-looking lashes.

Airbrush Makeup

With the advent of the high-definition camera, traditional makeup reveals every line, pore, and wrinkle. Airbrush makeup, applied in tiny pixilized drop-lets, smoothes away these problems. Tiny droplets are sprayed onto the face and body, creating a sheer, natural look that gives the illusion of "no makeup" and still makes you look flawless on camera. Plus, it won't rub off and lasts four to five times longer than traditional makeup does, so the makeup artist has fewer touch-ups to do. For men, airbrushing gets rid of the five o'clock shadow and looks natural. Jay Leno, David Letterman, and all the major newscasters appear warmer and not made up with airbrush makeup.

A trained airbrush makeup artist will know how to airbrush eye shadow, blush, eyebrows, and lips. For further information about camera-friendly makeup kits, salmon concealer and airbrush makeup, visit www.judithanngraham.com.

ADVICE FOR MEN

Men who tend to grow a heavy beard are smart to carry an electric shaver whenever they have a late afternoon interview or audition so they can remove any hint of a five o'clock shadow. Actors with facial hair should be sure it matches their hair color. An eyebrow pencil can be applied to achieve an even coverage.

YOUR TEETH: WHAT'S IN A SMILE?

According to behavioral scientists, smiling relieves stress and relaxes specific muscles in the neck, which helps to alleviate pain experienced in tense times. Research psychologists report that smiling makes us happy because the act of turning our mouths upwards changes the way air and blood flow through our heads, cooling our brains. A cool brain, according to the theory, is a happy brain.

It is possible to distinguish a genuine smile from a false one. When a smile is sincere, you will see that crinkly crow's-feet effect around the eyes, as well as a mouth that's turned up at the corners. A fake smile, on the other hand, will lack any sparkle or movement from the eyes.

Other than your eyes, the one feature of your face that is always in motion is your mouth. Is your jaw aligned? Do you look self-conscious when you smile because your teeth are crooked? When you do smile, do we see too much of your gums? Gum lines, by the way, are not attractive.

Do-It-Yourself Smile Analysis

Here's how to judge your smile:

- **Shape:** Does the shape of your teeth balance your facial features? If your eyes, lips, and nose are large, for example, tiny teeth look out of proportion.
- **Length:** The length of your two front teeth compared to that of your two laterals (the teeth just on either side of them) indicates age. Laterals are shorter when you are young. By age forty, laterals and centrals can be the same length. Changing your tooth length can make your smile younger looking.
- **Position:** Are your six upper front teeth (the ones that really show you when you smile) on the same plane? Any crooked or recessed teeth swallow light and make a dark spot in a smile.
- **Color:** Generally, tooth color should be uniform, but teeth aren't supposed to be solid white. That could look artificial. Teeth are typically more yellow at the gum line and transparent at the edge and darken naturally with age.

Tooth Menders

Advances in cosmetic dentistry make it easier to have a dazzling smile. Put your money where your mouth is in the most literal sense. We all notice when an actor's teeth have been improved. Clark Gable and Humphrey Bogart, Faye Dunaway, and Pierce Brosnan were not born with the teeth we have seen them show in their films; they were ready for their close-ups only after dental work.

You should consider veneers if you value durability and low maintenance; have gum problems, or have broken or very dark teeth. Although costly, veneers can last fifteen years with little upkeep. Veneers don't attract as much plaque as bonding but bonding is a less expensive procedure. Consider bonding if you want to fill in gaps, repair chips, or build up a receding tooth. You have to be fastidious about maintenance and daily care. Limit intakes of high-staining foods, such as soy sauce, balsami vinegar, red wine, graview, coffee, and dark fruit juices.

HANDS AND FEET

Hands are an important indication of your health and well-being. Chewed fingernails, rough, dry skin, excessive moisture in the palm area, frequent bouts of psoriasis, and discoloration reveal nervousness, a lack of care, and health issues. They are also quick to reveal our age. Care for them with regular manicures. For women, pale pink or natural nail polish is best for TV commercials, industrials, and soaps. Men should keep their nails clean, trim, and buffed for a natural rosy color. Apply a moisturizer after putting your hands in water.

Our feet take a beating. They become shock absorbers when we walk, engage in sports activities like tennis or hiking, and enjoy recreational hobbies like ballroom dancing. When our feet are in pain, our whole body reacts. Corns, bunions, neuromas, hammertoes, blisters, and other conditions that cause us to wince when we take a step can be treated with the help of a good podiatrist or an array of healing products at the local pharmacy. It is important to wear shoes that give good support and plenty of toe room. We recommend a monthly pedicure for cosmetic improvements and to release stress. Many nail salons offer massage and foot reflexology treatments.

FRAMED FOR LIFE

If you must wear glasses, remember that for every face there are suitable frame shapes. Use them to enhance your face and to highlight your best features. You should also consider your coloring when selecting frames. Whether your skin is warm-based (gold tones) or cool-based (blue tones), choose the appropriate colors. Chartreuse may be the hot color but if you are cool-based, it won't work for you. You may love pink, but if you are a warm-based person you will look and probably feel uncomfortable.

Your eyewear reflects you and your lifestyle. It is the accessory that people see first. The proper eyewear can help capture the look you want and make you feel more confident. Frame options are:

- **Oval face:** wide as or wider than the broadest part of the face—almonds or ovals.
- **Heart-shaped face:** rimless styles, very thin metals or plastics.
- **Square face:** rounder, narrower styles that soften the facial angle—narrow ovals.
- **Round face:** wider than they are deep—angular, narrow frames.
- **Oblong face:** top-to-bottom depth or decorative frame arms to add width.
- **Diamond-shaped face:** detailing or distinctive brow lines—cat-eyes or ovals.
- **Triangle-shaped face:** styles that draw attention upwards—bold frames, cat-eyes.

WARDROBE SELECTION

There is no point in selecting a professional wardrobe until you understand how vital the power of color is to your total package. Casting directors and agents want to see you in a color. If you only have enough money for one outfit, be sure it is from your color palette.

The Power of Color

All of us have specific colors—whether they are dramatic, understated, or neutral—that look better on us than other colors. Wearing the right colors next to your skin can have a rejuvenating, uplifting, and healthier impact on your overall appearance. You will know the colors are wrong if you suddenly look older, sallow, or blotchy, or if your cheeks seem drained of color.

Color triggers memory more readily than your name. If you see a casting director or an artistic director or a producer making notes during your audition, it is probably a record of the colors you're wearing. After auditions, clients will frequently say, "You know I really liked the girl in the purple jacket," or "Remember that guy with the red vest?" One actress who wore a rose-colored blouse to a commercial audition is convinced that the color was responsible for the callback and the booking. The connection and self-confidence she felt wearing it impressed those who hired her.

If you have pale skin and dark hair, the jewel-tone colors (sapphire blue, emerald green, ruby red) and the icy pastels (orchid, lemon, pink, pale blue) will bring out your natural blush. Muted rosy colors work extremely well with skin tones that have beige, pink, or ivory undertones. Yellow or peachy undertones suggest deeper pigmentation, and clear bright colors or richer and deeper golden-based hues work well with them. Some skin tones are so balanced that both cool and warm colors work well with them. Remember, there are no absolutes. Wearing what makes you feel good when you put it on should be the general rule. But bear in mind that you must wear the color, the color must never wear you.

The color you choose to wear to an interview can have a psychological impact on the interviewer. So choose carefully to avoid sending the wrong vibration. For example, red is associated with passion, ambition, desire, assertiveness, and self-sacrifice. It is the "I am" color. If you are meeting someone for the first time, be careful about the red you select. Avoid reds with too much yellow; they can overwhelm you. Reds with more blue in them (such as the wine colors, cranberry, and raspberry) or more brown (such as brick and terra-cotta) will be less intimidating. Red is also effective as an accent color in a scarf, tie, belt, pocket square, or suspenders.

Green has a cooler energy and, like the color of the forest, is calming, nonthreatening, balanced, and restful to the eye. The deeper shades of green (jungle, emerald, cucumber, and avocado) are terrific to wear to the interview and on camera as well.

Blue is the color of trust, loyalty, wisdom, and inspiration. Corporate executives in navy blue suits inspire confidence. If you want to appear credible and confident, wear blue.

Purple is the color associated with artists, writers, and spirituality. Michelangelo kept purple stained glass in his studio when he sculpted his masterpieces. Wagner wore purple robes to compose. Studies have shown that meditating on purple can reduce mental stress. So when you choose a royal purple to wear at the interview, you will be relaxing the pressure the casting director or agent might feel and, in turn, connecting to your creative center.

Yellow is so bright and dynamic that it can cause anxiety and hyperactivity. It is more effective in a print design. Large doses should be avoided, unless you have a tan to balance the color. Orange may be the color of geniuses, extroverts, good negotiators, and safety on the construction site, but not everyone can wear it.

White is reflective and can upstage your face. Gray represents passivity and noncommitment. Black, technically, is the combination of all the colors, and not a color at all. It is distancing, lacks vibration, absorbs color and light, and can drain it from your face. Black is best worn from the waist down. Both gray and black keep your energy contained and rob you of vitality. Neutrals like black, gray, brown, and deep navy can always be enlivened with colorful scarves near your face or with pocket squares, ties, shirts, blouses, and jewelry.

Actor-Friendly Colors for Monologues, Scenes, On-Camera Auditions, Photos, Interview

Pastels: Blue, pink, peach, jade, mint, aqua, orchid.

Oranges: Terra-cotta, rust, melon, deep coral, cinnabar, nutmeg, saffron, persimmon, mango, tabasco. *No bright orange.*

Reds: Ruby, brick, merlot, mauve, crimson, burgundy, maroon, garnet, deep rose, raspberry, cranberry, carmine, strawberry, watermelon, American beauty.

Blues: Royal, navy, indigo, blueberry, ocean, ultramarine, sky, cerulean, Wedgewood, robin's egg, periwinkle, hydrangea, iris, sapphire. Blues are extremely camera-friendly.

Blue Green: Teal, azure, aqua, emerald turquoise.

Greens: Forest, jungle, bottle, cedar, fir, pine, hunter, emerald, moss, khaki, avocado, jade, spinach, parsley. Avoid yellow greens, lime, and chartreuse.

Purples: Royal, plum, grape, lilac, lavender, orchid, pansy, amethyst, violet, eggplant.

Neutrals: Rich browns, camel, beige, navy, dark green, wine red, warm gray.

The Professional Closet

The first impression you make is what people will ultimately remember about you. How do you want to be perceived when you make an entrance or an exit? You may not get a second chance.

What you choose to wear on social occasions, to parties, to barbecues, and when hanging out with pals on the weekend should be comfortable and appropriate for the situation. However, meetings with industry professionals necessitate a pulled-together look, a separate budget, and sensible shopping that will afford you a number of choices that should never look dated. This clothing is also important for your photo shoot, auditions, and networking. Some training programs will hire image consultants to advise the graduates about what to wear for their scene showcases. Having outfits ready for last-minute meetings will be much easier if you heed this advice.

Professional Closet Items: Actresses

- Skirts with various hemlines, usually flared, pleated, or A-line: They should make you appear graceful and allow for comfortable movement. The hem can be at the knee, no shorter than two inches above the knee, and is proportionate to height, shape, and age. All skirts should be in dark colors: Black, charcoal gray, dark brown, navy blue, forest green, royal purple, or wine red.

- Tops in a variety of fabrics—cotton/polyester blends, Lycra/spandex, knits, microfibers, washable silk: Necklines should flatter the face shape. V-necks are the most attractive, especially if you have a round face. Other necklines are scoop, U, boat, cowl, square, scalloped, jewel. For young actresses, the tank, camisole, tube, shell, and halter are the basic shapes that work well in the photo shoot.

- Colors should be solid and complement the skin tones. Avoid turtlenecks.

- Shirts and blouses that are form-fitting, not bulky: Collars will give focus to the face and soften the jawline. The best colors are royal blue, ruby red, emerald green, amethyst, plum, and teal. Colors that are too light, such as pastels, are less likely to define the face shape. Avoid white and black.

- Sweaters that are fine close knits, not thick, like cable: Wear a sweater set, silk knits, cashmere or faux cashmere.

- Slacks that are pleated, full-length, with elastic waists or side zips: Choose soft fabrics, such as wrinkle-free twill, wool crepe, gabardine, and 95 percent acetate/5 percent spandex. The best colors are black, dark brown, charcoal gray, and navy. Avoid pinstripes. Off-the-rack purchases might need some tailoring. Slacks should not bag or sag and should fit well around the waist and hips. Bring the jacket you plan to wear with the slacks with you to ensure the right proportion and compatible colors.

- Pant suits: Allow for mixing and matching with different tops and accessories.

- Sport jackets or blazers that can be worn with different slacks and skirts: When buying any type of jacket, avoid exaggerated proportions. You always want to look longer and leaner.

- Shoes in dark, nonreflective leather: Pumps are conservative and don't distract from the line of your outfit. Short heels (two inches) are preferable for support and graceful movement. Avoid slides, backless heels, open toes, and strappy sandals, stiletto heels, and flip-flops. Wear neutral-colored pantyhose.

- Accessories that are minimal and appropriate: Avoid dangling ear-rings, large hoops, numerous bangles, flashy belts, and all reflective metals. Chunky necklaces and "bling" will upstage your face.

Professional Closet Items: Actors

- Shirts, long-sleeved, in poplin, cotton/polyester, washable silk, Ox-ford cloth, or corduroy: Dress shirts should be 100-percent cotton, non-button-down, preferably in shades of blue, green, peach, pink, orchid, or other flattering pastels to your skin tones.
- Sport shirts: Navy, burgundy, pine, crimson, purple, and rust.
- Sweaters that are not bulky, such as ribbed cotton polos or crew necks: V-necklines look best over a shirt and add more texture to the ensemble. A sweater vest with buttons or a button-front cardi-gan can add another layer. Best yarn quality is found in extra-fine merino wool and cashmere.
- Trousers that define your shape: No baggy pants. Fit is essential to looking pulled together. Pleated-front or flat front wool gabar-dines, chinos (nano-care fabric is extremely resistant to stains and wrinkles), plain or pleated-front, corduroy, pleated-front, plain-front, or side elastic adjustable waist. Best colors: Dark olive, dark green, coffee, navy, charcoal, black.
- Jackets made of medium-weight worsted wool for year round wear: Avoid fancy cuts, double-breasted, or four-button styles. Choose a clas-sic navy two-button blazer. As an option, get a sport jacket in a textured fabric like tweed, glen plaid, or herringbone. Avoid pinstripes.
- Suits that look good on nearly every body type: two- or three-button single-breasted in dark gray, navy blue, or dark brown.
- Shoes: All leather, either dark brown slip-ons like loafers or a quality pair of black lace-up shoes. Wear dark socks. Keep shoes polished and in good condition.
- Ties: Solid colors, rep stripes, or colorful prints that complement the jacket and the shirt.
- Pocket squares, suspenders, belt buckles to add a creative touch to the ensemble: Use in moderation, though, and avoid hats.

• Jewelry that is kept to a minimum so it doesn't distract: wristwatch, ring, lapel pin, and tie pin. Keep the throat area unadorned.

Before You Buy

Now that you have some information pertaining to actor-friendly colors and wardrobe selections, there are steps you can take to make sure your purchases are a wise investment.

Always do a closet review and discover what can be salvaged with a new hem, lining, alteration, buttons, trim, or color. If there are clothes in your closet that you haven't worn in more than a year, donate them to a homeless shelter. Get rid of what is no longer relevant or stylish, or doesn't fit. If you are squeamish about doing this, hire an image consultant who specializes in this area to assist you. The fee charged can save you shopping time and credit-card charges.

IMAGE CONSULTANTS

It is important to manage the impressions we leave with people in The Business as well as in our personal lives. Research tends to show that people who are well groomed, well mannered, and well spoken are assumed to be more competent. Yet, it is very difficult to see ourselves as others see us. News anchors, politicians, corporate executives, and other professionals with high visibility depend upon the expertise of trained image consultants who have extensive backgrounds in fashion, retail, marketing, and communications. The image consultant's role in helping to effect a change in appearance extends beyond wardrobe, makeup, and hairstyling guidelines to advice on nonverbal communication such as body language, eye contact, listening skills, and camera-ready techniques. The major objective of image consultants is to establish long-term relationships with their clients and to help them achieve a lifetime of inner and outer confidence. Those who seek image consultants to achieve success in their personal and professional development will always appear comfortable with who they are.

How Image Consultants Work

Your initial consultation with an image consultant will probably last two hours. You will discuss your experience, your career status, and what package you want to be selling. Your colors will be analyzed so you will be able to know the most flattering hues that complement your hair, eyes, and skin tones.

The consultant is trained to zip through your closet and eliminate the unnecessary, the unflattering, the unwearable, the out-of-date. You may discover there is a sensational outfit you've forgotten about, that shirts and skirts can be matched in snappy combinations, or that easy fixes—such as changes in trim, hemline length, or color—can improve your wardrobe. The consultant has a long list of resources that will help you to find what you need.

The consultant will address appearance issues, such as the best make-up, hairstyle, skin care, posture, fit, and wardrobe styles, and also refer you to well-researched photographers, duplicators, tailors, personal trainers, dermatologists, cosmetic dentists, and plastic surgeons if necessary. Their one-on-one session will help you assemble all the wardrobe essentials—best interview ensemble, appropriate accessories, and shoes, everything you will need to create a lasting first impression. Your best styles will be emphasized so you will know how you want to market yourself at the photo session.

Jill Bremer, the author of *It's Your Move: Dealing Yourself the Best Cards in Life and Work*, focuses on the ABCs of appearance, behavior, and communication. "If I've done my job right, people won't notice my client's grammar, clothes, or manners, but those things will all be working for them in the background to help project a confident and capable persona."

Image consultants usually charge their clients by the hour, and their rates vary widely. Charges can range from $75 to more than $300 an hour; a rate of $250 an hour is not uncommon for a highly regarded consultant in a major metropolitan area.

Whatever your specific needs are, there is a certified image consultant who can offer help and invaluable tools. The Association of Image Consultants International (AICI) is a worldwide, nonprofit, professional organization of men and women in the fields of fashion, image consulting, and related industries. You can learn more about this organization at www.aici.org.

Remember that there is no single recipe for creating your *image*. Everything will depend upon your physical type, your coloring, your individual flair and personality, and ultimately how you feel about yourself. Managing your image can be a lifelong process.

DEFINING STYLE

Everyone has a unique style, an essence, a way of connecting to others, to society, and to daily life. Style is determined by your personality, physical characteristics, preferences and goals, creativity, energy, and your sense of self.

Image Consultants Alyce Parsons and Diane Parente pioneered the concept of "universal style" for both men and women in the early 1990s. They discovered that we connect with one or more predominant lists of keywords that describe who we are and how we should be perceived. To better illustrate their thesis, we selected well-known individuals who exemplify the inherent traits in these seven basic styles:

Sporty: friendly, casual, unpretentious, comfortable with who you are, likeable

Sandra Bullock, Kyra Sedgwick, Jamie Lee Curtis, Joe Mantegna, Richard Gere, Philip Seymour Hoffman, Paul Giamatti, Michael Caine

Traditional: businesslike, conscientious, loyal, organized, reliable, trustworthy

Tom Robbins, Billy Graham, Jimmy Carter, Bill Moyers, Madeleine Albright, Brian Williams, Anderson Cooper

Elegant: refined, polished, cultured, poised, discerning

Sigourney Weaver, Audrey Hepburn, Cary Grant, Helen Mirren, David Niven, Gwyneth Paltrow, Grace Kelly, Jeremy Irons

Romantic: caring, compassionate, charming, sensitive, vulnerable, nurturing

Renée Zellweger, Hugh Jackman, Nicole Kidman, Jude Law, Brad Pitt, George Clooney, Meryl Streep, Judi Dench

Alluring: provocative, body conscious, seductive, sexy, enticing

Angelina Jolie, Salma Hayek, Heath Ledger, Viggo Mortensen, Halle Berry, Antonio Banderas, Shemar Moore

Creative: adventuresome, free-spirited, imaginative, original, fearless

Robin Williams, Billy Crystal, Johnny Depp, Bette Midler, Jack Nicholson, Cher, Tommy Lee Jones, Diane Keaton, Al Pacino

Dramatic: commanding, confident, intense, self-assured, sophisticated

Denzel Washington, Catherine Zeta-Jones, Michael Douglas, Angelica Houston, Annette Bening, Russell Crowe, Harrison Ford

If you are a Sporty Male, your wardrobe colors are earth tones such as tan, khaki, olive, moss, and chestnut. Your favorite fabrics are easy-to-wear Oxford cloth, denim, or microfibers. The fit is loose and comfortable. Your preferred hairstyle is short and carefree. You wear loafers or rubber-soled sports shoes. Daytime ensemble might be a sport jacket, button-down shirt or silk tee, and casual slacks. Labels you buy would include Perry Ellis, Banana Republic, Eddie Bauer, J. Crew, L.L. Bean, Nautica, and The Gap. The overall message you want to communicate is that you are comfortable with who you are, open, and accessible. And that is the message you want to communicate at your interview or when you are selling a product.

It is important to realize that we comprise all the styles to a greater or lesser degree. Can a Sporty Male be Romantic? Absolutely. Paul Giamatti is a perfect example. Take another look at *Sideways* and *Cinderella Man.*

The Romantic style for the actress is defined by a wardrobe featuring muted colors and pastels. Fabrics are fluid and lightweight like chiffon, challis, and rayon. The fit is loose and flowing. Hairstyles are soft with face-framing curls or natural waves. Makeup is delicate and luminous. Clothing includes flared skirts, jackets that are loose or fitted at the waist, tunics over slacks, blouses with round, ruffled, or lacy collars or cuffs. Shoes will have T-straps or ankle straps, or be open-toed pumps or ballet-inspired flats. The jewel box might contain pearl earrings and necklaces, cameos, floral pins, and a heart-shaped pendant. Designer labels could include Ralph Lauren and Talbots.

Can the Romantic Nicole Kidman be considered Alluring as well? Remember her sizzling performance in *To Die For* as the ambitious newscaster and then the Civil War heroine in *Cold Mountain.*

Technology has made it easy to shop online at thousands of retail and wholesale sites for the look that suits your style. Sites we enjoy include www.nordstrom.com, www.eddiebauer.com, www.salesandbargains.com, www.gap.com, www.llbean.com, www.coldwatercreek.com, www.jjill.com, and www.chicos.com.

KNOW YOUR SHAPE, SHOW YOUR SHAPE

Catherine Schuller is well known in the retail industry for the image work that she does with plus-size women. She is the empowerment editor for Amaze Magazine, an e-zine that is focused on lifestyles and fashion advice (www.amazemagazine.com) and helps women shop with a "wardrobe strategy, to know her shape, show her shape, and to find her figure type." She is also a former performer and plus-size model who speaks with great authority about the obstacles facing actors with curves.

In show business one's dress or suit size is a definite factor in determining the types of roles they will get. Someone once tweaked the saying and came up with, 'There are no small roles, only small waistlines wanted for them.' How often do you think an actor has been told, 'You've gotten too thin for this role?' I am stating the obvious, that the industry is all about thin, but what about the fact that acting represents and reflects life?

Only recently have there been roles with plus-size women and men in which the character's size is unrelated to what happens to them. The roles sometimes have not been created for a plus-size gal, but the producers want to take a risk and hire someone out of the norm. Like Camryn Manheim's character in The Practice (1997–2004). They kept her in a very simple suit, hair back, very tailored, and they didn't shoot her so that she looked too contrasted with the other characters. There wasn't any mention that she was a fuller-figured gal. No reference was made to food addiction or eating disorders. She just was who she was.

Find a happy medium between the excess and the holocaust victim. Look at your body and say, 'What do I want to draw attention to and what do I want to detract from?' With clothing, you can draw a neon finger right where you want people to look. Try a monochromatic outfit, empire line, tunic top over the hips. The ancient Greeks not only looked at the horizontal proportions but also at the vertical. They realized that the eye needs to see short over long, long over short. So, if you have a very narrow bottom, you need something a little bit more voluminous to balance that, and likewise if you have a bigger bottom, a skinnier top so it is not big over big or long over long. This way the eye never rests anywhere. Vertical proportions show how your torso and your legs relate to each other. Get to know yourself and work with that and don't apologize.

Anyone with larger legs should not be wearing a miniskirt. To the knee is very chic. Rolling up sleeves and three-quarter sleeves give you a diminishing line. Highlight your best body parts, especially if you are on camera. A lot of times stylists who work for the TV shows don't know about body shapes. They are used to dealing with skinny people. They don't even know there are large-size departments in the stores. A lot of times the plus-size actor has to educate the stylist.

If you are really going to stick with being a full-figured actress, then that is your type. Don't do monologues that are about skinny ingenues. Do something that shows your power, and owns it, and really expresses it. I find that most people jump on your bandwagon if you are there for yourself. You send the message that you understand yourself and who you are in your life.

For more insights from Catherine Schuller, visit www.catherineschuller. com and www.curvychick.com.

Larger is becoming more acceptable. In the entertainment industry, plus-size actors like Queen Latifah and supermodel Emme have become role models for actresses who thought they had to look like Twiggy to become successful.

Late-nineteenth-century musical theater superstar Lillian Russell was shaped like an hourglass and tipped the scales at nearly two hundred pounds. The world still fell in love with her. The press referred to her curves as "sonnets of motion," which added to Russell's appeal. Duels were fought to defend her honor, one love-struck fan jumped into Niagara Falls because he couldn't win her, and Diamond Jim Brady—the Donald Trump of his time—proposed marriage by pouring a million dollars into her silken lap.

We deliberately advise actors not to list their weight on their résumés. It fluctuates so rapidly that it will not be the same on any given day. Is the part you are auditioning for contingent on how much you weigh? Is there a scale placed in the casting office? Probably not. Besides, with exercise programs creating physiques that are more muscular and therefore heavier, it's more difficult, and less important, for casting directors to gauge weights.

Finding a New Shape

Actor and singer Russell Painter lost eighty pounds after he moved to New York City. He originally weighed 275 pounds and was wearing pants with a size 40 waist. The first major change he did was to increase his walking. On some days he would walk from Ground Zero to West 159th Street (approximately ten miles). As an experienced ballroom dancer, he would maintain his dance posture while walking. Focusing on pace, breathing, and posture he could turn a regular walk into an hour-long workout.

I found that, by taking these walks, I could get to know the city, practice my breathing techniques to help with my singing, work on songs or monologues, and reduce stress. I also bought two thirty-pound weights to use at home to help tone my upper body.

I went from eating one or two large meals a day to eating four, five, or even six small meals throughout the day, plus snacks. An average meal was whatever I could hold in my hand and eat while walking to an audition or a photo shoot. I eventually knew all the places to get a healthy slice of pizza (almost always something with chicken and some vegetable like broccoli or mushrooms), fruit, and lots of water. I would hit one of three of my favorite stores for a smoothie with a good amount of protein and a multivitamin enhancer. I made healthy choices in what I ate and they were all small portions.

I've gone from buying everything in large to actually wearing some smalls and a few mediums. My energy level has practically gone through the roof.

FINAL ADVICE

A schedule of interviews, auditions, classes, and rehearsals requires stamina. A balanced diet, rich in fresh fruits and vegetables, greens, and grains, is essential. Plenty of actors, including the biggest names, brown-bag it through the day, toting fruits, nuts, raisins, strips of raw carrot, celery and green pepper, wedges of cheese, containers of yogurt, and the indispensable spring water. They do this not because they are hypoglycemic or diabetic or to save the high cost of lunching in restaurants, but because they know how important it is to take good care of themselves. When you spend a full day at a studio or on location, you may have no control over what the food carts will provide, which might have an overabundance of quick energy fixes filled with sugar.

Getting your act together from head to toe represents a significant investment in your business plan. It is your primary responsibility to keep your package in the best condition.

CHAPTER 3

The Tools of the Trade

"**When I first look at a headshot, I'm drawn to the eyes and try to read what the actor is saying through them.**"

—Margaret Emory, Talent Agent, Dulrina Eisen Associates

You've found a place to live, set up your home office, recorded a professional-sounding voice-mail message, made room in your closet for the professional, color-friendly wardrobe, polished the perfect audition shoes, and have now saved up enough money for the most major investment: the photo.

THE PICTURE AND YOU

In-your-face marketing demands that you have a terrific promotional photo to use for all your headshots and on your letterheads, postcards, business cards, and the Internet.

Having your photo taken can be a nerve-wracking experience. Some of us don't even like to be snapped at family gatherings, much less having to pose for a photo intended to get us an agent or an audition. It feels so often like an artificial and manipulative situation with constraints and pressures to get it perfect. But we aren't perfect, so how close can we get to a true, aesthetically pleasing representation?

First and foremost, the picture must look like you—and not what the photographer thinks you should look like, with too much makeup, lighting tricks, and extensive digital retouching.

Looking comfortable in your skin is the key to a successful picture. Your physical attitude should be open and friendly. Your shoulders should be relaxed. Your hands, if they are going to be visible, should be in natural positions that are supportive, organic, and tasteful. They should never distract from the face. Your smile should be easy and sincere, with your mouth turned slightly upwards and your eyes sparkling with humor and warmth. Your eyes are a reflection of your quality, your energy, and your approachability. According to New York headshot photographer Matt Hoebermann, "Lighting is the key to successful photography. It is about the eyes in every shot. They are the windows of the soul."

If you already have a photo, do this picture test to determine if you need a new one. Hold your photo right next to your face and look in the mirror. Do you and the image in that 8 x 10 look like the same person? Does one of you look older, younger, tense, relaxed? Do you have freckles, laugh lines, or little puffs under your eyes when you smile? If you are concerned about puffy eyelids, dark circles, lines, bumps, crooked teeth, or other shortcomings, have them attended to by a plastic surgeon, dermatologist, or an orthodontist in advance of your photo shoot.

Choosing the Right Photographer

Almost inevitably, when you are trying to make it in the major talent centers, you will have to discard the picture you have had taken in Peoria, Battle Creek, or Billings. It's not that local photographers aren't talented; they simply do not have the frame of reference necessary to provide you with the photos that will do the job you need. Many photographers in New York, Chicago, and Los Angeles work with thousands of actors and know what the industry wants and expects. Professional photographers advertise in the trade papers: *Back Stage East* in New York and *Back Stage West* in Los Angeles, *PerformInk* in Chicago, and *The Working Actor's Guide to Los Angeles.* Reproductions (www.reproductions.com), which specializes in photographic reproduction for actors, publishes a free directory of photographers on both coasts.

Interview several photographers before you make a choice. Rapport between you and your photographer is essential. If you don't feel comfortable at the interview and aren't convinced the work is right for you, go on to the next photographer on your list. Sense where the photographer is coming from. Do you feel comfortable with this person? How does he or she see you? Sexy? Glamorous? Next-door neighbor? Corporate spokesperson? *Law*

& *Order* lawyer? Soap star? Be sure you and the photographer are on the same professional page. Avoid anyone who seems to be giving you a hard sell or trying to intimidate you by bragging about the big name performers in the portfolio rather than focusing on you.

Examine portfolios carefully and check out photographers' Web sites, and keep the following in mind:

- Do you like the work? Is the style so forceful that you feel the actor is upstaged? Ask to see some before and after shots. These give perhaps the strongest indication of a photographer's credibility.
- Pay attention to the lighting techniques in the shots. Lighting should frame your face and not hide it with shadows, harden your features, or make you look like you have a halo.
- Look at the backgrounds. The background must never upstage you! This means no brick walls, shiny wood veneers, furniture, strange geometric shapes, plants, busy wallpaper, tree trunks, and other distractions.
- Is the price reasonable? Photo session fees range from $250 to $1,200. What do you get for it? How many prints? Is a makeup artist and/or hairstylist included in the cost? Ask if the makeup artist and hairstylist will be with you throughout the session.

Finally, find out in advance how long the photographer allows for the sitting. You want to be sure you have all the time you need to make certain you get a photo that you'll think puts your best face forward.

Before the Shoot

Study yourself in the mirror and practice facial expressions. According to Paul Ekman and Wallace Friesen, psychologists at the University of California in San Francisco and developers of the Facial Action Coding System (FACS), facial muscles are capable of producing forty-three movements, which in turn can create 10,000 different expressions.

Careful self-scrutiny will enable you to discover that when you smile, you squint and your eyes disappear, or your gums show, or you wrinkle your nose and furrow your forehead. Be on the lookout for double chins. Do you hunch your shoulders? What is your best side? Whenever we sneak a glance at ourselves, in a mirror or a store window, we're always on the way to or from some place or busily talking with someone. Anything other than a candid snapshot catches us in a totally artificial moment—perfectly still. Shifting the emphasis and becoming aware of how your body sags or slumps when you're doing nothing may require a bit of practice. (See the discussion of the Alexander Technique in Chapter Five.)

Patricia Elliott, a Tony Award–winning actress, tells this story:

> I looked at myself in the mirror one day and I saw that I have, just by virtue of nature, very strong, very strict, cruel, cool, cold lines in my face. If my face is in repose, very often people will come up to me and ask if I'm okay, did someone die? And all I would be doing was concentrating on my scene for that day. So, after giving myself that long look in the mirror, I realized that just by raising the corners of my mouth a little bit it all went away.

Discuss wardrobe choices with your photographer and decide which are best for the session. Review the professional wardrobe guidelines in Chapter Two, "Getting Your Act Together." Since you are getting color photos, avoid black and white as wardrobe colors. Wear colors that complement your skin tones, hair color, and eyes. Remember that modified shoulder pads provide structure and authority.

Avoid prints, patterns, polka dots, stripes, brand logos, and bright upstaging colors like lime green, yellow, bubblegum pink, and neon orange. Don't wear jewelry and large buttons, particularly those made of mother-of-pearl or bone white, because they can steal the focus from your face. Fabrics should not be too sheer or lacy, shiny, or light-reflective. Opt for knits, rayon, and acetate blends.

Choose fabrics that are wrinkle-free and low maintenance. Press or steam your clothes in advance. When you pack them, use a garment bag so your clothing will retain softness and won't flatten or crease. If the photographer doesn't have an iron (ask about this when you make your appointment for the session), tote your own.

If you have curly hair and want a photo with straight hair, you don't need to book two separate sessions. You can achieve the different looks with the help of the hairstylist in one sitting. Men with facial hair might want to start the session with the beard, moustache, sideburns, or stubble, then shave it off for a clean-cut look.

Shooting Outdoors

Many photographers prefer to work in natural light. This is particularly true in California, where the climate and landscape are so conducive to outdoor photography. If you are more comfortable outside a studio, look for someone who has a track record of working outdoors. But realize that the weather has to be totally in your favor—not so sunny that you automatically squint, not so breezy as to play havoc with your clothing or hairstyle. If your hair frizzes when there is even the slightest bit of humidity, stick to the indoor shoot.

Getting the Most from the Photo Shoot

The success of your photo will depend upon the message you are trying to communicate. Decide in advance what roles you feel you are best suited for. Typecast yourself in episodic dramas, sitcoms, feature films, commercials, and soap operas. It is important that you have the "get me in the door" shot in which an engaging smile shows your personality and humor. Realistically, could you have auditioned for Holly Golightly? Forrest Gump? Eliza Doolittle? Stanley Kowalski? Scarlett O'Hara? Rhett Butler? Fanny Brice? Indiana Jones? James Bond? Rocky? Norma Rae? Think of the roles you were born to play or the types of roles you most enjoy playing. Contemporary, edgy characters? Romantic heroines? Are you all-American, ethnic, quirky? A girl-next-door or a seductive vamp? A rich society heiress? A politician? A corporate executive

Look at your current photo and write a first-person caption to verbalize the thought you are projecting. If nothing comes to mind, the photo is too general and lacking in personality. Visualize Barbra Streisand as Fanny Brice shouting "I'm the greatest star"; Vivien Leigh as Scarlett O'Hara defiantly declaring "I'll never go hungry again!"; Julie Andrews as Eliza Doolittle happily chirping "I could have danced all night." Your thought need not always be in the first person. Clint Eastwood just has to say "Make my day!" and we have an image of a taciturn, menacing, tough character with whom no one wants to mess. If you cannot think of that caption, toss the photo aside. If you can't tell what it's trying to say, casting directors won't either, and they don't have the time to wonder what character types you are capable of playing.

Now, here are some specific tips to help you relax and enjoy the shoot. Your ease and sense of self will come across in the photos.

- Plan to bring your favorite CDs with you. Most photographers have CD players in their studios. You should listen to music that relaxes you, gives you energy, puts you in a great mood, and triggers your imagination. Samples include ocean waves, new age, Sinatra, Norah Jones, Springsteen, Mozart, the Dixie Chicks.

Successful headshots (clockwise).
Schuyler Yancey
Jenny Strassburg
Kim Shively

- Carry along your favorite fragrance. If a scented candle or a spritz of some lavender or gardenia or green apple enhances your mood or inspires you, use it.
- Bring a photo of someone close to you. Just looking at it may release some tension. Try some deep breathing exercises and yoga postures prior to the shoot to get you limber and open to a deeper enjoyment of the session.

Remember the photographer is working for you.

After the Shoot

Your photographer will probably make the photos available for viewing on a disk and online and select some of the best ones for your consideration. According to photographer Matt Hoebermann, :

> You will be able to pick your favorites online and e-mail them to agents, casting directors, managers, and other industry professionals for their input. Many people, even your agents, will feel bogged down if you ask them to look at three-hundred-plus photos. It simply takes too long. You should edit them down to a reasonable amount, showing a variety of images you would consider using. You can send an e-mail link for each photo of you to the favorites list on your Web browser, but these have been known to reset themselves. As a back-up, write out a list of the images. Don't forget that with technology you can improve the photo easily. Digital retouching can whiten your eyes, diminish harsh lines or wrinkles, remove blemishes (even with expert makeup, blemishes are rarely invisible in a color shot!), remove stray hairs, fill in thinning hair, and warm up your hair color. Almost anything can be fixed, but retouch prior to ordering prints to save time and money.

Photos can be printed on a variety of papers. Choose semi-matte or matte finish, which have a popular and user-friendly, nonreflective tone.

Duplication

Despite the popularity of electronic submissions, you will still need a certain number of prints. If you look at the casting Web sites, they will tell you that you need to bring a hard copy with you. You will also probably want a certain number of photo postcards to send between your regular 8 x 10 mailings. Postcards are less expensive to mail, but unless you put them in a number 10 business envelope, you have no control over what they will look like when they reach the casting office. We have seen them show up with moustaches and lip prints added and torn corners. Be sure your name, contact information, and union affiliations are printed beneath your picture. You may also want to invest in a photo business card, which has a postage-stamp-size photo of you, along with your name and contact number. This is easy to carry with you at all times and especially handy to have at networking events or social occasions where you might meet someone who works in show business or who knows somebody who does.

Duplication and reprint providers advertise in *Back Stage* and other trade papers. Your photographer may work with a particular company whose work is consistently good. With the advent of digital reproduction, photos can be ready within a day, as opposed to the two weeks the process used to take.

Cameron Stewart, president of Reproductions, a New York and Los Angeles firm that reproduces headshots and creates postcards, photo business cards, and other images for actors, explains how the process works.

> The photographer burns a disk after editing a shoot or sends selections from the session to us via the Internet, and we post the shots online for actors to view. We send an e-mail notifying them that the session is online with instructions on how they can access the contact sheets. They can enlarge and edit the shots they like, select the font and size for the type they want to use, select a border if they want to use one, and place an order for retouching. After they have approved the retouching, they can pick up their print order within an hour.

> We understand that actors are thrown into the deep end of the pool in terms of the fact that they need to become advertising people and self-promoters. That is not what they are trained to do. Whatever we can do in helping them along the way in terms of design, or layout, or if somebody makes a mistake and they really didn't want their name that way, we will default to the actor. Every once in a while a blue moon rises over someone and we try to make that go away as quickly and painlessly as possible.

How many prints you order will depend on how much you will be using the Internet to electronically submit your headshots and how many hard copies you estimate you'll need for self submission or to give to your talent representatives. According to Cameron Stewart, "With the advent of online casting several years ago, actors no longer need the same number of pictures. Now they can spend the same amount of money but get fewer copies with better quality."

THE RÉSUMÉ

A résumé is an outline of your experience and training and should always accompany your headshot. Staple the 8 x 10 résumé to the back of your photo, print side out. It is your responsibility to attach it to the back of

Marta Reiman
Alluring headshot for
soap operas (above).
Smiling headshot for
commercial work.

the photo. Performers have been known to hand them to casting directors separately, waiting for the casting director to hunt for the stapler. That doesn't make a good first impression. Avoid gluing the résumé to the photo; in humid conditions, it buckles.

The Basics

Do not put the words "résumé" or "experience" on the document. Everyone will know what it is. Be sure your font sizes are reader-friendly.

Your Name

Your name should be in large bold letters at the top left or center. Simple enough, but are you happy with your name? If not, and if you are thinking about changing it, now is the time to do it, before you put your name out there in The Business or join a union.

Your birth name defines you. It represents your family history, ethnic roots, and the creative efforts of the parents who gave it to you. However, if it is difficult to pronounce, spell, or remember, it may not be the name you want for your professional career. You might think you are being typecast because of your ethnicity. Oscar winner Anne Bancroft might not have been considered for the roles of Annie Sullivan in *The Miracle Worker* or the lusty Mrs. Robinson in *The Graduate* if she had remained Anna Maria Italiano.

Changing your name can be a weighty decision. Consult with family members, close friends, and industry professionals. If you want to retain a connection to your family, try using your mother's maiden name or the name of a revered relative. Or, like Tom Cruise, simply drop the surname (Mapother).

Whatever you choose to be called, pick a new name and consistently use it. This is called common usage. Or, you can go through a more formal court procedure. In general, the court proceedings are relatively simple; the Web site www.soyouwanna.com outlines the process.

Once your name is changed, alert your state motor vehicle division and the Social Security Administration. You will also have to report the change to the IRS, utility companies, credit card companies, passport bureau, banks, and your voter registrar. You can seek help from a lawyer or a paralegal. Sites on the Web that can assist you include www.soyouwanna.com, www.namechangers.com, www.uslegalforms.com, and www.namechangelaw.com.

You should check with the actors unions—Actors' Equity (AEA), the American Federation of Radio and Television Artists (AFTRA), and the Screen Actors Guild (SAG)—before you go to the courts to be sure your new name is not already assigned to a union member. Actor Michael Keaton was christened Michael Douglas. Sometimes a simple change of one letter can make a big difference. Bette Davis changed the "y" to an "e"; Julia Roberts replaced her "e" with an "a." Once you've chosen a new name, embrace it, own it, and be proud to slate it.

Union Affiliations and Physical Statistics

Under your name list any union affiliations or eligibility and then your cell phone or voice-mail number; e-mail and Web site addresses are optional. Never include your home address or your home telephone number on your résumé. Résumés are passed around to many hands and, unfortunately, may end up with some people whose interest in your career is questionable.

Physical statistics include height and size, but with color headshots, it's no longer necessary to list eye and hair color. Height is important because, due to character specifications, many casting directors will insist on knowing it.

You don't need to list your weight. Men can put their jacket size, women their dress size. Weight fluctuates, but size indicates your physical shape.

Actors older than twelve needn't state their age or date of birth. Nor is it necessary to describe your age range—that's an old theater habit. If they want an actor to look forty–five years old, they'll hire an actor who is forty–five. If you sing, list your voice range (e.g. soprano, baritone, tenor).

Credits

The body of the résumé lists stage, film, and television roles. Because of the type of opportunities available, New York actors list theater credits first, while Los Angeles actors begin with film and TV work. It takes awhile to accrue credits, so early résumés often include roles played in college theater departments or conservatories and an extensive training section. As your career takes off, these will be replaced by small parts on soap operas or prime-time episodic dramas, Off-Off-Broadway showcases, and regional theater, and commercials or industrials.

Always begin with your strongest credits. If you have to prune high school roles that are no longer age-appropriate, snip away. Put the headings in all-capital bold letters. For THEATER, list—in three columns—the role played, the title of the play, and the place or director. For FILM, list the role played, the type of role (lead, featured, costar), and the production company, studio, or director. Next to COMMERCIALS, you can put "list upon request" if you are working in New York or Los Angeles. Casting directors in the major centers will ask you if you are selling or representing a product that would conflict with the commercial being cast. They might also want to see a DVD demo of any commercial work you have done. In regional markets, commercials and industrials are listed.

Next comes EDUCATION. Name the university from which you earned your B.A., B. F. A., or M.F.A. in theater or musical theater. Degrees in psychology, sociology, history, and English are also impressive. Actors have been told they shouldn't list degrees that have nothing to do with performing, but an actor who has another major is an educated and disciplined individual whose expertise in forensics, nursing, law, history, or biology might be useful on a daytime soap or an episode of *CSI: Crime Scene Investigation.*

The TRAINING section features scene study, on-camera techniques, and voice, dance, singing, and acting classes you have taken. We want to know where you studied, with whom, and for how long. For performers who have not done a lot of professional work, this section is the heart of the résumé; casting directors and agents will know the teachers and the schools. Judy Blye Wilson, award-winning casting director of *All My Children*, says, "The first thing I look at on a younger actor's résumé is training. If someone has not studied anywhere, it's not a good sign to me. With an actor who has had time to build a résumé, training and experience are both very important to me." Don't list the specific years you graduated or when you took the extra classes. The information is irrelevant and will date you.

SKILLS refer to your craft: types of dance, musical abilities, dialects, foreign language proficiency, stage combat, sign language, improvisation, clown work. Be sure that your knowledge of dialects is such that if you get an audition on short notice for one you've listed, you don't need a lot of time to prepare it. However, dialect coach Amy Stoller suggests that if you have six or seven dialects you could do with enough time to prepare, add the words "with notice" after them. Recently, a casting director released a breakdown for performers who could do real authentic duck calls, as opposed to duck sounds, for a New York Lottery radio commercial. The casting office for the feature film *I Am Legend* needed male and female professional-level modern dancers, acrobats, and/or free-runner parkour practitioners (parkour is an art or discipline that resembles self-defense in the martial arts), or very highly advanced yoga practitioners for non-speaking movement roles. Note: A driver's license is not a skill.

Finally, SPORTS should highlight your athletic abilities, from martial arts to in-line skating. Racquet sports, acrobatics, horseback riding, rollerblading, swimming, knowledge of how to use firearms, as well as any awards you might have won for athletics, get a separate category. But list only the ones you do expertly. In commercials, you'll be asked to dive off a high board again and again for repeated takes from a number of camera positions. Or you may have to ice skate for several hours, jog all day, play pool, throw darts, or serve a tennis ball in the noonday sun. Lying could truly be hazardous to your health.

Miscellaneous

If you have a valid Canadian or European passport, list that on your résumé. If you have a well-edited DVD showing three minutes of professional quality work, list its availability. Owning vintage cars, a versatile wardrobe, police or military uniforms, or a variety of wigs can provide you with opportunities to be seen for film or TV roles. However, the fact you work well with children and animals is a given.

Padding Your Credits

Wrong-headed advisers might suggest that you add a credit to look more experienced. Our advice is: Don't. This is a very small business and someone will inevitably discover that you are lying. You will regret it, lose credibility, and be embarrassed.

We love this true story by Oscar winner Michael Caine from his autobiography, *What's It All About*:

> I padded my résumé a bit by adding parts in plays that I had never even seen . . . I wrote down as part of my experience that I had played George in George and Margaret, a very popular repertory play. I was summoned to an audition, and when I walked into the theater the first thing the producer said to me was, "What have we here, then, apart from a bloody liar!"... The plot of the play centers on the fact that the entire cast spends the whole duration of the play waiting for George and Margaret to turn up, and they never do.

THE PHOTO-RÉSUMÉ

Adding a small photo in the upper left-hand corner makes your résumé a much more interesting marketing tool. One of the advantages is that you can now add a look that differs from the headshot. Perhaps the smiling, engaging commercial picture you attach to the back will be contrasted with a more glamorous or theatrical one on the résumé.

You can add a photo to your résumé using Microsoft Word on your home computer and print out résumés as you need them. Amanda Jones, describes how she created her photo résumé using Microsoft Word:

1. Open a new document in Word.

2. Format paper size to 8 x 10. Do this in File/Page Setup, on the Paper Tab. You may want to then switch to Print Layout in the View Menu for easier formatting.

Amanda Jones
AEA, AFTRA

EYES
Blue-Green

HEIGHT
5' 3", slender build

"It is not easy to find the chill in Genet's play... but the Cocteau production manages it. Credit an eye-opening turn by Ms. Jones. She is beautiful and scary, rational and deranged, somehow all at the same time. If your nanny-cam captured her, you would certainly have her fired, but you'd also keep the tape, just to study Ms. Jones's performance."

- Neil Genzlinger,
The New York Times,
"The Maids"

THEATRE

OFF-BROADWAY

Walking Down Broadway	Elsie	Mint Theater (Steven Williford)
The Maids	Solange	Cocteau Rep (Ernest Johns)
Uncle Vanya	Sonya	Cocteau Rep (Eve Adamson)
The Importance of Being Earnest	Cecily	Cocteau Rep (Ernest Johns)

OFF-OFF-BROADWAY

Fool	Nika	Gorilla Rep (Michael Lew)
Travesties	Gwendolyn	Perkasie Theater (Steve Keim)
Seven Reece Mews	Nora	Monday Morning Productions
Ah, My Dear Andersen	Various	Russian-American Theater
Hamlet	Ophelia	Million Stories (J. Michaels)
You Are Here	Rosie	TSI (Marc Bruni)
Romeo and Juliet	Juliet	Genesis Rep (J. Arellano)

REGIONAL

Business is Business (Brian Murray) Hampton	Germaine	Playwrights Thtr. Of E.
A Christmas Carol	Belinda Cratchit	North Shore Music Theater
Engaged	Minnie	Depot Thtr (Christopher Jones)
Arsenic and Old Lace	Elaine	Depot Theater (Chris Clavelli)
Bell, Book and Candle	Gillian	Sierra Repertory (Dennis Jones)
Picnic	Madge	Sierra Repertory (Frank Latson)
Sylvia	Sylvia	Tri-State Actors Theater
On the Verge	Alex	Tri-State Actors Theater
Magnificent Ambersons	Lucy	Oldcastle Theater (F. Latson)
The Man Who Came to Dinner	June	Oldcastle Theater (E. Peterson)
Abel	Wife	Moore Theater (Pavol Liska)

FILM AND TV

One Life to Live	Under 5 (Twice)	ABC
Black Mary	Supporting	Roman Moher Productions
My Stuffed Animal Is a Monster	Supporting	Joe Fiorello Films
Fisherboy (short)	Lead	NYU
Harry Otter (short)	Supporting	Ember Productions
Old Fashion Romance (short)	Lead	NYFA
Marley's Angels (industrial)	Supporting	NYU/HEOPOP

EDUCATION

BA in Theatre and Government (double major) from Dartmouth College

TRAINING

Acting:	Karen Kohlhaas, Clarke McCarthy, Charles Tuthill
Commercial Technique:	David Cady
Improv:	Billy Meritt/Upright Citizens Brigade
Singing:	Sharon Powers

SKILLS

Fluent German, conversational Russian and Japanese; English, Irish, Scottish, Russian, Polish, German, American South and Midwest dialects; knitting; ballroom, belly, jazz, ballet and Irish step dancing; valid driver's license

SPORTS

skiing (snow and water); skating (ice and inline); soccer

Kelley Rae O'Donnell
AEA, AFTRA, SAG *eligible*

Henry Downey Talent Management
Mari Lyn Henry   212 459 4545

THEATRE

The 6-Pack	Various	NY Neo-Futurists
1:23	Andrea Yates	LAByrinth Theater Co.
92 Jonquil Lane	Annie	Prospect Theatre Co.
Faith	Sandra	Push Productions (US premiere)
The 24 Hour Plays	Various	The Atlantic Theatre
You Can Clap Now	Miss. Stevenson	Chris McGarry (Hip Hop Fest.)
Celebrity	Various	John Gould Rubin
How To Catch A Monkey	Nurse, PETA, Kisser	LAByrinth Theater Co.
Stupida Boyz (sketch comedy)	Various	Moxie Films
Macbeth	Witch 2 & Murderer 2	Anthony Abeson
Second Hand Smoke	Mom	Matthew Maguire
Titus Andronicus	Lavinia	Dennis Reid

FILM

The Saint of Avenue B	Waiter (supporting)	Rene Alberta
On Your Mark	Sophia Wagner (lead)	Dylan Kidd (Thousand Words)
Acme Pictures Summer Project	Laura (lead)	Michael Nigro/Perry Grebin
Beyond Recognition	Diane Gold (lead)	Tom Muschamp
Spy, Inc.	Alex (lead)	Pawel Pawelczak
Eureka	Hera (supporting)	Meike Peterson
Oedipus	Lydia (lead)	Alban Kakulya
The Bench	Miss. Grace (lead)	Jacob Waxler
Damned	Gina (supporting)	James Murray

TELEVISION

Guiding Light	Airport Ticket Agent	CBS
The IT Factor	Self	BRAVO/Billy Hopkins

COMMERCIALS – CONFLICTS UPON REQUEST

TRAINING

B.A. Theatre, Fordham University
LAByrinth Theater Co. - Philip Seymour Hoffman & John Ortiz, Co- Artistic Directors
ACTING: Anthony Abeson * Deborah Hedwall * John Gould Rubin * Larry Sacharow *
Joan MacIntosh * Matthew Maguire
MOVEMENT: Saratoga International Theatre Institute (suzuki & viewpoints)
VOICE: Judith Jablonka * Sandy Kazan * John A. Harris * Joan & Doug Barber
DANCE: Broadway Dance Center, Steps, Princeton Ballet

SPECIAL SKILLS

British and American dialects (pick up dialects quickly), Aerobics, Jazz Dance, Modern Dance, Ballroom Dancing, Yoga, Stage Combat, Voice (alto/mezzo soprano); Sports: Roller skating, Hiking, Swimming, Deep Sea and Basic Fishing -- Reel Available (DVD/VHS)

HEIGHT
5'4

SIZE
4

Member of
LAByrinth
Theater Company

"There are powerful turns
from
Kelley Rae O'Donnell
as the woman railing against
the transformation of her
beloved adopted homeland
into a battleground"
-Ron Cohen, Backstage
on "Faith"

3. Using the Drawing toolbar at the bottom of the screen, click on the Text box button; then, using the arrow key, draw a text box across the top of the page. The box will contain your name, contact information, union affiliations, etc.

4. Left-click on the text box, then start typing your name (it should appear in the text box). You can format the text using the Formatting toolbar at the top of the page. Right-click and a drop-down toolbar will appear. Use this to format the outline color and thickness, fill color, size, and layout of the text box.

5. Go on to create three more text boxes: one for your picture, one for your credits, and one for your physical statistics, review quotes, and Web site information. I recommend using one text box for all of your credits and one for your physical statistics and other info because:

doing so helps you keep all of the text perfectly aligned; you can re-format the font of all the type of the box at once by right-clicking and using the pull-down menu; and it is easier to move around one box than a bunch of little ones. I use the Tab key to align the text in each column.

6. To add the picture, use the Insert pull-down menu; click on Picture, then From File, and then pull your picture from wherever you have it saved. You will probably need to re-size it. To do so, right-click on the picture to access the formatting options.

7. If you are using regular-size paper, be sure to reformat the picture to 8.5 x 11 before printing. This should push your résumé into the upper left corner of the page, which actually makes it very easy to cut down. I staple the résumé to my headshot first, aligning the edges of the picture with the top and left side of the résumé, then cut off the extra paper on the bottom and right side with a paper cutter (a great investment that makes cutting much quicker than it is with scissors, and the result is much neater).

The Toot-Your-Horn Column

You will note in the two examples of the photo-résumé that each one has a section under the photograph that contains additional items such as a positive review excerpt from a production or a connection to a theatrical company. This column is designed to contain complimentary notices, additional skills you want highlighted, awards, or membership in groups which use your talents as a writer, an actor, or a director. You may get a job as an on-set consultant for your special abilities. It is one more way to promote yourself to the industry.

Making Copies

You can print copies of your résumé on your computer. Having your résumé on your desktop at home allows you to update it and tailor it to the specific needs of the job you are trying to get. If you have an audition for a Broadway show, you can produce a résumé listing your theatrical credits. Select a paper that prints clearly and will stand up to a lot of handling. You don't have to use white—ivory or a pastel tint such as blue or green are attractive and generally cost no more. Avoid bright orange, dark red, forest green, or lime green, or other tones that will make it difficult to read the print. We used to caution actors about printing the résumé on the back of the photo. The lettering would bleed through and it was difficult for the casting director to write notes on the slick surface. Reproductions, the photo duplication service for actors, has a patent on heavy photographic paper with a fiber back on it that allows the actors to print their résumés directly on the back at home with an inkjet printer. The paper is fibrous and you can write on it.

Kevin Scullin
Photo Biz Card (above).
Double Photo Card
(below), showing two
character types:
rugged/ edgy,
commercial/ corporate.

Kevin Scullin

Actor/Voice Artist / Announcer
SAG AFTRA AEA
(212) 203-5113
comediusvox@aol.com

Kevin Scullin   SAG AFTRA AEA   (212) 203-5113

THE DVD

The DVD has replaced the videotape as the most effective way to show film or television clips. It is vital that you always record copies of television sitcoms, episodic dramas, soap operas, and commercials. You can use TIVO or another recording process to copy shows when they air. You can also request copies of commercials from the ad agency once they have aired. Whether or not you will have to pay a fee will depend on the producer's generosity. We suggest that you enlist the aid of an expert to help you in selecting your best clips. While you should be learning to develop your critical sense, it is extremely difficult to look at your own work objectively; a second, professional, opinion never hurts.

Creating a Demo

If you don't have professional credits as a resource, you can create your own DVD. Look for an inexpensive but reputable production facility that has some longevity and has been recommended by actors and agents. The suggested time limit for Demo DVDs is one minute, because casting directors won't have time to view work longer than that. You can also have a DVD that shows three minutes of your work to send to an agent or casting director who requests more examples.

Before you do the prepared material, slate your name, contact information, and any other physical statistics that are helpful, including height. Select types of material that show your strengths as an artist. You might want to perform two contrasting monologues that demonstrate a range of your abilities, show a sample of your dancing ability, or sing a Broadway ballad, contemporary pop tune, or operatic aria. Do some stand-up that you have written and performed in clubs. You can choose material from a role you've played, a part you've worked on with your acting or voice coach, or a piece you've written yourself. Your pieces should be contemporary (casting directors for film and television prefer contemporary material) and originate from a place of emotional truth. The scene should have energy, humor, and be within a comfortable age range. Movement should be minimal and motivated. End with a close-up on you and fade to black. Lighting and audio must be of top-notch professional quality.

Pay attention to every detail concerning the material you send out with your name and face on it. Prepare yourself as you would for any on-camera audition. Enhance your personal appearance with the help of a makeup artist, hairstylist, and wardrobe consultant. You want to make the best impression.

Always look at the playback. If you're not totally satisfied with what you see, do it again. This DVD is your commercial about a sensational unique product: you!

For the DVDs (commonly referred to as reels) you send through the mail, produce a professional-looking label on your computer with your photo and include contact information (note the example of Kim Shively's

DVD label in this chapter). Keep records of to whom you sent DVDs and when. If you want it returned to you, provide a stamped, self-addressed return mailer. Always try to keep a half dozen DVDs on hand so that you can hand deliver one to a potential agent or manager or casting director at a general meeting or an audition. Remember to put "DVD available" on your résumé and keep the DVD updated.

INTERNET CLIPS

You can also send a shorter, edited sampler of your reel via the Internet to producers, directors, casting offices, or agents. According to actress and master teacher Caryn West,

> The online demo reel makes access very quick and simple. And chances are your agent and casting director are sitting in front of a computer with a high speed line so this is the most effective vehicle out there. They can watch a demo while on the phone. This provides truly instant access, no matter where you are living.

Web sites where you can post your demo reel online include www. nowcasting.com, which puts your full-length demo reel online (up to five minutes) with Now Casting and also with the West Coast–based *Players Directory*. The reels can be played in Quicktime and Windows Media Player, so both PC and Mac users can watch them without downloading any programs. The cost includes a Web page (nowcasting.com/your name) and up to six photos, with unlimited uploads and changes, as well as a feature that allows you to insert a quick link in e-mails that opens only the pictures and résumé clips or reels that will make the strongest impression for the role you are up for.

The CD

What once was known as the audio tape is now a CD, the promotional tool used by voice-over artists, announcers, or character actors who are heard but not seen on TV and radio commercials as well as in video games, animated feature films, and animated series. You may wish to be considered for voice-overs if you have a distinctive speaking voice, with flexibility and range, and have mastered nonregional professional speech; if you are a whiz at dialects; or if you can produce trick voices, baby cries, animal sounds and do them consistently on cue. If you have these talents and wish to pursue voice-over work, you will need a recorded example of your vocal skills.

The CD is a compilation of commercials or narrations you have already broadcast. If you're just starting out, you will have to put a reel together from material that other actors have performed, or you may write your own copy—if you are good at that. Listen to commercials, select those you feel you should have been called in to audition for, record them, write out the lines, practice, then go to a professional studio to create your CD.

Julie Fulop-Balfour, who heads both the voice-over department and on–camera commercial division at the AKA Talent Agency in Los Angeles, speaks about the training that is necessary to enter the voice-over arena:

> It depends on the specialization. Some actors are vocal acrobats and can manipulate their voice to create animated sounds and characters. Their forte would be in animation. Some actors may be more soothing or have a deep baritone voice, so they specialize more in radio or the announcer type of voice-over work. Voice-over artists must be able to breathe life into the character or dialogue. It becomes a different style of acting. They need to be excellent readers, be able to take acting direction, and the delivery must be totally believable. You need to be a strong actor, so it would behoove you to get into a reputable acting class. It can take time to land that great animated project or start being the voice heard on a television commercial voice-over. So patience is a must!
>
> We are able to record our clients in house and send the audition in seconds. If a client is out of town, they can e-mail us an MP3 and not miss out on an opportunity. It has become so mobile and I cannot imagine doing business any other way.

Mark Oliver, an actor and voice-over artist (TCM announcer) who resides in Atlanta, built a voice-over studio in his home.

> The times when agents call you to ask you come in and audition for a voice-over are dwindling. Everyone now has MP3 capability. MP3 is a compressed file. What you record is compressed into a smaller sized file that takes less time to download and is easier to e-mail. IPods, for example, are MP3s.
>
> For Mac, I use Pro Tools, which is what they use in the big recording studios. For people who are starting and want to have a little audition system set up, I would recommend downloading Audacity, which is a free download of audio editing software. We are talking about professional industry standard software, so you can do broadcast quality jobs from home.

If you just want an audition setup, MP3 is the way to go. The quality isn't perfect, and you can have a little ambient noise, but they just want to hear you audition. Spend a hundred dollars on a microphone, and you are good to go.

There has to be some sort of interface between your microphone and computer. There are some programs that allow you to attach your mike directly to the computer via USB. And you have to have some kind of software to edit. You have to do a lot of research. It pays to have some audio engineer friends. They were my support group.

ONLINE MARKETING

Actors learn about job opportunities through a wide range of online and print resources. Some of the most prominent online listings and services include:

Players Directory

Known as the industry standard since 1937, the West Coast–based *Players Directory* (www.playersdirectory.com) is the only casting reference service to offer a biannual printed listing and a searchable Internet listing. The two-volume print directory is published in January and July, and distributed to all members of CSA (Casting Society of America) and CCDA (Commercial Casting Directors). Production companies, studios, and independent film companies around the world also purchase the directory and use the Internet component.

To receive print versions of or to access *Players Directory* online, you must be a member of an actor's union—Screen Actors Guild (SAG), the American Federation of Television and Radio Artists (AFTRA), or Actors' Equity(AEA). Members of a professional actor's union in a foreign country can also be included. The online listings are updated continually and include the actor's photo/s, professional name, representation, and résumé. Now Casting Inc. (www.nowcasting.com) provides an option to include a demo reel.

The cost for a directory listing is $75 per year per category; online listings are $60 per year per category. These fees entitle you to inclusion in two issues of the printed edition and one year online, and the online fee includes a free photo and the option to upload two others. The *Players Directory Online* is password protected and only legitimate industry professionals can access the site. They must sign a release stating that their use of the directory is for casting purposes only. Casting directors can search for an actor by name, special skills, categories (leading men, young leading men, leading ladies, ingenues, character men, character women, and children), and various other attributes.

Casting director Randi Hiller says, "The *Players Directory* has proved to be an invaluable tool in the meeting process. It helps to trigger my memory of actors I have not seen in awhile. It is enormously helpful when I need to pull together a casting session in a hurry and when I need fresh ideas and fresh faces."

The *Players Directory* is located at 2210 West Olive Avenue, Burbank, CA 91506; www.playersdirectory.com.

Actors Access/ShowFax

Before the Internet exploded with Web sites to inform the actor how to get a job, there was the New York–based *Player's Guide*. First published in 1942 as the directory for Equity performers, its circulation soon expanded to include AFTRA and SAG members. *Player's Guide* is no longer being published and its subscribers can now take advantage of Web sites powered by Breakdown Services, Ltd. (See Chapter Seven, "Cyberbiz," for more about this organization.)

These Web sites include Actors Access (www.actorsaccess.com), where union and non-union actors can find casting notices. Registration is free. Casting directors are also able to search through the Actors Access database by using information stored in participating actors' online profiles. Actors can place two pictures and their résumé online at no charge and then submit them electronically to casting directors looking for online submissions. Additional photos can be uploaded for a one-time charge of $10 each.

Through Actors Access Breakdowns, a casting director who selects your picture can view your résumé as well as any other pictures that you have in Actors Access. A casting director interested in having you audition for the role can create a schedule and automatically notify you of the appointment time and address via e–mail or text messaging on your cell phone. Through Actors Access, you can accept and confirm the appointment time or send a note requesting a different time than the one indicated.

Once you have the audition, visit www.showfax.com. Showfax is the company that pioneered downloading your audition material or sides. It is free when you register for Actors Access. A year's membership with Showfax is $68. If you want to make an electronic submission without being a member of Showfax, the cost is two dollars per submission.

TRADE PAPERS AND OTHER PRINT RESOURCES

Actors also learn about job opportunities by reading the trade papers. For more than forty–five years, *Back Stage* has been a reliable source of information every week for actors, singers, dancers, and others in the performing arts, both on stage and screen. Two weekly editions, *Back Stage East* and *Back Stage West*, include regional news, reviews, and casting notices relevant to East and West Coast readers and offers valuable advice, features, columns, profiles with well-established and emerging talent, and editorials that help professional actors stay on top of their careers.

BackStage.com, which charges a nominal monthly fee, posts daily casting notices and provides industry news in Chicago, Seattle, San Francisco, and other regions of the United States. The site also provides an electronic forum for actors to submit their headshots, résumés, and even their demo reels to casting directors and producers online. Casting notices are posted daily on the site. It might be a good idea to start an online subscription some months before you travel to New York or Los Angeles.

Ross Reports Television & Film is a sister publication of *Back Stage*. The bimonthly publication contains the names of production personnel and casting directors for all current prime-time network series, talk and variety shows, and daytime serials on both coasts. Also listed are films in preparation and development, TV and film companies, production facilities, unions, guilds, and professional associations. Talent agents and casting directors on both coasts are constantly updated. *Ross Reports* is available wherever theater books and publications are sold; on the Web, go to www.rossreports.com.

Sue Porter Henderson began helping actors in 1983 when she decided to publish the monthly *Henderson's Casting Directors Guide*, which lists more than 300 casting directors as well as producers of corporate videos, films, and television shows. She also publishes a list of personal managers living in New York, New Jersey, and Connecticut known as *The Personal Managers Directory* and a comprehensive, well-researched monthly listing of all of the union-franchised talent agents in New York entitled *New York*

Agencies. She has created a system of mailing labels geared to casting directors, agents, and managers, so actors can quickly affix them to their submission envelopes when doing a mailing. Twenty-five categories of these labels are sold at various theater bookstores and Barnes and Noble branches in New York City and can also be ordered at the Web site, www. hendersonenterprises.com.

The Hollywood Edition of *The Agencies: What the Actor Needs to Know* is published every month with all late-breaking changes. It also contains features on career guidance and viewpoints on the industry and is available from Acting World Books, P.O. Box 3899, Hollywood, CA 90078.

Casting Director Guide is a West Coast–based monthly publication run by actors for actors. If you become a member of www.nowcasting.com, you can download the guide. This very comprehensive book lists the names and addresses of more than 500 casting directors on both coasts and gives additional information about their audition do's and don'ts, likes and dislikes, how to submit, past and current projects, associates and assistants, important background, e-mail addresses and fax numbers. It is not sold in New York. You can find out more about the guide at www.nowcasting.com.

Theatrical Index is a weekly listing about play production—what's opening, what's on, what's in previews or rehearsal, and what's announced or projected for the future. For each show, the producer, the playwright, and the director are named, as is the casting director. Frequently there will be a brief synopsis of the play and capsule descriptions of available roles. Off-Broadway information is included, divided into the same categories. Talent and literary agents are listed, as are nonprofit producing organizations. For the use of union members, Theatrical Index is posted on the bulletin board of the Actors' Equity Lounge at 165 West 46th Street, New York, NY 10036. Single copies are currently $14. Information about subscriptions is available from the publisher, Price Berkley, 888 Eighth Avenue, New York, NY 10019.

Variety (www.variety.com) and *The Hollywood Reporter* (www.hollywoodreporter.com) are daily publications that contain up-to-the-minute news about what's going on in the entertainment industry both here and abroad. You'll enjoy pages of data on the grosses of movies, plays, records, cabaret, nightclub acts; the latest negotiations, production deals, features on who's hot and who will be, awards coverage, reviews, features, columns, and the new media.

Playbill, the program magazine of the Broadway theater, has an informative Web site (www.playbill.com) that aims to be the online resource for everything about live theater, including interviews with actors, directors and writers, casting opportunities, and news of upcoming shows and festivals. Sign up on the site for free. You'll also get access to discounted tickets for the best of what is currently on Broadway.

Dramatics magazine is published monthly (except in June, July, and August) by the Educational Theatre Association, 2343 Auburn Avenue, Cincinnati, OH 45219 (www.edta.org). A special February issue contains a Summer Theater Directory, articles on life in summer stock, and listings of summer theatre study programs to help readers find a way to pursue their passion for theater in the summer.

The *Season Overview* is a monthly updated listing of the major regional theaters in New York and throughout the nation. It is dedicated to bringing you the most thorough information available on the current and upcoming seasons of more than 180 theaters, including artistic directors, playwrights, addresses, Web sites, and e-mail addresses. For more information, go to www.theseasonoverview.com.

Hunter Bell, cocreator of the Obie-winning hit musical *[title of show]*, remembers how helpful the trade publications were when he first came to New York. "I would read *Back Stage*, *Variety*, and *The New York Times* to do research about opportunities. There was no Internet. I would also read *Theatrical Index*. I would go to the library and find out what every regional theater was doing and if I was right for it. I would have the highlighter and check off *Most Happy Fella* or *Last Night of Ballyhoo* and I would send them letters. I wound up doing two productions of *Ballyhoo*. It speaks to the merits of highlighting the *Theatrical Index* instead of sitting around in a diner with your friends complaining you can't get seen."

SOME OTHER HANDY TOOLS

If you don't know the territory, you need a map. As we have already suggested, you should be able to get some of these from the convention and visitors bureaus. In California, everyone swears by the Thomas Guides Los Angeles street atlases. You can also download driving instructions from the Internet, via Web sites such as www.mapquest.com. First, though, you need to gain a sense of the whole area and where those destinations you expect will be important to your career search are located in relation to the neighborhoods in which you can afford to live.

You've accomplished the first important steps: photos that look like you and enhance your marketability; photo résumés that are outlined and reader-friendly; photo business cards and postcards with two contrasting headshots. You have produced a DVD reel that highlights your acting abilities in monologues or production clips. If you are pursuing a career as a voice-over artist, your CD demos are at the ready.

Now, let's discuss where these materials should be sent to open some doors to professional opportunities.

CHAPTER 4

Buyers and Sellers

"The agent or the casting person is trying to avoid clutter. You have to find a way to break through the clutter. You have to devise a way of getting around their defenses."
—Gerald Kline, New York actor

By reading the trade publications, you will acquire a collection of leads: names and addresses of producers, directors, talent agents, casting directors, and managers. You could, of course, sit down and—in one colossal burst of energy—send, fax, or e-mail your photo and résumé to every one of them. That would be a "mass mailing." A more efficient way to proceed, however, would be to learn first what it is that these people do, what they are looking for, and where you might fit into that picture.

Newcomers tend to lump all agents and casting people into one intimidating, omnipotent group, like modern-day versions of the emperor Nero: Thumbs up, you're in; thumbs down, you're out. In reality, the people you hope to impress with your talent can be separated into two categories: they are either *buyers* or *sellers*.

TALENT AGENTS

Whether they confine their efforts to theater, films, television, or commercials or are active in all of these areas, agents are sellers. They are in The Business of selling the efforts of their talented clients to the buyers—casting directors, producers, and directors engaged in a particular project.

Actors, regardless of their age, are often heard to moan, "Oh, what I really need is a good agent to get me a job!" Such moaning arises from a misconception about the way things work in The Business—the notion that actors, totally passive and dependent, need only sit and wait for the phone to ring, wait for the Big Break, wait for someone to hand them their career. And yet, when Actors' Equity scheduled a free seminar on "How to Meet an Agent" and guaranteed that several prominent agents would appear and answer questions, only fifty-six actors (out of the union's thousands of members) showed up to take advantage of that opportunity.

Despite all the stories you may have read or heard about this or that powerful superagent, the plain truth is: The agent cannot get you a job. The only one who can do that is *you* says Kristene Wallis of the Wallis Agency in Los Angeles.

> I always remind my actors, 'You are not working for me. I work for you.' A lot of actors don't get that. The client's responsibility is to communicate with me. If I ask, 'Can you ride a bicycle, use a hula hoop, and breathe fire at the same time?' I'm asking because I want an answer. Yes or no is all I care about. Tell me the truth so I can tell the casting people the truth.

What agents can do is find out about jobs through their long-established contacts or relationships with producers, directors, and casting directors; via the Internet; or through descriptions supplied (at some cost) by Breakdown Services, Ltd. and its competitors. Agents then try to find clients who are right for the roles being cast.

An agent can submit you, by sending your picture and résumé (that's called "hard copy") or electronically, via e-mail, to the person or persons casting the project. If the person to whom your name is submitted agrees to see you, the agent can then arrange an appointment for an interview or an audition. If you get the job, the agent may then negotiate salary, billing, and other terms of the agreement (if it is an "over scale" job, meaning it pays about union scale). For handling all of these arrangements, the agent will then be entitled to 10 percent of your earnings for that job, after you have been paid. This last point is important. Agents work only on commission. The legal commission an agent may charge a client is 10 percent. Never have anything to do with any "agent" who asks you for payment in advance. The agent gets paid only after the client performs the job and has been paid for the job.

How Agents Work

Talent agencies are doubly regulated: They are licensed by the states in which they operate, and they are required to sign franchise agreements with Actors' Equity Association (AEA) and American Federation of Television and Radio Artists (AFTRA), the unions in which they endeavor to find work for their clients. To obtain a franchise, the agent must have a certain amount of previous experience and an excellent reputation in The Business. The franchise agreement permits an agent to submit clients for work in theater, television, and commercials.

Until recently, the Screen Actors Guild (SAG) also required franchise agreements with agents. However, during the 2002 franchise agreement negotiations, agents and the union were unable to agree on terms. As a result, a number of agents currently offer general service agreements to performers they represent for motion pictures. In April 2007, the Guild took its first steps in a new attempt to regulate Hollywood agents.

Some talent agencies specialize. For example, an office may work exclusively on commercials. Other offices, usually those with several sub-agents, are active in all fields. The majority of agencies work only with signed clients, a select number of performers whose work they know very well and whose names and credentials they submit for all jobs that might be right for these actors. Other agencies handle only freelance talent. They will submit the name of any performer whose work they know, for any job they think the actor can handle. As freelancers, these actors have not signed with any other agencies for that field of work. There are also agencies that work with both freelance and signed clients. When none of their signed clients is suitable for a role, they suggest freelance performers whose work they know.

A performer may sign with only one agent at a time in a particular field, such as commercials. That same performer may then sign with another office for legitimate theater and TV. If the office is large and active in all areas, a performer may be represented by three people within the same agency. If you hear an actor say, "I'm with William Morris across the board," that means the performer has a contract with a large, powerful agency and is represented by its staff in all areas.

Once you have signed with an agent, you cannot accept "go-sees," or audition calls, from other agencies (although you may wonder why your agent hasn't sent you up for the job). You may, and indeed should, continue to seek work on your own, but always refer any contacts you make to the agent with whom you've signed. "Of all the agents I've had over the years, only four or five jobs were initiated by my agents," says Tony Award–winning actress Patricia Elliott. "A lot of times I would let the agent know I had heard about a job and ask the agent to make the call. Most of my agents were grateful for the input."

Agents encourage even signed clients to keep track of the people they have met, and occasionally send them reminders to that effect, as part of their business. Many agents also let their clients know they should stay in touch.

"We like our clients to stop by," says David Elliott, a commercial agent with Don Buchwald Associates. "We may not be able to talk to you, we may be really busy trying to get you work, and may not have time for a conversation, but it's important that you come by. It is a people business, and you are the product. We need to see the product we're selling. There are benefits to showing up in person. People change, lose weight, gain weight, cut their hair."

Must You Have an Agent?

In New York, the answer to that question is, "Not necessarily." In fact, many people believe it is to the beginning performer's advantage to do so. The various agents you meet will almost certainly see you differently. One office may think you're perfect for roles described as the young executive type. Another office may categorize you as the down-to-earth, rural, homespun sort. You, of course, are positive that you can play both roles marvelously, as well as countless others. One petite young actress described her range as, "I can play anything but tall!"

What you are seeking, then, is a representative who will be aware of all the things you do well. Until you meet that savvy agent, it's up to you to keep in touch with all the offices interested in freelance talent. And make use of every opportunity to demonstrate your range.

In Los Angeles, on the other hand, one definitely needs representation. You need one agent for commercials and another for theatrical work, which in Los Angeles means TV and films rather than stage work. Plus you need ID. You must be cleared by security everywhere you go. You cannot gain admission to a studio lot unless you have a definite appointment, arranged by your agent, with a casting director or producer.

Performers joke that it's easier to break into Fort Knox than get an agent. However, informal arrangements—known in Los Angeles as *hip-pocketing*—have recently come into practice. These are trial relationships between agents and young performers who show promise. Such agreements are based solely on a handshake; no contracts are signed. This gives both parties time to get to know each other professionally. The agent can learn whether that performer is sufficiently focused, disciplined, and hungry about pursuing a career, while the actor learns what kinds of roles this agent considers suitable for him or her.

Who Becomes an Agent?

We polled agents across the country. The majority of them have had previous experience within the industry and have worked as subagents for larger offices. Many of them have been in business for a long time. Since no schools offer courses in talent agenting, hands-on experience becomes the best and only teacher. Aspiring agents may start out as interns, assistants, or in the mailroom of a large agency. They're avid readers of all the trade papers; they go to see plays, movies, workshops, everything that's happening in The Business they wish to work in. They know the best way to learn the job is to do the job.

"I got into The Business in 1986," says agent Kristene Wallis. "I went to work for one of the top voice-over agents in Los Angeles. I thought I'd just be his secretary, but I realized if I didn't learn how to do the recordings there'd be no auditions, and the clients would lose out on opportunities. It was wonderful; nothing but celebrities. James Garner was one of his clients, and so were Glenn Ford, Barbara Eden, Frank Langella."

Talent agent Margaret Emory, adds, "Even after being an agent for fifteen years, I still learn new things every day. Each client brings a variety of needs. How to meet these for each client is the creative genius of an agent."

What Do Agents Want?

We asked agents what they looked for in new talent. *Charisma, personality, uniqueness,* and *ability* were the words they most often used.

"I always sit and talk to people. I try to find things on their résumés regarding their interests. I try to make the atmosphere comfortable. Even when they are doing the monologue. It is not a test. How do they handle the words, how do they make sense of the sentences?"

—Marilynn Scott Murphy, talent agent, Professional Artists, New York City

"Talent turns us on. We can spot it coming through the door. We look for honesty and self-confidence, not cockiness. We look for intelligence, consideration of others . . . and a measure of insanity helps."

—Peggy Hadley, Peggy Hadley Enterprises, Ltd.

The agent can pay the rent and the electric bill and the cost of Breakdown Services only if and when the clients are working. Of course, every agency wants the next new person who comes through the door to be a potential money maker. Yes, indeed, they want to see dollar signs.

We also asked what turns agents off. Over and over they cited the same unattractive traits: greed, overt aggressiveness, egomania, ignorance, stupidity, and a sloppy appearance. We think they were very clear about what they *don't* want to meet.

The Right Agent for You

Every performer would love to be represented by an agent who is dedicated, powerful, and willing to invest limitless time on the client's behalf. Signing with such a "dream agent" may not always be possible, particularly when you are new in The Business. Certainly, no reputable agent will want to sign a client whose work he or she doesn't know and appreciate.

You and the agent should be clear with each other about the contacts you are expected to make on your own. Be realistic. There will naturally be greater incentive for the agency to make phone calls on behalf of a client whose earnings may be ten times what you can command at present. Therefore, it is smart business practice for you to continue your independent efforts to make yourself known to the potential buyers of your talents. The fruits of your own efforts will affect the representation you get down the road.

Find out whether the agent wants to hear from you about job ideas, or prefers that you wait patiently for his or her calls. Two working actors who understand the value of marketing themselves were both impressed by the advice they received from Nancy Curtis, co-owner of Harden-Curtis Associates. According to actor Sean McCourt (*Mary Poppins*):

> She told me now it was time to turn on the gas because I was on Broadway. She gave me a tutorial on how to use her as an agent. She said, "This is how not to bug me, but how to stay in contact every single day." Nancy would have me set assignments for her that were realistic but constant. I had the order of casting directors I wanted her to call.

Every day at four-thirty I'd call her and ask who she'd called. She would either say, "Oh, I didn't get to it," or, "I left a message," or "They weren't interested." It was incredible, and I got lots of people to see the show.

Actor Patrick Boll, who sends promotional material about every job he does, whether it's a showcase, a reading, or the tryout of a fresh new musical, such as the recent *Man in the Flying Lawn Chair*, e-mailed us: "As my agent, Nancy Curtis, says, 'To have a career as an actor, every day you need to do s*omething*.' Today it's my mailing. Tomorrow, who knows?"

It's important to clarify how the agent views you. Are you the upwardly mobile executive or the homespun hero, or both? And how many actors like you does the office already represent? If there are too many, does that mean you should seek representation elsewhere? Or does the office hope to corner the market for a particular type, so that if, say, Young Bride A is busy, Young Bride B will be the nex t choice for a job, or Young Bride C? These are subtleties that you should discuss openly with an agent. It's not easy to think about such things when you're beginning your career. But your chances of building a successful career improve if you pay attention to such details.

Signing with an Agent

Be sure that the agency with which you're signing is franchised by AEA and/or AFTRA. We assume, also, that you feel comfortable with the agent. Mark Teschner, Emmy-winning casting director of *General Hospital*, says:

> I think that in a town of illusion and fantasy, where it is sometimes difficult to separate truth from fiction, all actors who are approached by an agent or manager should do their homework and check the credentials of that person with the unions and the Conference of Personal Managers, and also find out who their clients are. I think that an actor will have a sense or a "vibe" that someone is not legitimate, and you will have to trust that, because all that actors really have to go on is their instincts.

First-time agreements, which are standard agency contracts, may be for a period of one year. That is considered sufficient time for you and the agent to test the relationship. However, each agreement has an "out clause," to protect you if you begin to suspect that the agent's initial interest has cooled too quickly, and to protect the agent if in some way you fall short of his or her expectations. Casting director Mark Teschner firmly believes,

A good agent is one who has good taste. There are many agents with many sensibilities, and it's very hard for an actor to find an effective one. An actor wants to be represented by an agent who 'gets' them and what they are about, who is passionate and committed to working with that actor and developing a career. But even that isn't enough if the agency doesn't have solid, respectable relationships within the casting community.

PERSONAL MANAGERS

The personal manager is another type of seller who works with a select group of signed clients. Managers need not be franchised by any of the unions or regulated in any way. Established in 1942, the National Conference of Personal Managers Inc. serves as a board of ethics and standards, and aims to advance the integrity of the group.

Managers frequently work with a small number of agents with whom they are close, or they may sometimes go directly to casting directors, producers, or directors to get their clients' work seen. As talent manger Jean Fox, a partner with Fox Albert in New York, says, "Managers are supposed to rely on agents to get appointments with casting directors. But if you believe in somebody and you can't get an agent to support your belief, then you have to go after it yourself." A manager may not sign the deal; only an agent can do that. Managers, therefore, will either work with agents with whom their clients are signed, or seek the services of a theatrical attorney.

Personal managers can be extremely useful in guiding a career, because typically their contracts span two or three years. Arguably, theirs is the longer view of a talent's possibilities. They have the expertise to find and develop new talent and create opportunities for those artists they represent. They build an identifiable image or personality for a client. Managers are expected to have a great many close contacts with important, powerful people, such as packagers, studio heads, and executive producers. According to Ms. Sam Downey, a partner with Henry Downey Talent Management:

There are many obvious traits that make a good manager: organizational skills, sales ability, business savvy. But to me, the single most important quality any manager can possess is belief in the clients. When I meet a potential client I have to feel something about them— that they are special, or that we have a bond. If a manager truly believes in her client's talent, you will hear it in her voice and see it in her eyes and there is no stronger sales tool! A good manager starts out with a firm set of work ethics in place. They have expectations of how they want to do business with their clients. They want them to return calls quickly, they want them to be prepared, they want them to take advice and basically work as a team. Client and manager should be in constant communication with each other because you are trying to accomplish the same goals.

If a personal manager expresses interest in you, make certain that he or she is experienced enough to have amassed impressive connections. Find out all you can about their credentials: Who do they know? Who do they work with? Who can they get to "take a meeting" with you? What's their track record?

Like agents, personal managers are paid after the client has done the job and received his or her check. A reputable manager never demands payment in advance. The client agrees to pay a certain percentage of his or her gross income to the manager, who will provide advice, counsel and direction in the development and advancement of the client's career.

Talent managers on the East Coast belong to the National Conference of Personal Managers, and information about members is listed in *Henderson's Guide to Personal Managers*. Managers on the West Coast belong to a separate organization, the Talent Manager's Association (TMA), which has its own Web site, www.talentmanagers.org.

PERSONAL PUBLICISTS

Publicity is a means of bringing yourself to the attention of others. The publicist is also a seller, working to develop and sharpen your image, draw attention to your activities and achievements, and create the kind of "buzz" that attracts opportunities for advancement by making people aware of you. Smart publicity often determines whether an actor gets noticed or not. It must also be said that there has to be something to publicize. Publicists cannot generate press or create requests for personal appearances if the performer has no significant projects going on. So, if you are thinking of hiring a public-relations pro, make sure the timing is right, when something you've done will be getting a lot of attention.

A good publicist can give you feedback on your appearance and demeanor, and explain the best techniques for dealing with the press. These professionals have extensive media contacts as well as writing ability. Such expertise can be invaluable to your career.

Publicist Sarah Kuhn, for example, says she always tells clients who are appearing in films to keep a journal on the set and write down funny things that happen and things they really enjoyed about making the film.

> Because that really helps when the time for talk shows comes and you have to pull those anecdotes out. Actors should remember that when you're doing an interview, you're at work.
>
> It is important to make certain decisions ahead of time—for example, how much are you willing to share about your personal life? If there's a topic you don't feel at ease with, avoid that topic or simply say that you don't talk about that subject. Some questions may not be phrased in the best way possible, and it's important to listen carefully to what the interviewer is asking. Don't be afraid to take a minute to pause and think about your answer before you launch into it.

Musical theater star Karen Ziemba (*Curtains*) received rave reviews for her performance in *Contact*, for which she won a Tony Award. For the awards ceremony, Karen's publicist helped select the right designer gown and accessories for her, borrowed fabulous jewelry, and did everything to promote an image of stardom. She also made sure the press photographers knew where Karen was at every party and arranged for photo opportunities of her client with properly noteworthy personalities.

Publicists average about $3,000 a month, though the fee depends on the size of the company. "You are probably looking at a three-month commitment before you start to feel the impact of the publicity," according to publicist Sarah Kuhn.

Good publicists will be known in the industry. Your agent, manager, or fellow actors may be able to refer you to several who are capable. Interview a number of people until you find the one whose track record, media plan, and personality most appeal to you. This community also has its share of charlatans. Beware of flacks who are best known for staging outlandish publicity stunts, like faking celebrity romances—usually between two of their clients. Such flamboyant, phony tricks might even damage your credibility.

If your goal is to move from daytime to prime time, it may be essential to engage a publicist. However, be sure that person understands exactly what you're aiming to accomplish and can deliver what you want.

HOW TALENT CAN BE DISCOVERED

The alert agent or manager does a great deal more than sit in the office, download Breakdown Service listings, make phone calls, and hope an irresistible new talent will drop off a photo or résumé. The good agent—the one you hope to sign with—is in energetic pursuit of talent. That means doing things like going to showcases to see new performers work, and attending graduation showcases at respected acting schools. It means leaving the confines of the city to see work in regional theaters, at drama festivals, or wherever there's a play or acting company that sounds adventurous and fresh. Agent Marilynn Scott Murphy explains:

> When we go to see our clients in shows, usually we add to our roster some people who work with our clients. We do go through the mail and a few times a year we hold auditions in my office. People who have sent in their photo and résumé and look interesting, I will have them come in and do a couple of monologues, or if they sing, an up-tempo ballad and a monologue.

A performer could not ask for more than the chance to be discovered working in a professional situation. For Marin Mazzie, her role in *Carousel* at the Barn Theater in Augusta, Michigan, provided that opportunity. The star of the show was Tom Wopat, whose appearance on Broadway in Cy Coleman and Michael Stewart's *I Love My Wife* had carried him to Hollywood and a career in film and on the TV series *The Dukes of Hazzard*. Wopat's agent traveled to Michigan for the opening, and was captivated by Marin's performance. The agent went backstage to see his client, made certain to meet Marin, and offered to represent her as soon as she came to New York. She made the trip at the end of the summer season. It wasn't long before she made her Broadway debut in the Tony Award–winning musical, *Big River*.

HOW TALENT IS NOT DISCOVERED

Talent is not discovered or eased along the path to stardom by means of the "casting couch." It's not necessarily difficult to spot a set up, according to Mr. Carmen LaVia, Vice President, Fifi Oscard Agency: "There are people who, when you ask them what time they'd like to see you, say, 'Six o'clock in the evening.' Then you know they have a very wrong focus."

Legitimate talent agents and personal managers do not advertise in the employment classifieds of any local newspaper, or in the trade papers, or on the Internet. Any ad that solicits "new faces" for modeling or for films, implies that experience is not necessary, and suggests that high salaries await the first people to respond, was placed by a phony.

Beware of any person claiming to be an agent or manager who asks you to read sample copy for a dramatic scene or a commercial test—and then says that you have talent, but that it needs to be "developed." Such a person will typically suggest that you attend a particular school or study with a particular coach to whom he or she recommends all "clients." Such a person is almost surely a phony (getting a kickback from the recommended school or teacher), and not someone who can help you in your career.

SMELL THE SCAM

There have been get-rich-quick schemes since the dawn of civilization. That great nineteenth-century showman P.T. Barnum declared, "There's a sucker born every minute." And W.C. Fields drawled, "Never give a sucker an even break."

The Business, where so much money and celebrity are waiting to be won, is particularly fertile ground for take-the-money-and-run gimmicks that may appear legitimate on the surface but are in fact fly-by-night operations. Buyer Beware becomes Actor Beware, or Parent of Child Performer Beware. Let us examine some of the more common fraudulent schemes.

Be wary of ads for guides and publications promising to do more for the newcomer than established guides can do. The wheeler-dealers who placed the ads will offer to get information about their "personal" clients to "influential" people. Such ventures are usually rip-offs of one sort or another. Newcomers may be excited and flattered by the idea that some star-maker could be taking an interest in their career. But the venture is a money-maker's scheme—for the person collecting the checks. Newcomers must face the fact that they are the only ones who can create interest in their career. And they have to do that by working hard for themselves.

The advent of cable TV brought a new wrinkle to the scam: For a hefty fee, one TV ad promised to telecast performers' pictures during daytime, on public access channels, for casting people to view in the comfortable privacy of their offices. An unsuspecting performer might not realize that casting people work in their offices during the day. They're not looking at talent on public access TV. They are interviewing actors, in person, by appointment. The only audience for such a telecast would be the talent's family or people interested in talent for other purposes.

One "production company" rented a nicely furnished mansion in a posh neighborhood in southern California. They decorated the walls with giant posters of Hollywood stars to suggest to wannabe stars that they, too, could be as successful as the legends they were staring at. Applicants who filled out the New Faces Application Sheet later learned that the operators were wanted for fraud and theft in seven states.

Today, you can also be hoodwinked on the Internet by shady operators who bait the hook with promises of international fame. Such con artists have already fleeced many people with other schemes, selling them phony antiques and nonexistent real estate, or offering no-cost bank loans—while obtaining vital personal information about their "marks." What's the fastest-growing crime problem in this country? Identity theft! Don't fall for it.

The high-stakes glamour of the entertainment industry attracts Internet schemers who prey on the gullible, vulnerable, desperate actor. Already, the Internet is home to thousands of state-of-the-art Web sites hawking "exclusive" listings of amazing auditions, star searches, and links to "top" managers. Best of all: "You can join for free!" But scroll down and you'll come to the monthly service charges, annual fees, or a three-year contract. Taking advantage of such an "opportunity" to climb the ladder of stardom could cost you more than $2,000—and not get you a foothold on the first rung.

One ad solicited photos of female actors to appear in an adult film production in a southern state. This work was for "serious people who didn't mind performing in scenes in adult situations." This scam was alarming on two counts: The term "adult situations" is a euphemism for porn; and once you submit your photo on the Internet, you have no control over where that image will end up. There is no regulation on the Internet. What appears legitimate at first glance could prove damaging to you in all sorts of ways. So, beware, and be skeptical. That online stranger who wants to show your beautiful child's photo to a "select coterie" of agents seeking young talent is not a bona fide talent scout. We'll say it again: The Internet is global and unregulated, and you have no idea where that picture could show up.

Rip-Off Protection

When you're in doubt as to whether people offering to build your career, make you a star, put your name in lights, and so on, are all they claim to be, feel free to call or e-mail any of the talent unions: Actors' Equity Association (AEA), the American Federation of Television and Radio Artists (AFTRA), and the Screen Actors Guild (SAG). You can also contact the local Better Business Bureau or Volunteer Lawyers for the Arts. Report any shady activity you uncover to your elected representatives and to the office of the attorney general of your state.

We cannot overstate the need for skepticism and caution. If an offer sounds too good to be true, it probably is. If you have to pay a fee up front so the whole world can become aware of your talent, it's a scam.

CASTING DIRECTORS

The casting director (CD) is a talent buyer, and your major link to the people who are in a position to hire you. It has been said that the best casting directors are those who have done some acting, for they are uniquely tuned in to actors' problems, and to what goes into the creation of a memorable performance.

Good casting directors go to see as much work as possible, remembering all the good actors in the production. Moreover, they know that a mediocre performance is not necessarily the actor's fault, but can be the result of bad direction and/or miscasting.

The casting director is engaged in a never-ending search to find the right actor for the right job. Always under the gun to meet a production deadline, the casting director needs an encyclopedic knowledge of actors and the talent pool. It also means that after spending eight or nine hours at a desk, looking at pictures, interviewing actors, and hearing them read, a CD's evenings are spent going to plays, showcases, cabarets, and comedy clubs as well as watching movies and TV.

The casting director is always seeking the talent no one else has found, the ones who, according to Judy Blye-Wilson, award-winning casting director of *All My Children*, "have an imaginative way of lifting the words off the page. By far the most rewarding part of my job, is to find and cast new talent, and to watch them grow and develop into being really skilled and successful."

Casting directors frequently have only two weeks in which to cast twelve or more characters. That means there's no time to do any pre-screening, and there are at least a dozen people to please—among them producers, writers, directors and network programming executives, each of whom has a different mental picture of what actor would be perfect for each role. "I may read two hundred and fifty actors for one role," says Mark Teschner. "The philosophy is that if there is someone who might be remotely right, I would rather take the extra five minutes to read them."

Casting directors who work in television, theater, film, and commercials synthesize their personal impressions about each character, gathered from careful examination of the script and ideas they receive from the producer, the director, and the writer. Then they make recommendations. The casting director's greatest reward is completing a job, looking at the results, and saying, "Yes, that was the person for the role." The CD also gets the satisfaction of knowing that this production—this role—could be an actor's launching pad. "We want you to be fabulous! The casting director is your friend. We can't do this without you. Find something about the process you enjoy," says Nancy Piccione, casting director, Manhattan Theatre Club. Adds Gayle Keller, independent casting director, "We are your cheerleaders. We want you to be great."

One respected casting director who loves discovering talent reflected on the nature of the job this way:

> You can't always predict at a screen test what will happen. Sometimes you see a spark in someone on camera, or you see something that is ready to explode, and you must let it happen. There is almost a psychic need to get inside what an actor can do. You can't always tell from the audition alone, just because of nerves. So I am a firm believer in the interview process. It's important to look deeper, to see something of who the actor is, to try different approaches to reach beyond the nervousness, to get to the divine spark.

In a career that has spanned three decades, West Coast casting director April Webster, of April Webster and Associates (CD, *Lost* and *Criminal Minds*), has won an Emmy and two Artio Awards. She's the casting director who discovered Kevin Costner's headshot in the extra files at Zoetrope, called him in to read, and the rest, as they say, is history. Her advice to actors who are called in for readings and want to ignite that spark: "The best thing I could say would be to be as present as you possibly can be, not to be thinking about what the end result of the meeting is, to stay in the process of what you're doing. I find that when people do that, in general, you see them. You really see them."

A casting director may have a permanent position on the staff of an advertising agency, a network, a series, or a busy packager or production company. In that capacity, casting directors actively seek out talent and will frequently travel from their home base to get a glimpse of it. They will be in touch with coaches at professional schools, and with directors of college theater programs. They will maintain contacts with agents and talent scouts across the nation and even pay attention to productions in foreign countries. Interesting talent is what they are after—the stars of tomorrow, able to grab an audience's attention and hold it, for thirty seconds, for two hours, or for the duration of a story line.

A Different Bailiwick

Lesley Collis does not cast for theater, TV, or films. She is the casting director for the world's largest toy company, Mattel. Over the past twenty-five years, she has cast thousands of actors for Mattel Toy Fairs, most of them young and just starting in The Business. Many have gone on to high-profile careers, among them Vin Diesel and Lauren Graham of *Gilmore Girls*. Lesley is also a successful actress, musical theater performer, and director. As she tells it:

> I look for actors who have good improvisation skills, and a sense of appropriateness backstage. I prefer an actor who has done some regional theater, Off-Broadway, some touring. This is a wonderful opportunity for young actors to get their foot in the door and make some money. This corporate industrial area is not covered by any union jurisdiction.
>
> As we are presenting products not yet on the market, we require a high level of confidentiality. I look for actors who understand that. For the audition, I use old scripts and just tweak them for the audition process. It is a foreign type of dialogue for most actors—talking about mechanics and advertising strategy. After the cold reading, the actors do an improvisation. They look at the toys in the waiting area, choose one they relate to, then present it to me on camera and talk about all the fun and marketing features of that toy.
>
> It is the hardest thing in the world to do. It separates those who can act from those who can't. It shows me how they speak extemporaneously, how their mind works. Everyone says it is the hardest thing they have ever done.

I also ask them to tell me a bit about themselves. I want a sense of their personality. Because if they are very much involved with themselves, very one-note in terms of background, they are going to be boring to be around. I am in awe of the people I hire because of what they do.

Lesley has worked with the same agents and managers for years. "They know how difficult this job is, and they don't waste my time." She attends showcases, opens every piece of mail, and is on site all through rehearsal time. She says, "I love making that call and saying, 'You booked it!' That gives me as much pleasure as if it were me getting the job!"

Jenny Strassburg is one of the performers recently cast by Lesley Collis. "Working for the Mattel Toy Fair was my first professional job as an actor out of college. I was told from the beginning that memorization was a key element of the job, because of the lengthy scripts, so I memorized the script I had for the audition. Being so familiar with the script, I was able to be more confident and take direction and adjustments." She got the job.

After a week of training at corporate headquarters, I was flown to Los Angeles for the show, which lasted nine days. The job is not union-affiliated, but working conditions are excellent, with lunch and dinner breaks, as well as breaks throughout the day.

The typical show lasts from around seven A.M. to six P.M., depending on buyers' schedules. I've done two different show formats. The first is gallery style, where actors/marketers are assigned to a specific product or line of products, which they demonstrate to buyers.

Format Two is more conversational and less formal. Buyers can choose which products they'd like to learn about. This format is more like a "show." Buyers are seated in a conference room, and the products are brought up in front of them while the actors/marketers tell them about the toy and show them how it works. With both formats, it is the actors' responsibility to bring the marketing information to life, so the client is engaged and the toy is sold!

Long hours and lots of energy are required, but it's also fun. What's better for an adult than to be paid to play with toys?

Independent Casting Directors

The independent, or freelance, casting director is employed on a per-project basis by the director of a film, play, commercial, or other vehicle requiring talent. Like their on-staff colleagues, these experts have extensive experience, know the talent pool, and will also go exploring for new performers. An independent casting director may be involved in the initial casting of core characters for a new series or soap opera, and then hand over the day-to-day casting chores to a staff casting director.

Independent casting directors, however, are less likely to invest much time in developing young actors, and they will not set aside time to meet actors unless they feel they would fit well into a particular role.

Laura Verbeke, an independent casting director who has done many years of extra casting, was always impressed by the fact that the directors she worked for really loved to upgrade qualified people to SAG membership status.

> Filmmaking is about collaborating and that's what I love about it. I had a woman with incredible theater experience, who was not a SAG member. We'd looked for months for someone to play this scene with the leading actor. She had several interviews with the director and was upgraded three days in a row, and is now a member of SAG.
>
> People I work with look forward to the opportunities. Their chances of being seen are better because the scenes are small. I rarely run into the problem of the "cattle call" and abuse that is associated with being an extra.

She advises actors to send a good headshot and résumé –through regular mail or via the Internet. "That is still the best way for an actor to get a chance. We will always need people with special skills. Some people don't want to do background work. But it is a way to become a member of SAG, and to learn if you are interested in working in film and TV."

Finally, a caveat: Please remember that a Casting Director is not to be called a Casting Agent—that is a contradiction in terms. The terminology is Casting Director and Talent Agent.

CHAPTER 5

Training Is Everything

"Training is everything. The peach was once a bitter almond; cauliflower is nothing but cabbage with a college education."

—Mark Twain

Luck is best defined as the marriage of preparation and opportunity. In acting, as in many fields, training and preparation are one and the same. You can decide to become an actor, singer, or dancer as early as the age of three or as late as when your children are grown and it's your turn to live your dream. But no matter when you feel the desire to act, no one can hit the ground running without a foundation. All actors start their journey by learning the craft, whether by going to a high school of performing arts, majoring in theater or musical theater, attending graduate school to get an advanced degree, taking weekly classes with well-respected teachers, or making the leap from a small regional market to either coast and researching which teachers or schools will help them to continue to improve their audition skills in front of the camera or on stage.

The incomparable acting teacher/actress and author Uta Hagen once said, "You don't stop learning until you are dead." Casting director Jackie Briskey declares, "A good actor never graduates." You can come to New York or Los Angeles well versed in the Meisner Technique, certified in stage combat, and proficient in dialects. Your résumé may list a variety of roles, from Shakespeare to Shepard. You can be confident in your audition techniques for the stage and be equipped with at least six monologues and songs that demonstrate your range, but how will you react when the casting director wants to know if you have anything that is more comedic and age-appropriate? And can you do an improv about the character you hope to play, find more "colors," make her more like Eve Harrington in *All About Eve* and less like Scarlett O'Hara in *Gone With the Wind*?

To prepare to be an actor, your start-up budget should include money for ongoing classes with good teachers and coaches who are known and respected in the industry, because with limited professional experience reflected on your résumé, agents and casting directors will be looking very closely at its "Training" section to gauge your dedication and readiness to learn and improve your craft.

THE VALUE OF TRAINING

Broadway actress and singer Donna Lynne Champlin, who has appeared in *Sweeney Todd*, and Hollywood Arms (www.donnalynnechamplin.com) explains why training and the acquisition of skills is essential to the life of the working actor:

> Training is essential. Not only for the technique and education you get from it, but also for the confidence it gives you when you walk into an audition. Getting training is like going into a hardware store with an empty toolbox. Each class, each teacher, each experience, offers you a new tool to put into that box. And by the end of your four years you find that some tools you use over and over, and some tools you may only use once, if at all. But when you get into the professional world where time is literally money—it is a hell of a lot easier to quickly and calmly solve the problems that come your way."
>
> Any skill you pick up can and will help you as an actor. Whether it's speaking another language, reading tarot cards, or playing the zither. I look back now on the things I'm so grateful to know how to do, and yet at the time I was learning them, I thought it was a complete waste of time for someone who "just" wanted to be an actress. For example, in our Carnegie Mellon University (CMU) movement class we studied "neutral man" for what seemed like forever. For months we would do the simplest things, like pick up a pencil or get up from the floor as "neutrally as possible." This was also the same class in which I learned commedia dell'arte. It just couldn't have been more torturously boring,

and I remember one day in a fit of frustration I said, "When are any of us ever going to need to know how to do this in an actual show?" And the teacher just smiled at me and said, "You just wait and see."

And lo and behold, my entire character of Pirelli in *Sweeney Todd* was based on the principles of neutral man and commedia dell'arte. Yes. There was a big mea culpa thank-you note, dinner on me, and a pair of comps to the show for that one. Not only did those four years at CMU teach me what techniques worked (and did not work) for me acting-wise, but they also gave me priceless social and emotional maturing that I desperately needed. Had I gone straight to New York from high school, I would have been devoured in more ways than one.

The Importance of Classical Training

An actor's training should emphasize the study and, most importantly, the production of great classical plays. Oscar-winning actress Estelle Parsons strongly believes that everybody in America would be a lot better off if the classics were taught properly from the first grade on, as they are in England. The works of Shakespeare, Eugene O'Neill, Tennessee Williams, and the greatest dramatic literature in the English language are simply not taught here the same way.

In his book *Classical Acting*, Malcolm Morrison, dean at the Hartt School at the University of Hartford, makes a strong case for studying the classics:

> These plays are highly structured, representative of their times and authors, deal with enduring themes—often expressed in heightened, literary language—have stood the test of time, and are not related to colloquial and modern experiences. Shakespeare, Molière, Sophocles, Shaw, Ibsen, and Chekhov, though they wrote in very different styles and for different purposes, would all have to be included.
>
> The themes that appear in classical plays are common to being human in whatever age. Courtship, mistaken identity, honor, are still as much an issue today as they were when any of the plays of Plautus, Shakespeare, or Molière were holding their audiences. The challenge to the modern actor is not primarily in discerning the themes of a play or in recognizing what is human or true in any of them, but rather in the language and structure of the play itself and in the specifics which contribute towards the context in which the events are played out.

Character actress Jayne Houdyshell, a Tony nominee for her work as Ann Kron in *Well*, says that when she plays someone who has to be "real" and at the same time project that reality to a 1,200-seat theater, she uses her training in the classics and all that vocal and text work that she had as a student in acting school. "I developed a deep respect for what the British were doing in terms of training. The acting school curriculum was very appealing because of the particular emphasis on technique, text, period work, and the classics."

TRAINING PROGRAMS FOR ACTORS

When you are looking for academic training, we recommend the Directory of Theatre Training Programs, which is published every two years, offers information on admissions, tuition, faculty, curriculum, facilities, productions, and philosophy of training at almost 500 programs in the United States, Canada, and abroad.

Another excellent resource is program Web sites, where you'll find in-depth material on faculty, famous alumni, guest artist programs, auditions for acceptance, affiliation with a professional theater or summer theater, and, of course, scholarship assistance.

In addition, actors in New York or Los Angeles have the opportunity to study with some of the finest talents in The Business. Every year, *Back Stage* publishes a list of more than 200 New York–area stage and film acting schools, teachers, and coaches. Entries are divided into Acting Technique, Children/Teens, Comedy/Improv, Monologue/Audition/Coaching, and On-Camera (Film/TV/Commercial). Each of the entries provides names of teachers and schools, locations and contacts, Web sites and e-mail addresses, the average number of students in a class, and whether auditing is permitted.

University Programs

According to Tony- and Emmy-winner Debra Monk, the best advice she ever received when she started in The Business came from a teacher in college, who said, "You are not ready to go to New York. You really need to get your Master's degree because you need more training and you may not make it. So by the time I came to the city, I had a real basis of training. If you don't have a passion to do this, it's really, really hard. I was able to hold on to my passion, and I still have that, and my training, which is ongoing."

David Hyde Pierce, four-time Emmy winner as Niles on *Frasier* and Ms. Monk's costar in *Curtains*, one of the last musical collaborations of John Kander and Fred Ebb, studied acting at Yale. He was advised to go to New York before spending any more time and money on training. "So I went to New York, and in some ways I wasn't ready. There was a lot of training I should have had, and you can go back and read the reviews and see that that's true."

In the *Directory of Theatre Training Programs*, founding editor-in-chief Jill Charles includes her comprehensive analysis of the differences between undergraduate programs for actors entitled "T.B.F.A. or Nor to B.F.A: Choosing a Theatre Program."

> One of the great arguments for choosing a liberal arts B.A. degree over a B.F.A. is the importance of learning to think, and of being exposed to a variety of subjects and ideas. At age twenty, it is hard to draw on life experience when working on a role—you just haven't had that much of it. Studying a broad range of subjects, considering different points of view, being exposed to different philosophies—all can enhance a student's understanding of the world, and thus his or her ability to bring truth to a wider variety of roles.

As B.A. proponents contend, focusing exclusively on theater for four of your most intellectually fertile years can be a narrowing experience. But if you are determined to enter the profession and don't want to let those four years go by without accumulating essential skills, then a B.F.A. (bachelor of fine arts) degree makes sense. It is the responsibility of a good B.F.A. program to ensure that its students are challenged to think, to read, and to acquire a broader view of the world.

The University of Central Florida in Orlando offers B.A.s in theater, B.F.A.s in acting and in musical theater, and M.F.A.s in acting and musical theater. John Wayne Shafer, associate professor of theater, believes that "Most people spend more time shopping for a new car than they do for a degree program. This is unfortunate. The impact of this educational purchase on their lives will be far greater than that of a car." He continues:

> Our B.F.A. is based on a conservatory-style system of training. We have stripped as many credits as possible from our general course of study and funneled them directly into the professional aspirations of the student. Our B.A. Theatre Studies program is a liberal arts–based program dedicated to producing graduates with a unique

skill set designed to help them achieve their dreams and goals. It supports the belief that a student benefits more in the long term from a curriculum that has a broader educational base. Most parents are more comfortable with a B.A. in philosophy because it tends to give a student wider options later in life.

Disciplines Working Together

In 1986, the Florida legislature created the New World School of the Arts (NWSA) in Miami as a "Florida Center of Excellence" in the visual and performing arts. An educational partnership of Miami Dade County Public Schools, Miami Dade College, and the University of Florida, the school provides a comprehensive program of artistic training and academic development for careers in dance, music, theater, musical theater, and the visual arts. Through its partners it offers high school diplomas, Associate of Arts degrees, and Bachelor of Music and B.F.A. degrees.

Patrice Bailey, Dean of Theatre at NWSA, recruits students at theater conferences such as the Southeastern Theater Conference (SETC), auditions potential students on site, and receives applications via the Internet from all over the world:

> We are trying to encourage the disciplines to work together. Music majors play for the high school musical; actors love to work with the dance division; dancers perform in the musicals. I have a performance artist who works with the students and offers a performance art class. New World is about creating artists and the future of art, and also about creating leaders in the arts. We also hire professionals as teachers. People who have been in The Business or who are still in it discover the love of teaching and come in and share that with everybody.

INDUSTRY SHOWCASES FOR STUDENT TALENT

Dozens of undergraduate and graduate programs bring their students to New York, Los Angeles, or Chicago to help them showcase their acting and singing talents and training for an invited audience of casting directors, talent agents, and managers. Many schools outside New York will hire professional showcase consultants to come to the campus and prepare students for this exciting opportunity to be seen—and possibly secure representation or be interviewed by casting directors for current projects. Students receieve advice about up-to-date, professional-quality color photos and well-formatted résumés. Actors making this transition into the "real world" of The Business should be prepared with at least ten monologues, know something about who the agents and casting directors are, understand protocol like thank–you notes and follow-ups, and realize that their work is just beginning.

Talent agent Margaret Emory describes why an industry showcase from a reputable training program that she attended was a major disappointment.

> In an effort to entice us industry folk, the material included scenes from then-current movies and television shows. The showcase, catering to the most commercial aspects of the industry, left nothing to the imagination of the agents and casting directors attending. The banquet of talent offered was a misconceived recipe wasting flavorful ingredients, rather than a fine stew celebrating the talents of dedicated artists who had devoted three years to rigorous conservatory training in Shakespeare, Molire, Shaw, and Ibsen. It seemed odd that all the training should come down to a two-minute sampling of the latest Quentin Tarantino flick.

Suggestions for a successful industry showcase include:

- Choose material that has humor and energy. We want to be entertained.
- Roles you play must be age-appropriate and realistic for your physical type.
- Wear clothing that flatters your shape and fits well. (see the chapter two "Getting Your Act Together.")
- Length of the scenes should not exceed three minutes; monologues, two minutes.
- Songs you select from musicals should be for roles you can play now.
- Length of the whole program should not be more than one hour and fifteen minutes.
- Directors should not have all of the graduating actors sitting onstage watching each other. We like to see you make entrances and exits. Actors sitting on stage steal the focus from those who are performing.
- Invitations should be sent out at least four weeks prior to the date. Promotional fliers on Breakdown Services should appear two to three times the week before the scheduled performances.
- Students at the school can participate in a phone tree to call the

invitees and see if they are coming. This provides an opportunity to contact them directly with sincere motivation and to know immediately whether the response is a yes, a no, or maybe.

The chair of the training program usually gets "callback sheets" after the showcase from industry professionals requesting interviews, photos, and résumés of actors who captured their interest.

The agent or casting director may also leave a message for a student to contact them when he or she has relocated to New York or Los Angeles. Some actors may not get callbacks. Don't take it to heart if it happens to you. All it means is the industry people couldn't find a slot for you at their agency, or they just don't know how to place you. When you are financially able to move to New York, Chicago or Los Angeles, it will be your responsibility to connect with those people who saw your work.

AUDITIONING FOR GRADUATE SCHOOL

Charles Tuthill teaches a grad school prep class at the Actors Center in New York. The course includes several sessions with a voice teacher to help students improve breath support and vibration. On his Web site, www.charlestuthill.com, he addresses what you should know about the grad school audition process.

He encourages his students to apply to many schools, since admissions are so competitive, and he includes a list of overdone monologues for men and women. Examples from Shakespeare's plays are included to help you prepare for those selections. He offers this advice about monologues:

> It is my experience that the most successful auditions are those that include a very realistic modern piece by writers such as David Hare, Arthur Miller, Edward Albee, Sam Shepard, Suzan Lori Parks, and August Wilson.

> "When it comes to Shakespeare, there is hardly a monologue they haven't seen, so don't get wrapped up in selecting one that is unknown. Focus your attention on bringing yourself to the material and making it your own.

> Remember, you are going to be paying this school a lot of money to train you. Be concerned about whether or not this is the right school for your development as an artist.

At the interview, the faculty gets the opportunity to ask you why you want to go to do advanced training. Tuthill suggests that you prepare yourself to talk about the things you enjoy. "Stay away from talking about the theater, but talk about your hobbies, sports activities you enjoy, novels, or recent vacations. It will put you at ease so that the teachers can get to know you on a more personal level."

CONSERVATORY TRAINING

Jayd McCarty, the director of programming at the Actors Center, a highly regarded conservatory in New York City , provides an overview of one approach to conservatory training:

> If you want to act in more than just film and television, there are many more demands on you than how you look or what your type might be. The only way you can get around that is training. Because the community of actors is so large, the only thing that really sets you apart is your training.

Asked whether actors can be successful relying solely on their instincts, McCarty responds:

> Perhaps in theory, but I have never seen it myself. I have seen people come through here who, on first look, appear not to be very talented or capable, but it is very hard for us to tell until we start working with them in a classroom, because who knows what they are going to turn into? Once you start to remove that scar tissue and socialization and get them to understand the possibilities within themselves, that they are worth so much more, I find people who I thought had no potential at all become the most incredible actors. I have also seen the other happen. People come in who were really slick and glossy and had good instincts and didn't go very far.

In addition to individual classes, the school also has a nine-month conservatory. It differs from other programs in that:

> J. Michael Miller created the conservatory on the foundation of the studio teachings of Michael Chekhov. It is the same teaching that two-year students at Yale or New York University experience, but it is condensed into a year that is incredibly intensive. The classes are put together so that all the teachers work synergistically. We do lose people for whom it is too hard and too intense. People will start not being able to come to class, manifesting disasters in their lives, illnesses, psychological problems affecting their bodies and their minds, and it is a way of saying they are not ready to do the work.

According to McCarty, no more than fourteen actors are admitted to the conservatory, and they have been known to stop at eight if it is a really good peer group. As for the audition process, it is handled as follows:

> Anyone who studies here auditions for us. It is not only a weeding-out process, but it is a chance for us to tell actors what we currently see in them and what can be developed. Actors call our office and arrange a meeting. We tell them what to prepare for the audition. If they are new, they prepare at least two monologues. The most important factor is that they are connected with the material. What they choose is a good indication of where they are in the program. We ask for a classical piece—Shakespeare, Molière—to see how they can handle language.
>
> At the initial meeting we ask what has brought them to us, what it is they want to work on. We can tell a lot about their self-awareness, if they are really honest, about what they are coming up against in their process, whether they are ready or not to enter this kind of training. We work with them in the audition. It is very much a working session.
>
> How willing are they to work with us? Then we sit down and talk and do an evaluation immediately. We have no problem saying we are uncertain, we need to see more, and they should come back with a specific piece that Michael Miller will assign them, something that will help them to get in touch with themselves. We always ask them about their interests, hobbies, athletic abilities, things that are not directly connected with them as an actor.
>
> So we can see the person up there. Then we can teach them almost anything else. But they have to be willing to get up there and be honest on stage.
>
> We evaluate the training for the conservatory students throughout the year. For individual classes, which are three-hour sessions, two to three times a week for ten weeks, we will tailor the needs of a group. We create what the students want. It is very hands-on. We enter into a relationship with these people.

Joey Sorge, actor, *Drowsy Chaperone* says of his experience at the conservatory:

> I came to New York and studied at the Actors Center. I worked with Joanna Merlin and great people. I picked what I needed—Clown, Shakespeare—and I am stronger for it. As opposed to having someone strip you down and build you back up again.

Hunter Bell, cocreator of [*title of show*], graduated with a degree in musical theater from the Webster Conservatory in St. Louis.

> The program at Webster is great, because it is designed as two majors. One is regional theater for kids who basically want straight acting, and the other is for musical theater. The regional theater students had the same classes we did and vice versa, so I got all that Shakespeare and classical training—and I am glad for that. I'm asked if a conservatory is the right thing. It depends on the individual, but it was right for me. I value training. I am not saying it isn't possible to succeed without it. There are many paths in this business. I wanted some time to get better, time to learn, and it has influenced me and my writing.

ON-CAMERA TRAINING

Many acting schools and some conservatory programs prepare actors for television and film by offering on-camera training. On camera, it's especially important that you have a solid foundation in scene study and script analysis so that you can interpret the material and make choices that are less about theatricality than about truth and credibility. The camera never lies. If you play a scene "over the top," you will look like you are doing too much, and you may "upstage" your character by calling attention to yourself. If you lack confidence in your choices or transitions, you won't register or make an impression.

Rob Decina, the casting director of *Guiding Light* and an adjunct professor of communications at Pace University in New York City, has written a primer for actors who need to master the skills and techniques needed for on-camera auditions. In *The Art of Auditioning: Techniques for Television* (Allworth Press), he takes the actor through the steps necessary to achieve success.

> I always like to think that talented people will rise to the surface no matter what path they take. I personally love training. I think it is valuable because it is what you rely on and lean on when times get tough, and they get tough in daytime TV. There are people with natural ability who are able to learn on the job. Crystal Hunt (ex-Lizzie) was eighteen when she got the contract role. When she started she had very little experience, very little training, but she was exactly what the executive producer had wanted in terms of the look, and in terms of her own background, which was similar to the character's background.

She was able to learn on the job, and she worked with an acting coach whose guidance gave her confidence, and she improved in the role.

The "perfect" audition starts for me when I go to the waiting room and meet the actor and get a vibe that this person could be right for the role—that physically they seem right to me. They enter my office and ask smart questions—or they don't. In the best case, they have made choices about the scene, and they play those choices and it comes alive. They become a thinking, feeling, living being in character. Ideally, an actor is physically what I am looking for and makes choices about the scene without seeking them, based on smart thoughts and feelings. And if I need to make adjustments or notes, they are open to that.

Rob also shares some important technical advice:

Something to remember about on-camera auditions is that many times the casting director is operating the camera as well as reading with you. He would not have the ability to move the camera while you walk in the space and simultaneously say lines.

Always speak directly to the reader, not the camera, unless instructed to do so. One trick to doing an on-camera audition is to remember to drive the audition scene. I find that tapes of an actor play out slower than the action seemed to play in real time. Technology gets in the way of pacing. You always want to pop off the screen, so driving the scene is a suitable way to fight this technical problem. Keep your energy up.

Peter Miner is an award-winning television director who has been teaching actors the art of the on-camera audition for many years.

Sanford Meisner defined acting as "behaving truthfully in imaginary circumstances. You'd better be doing just that when you are working as an actor on camera because the camera is a very efficient lie detector. If you don't behave truthfully, if you underline, exaggerate, indicate, to make sure the audience "gets it," the camera records an actor "acting." The audience sees a lie and stops believing. As Spencer Tracy once said to a young actor, "Acting is okay, as long as you don't get caught at it." Ben Kingsley put it more simply: "The camera's allergic to acting."

So, how can you be an actor and not have the camera catch you acting? First, you have to do your homework, make choices about your character's background, desires, needs, flaws, and the obstacles he/she faces. You learn your lines so well that you don't ever have to be thinking, "What do I say next?"—unless it is the character's thought. Then when the camera rolls, you let your homework go, trusting that it will be there when you need it. You think only as the character, never as the actor. You listen as the character and you never know what's going to happen next unless the character does.

When you're acting on camera, you'd better not be playing a scene, you'd better be having an experience.

David Vando, author of *Shakespeare for the 21st Century* (Angel Management), teaches Shakespeare for the Contemporary Actor at the New York Film Academy (www.nyfa.com), which combines acting techniques and onscreen work in a one-year program. For the first four months, students train to achieve the techniques, emotional availability and physical work needed for film acting; by the end of the year they will have performed in film or video shoots which may involve original work created by the students in collaboration with their instructors. David devoutly believes in the old adage that "if you can act Shakespeare, you can act anything." He continues:

An overwhelming number of the world's greatest actors have had a significant kinship to Shakespeare and that has been instrumental in developing their craft. Actors starting out today have some wonderful opportunities to introduce themselves to Shakespeare at theater festivals and regional theaters throughout the country. Seeing Shakespeare being performed on the stage is a unique learning experience not to be missed.

There are many other lessons to be learned from Shakespeare, the most important of which include to act naturally, like a real human being. He put every human type imaginable on the stage: kings, queens, witches, bawds, beggars, fools, the evil and the saintly. To bring life to these characterizations, we are compelled to call upon our own humanity from the depths of our souls. The other important lesson is to be honest to our inner emotions, or as Will would say, "To thine own self be true.

We highly recommend that you study Hamlet's "Advice to the Players" speech to understand not only the importance of the vocal and physical training in Shakespeare's day but, as David Vando suggests, its contemporary relevance. Practice reading it aloud. Note the phrasing, the language, the metaphors, and the words of wisdom that we are still using today.

> Speak the speech, I pray you, as I pronounced it to you, trippingly on the tongue. But if you mouth it, as many of your players do, I had as lief the towncrier spoke my lines. Nor do not saw the air too much with your hands, thus . . . but use all gently. For in the very torrent, tempest, and (as I may say) whirlwind of passion, you must acquire and beget temperance, that may give it smoothness.
>
> O! it offends me to the soul, to hear a robustious periwig-pated fellow tear a passion to tatters, to very rags to split the ears of the groundlings, who, for the most part, are capable of nothing but inexplicable dumb shows and noise; I would have such a fellow whipped for o'erdoing termagant; it out Herods Herod; Pray you avoid it.
>
> Be not too tame neither, but let your discretion be your tutor; suit the action to the word, the word to the action, with this special observance that you o'erstep not the modesty of nature, for anything so overdone is from the purpose of playing, whose end, both at the first, and now, was and is to hold as t'were the mirror up to nature, to show virtue her own feature, scorn her own image and the very age and body of the time, his form and pressure.

THE TEACHER'S VOICE

A good class develops and invigorates the "acting muscles, including imagination, humor, sense memory, emotional range, style, movement, timing, speech, and vocal variety. It's where you stretch, get out of your comfort zone, and discover new ways to enhance the author's words and create more complex characters. The right class can help you perform better monologues; relax in front of the camera; teach you techniques to strengthen your mind, voice, and body; improve your cold-reading skills and auditioning technique; and give you greater self-confidence.

> I find in today's world that actors starting out are already loaded with emotional accessibility. They need to know how to arrive at it, not by isolating it, but by saying 'my character doesn't want emotion.' Emotion gets in your way. How are you ever going to get anywhere if you are emotional all the time? If you work against it, you will go where Blanche DuBois *(A Streetcar Named Desire)* goes or where Eddie Carbone *(A View From the Bridge)* goes. You will fall apart emotionally

if you work as you would in life to try to achieve something under insurmountable odds.

The legendary teacher Stella Adler believed that a teacher must not only inspire the actor but also agitate and stimulate what's already there. She taught many of the greatest working actors how to analyze a script. New York–based acting teacher Catherine Gaffigan believes her curriculum covers enough in two years, and then encourages her students to move on and not "hide out" in class. "My job is to get them ready to get out there and become employed.

Don't hesitate to ask casting directors, agents, or other actors for referrals. Some teachers accept students based on auditions; others allow audits or schedule orientation sessions about their teaching philosophy. There is no benefit in studying with a celebrity teacher or the one whose class is most difficult to get into unless that person is someone whose work you respect, with whom you feel a connection, and who demands the best of his or her students. If you find that you are not challenged enough in the class, leave.

Alice Spivak, acting teacher, coach, working actress, and coauthor of the book *How to Rehearse When There Is No Rehearsal: Acting and the Media* (Limelight Editions) compares taking classes to going to the gym. Training is particularly vital when an actor has very little time to rehearse, she says, especially when working on television or in film.

You're maintaining your reflexes through training, your muscularity, and at the same time you are trying to stretch a little further. Serious actors never stop studying. It is a never-ending study. My book speaks to the problems American actors have today. The Brits, Australians, Irish, and Canadian actors are taking over American roles. They are trained and have considered the theater their first love. They come out of the theater and the classics. They can take something as minimally written as almost anything for TV and make something of it by adding a dimension, creating subtext for it, and rounding out what seems to be very little information.

Actors in America are being influenced to take very limited courses of study. They are learning how to get the job more than how to do the job. They are not learning how to develop a character or about technique.

Terry Schreiber, acting teacher, director, and author of *Acting: Advanced Techniques for the Actor, Director, and Teacher* (Allworth Press), revealed in his article "Acting as a Sane Obsession" (*Back Stage*):

> During my thirty-eight years as a professional acting teacher, I have encountered too many actors who have been emotionally hurt by teachers and mentors who feel they must strip actors of their ego and rebuild them—or worse, prey upon their neuroses. . . .
>
> Whichever technique an actor uses, what's important is that the actor use only experiences he or she has already resolved psychologically and emotionally. And it is the job of the teacher—or director—to recognize whether a particular place is a safe one for an actor to go to. Has the actor found closure? Can the actor visit a "source" objectively? Drawing on unresolved issues is apt to create a very unhealthy personal life for the actor; nine times out of ten, there's a direct line from such acting to neuroses.
>
> A teacher, therefore, assumes enormous responsibility for creating a safe environment. It must be a nonjudgmental place where actors can take risks but where they aren't really forced to. We attempt to understand the 'blocks' that stop actors from opening up their feelings, so they can fulfill the requirements of all the roles they possess the potential to play.

Actor Edward Norton *(The Painted Veil, The Illusionist)* has this to say about his former teacher:

> Terry understands that every individual actor will best access his gifts in different ways, and also that the modern actor will inevitably be called upon to tackle a wide spectrum of texts, styles, and collaborative dynamics. No method, no theory, no dogma, or technique covers it all or works for everyone, and Terry urges students to be 'multilingual actors', to develop a toolbag that gives them confidence in every situation.

Karen Kohlhaas is a New York City theater director and a founding member of the Atlantic Theatater Company and senior teacher at the Atlantic Acting School (www.monologueaudition.com). She also teaches monologue workshops for auditioning actors, and is the author of *The Monologue Audition: A Practical Guide for Actors* (Limelight Editions) and producer/director/writer of "The Monologue Audition Video," a two-hour

DVD that features a demonstration of her monologue rehearsal technique.

David Mamet said: "Playwrights create chaos, and actors create order." That thought has stayed with me as a director and teacher. I think you can look at any actor and you can say he's playing the problem or playing the solution. Acting that fights for a solution is heroic and thrilling, and involves the audience on the deepest possible level.

We apply the same principles in monologue class. Monologues are often about a huge problem that has been building up for a character for some time. The danger is always to get sucked in to playing the same note of desperation or anger throughout. This makes the monologue repetitive and predictable. Along with finding the acting solution for each character, we also give the monologue staging that has variety.

Howard Fine, the Howard Fine Acting Studio, Los Angeles (www.howardfine.com) says:

Great acting is very difficult but it looks easy, so everyone thinks they ought to be able to do it. That is why everyone thinks they can act, because they can't see where the technique is. The late Uta Hagen, my mentor, was once asked after a performance of the last play she ever did [Six Dance Lessons in Six Weeks, with David Hyde Pierce at the Geffen Playhouse], "How do you do it?" She said, "Would you ask a violinist after a concert how they do it? How would you expect me to explain my technique in a few minutes?

If technique is used incorrectly, it puts the actors in their heads. What it should do is free them up that their instincts can really live. Our goal with technique is spontaneity. That is what got Uta excited about the work. She went to see Laurette Taylor as Amanda in The Glass Menagerie, and to her dying day, she refused to ever play Amanda because she had seen Laurette Taylor. She went to the play several times and would bring friends and she would prepare them to see Laurette do this and that and such and such, but she didn't do that at that performance. Uta realized that Miss Taylor was still playing Amanda in those given circumstances but something different was hitting her emotionally in every single performance. There are two kinds of actors: those who play it the same way no matter what; and those who really know how to live the life so every single performance has something different.

I tell my students, "If actors finish a scene and there's nothing happening inside of them and they're not drained—I don't care if it's comedy or drama—they didn't do it." You can tell when they're working completely externally, without any real, soulful connection to what they're doing. You can tell if somebody is relying on vocal gymnastics; you can tell if the work is preset and preshaped instead of really alive. The eye will always go to what's really alive.

Uta used to say, "It is not about losing yourself in the role; it is about finding yourself in the role." So much of my work is about giving the actor the tools to work on their own, the tools to look through their own life and take an inventory of their own meaning, to make the strongest connection to a role. To be an interesting actor, you must become an interesting person. To be a great actor, you must be insatiably curious, fascinated by life. And respect your craft. Respect it the way you respect any other art form, because you don't have instant mastery. I'm still learning. We are all still learning, all still growing. It is lifelong.

Ivana Chubbuck, Ivana Chubbuck Studios Hollywood (www.ivana-chubbuck.com), wrote *The Power of the Actor* (Gotham Books) and is the creator of the Chubbuck technique.

You're not going to have longevity in your career, and you certainly won't be acknowledged by your peers, if you don't do the training.

Actors have to be aware of who they are as people, know what pushes their buttons and what makes them tick. All people are limited to their own life experiences. You can't play anyone and everything. Imagine Benicio Del Toro (Oscar winner for *Traffic*) playing the stodgy dean of an Ivy League school, or Dame Judi Dench (Oscar winner for *Shakespeare in Love*) playing a prostitute in the "hood."

Actors have to understand who they are and what they are selling. Training will force you to focus on being the best version of your type. You must supply all the colors, all the dimensions, all the layers and texturing of who you are as it relates to the character on the page.

The director of a movie and the producers of a television show will determine if you are the right type. These powerhouses are human and can change their minds. If you give them a great audition, you can have that power. It happens all the time.

Example: Charlize Theron, with whom I worked on the auditions for *Devil's Advocate*. She was the wrong type and age and had very few credits, a virtual unknown seeking a starring role in a big film. We worked on the audition and maintained the essence of all that is Charlize. She auditioned ten times, with the director and the studio saying she wasn't the right type, and they probably weren't going to cast her. However, they were haunted by her authenticity and couldn't get her audition out of their heads. She got the role because her audition changed their minds. This part turned out to be the pivotal role that created her successful career.

I worked with Béyoncé Knowles on the film *Dreamgirls* for many hours, over a period of two months, before the rehearsal schedule began. We continued to work during the actual shooting and on set for the particularly wrenching scenes. She knew that in order to get to the places she wanted to go she had to be open and available. The result was amazing.

When I am teaching in the class, I do not believe in coming from a "guru-esque" place. I create an atmosphere of "we are all in this together to make sense out of this crazy world and to grow, continue to learn, explore, change, discover and evolve.

Marilyn Mcintyre has been a working actress for more than twenty-five years. Howard Fine asked her to develop a "Personalization" course for actors who have difficulty with emotional availability.

If you are an actor who is only looking for the next job, then the chances of really committing to training are going to be less; if you are looking to have longevity and depth in a career and also be able to use your acting skills in all the different media, you have to train. It costs money to do this training. But if you are a smart actor, you have to factor that into your budget. For those of us who are in it for the long haul, we are the 'marathon runners' of the performing arts. Training gives you freedom.

Your life experience, all of what you have gone through, you need to work on that and make peace with that. It is crucial for actors to be really present in their own lives and circumstances before they can make the "actor's leap of faith" into the fictional world of a character. I think we have all seen certain people who have an "aerial view" of their own lives. They keep themselves on the outside, constantly watching, judging, and attempting to control everything, all the time, therefore not really being aware of the moment or what is happening around them. What I love about the actress Helen Mirren (Oscar winner, *The Queen*) is that she never judges her characters. She doesn't maintain a safe distance or an "aerial view" of a character, even when the fictional circumstances are bleak and complicated and we know that it will cost her something to go through this experience.

As actors, we must face the flames. We are the "firepersons" of emotions. When everyone else turns and runs, we stay to face the heat. That's why we must work on our emotional and psychological health and well-being to keep our vessel open and sensitive.

Caryn West is a working actress who teaches a variety of courses on both Coasts that include audition skills and a comedy-intensive. She considers herself to be a protégé of Steve Kaplan, who teaches a highly regarded comedy course (www.kaplancomedy.com).

My favorite comic character is Wile E. Coyote. In the Roadrunner cartoons. Wile E. wants to get Roadrunner, devises all these ways to do that, and then gets foiled in his plans. He drops down into the Grand Canyon in an explosion. You never see him in the ICU, and the next day he has a better plan. We root for him even though he is probably going to fail. He never gives up, has a passion, and his pain is temporary. In life, pain, death and destruction will affect us all, but in comedy we defy all those things. Wile E. is always optimistic and that is the root of comedy. He is oblivious to the one essential fact that he is slow and will never catch the roadrunner.

Stereotypes are good. Stock characters, like those in the commedia, aren't well rounded. If you watch *Cheers,* not one of those characters ever evolved into a different kind of person. Sam Malone played by Ted Danson was a womanizer till the end and never able to commit. Kelsey Grammer played Frasier for eighteen years, and he never changed but remained pompous and unable to have a lasting relationship. That is the essence of comedy.

The actor who thinks he is smart will know where the laugh is and sort of be 'winking' because he knows the joke. And that kills comedy. Lucy never knows how stupid she is; Lucille Ball has to play her like she doesn't know she is dumb. Wile E. can't know that he is too slow. He has to forge ahead not knowing something about himself. Doris Roberts [Marie on *Everybody Loves Raymond*] can't know she is negative and controlling. She has to play it like she is well intended and so are her comments. You have to embrace this "not-knowing-ness." The actor knows the flaw; the character doesn't.

In comedy I think it is about overcoming bad situations and remaining optimistic as opposed to giving in. In *Some Like It Hot,* Joe E. Brown is in love and wants to marry the woman, who says there is one problem. When he asks what it is, the character says, "I'm a man!" The greatest end line in movies is Joe E. Brown's, "Well, nobody's perfect." It is the classic optimistic ending.

THE ESSENTIALS: THE BODY AND VOICE

"Whatever the art you may wish to learn . . . acrobatics or violin playing, acting, singing, dancing . . . there is one thing that every good teacher will always say: Learn to combine relaxation with activity; learn to do what you have to do without straining; work hard, but never under tension." —Aldous Huxley, novelist and essayist

Whether you are training for theater, television, or film, movement skills and a resonant, well-modulated voice are essential to your work as an actor.

The Alexander Technique

Australian-born Frederick Matthias Alexander (1869–1955) discovered this functional approach when doctors couldn't cure him of his recurring loss of his voice. Given his profession as a Shakespearean reciter, this was a significant liability. Through self-observation and self-sensing, he became aware of his unconscious propensity to pull his head back and down, which exerted pressure on his neck. Once he began controlling this habit, he healed himself of throat and vocal troubles and the respiratory and nasal difficulties he had suffered since birth.

He organized a method for converting such faulty use of the body into improved coordination; this method became known as the Alexander Technique.

The first step is to become aware of your detrimental habits through your own body awareness. An Alexander teacher gently uses his or her hands—while you are bending, sitting, standing up, walking. Although your whole body is involved, the emphasis is on the head-neck relationship, which Alexander called "Primary Control." The teacher lightly steers your head into its proper position on the tip of the spine, which leads to optimal lengthening of the spine and more fluid movement in general.

The second part of changing a habit is getting rid of the established, old pattern of unnecessary muscle-tightening. When you learn to stop yourself from "tightening up," you leave your body free to act naturally and easily, allowing the neuromuscular system new freedom.

Tense responses develop through what the technique calls "end-gaining." When you end-gain, you rush unconsciously for an immediate result, such as sitting, instead of consciously going through a process in which there is nothing to force, only muscle tension to give up. When you break from the old pattern, you can make intelligent choices during your actions. Instead of plunging unreflectively toward an end, you continue to allow moment-to-moment awareness.

The third element is verbal feedback. You learn the following words from the teacher and internalize them by repeating to yourself as you move: "Let my neck be free, let my head go forward and up, let my torso lengthen and widen, let my legs release from my torso, and let my shoulders widen." These gentle mental reminders lead your movement toward more expansion. In turn, you will find yourself experiencing increased energy and emotional availability.

Tom Vasiliades, the director of the Alexander Technique Center for Performance and Development, teaches individual and group sessions in New York. In the sessions, students wear comfortable clothing. During part of the session they lie down while he helps them let go of excessive habitual tension without the demands of being upright. In another part of the session he helps them practice the technique as they are doing everyday activities. The results are often dramatic relief from chronic pain, improved breathing and vocal production, enhanced performance, movement with ease and stress reduction.

Actor Alan Rickman acknowledges that "with the best intentions, the job of acting can become a display of accumulated bad habits, trapped instincts, and blocked energies. Working with Tom and the Alexander Technique to untangle the wires has given me a vision of another way. Mind and body, work and life, all of it together. [It creates] real imaginative freedom."

For more information about the Alexander Technique, visit www.atcpd.com.

Posture, Movement, Body Language

Movement skills are organic to the development of characters for the theater, television, and film. They are an essential part of the actor's tool kit.

Actor-director Erika Batdorf, in an essay included in *Movement for Actors* (Allworth Press), writes: "Film actors need even more training than theater actors, if they want range. In theater, one can rehearse with the text for longer periods of time. With film, one's bag of tricks has to be large and immediately accessible." She points out that you don't want to be typecast by the slump in your shoulders or a protruding chin.

> Character development . . . involves changing tension levels, spinal shape, extensive gesture change, subtle head-eye relationships, rhythm, and breath.
>
> As an actor, even if you use the most profound psychological approach, if your body does not respond, your acting will misfire. If you can access the larger, deeper parts of the body consciously, then you have a large-enough container of these feelings. You can place [them] into the muscles of the legs or the back, you can deepen the breathing, you can engage a more believable whole-body response.

New York–based stage and film actor Cathy Haase, in *Acting for Film* (Allworth Press), notes that today's film actors need more movement skills than ever.

> The body is a huge, intelligent playing field for an actor, but the constricting nature of some camera setups can make you forget that you even have a body, especially if you have been doing a lot of work focusing on the mid-chest and up.
>
> Whereas before you had to tap-dance and sing, now you have to be able to ride a motorcycle and shoot a pistol. These days women are in the military, in combat, are first-responders, carpenters, and construction workers. . . . As women break down the barriers of physical prowess in the working world, actresses should consider what the physical demands of future roles might be and train accordingly.

West Coast–based on-set coach and choreographer Paula Thomson teaches dance and movement at California Stage University at Northridge. Her classes include body alignment work using the Alexander Technique. She says if your body alignment is skewed, you can't access all your energy. But the most common problem she sees is that actors lack core strength: a center in the lower abdomen and lower back stable enough to support them. As a result they can't open their chests and diaphragms enough. She recommends movement training at a conservatory.

Other approaches to body awareness include the Pilates, Feldenkrais, and Laban methods. What's important, she says, is to find someone who can help you identify and change your physical habits. She also recommends a movement-improv class, or "someplace where you can get the kinks out and find freedom within your own body, even if it's salsa dancing. Any kind of improv especially helps actors to learn to trust their unconscious, autonomic responses."

Training the Speaking Voice

"At the John Murray Anderson School, we performed in a play a week. We learned about voice. When we began, my small voice and my New England accent made me a poor candidate for success. All regional accents limit an actor's possibilities."

—Bette Davis, Oscar-winning actress

Do you have any idea what you sound like? It is your responsibility to have a resonant, well-modulated voice on the phone and in person. Breathy, high-pitched, whiny, inaudible monotones announce the amateur and destroy our confidence in your ability. Take a lesson from Eliza Doolittle. She never would have been anyone's Fair Lady if she hadn't learned to match her voice to her look.

When casting directors or agents call your voice mail, they should hear a warm, friendly, casual, accessible, and self-confident announcement of who you are.

Lucille S. Rubin, PhD, president of Professionally Speaking, is a voice, speech, and performance coach. She helps performers develop voice skills such as elimination of harsh, strident, and nasal tones; banishing monotony, breathing with ease; finding an optimum pitch level, releasing throat and jaw tension; fighting vocal fatigue; using vocal variety; and maximizing vocal potential. She has coached performers in Broadway shows, regional theaters, and red-carpet TV hosting. Dr. Rubin teaches stage voice at New York's Circle in the Square Theatre School. "One of the things at Circle in the Square (www.circleinsquare.org) that pleases me is that voice and speech are separartely taught. As a speech teacher you have to hear every single sound, how many sounds we have, not just the five vowels— a, e, i, o, u—but twelve to fifteen vowel sounds plus all the diphthongs, plus at least twenty-six consonant sounds." She makes a chart for each student to ensure that when each one speaks she can accurately identify each sound.

Dr. Rubin is a founding member of the Voice and Speech Trainers Association (VASTA; www.vasta.org), and she wrote the organization's guidelines to help raise the standards of voice and speech coaching and training.

Her biggest complaint today is pitch. Students think that a low pitch is natural.

"Even if they have reasonably good articulation, we still don't hear what they say because they are muttering." She recommends a simple exercise to find your most comfortable and effective voice.

Hum for three minutes in the morning, with your lips closed and your teeth unclenched. Maintain a low volume and smooth air flow, and explore your pitch range by using all your notes.

Once you've found your natural voice, you can move on to a strength-training exercise. Align your body by imagining that a string at the top of your head is lifting you up. Now open your mouth and drop your jaw. Then start to speak. If you want to be sure you are keeping the anchor in your voice, put a hand on your chest to feel the purr.

Actors can have an audience in the palm of their hand, if they can get the audience to breathe with them. It is a trick that requires steady, slow breathing and a carefully measured speech pattern.

The areas of training that are mandatory for professional voice and speech mastery include both voice production skills (respiration, phonation, resonance, articulation) and voice perception skills (quality, loudness, rate and pitch).

Actors will sound more professional in all media if they consider training in the following areas, according to Dr. Rubin

- **Body alignment.** Today's actors like the "blue jean slouch," with hands in pockets, along with the "cool" chest crumple. Head pecking is used for vocal emphasis. Recommended studies might be Feldenkrais or the Alexander Technique.
- **Elimination of glottal attacks and breath-holding patterns.** These problems are the real giveaway of an untrained voice. Breath-holding is boring. It leads to false pauses. Actors need to get in synch with their breath rhythm.

- **Relaxation techniques.** These techniques help get in touch with free breathing and help centering. Centered breathing assures a full voice and encourages emotional connection. Running out of air and yet continuing to talk invites vocal misuse and abuse.
- **Opening the throat.** Finding jaw space, a soft tongue, a flexible palate, and an anchored larynx adds resonance and vocal color to the voice.
- **Blending resonators.** Blending determines how much bottom or how much top you put in the resonator you decide to use—the mouth, the chest, the throat or the nose—and adds to the "color." Very deep low notes are black; middle range (horn sounds) may be more lemony. There is always some deep purple. If you blend your purple with your lemon, you will save your voice, especially when you have to scream.
- **Forward tone focus and mask resonance.** This gets the voice out of the throat and aids ease of projection.
- **Finding optimum pitch level.** The best pitch is the range in which the actor's voice works most efficiently, with the least amount of effort.
- **Neutral vocal quality.** Vocal actors need to find their own voices, but if that voice is nasal, denasal, thin, strident, harsh, throaty, or chesty, they need to find voice appeal as a neutral quality. If they start with a neutral voice, then they can readily find choices for each character.
- **Extended pitch range and pitch variety.** American speech is characterized as fairly monotone. Inflecting is a hard leap for many actors, but once they are free from their three notes, they sense they are more emotionally connected.
- **Articulation skills.** This includes study of the International Phonetic Alphabet (IPA). Once actors have mastered the IPA, they can more readily learn dialects and accents. Using toned endings of words, placing the tongue to avoid distracting sounds, shaping the mouth, lips, jaw, and tongue to provide resonance changes, and putting all the sounds in the words—all these add up to sharper diction. The untrained American actor thinks that slurred speech is natural and cool, but the trained actor knows better. Accents and regionalisms disappear when an actor knows the IPA.
- **Avoiding vocal fatigue.** Actors need to know what is making their voice tired. They can find out by seeing an ear, nose, and throat specialist. It's important to identify vocal habits that bring about vocal fatigue and replace them with healthy behaviors.

- **Having a voice warm-up, tune-up, workout, and cool-down.** A coach can help design a personal program to best fit an actor's personal vocal needs, or a particular character they are playing. Knowing the warm-up is essential, but doing it is what brings about change. It's like going to the gym. You've got to keep your muscles in shape, and the vocal folds (cords) are one-inch muscles. They need daily workouts.
- **Ace-ing the audition.** The voice and the body are the two things that reflect acting talents. Many actors revert to what they call "honesty" and "truthfulness," which is usually small in scale, low volume, lazy diction and lots of husky-voiced screaming. Vocal training is all about finding new choices.

Kristin Linklater is a founding member and the artistic director of the Linklater Center for Voice and Language. She is a professor of theater arts and currently serves as head of acting of the Graduate Theatre Division of Columbia University in New York City. Her work is most widely known through her books *Freeing the Natural Voice: Imagery and Art in the Practice of Voice and Language* (Drama Publishers) and *Freeing Shakespeare's Voice* (TCG). Teachers she has trained are employed in many professional actor-training programs in the United States (visit www.thelinklatercenter.com).

Kristin is dedicated to the release and development of voices that tell the truth and reverberate with the necessary passion to bring the stage to life. She advises all actors to do a forty-minute warm-up before a performance. Speech and language reside in the entire body. The body must be warmed up so that it's loose enough to support the voice from every extremity and from everywhere else. She emphasizes that the voice doesn't come merely from the upper body.

Learning Dialects: The Stoller System

Amy Stoller is an actress and the director of Dialect Coaching and Design by Amy Stoller (www.stollersystem.com). She has played leading and featured roles Off-Broadway and in regional theaters. She began coaching informally when fellow students at an acting studio, impressed by her dialect skills as an actor, asked her to help with their accents for class work. Since 1995 she has been a dialect coach in New York City and is a member of VASTA.

> Accent has to do with pronunciation of the speech at hand. Dialect includes not only accent but all the other linguistic considerations—grammar, syntax, possibly register (formal or informal), and there are

also things that shift over time, so that a dialect will differ from one end of a century to the other. Some of the things that I consider when I am doing my research include geographical location, ethnic background within that location, the era in which the play is set, the characters' social status, and their education level.

A good knowledge of accents and dialects can inform an actor's choices, but it should never dictate them. It is a tool at the actor's disposal. I use the International Phonetic Alphabet (IPA) as my personal notation system, and I usually use it as a teaching tool for actors who come to me with beginning levels of experience and training. Every symbol represents one specific sound. For someone who is coming to me with no training or experience, I start with what I call "vowel and consonant kindergarten."

Very often actors don't know what vowels and consonants are from the point of view of the speaker; they know them from the point of view of the writer. So I will start people learning what's a vowel, what's a consonant, in speech terms, and what are the parts of your articulatory anatomy—your tongue, teeth, lips, and the roof of your mouth—and how do you use them to make different sounds? Then we can talk about what happens if you need to speak in an accent different from your own. Once we get to the text work, I address the intonation pattern and breath placement or resonance.

I will get calls from actors who say, "I need accent reduction." And I will say, "No you don't; you need accent acquisition." I don't believe in trying to erase a performer's individual accent or speech pattern, which I refer to as home-speech or heart-speech. That is integral to the actor's core instrument.

What should actors do about listing dialects on their résumés? On my own acting résumé, I list a handful of the accents that I know I can do at the drop of a hat. If you call me at ten o'clock at night and say, "You have an audition at eight a.m. tomorrow, when you need this accent," I know I can wake up and do it. Other accents I will list "with notice," which means I will need a couple of days' warning if you want me to bring in Romanian, Indian, or Tennessee Mountain. I recommend that actors only list specific dialects on their résumés that they can do with twelve hours' notice. I don't believe in misrepresenting your skill level on the résumé.

CLOWN SKILLS AND PHYSICAL COMEDY

According to Jayd McCarty at the Actors Center, any actor who has problems being sentimental, "schticky," presentational, or dishonest will benefit from a clown class. "You cannot lie. It is the most terrifying work I did in actor training. You have to be honest. You cannot be funny."

Geoffrey Rush (Oscar winner, *Shine*), Gates McFadden (*Star Trek: The Next Generation*), and Julie Taymor, Broadway director (*The Lion King*) are graduates of the Lecoq program, based on work created by the late Jacques Lecoq, a French actor, mime, and acting instructor. His work with commedia dell'arte in Italy, where he lived for eight years, introduced him to ideas surrounding mime, masks, and the physicality of performance. Julie Taymor went to Lecoq's school in Paris at the age of sixteen.

> The work at Lecoq's was about getting disciplined with the body. It wasn't just mime. It was work with the Neutral Mask, character masks, abstract masks. With Lecoq, the body is a complete resource you can use to express anything. What is it about "sad" that makes the body hard or soft? What rhythm does "sadness" have? Your body becomes a tool. Your body is like paintbrushes. How and when can we be a fat person or a thin person? What is it about a thin person, what is it about angularity, what is it that makes someone feel thin? You should be able to transform your body.

Lucas Caleb Rooney, cocreator and star of *Creation: A Clown Show!* is a classically trained actor who incorporates a bit of clowning in whatever roles he plays and also teaches it at the Actors Center. "Clowning to me is the basis of all acting. It's about being the most vulnerable, the most honest you can be. Whether you have on a nose or not, it's still clowning. It's the core expressive creature that most people's urge to perform comes from."

IMPROVISATION

Improvisation is an essential component of the actor's tool kit. It has been defined as the art of acting and reacting, in the moment, to one's surroundings. Using a highly tuned imagination to invent new thought patterns or new behaviors can release creative blocking in rehearsal and flesh out the life of the characters you are portraying.

According to Constantin Stanislavski, an actor who improvises a scene relies on his instincts to define a character's response to internal and external triggers or stimuli and avoid "mugging" and "indicating" to communicate his objectives. It is particularly helpful in its focus on concentration.

Film directors including Mike Leigh use improvisation to build characters and story lines. A broad outline with given circumstances is presented to the cast, and they must be adept at creating dialogue and actions and believable emotions to support the outcome. The actors chosen for projects such as these must be good at thinking on their feet, be able to be emotionally available and flexible, have a knowledge of theater games and storytelling, and be observers of the life around them and in tune with what is going on in the world.

Sir Anthony Hopkins believes that if you learn the basic text and it's very well written, and you learn it thoroughly, you can improvise around it.

> I was doing a scene in *The Bounty* where I have to get all of the crew together and really lash into them because they are mutineers. I have to really read them the riot act. I remember we had few lines and we kept the camera rolling and all this new stuff came out that I was improvising. I made up a whole speech. They seemed to like it, because it's still in the film.
>
> So you have to have freedom to improvise. On *The World's Fastest Indian,* there were scenes that I loosely added. Director Roger Donaldson did a couple of takes and I'd improvise around those, and what he didn't feel was necessary he would cut out in the editing room. It gave a sort of gravy to the part; it gave the sauce and the seasoning to the scene. It's like improvising in jazz or adding a cadenza in a piano concerto."

Tony-winning actress Frances Sternhagen studied with the late Sanford Meisner at the Neighborhood Playhouse. Meisner taught students improvisation skills that Sternhagen believes improved her acting technique.

> I work from the outside in. I like to start out with how the character looks and feels and how he walks and talks. The inside is where you use yourself and how you really feel and align with what's going on in the character. The improvisation method actually released me and made a difference in my acting, so that I was able to infuse the character with my own emotions and be the character.

The Second City

The Second City evolved from the Compass Players, a 1950s cabaret-style show started by undergraduates at the University of Chicago. The troupe chose the self-mocking name "Second City" from the title of a disdainful article about Chicago that appeared in *The New Yorker*. The first revue show premiered in 1959. While the style of the troupe's comedy has changed with the times, their format has remained constant. The revues feature a mix of semi-improvised and scripted scenes. New material is developed during unscripted improv sessions, where scenes are created based on audience suggestions. A number of well-known performers, including Bill Murray, James Belushi, Bonnie Hunt, Amy Sedaris, Steve Carell, and Tina Fey began their careers as part of the troupe and later moved on to television and movie work. In the mid-1970s, Second City Chicago became a source of cast members for the *Saturday Night Live* television show, which borrowed many of the troupe's writing and performing techniques.

Second City also has several schools of improvisation, most notably in Chicago, Toronto, and Los Angeles. Various alumni and notable performers have taught at these institutions.

The Upright Citizens Brigade Theatre

Located on both coasts, the Upright Citizens Brigade Theatre (UCBT) is one of the largest and most well-respected places for studying improv comedy in the nation. It is there that long-form improvisation and sketch comedy are taught by working professional comedians and experienced UCBT trained improvisers. Del Close, called the Legendary Guru of Comedy, developed what is known as the "Harold," the original long-form structure, which is outlined in his book, *Truth in Comedy: The Manual of Improvisation,* with Charna Halpern and Kim Johnson (Meriwether Publishing). To perform a Harold, a team takes a single suggestion from the audience, spins the suggestion into a set of ideas through an opening, which then inspires a number of scenes and group games. Characters, ideas, and games return throughout the Harold and eventually connect.

The students and teachers of UCBT have gone on to write, perform, and/or produce for *Saturday Night Live, Late Night* with Conan O'Brien, *The Daily Show* with Jon Stewart, *Mad TV, Road Trip*, and numerous other television shows, as well as films and commercials.

WORKING WITHOUT A NET

An issue of *Emmy* magazine reported that cable networks are moving into the comedy realm with original, improvised comedies that combine reality and script, in the same vein as HBO's *Curb Your Enthusiasm.* Eric McCormack (Will of *Will and Grace)* was an executive producer of *Lovespring International,* Lifetime's improvised comedy about a zany group of employees and their clients at a dating service. The show featured an impressive cast of improv veterans, including Jane Lynch, a former member of the Second City comedy troupe, and Wendi McLendon-Covey, a member of the Groundlings improv troupe who stars on the Comedy Central "improvedy" *Reno 911!*

Oxygen has debuted *Campus Ladies*, which follows the escapades of two middle-aged and often clueless housewives who experience college life and partying for the first time. The stars developed their characters as members of the Groundlings. They exec-produced the show with Cheryl Hines, an Emmy nominee for *Curb Your Enthusiasm).* She says:

> When I was coming up, everything was about the script. Improv was a tool to strengthen your acting abilities. But these improvised shows are more about the actor's voice than the writer's. Larry David [creator, executive producer, and star of *Curb Your Enthusiasm]* has always told me that actors who are great improvisers can say funnier things than he can write, especially from a character's point of view.
>
> Some improvised shows can get into trouble because the structure isn't there. Larry taught me that you still need a very strong A- and B-story.

"Not every actor can thrive in this form, so the ones who can are doing really well," says Michael C. Forman, who coproduced *Lovespring* with Eric McCormack. "It's really about actors who have the creative ability to work in a more dangerous situation, without a net."

Whether you decide to get a B.F.A, opt for a four-year conservatory program, head for the major industry centers after high school graduation, pursue a master's degree, or select your own curriculum of specialized acting classes, you will always be learning and growing during rehearsal, performance, and between engagements. Training is everything that helps you prepare for the audition, get the job, and keep it.

POSTSCRIPT

More than a hundred years ago, the character of Nina in Anton Chekhov's *The Sea Gull* passionately declared to Constantin at the end of the play that acting gave her a reason to live, brought her happiness and fulfillment, and fed her soul.

I've become a real actress. I take pleasure in my performance. I delight in it. I'm in a state of intoxication up there. I feel I'm beautiful. And now, while I've been staying here, I've kept walking round, walking and walking and thinking and thinking—and I've had the feeling that with every day my spiritual strength has grown. I know now, Kostya, I understand now, that in our work—and it makes no difference whether we are acting or whether we're writing—the main thing is not the fame, not the glory, not all the things I used to dream of; it's the ability to endure. Learn to bear your cross; have faith. I have faith, and for me the pain is less. And when I think about my vocation, I'm not afraid of life.

CHAPTER 6

Looking for Work

"If opportunity doesn't knock, build a door!"   —Milton Berle

The Business of being an actor, whether you are employed or not, is a full-time job. Serious pursuit of your career demands diligence in developing your talents, looking for jobs, being able to perform on cue, and packaging yourself correctly. It really requires a total commitment.

However, if you are well prepared, looking for work needn't be a daunting task. The recognized way to open *and* build doors is through some intelligent work on your part—making the rounds, knocking on doors, making cold calls, networking. In the forties and fifties, actors would sit in the waiting room of a producer's office, hoping to be there at the right time, when the producer would come out and say hello and possibly point to someone who was right for the next new show. They called it "making the rounds."

Back then, actors in New York would also hang out in the drugstore of the Astor Hotel on Broadway and Times Square; they'd commandeer one of the dozen pay telephones, take out a note pad and a roll of nickels, and make calls to agents and casting people, hoping to take advantage of whatever tips they'd heard over coffee. The NBC Cafeteria, on the main floor of 30 Rockefeller Plaza, and Colbee's in the CBS building at 485 Madison Avenue, were crowded with radio people from the shows that originated in the studios on the upper floors of those buildings. Assertive actors would have a friend, an agent, or a relative call and ask for them during the busy lunch and cocktail hours so the switchboard operators would page them—it was a good way to advertise themselves.

According to character actor Gerald Kline, "Now, it's about getting off an e-mail at the right moment. It's not so different; it's just different in the tools. But the overall concept of how one does business is really the same. It's still a battle to get that personal contact."

As actor Marc Baron says, "I was stand-in for Dustin Hoffman on *Family Business*. He told me something I will never forget: "'Marc, you have to make the work!'"

INTRODUCTION TO NETWORKING

Promotional materials are essential for "getting your foot in the door." You may send your photo and résumé to the casting directors and agents listed in *Ross Reports* and *Henderson's Casting Directors Guide,* both reputable sources. The photo, of course, should do you justice, and your credits should spell out your experience and training.

You'll want to use another photo on postcards—to send personal notes of what you're doing. Invest also in a business card with your photo on it. You never know who you may meet at industry parties, or when you'll reconnect with a writer, director, or a working actor, perhaps one from your training program. It's tacky to offer your 8 x 10, but a business card is easily tucked into a wallet. Keep notes. Build your own database so you can stay connected to the new friends you make, people who can open doors. For more about preparing your promotional materials, see Chapter Three, "The Tools of the Trade."

Read the trade papers for specific casting news, such as "open calls" held by casting directors when they need people for "atmosphere." All of the trades offer online subscriptions. For a fee, you can also register with online submission services such as ActorsAccess.com, NowCasting.com, and LACasting.com (see Chapter Seven, "Cyberbiz"). Both the American Federation of Television and Radio Artists (AFTRA) and the Screen Actors Guild (SAG) have recently created online talent directories at no cost to their members.

Networking Facilities

You probably won't have to look far to find events where you're likely to meet other actors, casting directors, producers, and other people in The Business. The Actors Connection has for many years offered seminars at

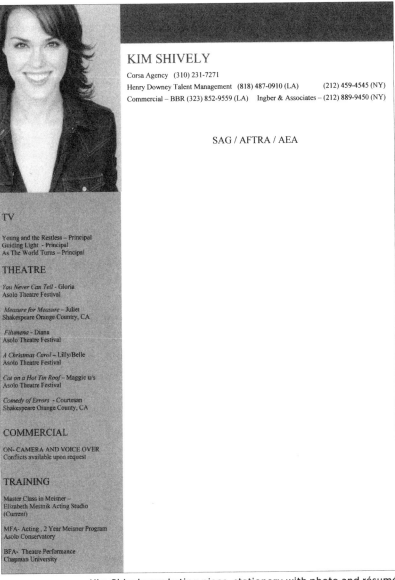

KIM SHIVELY

Corsa Agency   (310) 231-7271

Henry Downey Talent Management   (818) 487-0910 (LA)   (212) 459-4545 (NY)

Commercial – BBR (323) 852-9559 (LA)   Ingber & Associates – (212) 889-9450 (NY)

SAG / AFTRA / AEA

TV

Young and the Restless – Principal
Guiding Light - Principal
As The World Turns – Principal

THEATRE

You Never Can Tell - Gloria
Asolo Theatre Festival

Measure for Measure – Juliet
Shakespeare Orange Country, CA

Filumena - Diana
Asolo Theatre Festival

A Christmas Carol – Lilly/Belle
Asolo Theatre Festival

Cat on a Hot Tin Roof – Maggie u/s
Asolo Theatre Festival

Comedy of Errors - Courtesan
Shakespeare Orange County, CA

COMMERCIAL

ON- CAMERA AND VOICE OVER
Conflicts available upon request

TRAINING

Master Class in Meisner –
Elizabeth Mestnik Acting Studio
(Current)

MFA- Acting , 2 Year Meisner Program
Asolo Conservatory

BFA- Theatre Performance
Chapman University

Kim Shively marketing piece, stationery with photo and résumé

which actors' work can be seen by casting directors and agents. That is no guarantee of employment, but it provides an opportunity to get work, and it has been a door-opener for many actors. Actors Alliance pre-screens actors by having them audition for the chance to meet casting people in one-on-one sessions. For a nominal annual fee, actors get a chance to show their talent and to interview with CDs who cast for theater, film, and TV.

The Drama Book Shop, at 250 West 40th Street in Manhattan, is a show-business treasure trove for play scripts and all kinds of books about theater, TV, films, and more. On entering the shop you'll see lots of brochures for classes, coaches, and theater companies, all promoting their work. The shop sponsors monthly seminars, panels, and book signings with high-profile casting directors, agents, playwrights, teachers, and artistic directors. At one event, Rob Decina, casting director of *Guiding Light*, gave the audience insights on auditioning for soaps. In another, veteran acting teacher and director Walt Witcover demonstrated how he works with actors at the launch for his book *Living on Stage* (Back Stage Books). Emerging theater companies can rehearse and showcase original work in the store's Arthur Seelen Theatre.

Every autumn, Back Stage East presents ActorFest in New York and Back Stage West produces the event in Los Angeles. At these gatherings, acting schools, coaches, support services, career consultants, photographers, publishing companies, trade publications, and labor unions promote their activities. For a nominal fee, you can sign up for career seminars and focus sessions at which casting directors and agents share their expertise on auditioning, marketing strategies, and reaching your goals.

Another place to learn about auditions, interviews, and jobs is class. Well-known monologue coach Karen Kohlhaas referred one of her students to a playwright, who used him in a showcase. Classes can also provide the opportunity to perform in industry showcases, where casting directors and other influential professionals will see you in short performances. New York's Terry Schreiber Studios, where casting directors frequently hold open calls, auditions actors taking its classes for its annual series of four plays. Twice a year Mary Boyer, who teaches at MTB Studio in New York, directs industry-only showcases featuring the studio's students—one of whom was recently cast in a series.

Polishing Your Skills

Performers who can act, sing, and dance become triple threats, because American theater today produces far more musicals than straight plays, and successful musicals typically enjoy long runs—for example, *Phantom of the Opera*, *Legally Blonde*, *Curtains*, *Beauty and the Beast*, *Chicago*, *Rent*, *The Drowsy Chaperone*, *Mary Poppins*, *The Producers*, *Wicked*, *Mamma Mia!*, *Jersey Boys*, and *Spamalot*. There are lots of jobs in these hit shows on Broadway and in their touring companies.

Singers take classes in vocal technique as well as theatrical performance. To ease budget strain (learning to sing can be costly), you might
consider a group workshop, where singing lessons cost less than private
classes. For beginners, these two-hour sessions can also be less stressful
than solo lessons. It's comforting to realize you're not the only one who
hits wrong notes, as well as edifying to hear how easily others connect
with a song and keep working on it until they reach performance quality. You might consider bartering lessons—offering your talents in another
area, such as organizing clutter or computer design—to a colleague who
knows how to sing and is willing to teach you the skills involved.

Body movement is an essential element of the actor's training.
As writers of books on body language have made clear, movement is a
function of character and emotion. A dance class, therefore, may be more
useful than calisthenics for career purposes. And if you supplement your
ability to move well with a knowledge of contemporary dance steps, you'll
increase your chances of work.

You may also want to take workshops in soap opera, commercial,
and film technique. Begin with the area you believe will offer you the most
immediate opportunity for work. When you feel you've become skilled
and "employable" in one discipline, move on to another.

For more information on the value of training, see Chapter Five,
"Training Is Everything."

Knowing Your Field

You should get to know the life stories of well-known performers and the
literature of the theater. If you don't already have a library card, get one.
It costs you nothing. Read plays in their entirety, not just the scenes that
may be assigned to you. You may discover a part that seems to have been
written just for you.

Thanks to the generosity of the late producer, theater owner, and
actress Lucille Lortel, your New York City Public Library card admits you
to the Theater on Film and Tape (TOFT) Archive at the New York Public Library for the Performing Arts at Lincoln Center in Manhattan. The
world's foremost collection of films and videotapes of live theater, under
the guidance of librarian Betty Corwin, is a vast archive of Broadway, Off-
Broadway, and regional theater productions as well as related items, such

as interviews, documentaries, lectures, and awards programs. As Donna McKechnie, the original Cassie in *A Chorus Line*, learned when she directed a revival of *Company* a few years ago, "Thank God for Betty Corwin and the Lincoln Center Library. Without the *Company* tape, I'd never have been able to re-create Michael Bennett's work, his brilliant conceptual staging." The library's costume collection is equally spectacular.

A recent interview with Betty Corwin, produced by the League of Professional Theater Women's Oral History Project, can be viewed on request at the library. Throughout the year, the Library's Bruno Walter Auditorium offers theatrical, musical and dance events; these include interviews and discussions with major authors, directors and composers, performances by internationally known players, celebrations of achievements in dance, song, or other aspect of the performing arts. There is no admission charge for these opportunities to see artists of such high caliber and to hear their stories. Your library card is your ticket of admission.

The Donnell Library, at 20 West 53rd Street, in Manhattan, is the NYPL's Media Center. Here's where you'll find the largest collection of films and recordings, as well as a grand new theater, which is available for public performances.

Let's Talk About You

What can you say about yourself in sixty seconds? Have you any idea how long a minute is? The late Tony Randall, the compulsively neat Felix Unger in the TV series *The Odd Couple,* was noted for his infallible sense of time. Legend has it that immediately after his first read-through of a sixty-second spot, he called out to the director, "I'm a second over, Rick, I know where to pick it up."

You need a sixty-second pitch for yourself that provides all your relevant information: training, experience, background, recent credits, special skills, athletic abilities, hobbies, and roles you want to play. Write it down. Read it aloud. Don't rush. Be as relaxed as if you were talking to a good friend. Time it. Learn your words. From then on, whenever you meet an industry professional socially, you will always be prepared and at ease. Use the same material if you're asked to do an on-camera personality test. Practice telling your story. Practice will translate into confidence, and your confidence will be impressive.

Speed Networking

Twice a year, the New York Coalition of Professional Women in the Arts and Media (www.nycwam.org) sponsors the Blatant Self-interest Networking Event. A distinguished guest speaker talks about her work to union members, writers, composers, lyricists, producers, and directors. Each attendee then has thirty seconds to give his or her pitch.

Former Coalition president and director Melanie Sutherland has come up with Networking Intensive, a variation on the above theme, in which ten couples sit facing one another at long tables. They have ten minutes to introduce themselves, talk about what they're working on, what they're seeking, and to exchange business cards. After the ten minutes are up, the couples separate and move on to a new table and the ten-minute dialogue process repeats—and keeps repeating until everyone has spoken with every person at the event. Participants usually leave Networking Intensive sessions feeling exhilarated—and armed with more new contacts than a year's worth of party-hopping and chance encounters could have provided them. Union members may bring guests; there is a nominal fee for the sessions, and reservations are required (though you can take your chances as a walk-in).

Knocking on Doors

Here is where the sensitive artist must become the energetic, alert entrepreneur. Is it possible, in this era of tight security, when every visitor's name must be on a list at the lobby desk, to make cold calls? To drop in at an agent's or a casting director's office? According to many veteran actors who've tried it, you never know. Making the rounds is strictly a New York means of looking for work. You cannot do this in Los Angeles, where you cannot gain entrance to a studio without an appointment. Actor Gerald Kline tells the following story.

> I had an audition in a building with a lot of offices listed in the lobby directory. Mostly production houses. I don't know what they produce, or whether they use actors, but I have a couple of photos and résumés with me, so I knock on one door and ask if they use actors. The fellow says no. At the second office, the fellow says yes. I ask if I can leave my picture and résumé, and he says, "Sure." I don't know what's going to happen from that, but OK. I knock on another door, someone opens it and says, "Come on in." They may have thought I was there for some

other business, but I see scripts on the coffee table and I'm sitting next to two guys who are there to audition for something. Someone comes out and tells me they're doing an industrial film, looking for a doctor for a very short scene. Now, those other actors are much younger. I say, "Well, I'm just here to drop off my photo and résumé, but I could be that doctor." And son of a gun if they don't talk to me, and the next day they call, and I've got that job!

"Snail Mail" and Cover Letters

"Forget sparkles, sprinkles and all that. I will read it as long as it is legible. Sometimes I'll look at a picture and there'll be nothing on the résumé, but something in the cover letter will strike my fancy and I will take a chance. They have to start somewhere."

—Carole R. Ingber, commercial agent

The main way that actors reach agents and casting directors is by sending in a photo and résumé—either electronically or through the mail. While electronic submissions have become increasingly popular, many agents and casting directors find that a "hard copy" is easier to handle. They can easily browse through pictures and résumés sent by mail, study the credits, and get some idea of who the actor is as a person.

If you choose to send your photo and résumé, use a 9 x 12–inch manila (or colored) envelope. Always write "Photographs. Please Do Not Bend" on the outside of the envelope. Include a cover letter—a brief note introducing yourself. Keep it short and simple. Mention the name of the person who may have suggested that you contact the agent or casting director, and request an appointment. This is the time to use every connection you have: teachers, relatives, fellow college alumni, mutual friends, even neighbors. Make sure your referral is legitimate: You're trying to establish credibility. Consider this the equivalent of a "cold call" on a prospective client.

You won't establish credibility by addressing the person you hope to meet impersonally, as "Dear Sir" or "Dear Madam."It's better to use the person's last name in your salutation. Nor will you score credibility points by using a paste-on name label for your return address, or lined paper torn from a spiral-bound notebook.

Your stationery should be attractive, your words easy to read. Try to type (computer-process) your letter neatly. If there's no computer around, handwritten notes will do, provided you write legibly. And don't bruise the language with misspellings, improper grammar, incorrect usage, and malapropisms! One actor's letter contained the line "This is a funny anti-dote I heard the other day." If he didn't know he was telling an *anecdote*, how much in the way of "smarts" would he bring to a role? Why should an agent risk reputation and credibility by submitting the actor's name? The only "antidote" the letter contained was an antidote to work.

Make certain you spell the recipient's name correctly. Mari Lyn, for example, and not Mary Lynne, Mariann, Mary Lou, or Merry Lynn; Mary Jo, not Mary Joe. Know the sex of the person: Sam, Carmen, Leslie, Jo, Terry, and Pat could be men or women, but, as it happens, they are Ms. Downey, Mr. LaVia, Mr. Moonves, Ms. Bonney, Ms. Berland, and Ms. McCorkle. It's part of your business to find out such things. For more on preparing materials, see Chapter Three, "The Tools of the Trade."

Your Contact List

As we said earlier, you may send your photo and résumé to the casting directors and agents listed in the *Ross Reports* and *Henderson's Casting Directors Guide,* and in special issues of the trades. We are not in favor of mass mailings. Don't feel you have to reach out to everyone at once; this is not a race. Besides, what would you do if everyone—or even ten people—answered and invited you to an interview on the same day? Take time to compose your letter with care. Impart something of your personality, keeping in mind what you may have heard or read about the preferences of each office. If you know an agency wants only musical talent, and you're not ready to sing in public, put that office at the bottom of your list with a note to yourself to contact them when you've learned a couple of songs.

It's possible that you might want to see more than one person at the same office. In that case, wait a week or so between submissions and vary your cover letter. Consider sending the second person a photo postcard with your contact information and a cheery note: that would be less expensive and more visible than a second copy of your 8 x 10, and the first contact might happen to see your card and remember receiving your material.

Next, go through your list of leads to find casting directors who regularly cast series, soaps, and any other shows that use dramatic talent. Memorize their names; you can always get the latest information from the applicable unions. Select the casting directors who audition actors for shows that use your type, and send them your photo and résumé with a charming cover letter.

Advertising-agency casting departments and production houses with on-staff (or freelance) casting directors should also receive your packet. If you have a DVD, mention it in your cover letter. Do not send unsolicited material.

After about two weeks send a postcard as a reminder, and ask again for an appointment. Be pleasant and positive; remind them that you submitted your material a short time ago and ask when it will be possible to meet.

We advise against telephone follow-ups. Agents are trying to get work for clients they represent; casting directors are trying to accommodate agents and see people for specific roles. They have no time to talk to people they don't know. Your call is an interruption. They will call you if they are interested.

If you feel that you *must* call, you'll be lucky if someone answers the phone. Know what you want to say. Don't stammer or apologize. This is when your memorized one-minute "pitch," or a similar prepared statement of purpose related to the job at hand, would be appropriate. You'll get one of three answers: "Your picture is on file, so don't call us, we'll call you." "Call back in about two months." "We see people on Thursday at four o'clock." Note the response you get in your records, and date it.

The late Fifi Oscard, owner of the Fifi Oscard Agency, Inc., once "made the best of it" when she had to deal with a persistent caller—and everyone came out ahead.

> A salesman for the Kimberley Clark Corporation who wanted to be an actor visited me every day with a long-stemmed rose and a martini. He was so intent on launching a career. Finally I started sending him out. Not only did he book some terrific accounts, he became one of the highest-paid voice-over performers in the industry!

Promotion with Pizzazz

It's part of your job to publicize yourself in a way that reminds people of who you are and what you do. It would be even better to go beyond that and demonstrate a bit of imagination and a sense of humor. Actor Gerald Kline tells this story:

> Years ago I was working on *The Muppets Take Manhattan*. I knew a couple of people who were stand-ins, and they said, "Do you want to

meet Miss Piggy?" I said, "Sure." I was playing a construction worker, so I had on a plaid shirt, hard hat, all that stuff. We went to the tailgate of the prop truck. I had my camera with me, and we took pictures of each other, me and Miss Piggy looking at each other. I had a postcard made of that shot that said, "Kissy, kissy, Gerald Kline." That card got me lots of work..

Keeping Records

As you can see from the paperwork involved in beginning your job search, it is important for you to keep a file of all the people you try to see. Actors use index cards, a personal computer program, an accountant's notebook—what's important is that you know to whom you sent your photo, when, whether you received a response, and what it was.

You'll probably be sending different packets of your material to producers of regional theaters, industrial shows, to people you know—the possibilities are endless. And at times the paperwork will seem to be, too.

To lighten the load, you might want to consider ActorTrack, a comprehensive record-keeping program created by two working actors, Kristina Hughes and Brian Vermeire, that allows the actor to keep daily records of everything, from appointments and submissions to income and expenses, reports on meetings, mailings, what you sent to whom, callback reminders, and more. You can visit their Web site' at www. holdonlog.com.

Leslie Becker provides similar tools and covers the same territory in her book *The Organized Actor*. However, the focus is more on the beginning actor, offering career direction and analysis. She offers a newsletter on her Web site www.organizedactor.com.

We cannot overstate the benefits of keeping records—not only when you're trying hard to contact people who can employ you, but throughout your career. In addition to keeping track of your income and expenses, you'll also want to keep tabs on the work you're doing, as well as the work you want to be doing. Some very successful commercial performers tell us they go over their records every thirteen weeks (which is a commercial *cycle*, or period of use) and when they see that someone they've worked for in the past hasn't even called them in to read, they know they have to "get in touch" all over again. Even the busiest performers are always looking for work.

As you invest in photos, résumés, and all the tools of the trade, you will need records of these expenses. You'll need records at income-tax time, but also if you apply for unemployment insurance compensation. Freelance performers may work for dozens of employers a year. It's in the performer's interest to know exactly what those dates of employment were. Unemployment insurance requirements differ from state to state and have been known to change frequently, depending upon the general employment picture. Don't rely on your employers to keep those accounts accurately or to get the paperwork done on time. The office staff may be temporary, and (like you) as soon as the project is completed, pack up their supplies and go on to the next assignment. They can make mistakes, which can cost you money, as well as the time it takes to get the mess straightened out.

Rates of unemployment compensation differ from one state to another. Because the cost of living in New York is so high, unemployment compensation is higher there than it is in California. New York is among the states that permit phone-in registration, instead of requiring you to appear in person at the unemployment office to file for benefits. That is not true of California.

OPPORTUNITIES FOR ACTORS

While conducting your general mailing effort, you should continue to read the trades for specific casting news. Here are some of the types of opportunities you will come across.

Open Calls

For scenes requiring crowds of people who look as if they belong together, for example at a wedding, in a courtroom, or at a graduation or awards ceremony, casting directors, producers, and/or directors will hold an "open call," usually in a large theater or auditorium. The casting director chats with the actors in groups of three or four. Polaroid shots are taken and stapled to the performer's photo and résumé. Decisions may be made on the spot, or whenever the proper-looking group is finally assembled.

Open calls are also held when casting directors or producers are looking to cast a very special role and have been unable to find anyone that the writer, the producer, and the directors can agree upon. An open call means just that: Is there anybody out there who can do this job?

In such cases, character descriptions are almost always provided. Read the description carefully and try to look like what the production people say they want. Bring your photo and résumé. Have a monologue prepared in case the people behind the desks show interest and want to see your audition skills. This is a chance to sell yourself; bring everything you think will help you make the sale. You may not need it, or even get to use it, but you must be prepared.

One reason casting directors are not enthusiastic about open calls, aside from the possibility of attracting eccentrics, is that amateurs flock to such events out of curiosity. An open call was held for *General Hospital* some time ago. The ad appeared in *Back Stage*. Criteria were clear: a beautiful, upscale, Grace Kelly type, twenty-five to thirty, not over five feet eight inches. The actress should have some experience and be able to relocated to California if selected. Interview times were 10:00 A.M. to 1:00P.M. and 2:00 P.M. to 6:00 P.M. at ABC headquarters in New York City. It was a frosty February day, but at 6:00 A.M. young women started lining up outside the building. Wearing short skirts, high heels, and borrowed furs, they shivered in anticipation of the chance for soap stardom. ABC pages, carrying cardboard signs stating the qualifications for the part paraded up and down in front of the building. No one left the line. Some of the hopefuls had driven up from Philadelphia, New Jersey, even as far away as Washington, D.C.

One thousand women passed through the revolving doors. Of these, twelve were asked to go to another room and read the script. None were chosen. Few were prepared or experienced enough to handle the creation of a character on a network soap opera.

Despite the long lines, the people who should have stayed home, the impersonal treatment, there are happy endings to open calls. One young woman who stood in line with her friends at the open call for singers for the San Francisco production of *Phantom of the Opera* had never sung professionally, although she had won vocal scholarships in her hometown. Her fine voice attracted the attention of the casting director, who invited her to return for a callback. Director Harold Prince was impressed by her range and ability; he approved her for the chorus, and later chose her to understudy the smaller women's parts.

Tony- and Emmy Award–winning actress Debra Monk (*Curtains*) once went to an open call for director Tommy Tune.

There were eight hundred people there, and I got down to the final eight. When I was through, Tommy came over to me, put his arm around me, and said I was wonderful. I knew I wasn't selected, but I remember how good I felt that he took the time to make me feel that I had talent.

Misty Foster was a nonunion actress in her senior year at Marymount College in New York when she saw a notice for an open call.

I got up at four that morning because Ripley Grier Studios opens at around five fifteen. I took a cab. I was the first person there. Period. The building is unlocked so you can sit in the lobby. I started a non-Equity list, and around seven A.M. they let us go upstairs. They see Equity people first, then Equity membership candidates, and then if they have time, they see non-Equity. They usually honor the non-Equity list that we create.

I went on the first day of the call because it's usually easier to get seen then. I was seen around lunchtime, which was really lucky. I usually don't get seen until after four. I performed a song in the style of the show for the casting director. I had been taking voice lessons so I felt really prepared, and I had done the "given circumstances" homework for my song, too. I picked a song that showed off my acting just as much as my range, and I just had fun. That's the most important thing. Treat it like a performance. So . . . I did!

Amanda Jones had made a list of dream jobs. Working for the Mint Theater in New York City was at the top.

The day I received my Equity card they were having an open call at [the Mint]. It didn't seem too promising. The call had already started and none of the character descriptions sounded quite right for me. Nevertheless, I was dressed appropriately and I knew that they were using sides instead of monologues, which is sometimes a sign that theaters are actively seeking people to fill roles from an open call instead of fulfilling an Equity requirement.

Surprisingly, the call was not full. I picked up the sides and immediately knew which character I wanted to play. I had a dynamic and enjoyable audition for the director; got called back a few days later; and twenty minutes after I left the callback, I got a phone call offering me the part! The casting director—who was not at the open call—didn't want to call me back because she didn't know my work, but [the director] fought for me because I was the only actor they saw who understood the part.

Over time, attending any and every open call may prove discouraging; but a focused approach—reading and seeing as much as you can, and attending calls held by theaters, directors, or casting directors whose work you know and admire—will save you time and energy and will make you familiar to the people you really want to know.

Talent Searches

More structured and specific in nature than the open call is the talent search. ABC Daytime Programs launched a search to discover the best actors from culturally diverse backgrounds and to find performers with disabilities. Opportunities for leading roles on daytime dramas were presented to actors in regional markets, who would not ordinarily be aware of them. Actors were submitted by agents, and appointments were set up. Actors without representation were able to submit themselves. Each actor was asked to perform a two-minute monologue. Finalists were assigned a specific soap scene, which was recorded.

Pictures and résumés are reviewed in advance of the appointment for a talent search. Judy Blye-Wilson, award-winning casting director of *All My Children*, says she "cannot emphasize strongly enough how important the photo and the résumé are. They must be professional and well packaged. Visuals or DVDs must be well edited and demonstrate your best work."

Equity Principal Auditions (EPAs)

In its continuing efforts to provide access to employment, the Actors' Equity Association requires producers to set aside time for open casting for Equity members and for Equity membership candidates. Admittedly, the producers may already know whom they want, but they can always change their mind if they see somebody terrific. Many fine actors have been hired from EPAs. It is said that Nathan Lane is famous for building his career with equity principal auditions (EPAs). He was voracious, and went to every single one of them, whether he was right for it or not.

For the EPA the actor comes prepared with an audition selection, a monologue of two minutes or less. There is no limit to the number of people who may sign up, but only the first 115 are guaranteed to be seen on a day. There is no carryover of names. If you don't make it the first day, you must come in early the next day and sign up again. Actress Kim Shivey recalls her first experience with an EPA.

My first EPA was for Belle in *Beauty and the Beast*. I had great dreams of being Belle. I can sing it. It is in my range. I thought, "This is it," which shows how green I was. I wake up at four in the morning, hair in rollers. I take the train in from Brooklyn. I am totally nervous. Little outfit. It is cold. I waited on the sidewalk two hours with a lot of other actors who were smoking, talking. People brought chairs to sit on. They let you in at nine A.M., and you sign up for your time. [Once they had their time, some] people left for work. I got an early time. For my segment they said, "Okay, everyone line up because we are going to do typing." I was hysterical. A typing test? Is there typing in Beauty and the Beast? I had never seen the show. They lined us up and said okay, you stay, you go, et cetera. Are you over five-foot-six? You have to go. No one over five-foot-six because Gaston is short. You have to fit the costume.

Other Ways to Open Doors

As the following two actresses learned from experience, one way to find new opportunities is to become part of an artistic community.

One of the smartest things I did was to intern at an up and coming theater company called The New Group. I volunteered for free and quickly proved myself to be reliable. After I'd spent awhile in the office, they asked me to join their playwright development lab, enabling me to meet a ton of writers. One of those writers ended up recommending me for one of her shows, which was being produced regionally, and that is how I got my Equity card! In addition to interning, I did everything in my power to work in the theater as much as possible. Even if that means working for free, doing showcases, do it! Some of the worst shows I've been in provided amazing contacts that bore fruit in years to come. Of course, if you go to an open call or audition and you sense that the people are talentless, or abusive or unprofessional, leave. But if you feel you can learn something from the experience, do it. Some people change fields within the profession. One of my actor friends is now an award-winning playwright, one works for Williamstown; one directs all over the country. Which brings me to another point: Be gracious, hardworking, and kind to those you are working with. You never know where they will end up, and this is a very small world.

—Jenny Mercein, actress

Living Voices is a Seattle-based theater arts organization (www. livingvoices.org). Programs are about real people and events, thus showing today's young audiences history's relevance to our lives. These interactive scripts have been called "historic moments brought to life."

> **The amazing thing about my Living Voices job is that it came to me because I was connected to my artistic community. Jen Grigg, who I had met at the Actors Theater of Louisville, had worked for Living Voices. After I had been in New York for about a year or two, she e-mailed me to say that Living Voices was looking for actresses in the New York area, and if I was interested I should contact them. I did immediately. The interview was really just a chat about the company, the script, my background, questions I had. It was apparent they'd spoken to Jen about me. It seemed they took recommendations from their actors and colleagues seriously. I've been with them for a year and I love it.**
>
> **Which brings me to networking. In the past year I've realized what that means. It means striving to be the kind of person you would want to work with, and like-minded people will be attracted to you, and you will find your niche.**
>
> —Jamie Askew, actress

Additional Opportunities for Actors

You can find many other outlets for your acting talent, often in venues that might not come immediately to mind. Consider the following.

Commercial Print

Rather than use fashion models, the medium of commercial print uses "real people"—that is, actors who have a less slick, more believable look—in magazine and newspaper ads for products such as cereals, vitamins, cold remedies, insurance, and so on. It also uses actors to portray professionals such as doctors, teachers, and nurses. There's a growing need for ordinary faces due to the rapidly increasing number of advertising venues—the World Wide Web, cable TV, cell phone broadcasts.

What it comes down to, says Randy Ladner, an actor and a commercial print model, is that "photographers love actors because they take direction easily, so the shoot doesn't take a lot of time."

For this work you need a great "real person" headshot that looks like you, and a "comp card," which is like a gallery of your faces and characters. If you have friends with digital cameras, have them take pictures of you in various characters. Make copies.

There is no union covering this area, as yet, although agents do submit clients to photographers. Therefore, fees are negotiable. But if the ad moves to the Internet, there can be another payment. A print job can sometimes turn into a commercial; your image may be used on a product box. Any of those extra uses can mean extra payment, wherein terms of usage must be stated.

Finding work in this area, according to Randy Ladner, is as straightforward as "calling agents, asking if they have a print department, and telling them that you do commercial work and would like to work with them."

Student Films

Each issue of *Back Stage* carries notices of student films and describes the roles to be cast. This work can be useful to you in learning how to relax and be comfortable acting for the camera. It's also a way to get "film" on yourself, which is something so many casting directors now request.

Combined Auditions

From February through March, more than 200 regional theater companies convene to hold performer auditions for their upcoming season. Equity performers are eligible.

- **United Professional Theatre Auditions.** For information on registration, fees, and the audition format, write to: Audition Coordinator, United Professional Theatre Auditions, 51 South Cooper Street, Memphis, TN 38104. Phone: (901) 725-0776. Fax: (901) 272-7530. E-mail: upta@upta.org. The Web site (www.upta.org) may tell you what you need to know before you apply.

- **Southeastern Theatre Conference.** This is the largest combined audition in the country. For information, write to: SETC, P.O. Box 9868, Greensboro, NC 27429-0868. Phone: (336) 272-3645. E-mail: april@setc.org. Web site: www.setc.org.

- **New England Theatre Conference.** You can request an application by mail. NETC Auditions, New England Theatre Conference, 215 Knob Hill Drive, Hamden, CT 06518. Phone. (617) 851-8585. E-mail: mail@netconline.org. Web site: www.netconline.org.

- **StrawHat Auditions.** You can reach them at StrawHat Auditions, 1771 Post Road East #315, Westport, CT 06880. E-mail: info@strawhatauditions.com. Web site: www.strawhat-auditions.com.

URTA is the acronym for the **University/Resident Theatre Association**, which also holds national auditions and interviews in the spring. Actors, directors, playwrights, and stage managers are eligible, as are set, lighting, costume, and sound designers. For information, contact: University/Resident Theatre Association. Phone: (212) 221-1130. Fax: (212) 869-2752. E-mail: URTA@aol.com. Web site: www.URTA.com.

Theatre Communications Group (TCG) is the national organization of not-for-profit theaters in the United States, offering opportunities in all aspects of performance and production. It would be impossible to enumerate them here, but TCG's *Theatre Directory*, published annually, lists every one of those theaters and describes their special interests. It gives all contact numbers, the names of the theaters' artistic and managing directors, and much more. It may inspire you to think about your career in a fresh new way. TCG also publishes the excellent *American Theatre Magazine*, each issue of which is loaded with information about who's who and what's going on in theaters, colleges, and universities across the nation, as well as what is being done in theaters overseas. From time to time the magazine publishes complete scripts of new plays that have attracted attention, and would doubtless be ideal for scene study. You can visit the TCG Web site at www.tcg.org.

Playing Sick

Did you know two-thirds of the country's medical schools now use actors to help young doctors perfect their bedside manner? In New York, the Morchand Center for Clinical Competence at Mount Sinai Medical Center recruits and trains the actors, many of whom have performed onstage and in TV commercials, and particularly on soaps.

The actors are given a detailed personal and medical history of the patients they will be portraying. They're also given checklists or guidelines to keep score on the doctors. The medical students and residents know that the exam is being videotaped by hidden cameras and that they will be graded. According to the experts, good personal skills—treating patients with respect and empathy—not only means better medical care, but higher patient satisfaction.

The actors-as-patients program has become so well known that actors now have to audition for it. . Schools in smaller towns, far from Hollywood or New York, have their talent pool, too. They hire people from amateur theater groups, as well as students from local college and university theater programs.

Keeping a Journal

Set aside a part of each day to record your thoughts, feelings, ideas, discoveries, observations, and adventures in your working actor's journal. It will keep you grounded and enable you to assess what's going on in your professional life. Find a quiet place in your home, visit the nearest coffee shop, or retreat to the stillness of the local library. Do this in the morning or at the end of your day. Victoria Moran, author of *Younger by the Day,* considers a journal "a notebook for plotting your strategies, writing your affirmations, recording your insights, and putting you in touch with inner wisdom and intuitive glimmerings you might not have accessed otherwise."

Let's suppose that your tenacity gets you a meeting with a respected agent, a reading with a casting director for a series, a callback for a commercial, or work as an extra on a soap set. These situations are rich with incidents that should be chronicled. Was the agent distant or interested in "repping" you? Did the casting director ask about your availability or tell you to send in the next person on your way out? How many actors were at the callback? What did you learn from these experiences? Record what you observed on the soap set: How the director called the shots, related to the crew, handled the stars. Every audition is its own story; getting cast is the icing on the cake.

The Life Coach

In a business where so much seems left to chance and so few are prepared for success when it happens, life coaches say they help clients define and pursue career and personal goals. According to Phil Towle, who is both a psychotherapist and a life coach, "The difference between coaching and therapy is that psychotherapy is about helping people heal their wounds and coaching is about helping people achieve the highest level of fulfillment, or happiness, or success, whether they're wounded or not."

Life coach Leslie Becker (www.organizedactor.com) explains how the process works.

I think people are looking for guidance, for structure, to create a life full of joy and love and giving and contribution. We coaches are there to say that you can create the life you want and here is how you do it.

We start by getting clear on what you want and come up with five or six very specific goals that you are passionately committed to working toward in the next three to six months. For the person whose goal is to win a Tony Award, we back up from that and see what it will take to achieve that goal.

You want to walk into every audition behaving as if you are already that series regular or that Tony Award winner. You don't become that if you don't try, even early on, to exhibit the skills and have that mindset. Somebody who comes to an audition with the thought in their head that they are a future Tony Award winner projects a different presence than someone who goes, "Oh, will you please see me?"

Festival, Anyone?

Inexpensive digital cameras and desktop editing software are making it easy for aspiring Eastwoods or Clooneys to realize their dream. SAG and AFTRA have devised new low-budget production contracts to encourage independent filmmakers, and to encourage actors to try their talent behind the camera.

Once you've made a movie, what then? Well, you can enter it in a film festival. Not Sundance, necessarily, but there are thousands of others.

Here's one performer's story. Sally Nacker, the lead in the independent film *Sara Goes to Lunch*, flew from New York to attend the California Independent Film Festival in Livermore because the director and producer were unavailable. The director had given her a "cheat sheet" of technical information about the film in case there were questions after the screenings.

The owner/founder of the festival welcomed all of us. He said, "Be sure to introduce yourself to the other filmmakers and invite them to your screenings here." His advice was one of those whispers that resonate and stay with you.

Taking this advice, I introduced myself to people all during the run of the festival, giving them the postcard I'd put together for *Sara Goes to Lunch* and inviting them to my screenings. Everyone I invited attended!

I made sure to see the other filmmakers' films. Afterward, I collected the postcards from their films to take home with me. The filmmaker's contact is on the postcard, along with information about the film. At home, I placed the cards in a binder that became a scrapbook for *Sara*. I wrote "thank you" and "pleasure meeting you" notes via mail or e-mail to each filmmaker.

It was at this festival that I met the award-winning director of photography and the director of my new film! I'd invited them to the screening of *Sara*. On closing night I handed a gentleman my camera and asked if he'd take a picture of the three of us. I kept in touch with them. Then, in March, when the director was casting his new film, he contacted me. My New York agent put my audition on tape, and I booked the lead and shot the film in San Francisco!

Very few actors attend these festivals. The filmmakers attend, and so do directors and producers. It's really important to attend them as actors. The process is invaluable. The directors see how "you" are, your presence, off-screen as well as on. It is so vital!

A company called Withoutabox (www.withoutabox.com) maintains a database of almost 3,000 festivals in more than 200 countries. Founders David Straus and Joe Neulight have recently acquired a rights database company that links filmmakers and distributors. There's a lot of activity in independent films these days.

Expecting overnight box-office success or wide distribution is hardly realistic, but as Sally Nacker's story shows us, the opportunities are there. Networking—and all the other strategies discussed in this chapter—can open those doors.

CHAPTER 7

Cyberbiz

"A lot of actors have chosen to say I am not going to allow myself to wait until someone gives me permission to work. I will write or direct. I will tape something and put it up on YouTube or IFILM. I will create my own work. That is the miracle of the Internet and I see the future of that becoming a channel for actors to express themselves."
—Robert Petkoff, working actor

We have shown in previous chapters how accessible everything is these days online. You can find an apartment, set up your home office, phone friends and colleagues from your computer, decide how you want your headshot to look, organize your career with software like Performer Track, send casting offices and agents your DVD reels, shop for bargains, find a monologue, check out the work opportunities in regional theaters, buy a car on eBay, and ultimately make a connection with the movers and shakers, star in your own movie, and create your own online presence. And as we write this book, more cyber entrepreneurs are exploring and researching ways to create a better mousetrap and lure millions all over the world to come for a visit and stay and see some payback for their work.

The Internet has a huge impact on the ways actors conduct their business. E-mail has become the major way to communicate with agents, managers, producers, directors, artistic directors, union offices, and newfound industry-connected contacts you have cultivated at film festivals and other networking events. The Internet has created new ways for actors to market themselves, and made it much easier to connect with the powers that cast projects. In addition, actors have created survival businesses as Web site designers, computer graphics experts, technological consultants at places like Apple's Genius Bar, or starting actor-friendly sites helping talent to find jobs.

ONLINE MARKETING

Actors are finding the Web to be an invaluable tool, whether they are utilizing online marketing services, creating their own Web sites to market themselves, or putting their work out there on MySpace and YouTube.

Actor-Friendly Web Sites

Actress and entrepreneur Deborah Corbin used her computer skills to create a marketing business for actors. She empathized with the actors who were frustrated by clerical responsibilities and she wanted to relieve their stress so they could continue focusing on their craft. So ActorMail.com was born and today it posts casting notices in addition to designing the cover letters, letterheads, résumés, and flyers, and providing mailing labels, photo reproductions, custom lists, envelopes and postage, all for a nominal monthly charge.

Former actor and casting assistant Marc Levine and his computer-and-film-production-savvy partners Marc Miller and Rob Gillin realized the need to develop a Web site that would showcase actors, dancers, choreographers, stand-up comics, and filmmakers. They spent a year developing and researching what would be the key components that would satisfy their objectives and launched www.sceneinteractive.com. For a $50 setup fee and the monthly charge of $9.95 for hosting and maintenance, actors can establish a presence on the site, which provides a place where industry professionals can browse for talent. "Instead of having to scour the classifieds or pick up a phone, we provide talent a tangible way to market themselves online," Marc explains. "One time a director from Paramount called in an actor for a film. He didn't have to sign up to reach the talent or pay us a fee. Disney contacted a young actress/dancer with Broadway credits after reviewing her color photos, résumé, and taped monologue. Her talent agent has a link to us."

Actors can submit hard copies of their DVDs and the service will put it on their talent pages. A young actress/dancer with recent Broadway credits has an acting profile, color pictures, and an acting video on the site. Actor Jason Grossman has a résumé, a voice-over samples, and two contrasting monologues. As Marc says, "Agents may not be able to attend an actor's showcase, but with two mouse clicks they can see what a performer looks and sounds like."

Creating Your Own Web Site

Actor Patrick Boll, whose home page appears on page 168, realized that in this age of information a Web site would provide instant access to his work. He was also inspired by a friend's Web site that was professional, well put together, and informative.

"I went to Yahoo and found the section on building your own Web site. They have their own site-building software that I downloaded for free and I began to build my site page by page. Many other servers out there will also provide you the means to create your own Web site.

"I went to other actors' Web sites for inspiration. I got some great ideas for the way I wanted my site to look and what kind of information I wanted to share. My Web site is an extension of myself and my résumé. In a professional way, it gives viewers a more in-depth look at who I am as an actor and a person and the kind of work I have done over the course of my career."

Some basic tips for designing your own Web site are:

- Secure a domain name that serves as your site's address.
- Your home page should clearly lay out the site's features.Make it easy to navigate. Define what information is available and let one mouse click get you there.
- Content should be well written, organized, and concise. Avoid bells and whistles.
- A Picture Gallery should feature two of your best color headshots, showing two different looks. It can also contain production stills from recent work. Always title your shots and date them. Keep the photos updated. Make sure that a high-resolution (300 dpi) version of your headshot can be printed or downloaded.
- As you collect DVD copies of your work or voice-over demos, include them on your site The more material you have, the more storage space you'll need. You can purchase additional space as your needs grow.
- Be sure your résumé is in a compatible format that can easily be printed from the site.

- Have contact information available—a link to your e-mail address or phone numbers for your agent or manager.
- Keep it professional. Your site is a reflection of you. The same rules you set for your photo and résumé apply to your Web site.
- Make sure you can easily add details of your most recent work, including review excerpts and featured articles, and upcoming appearances.

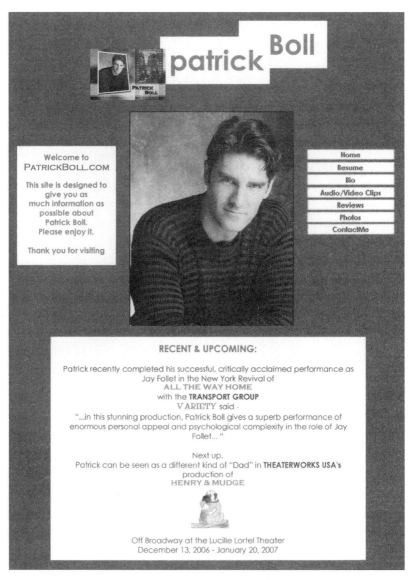

A well-conceived home page

Set up much higher-quality versions of DVD reels to have at the ready to facilitate casting directors who might like a short reel for electronic submissions. And remember, put your Web site address on your business card, postcard, letterhead, and résumé.

Casting Director Stephanie Klapper admits she looks at actors' Web sites. She told Back Stage about how having a professional site paid off for an actor:

"The director was in one stage, the producer in another, and I was somewhere else. I found the actor on his Web site, told the others to look at it. They did and we all agreed he was the best choice."

The iCard

Actor Joey Sorge *(Drowsy Chaperone)* wanted a fast way to promote his career. When he was working in Los Angeles he discovered that the Apple Store at the Grove held a free class called "The Mac in Your Acting Career," and that for an annual fee, Apple allows you to store pictures, important documents, and music on its server. He also learned how to create postcards with pictures from his own library and send them to agents and casting directors. To create an iCard, a postcard that he could send electronically, for his appearance on Night Stalker, Joey went through the following steps.

1. I went to the Web site of the network on which my episode of *Night Stalker* was airing and, using PhotoShop, copied and pasted the title of the show onto a copy of my headshot.

2. I saved that picture on the Mac server. This allowed me access to it when I went to www.apple.com/dotmac and sign in.

3. I went to the iCard section and clicked on "Create my own iCard." There I found all the pictures I had saved on the server as options to

Help solve my mysterious death as "Jeremy Steckler" in "The Night Stalker" Thursday, October 6th, 9/8c on ABC!

Thanks,

Joey

The iCard Joey Sorge

use for the card. I chose my picture, followed the instructions, typed a message, picked a font, and sent it to myself as a test e-mail.

4. I double-checked the e-mail once I received it. Then I went through my address book and sent it to people in the biz. It is that simple!

MySpace/YouTube

The Internet has given performing artists more power than ever. They can create their own content and present it to millions of people for minimal costs. They can also market themselves through such social networking sites as MySpace and YouTube.

MySpace, owned by News Corp., was originally launched in 2003 as a marketing tool for unsigned bands. The site now provides more than ninety million registered users with a forum in which to share photos, videos, and information and is the world's fourth most popular English-language Web site and the fifth-most popular Web site in the world. MySpace does have drawbacks, which include scamlike e-mails from illegitimate casting directors and fake modeling agencies and aggressive solicitations from headshot photographers and other service providers. Even so, many actors consider MySpace to be a great creative outlet.

As the world's thirteenth most popular Web site, YouTube is taking the Web by storm, attracting six million individual users daily watching more than 100 million videos. Conceived in 2005 by former PayPal employees, the site allows anyone to post a video, and 60,000 new videos are added each day. Some actors are using MySpace and YouTube to post their amateur films, reels, and résumés, and to audition for roles cast across the country. Actor and director Tom Kiesche uses MySpace to host his reels. "I can gain a little exposure and I have yet to see a downside," he explains. "I can trace one feature film audition to my presence on the site."

Casting directors, producers and even network executives are waking up to the talent on these sites. One network's executives regularly troll video-sharing sites for new talent. It is only a matter of time before a major piece of casting or the discovery of an exciting new talent will result.

CASTING ONLINE

The Internet is also proving to be a boon for casting directors, many of whom are finding the talent they are looking for on sites like Actors Access and Now Casting.

Breakdown Services, Ltd.

Founded by Gary A. Marsh in 1971, Breakdown Services, Ltd., is a communications network and casting system that provides a means to reach talent agents, managers, and actors when casting a project. Offices are located in Los Angeles, New York, and Vancouver and affiliate relationships are maintained with sister companies in Toronto, London, and Sydney.

A Breakdown is a description of all the speaking and nonspeaking roles, with an indication of the size of each role. The Breakdown includes a short synopsis of the plot and production information—start dates, producers, writers and directors. Staff writers read scripts provided by the casting directors and create approximately thirty television and feature film breakdowns a day, covering episodics, pilots, feature films, movies for television, miniseries, commercials, print projects, theater, student films, industrials, reality TV, and other types of projects that require acting talent. Breakdowns are posted at www.Breakdownexpress.com. Talent representatives view them and submit their clients' pictures, résumés, and videos via the Web site to casting directors.

Here is an example from the Breakdown released by Kathleen Chopin, the New York–based casting director for the miniseries *John Adams*, starring Paul Giamatti and executive produced by Tom Hanks and others for HBO. The start date was February 2007 and the locations listed were Virginia and Budapest.

> Edmond-Charles Genet] 25. Very bright, very young–and very, very spoiled, with the arrogant look and manner of an upstart. His father was a royal official, his mother a lady-in-waiting; and he grew up in Versailles, learning the gentlemanly arts of fencing and horsemanship. SEEKING NATIVE FRENCH SPEAKERS.

Casting directors will also designate whether to submit the submissions electronically or to send a hard copy or both. In this case, Ms. Chopin only wanted to see hard copies. If Breakdowns are requested electronically, thousands of postage stamp-size headshots with clickable résumés and e-notes might be sent via the Internet to the casting director. It is important that talent agents and managers take this into consideration and select the handful of clients who are truly appropriate for each role.

A soap opera might release this kind of Breakdown for an under 5 role (a part that has only one to five lines of dialogue).

> [Alistair's Assistant] Caucasian brunette female, late 20s to early 30s. She works for Alistair and pretends to be Beth in order to trick the office. In bold, Actress must be 5'6", 110 lbs., size 0/2 and wear a size 8 shoe. Please include height on submissions. Works in two weeks. SUBMIT ELECTRONICALLY ONLY. NO PHONE CALLS!!

The physical requirements in this Breakdown above are so specific that the electronic volume of submissions would be manageable.

Probably one of the most entertaining Breakdowns ever released appeared on April Fool's Day a few years ago for *CSI: Middle Earth*, the pilot. The executive producer was Barliman Butterbur, the casting director was Gollum Smeagol, and the interviews were scheduled for that day.

> Please note, due to severe time constraints placed by the producers on casting there will be only 5 minutes notice given for agents to get clients to the appointments. Be on your toes and wizard your clients to us. Location: Valencia and New Zealand. Submit electronically only ASAP to Gollum Smeagol, Hobbitswehatethem Casting.

Breakdowns for New Media

There have been new casting opportunities on Breakdowns for programs that will only be seen on the Internet.

One such Breakdown issued was for *Quarterlife*, a pilot for an hour episodic drama seeking six series regulars in their mid-twenties. The synopsis described "a magazine editor who sends her friends into fits when they discover she keeps a rather insightful blog about them as a Web site called 'quarterlife.'"

A major network released a Breakdown for two leading characters who would star in Webisodes for *Webcast purposes only*. The call was for nonunion talent who had excellent improvisational skills and was described as an incredible opportunity to be a part of a *brand new venture*. The characters would be creating a compelling video blog (vlog) for upcoming DVD releases of the network's series.

Actors Access

Breakdown Services also operates Actors Access, www.actorsaccess. com, a site on which casting directors can send information directly to actors. Registration is free, and actors can place two pictures and their résumé online at no charge. They can upload additional photos for a one-time charge of $10 each. Actors also create a personal profile about their acting experience, background, training, skills, sports, physical type, and union affiliations, ethnicity, and age range. Actors Access automatically notifies them via e-mail when a Breakdown is posted for a role for which their skills and attributes are suited. Or, after reviewing the Breakdown of available roles, actors can submit themselves via the Internet or mail pictures and résumés to the submission address.

When casting directors select your picture they can view your résumé and any other pictures you have in Actors Access. If there is interest in having you audition, they can create a schedule and automatically notify you about the appointment time and address via e-mail or text messaging on your cell phone. You can either accept and confirm the appointment time or send a note requesting a different time that is more convenient.

Extras Access

This site, www.extrasaccess.com, allows actors who do background work the opportunity to respond directly to casting notices for jobs. These actors create an online profile that has been designed specifically to meet the needs of those who do extra work, and post multiple three-quarter body shots and as well as photos showing various looks—in uniforms (nurse, policeman, military) or with a vintage car or a unique pet. Extras receive an e-mail notification whenever a project is posted that matches their profile.

Showfax

Professional actors use Showfax, www.showfax.com, also operated by Breakdown Services, to get their sides (audition scenes). Upon getting the date and time for the audition, actors can visit Showfax and download the script pages which contain directions where to begin to read and end. They are assured that the sides are current and that they will get instant updates if they are revised.

A year's membership is $68. As members of Showfax, actors can submit a picture and résumé electronically for specific roles listed on Actors Access at no charge and e-mail any picture or résumé they have in the system to anyone, anywhere, anytime. There is also no fee for unlimited electronic submissions to casting directors.

Performance Video

Another offering from Breakdown Services, Performance Video (www.performancevideo.com) allows you to place as many one-minute reels as you wish online. Your talent reps are able to submit the reels when responding to Breakdowns and you can submit them yourself when using Actors Access.

Now Casting

Now Casting, Inc., www.nowcasting.com, based in Los Angeles and created and run by actors, lists casting notices for feature films, episodics and sitcoms, commercials, pilots, indie projects, theater, low budget features, and student films. While the bulk of the notices are for projects in Los Angeles, Now Casting is expanding its reach to New York City. Now Casting is also the portal to the *Players Directory* online (see Chapter Three, "The Tools of the Trade").

Free registration includes access to audition sides, and posting of a complete profile with six headshots and résumé. Your agent and/or manager can use the site to submit you to casting offices and you can e-mail your profile to anyone.

A professional package costs $10 a month and also includes access to casting notices plus the ability to post your own Web site and a demo reel of not more than five minutes. Thom Klohn, director of industry relations for Now Casting's reel-hosting service, cautions actors not to get too creative when preparing these reels. "You want your online demo, which has to be viewed through streaming video, to be short. You can't fast forward it, like you can a DVD."

ONLINE CASTING VERSUS HARD-COPY SUBMISSIONS

In a business that is all about hurry up and yesterday, casting choices on the Internet would appear to be far more efficient than wading through hundreds and hundreds of hard-copy submissions. In some cases, that's true; in others, it's not.

Terry Berland, a West Coast–based commercial casting director, is among those who believe that the Internet makes casting much faster. "We e-mail back and forth with our clients. We don't have to stop what we are doing for lengthy phone conversations. When we send a casting notice nationally or internationally, we will get our submissions in a matter of minutes. Less paper and photos are exchanged. Our clients are used to quick results."

However, some casting directors still prefer hard-copy submissions. Judy Henderson, CSA, is an award-winning casting director who casts for theaters, features, video games, and interactive programming. She says she uses the "online stuff, but I prefer to work with the hard copies, because I'm not chained to the computer that way. Also when I want to get the pictures of the actors online, I've got to print them out, and it's a heck of a lot of paper and a lot of waste."

Jane Alderman, a casting director in Chicago, says that electronic submissions don't lessen her workload.

> If I am doing a movie with forty parts, I want hard copies. I am not going to sit at the computer and sift through all that online material. I would be there forever! I will say that if I'm in a hurry and I am just looking for a handsome guy who can handle three lines and they electronically submit three to five guys, I can look at them on my screen all at once.

You can understand why casting directors might prefer hard-copy submissions given that thousands of submissions are the order of the day for roles in a single commercial or a feature film. No casting director has the time to review that quantity when there is a definite time line on the project being cast.

Laura Verbeke, a former casting associate at New York–based Amerifilm Casting, believes that sending a hardcopy headshot and résumé is still preferable. But with the increased popularity of electronic submissions, she sometimes uses Actors Access and more often Casting Networks (www.castingnetworks.com), a presence in Los Angeles, San Francisco, Miami, and Chicago. She explains: "We can e-mail actors we choose or contact them directly through the information on their résumés.

Laura advises actors to heed the request of casting directors who include with their Web listings a "please do not submit" request for talent who is not appropriate for the project. "If actors neglect to follow that advice it is not to their benefit. I know the logic behind it, 'in case something else comes up,' but if that does happen we will do another posting."

Rob Decina, casting director for the soap opera *Guiding Light*, uses Breakdown Services to receive electronic submissions.

> I can put out a Breakdown in the morning and access submissions

in a couple of hours. Those submissions are ninety-five percent of the casting process. They are listed by agency, so you can start with submissions from the agencies you prefer. The process of reviewing a résumé online can be technically involved, and downloading a résumé and printing it sometimes can get to be a drag. But you can easily click on a picture and enlarge it. So, the lesson is, you better have a good picture if you are getting submitted electronically.

Danny Goldman, West Coast–based commercials casting director echoes that advice. "What stands out, because we get *thousands* of [electronic] submissions a day is a very compelling headshot that's eloquent and says something about the person."

If you do get an appointment from an electronic submission, don't forget to bring a hard copy of your photo and résumé with you to the casting director's office. New York–based casting director Liz Ortiz-Mackes urges actors to always carry several hard copies of their photos when they audition for her. "My clients like to take something home. They like to take the pictures in a 'goodie bag' they can refer to during the decision-making process. Also, what about the next project? An actor will want to have a photo in a casting director's files for future reference."

THE IMPACT OF TECHNOLOGY ON THE ACTOR

Actors were asked at a focus session how the advances in technology had helped them in their job searches. Most agreed that it was more efficient to have audition material, scripts, and sides e-mailed as attachments, to electronically submit their photos and résumés, DVD reels, and CD demos directly to casting offices, and to access hundreds of actor-friendly Web sites full of resources, leads, and links to expand their knowledge of The Business and get work. Annie McGreevy, who has had a successful career on both coasts, admired all the technological advances but felt that the personal connection was being sacrificed.

> The Business is impersonal now. Years ago you used to go into your agent's office and you would run into fellow actors and you'd go for coffee. There was a sense of community. You felt like your agent was looking out for you. I don't feel anyone's looking out for me. I feel like I am scrambling to catch up. It used to be that the agents would really work for you and advise and help you. They were really involved in your career. And I don't find that anymore.

Even so, for better or worse, actors are living in a high-tech society where they can use their cell phones to watch live television, listen to commercial-free radio, receive picture mail, and view "mobisodes," one to three minute television episodes specially made for viewing on a mobile phone. The BlackBerry, RazrV31, and the Palm Treo can play a variety of media. Search engines like Google and Yahoo! are positioned to be the choices the next generation of Web surfers will use to find, view, pay for, archive, and interact with the media.

All this technology presents new opportunities for actors, and Mark Carlton, SAG's National Chair of the New Technologies Committee, shared his knowledge of what lies ahead in an issue of *Screen Actor*.

> Because we are now faced with a plethora of delivery platforms— from iPods and cell phone "mobisodes" to Video on Demand and almost as many proposed business models that seek to profit from them, actors must educate themselves if they want their fair share of the revenue stream.

> New tech means new employment opportunities and income. The burgeoning electronic game industry is an example, hiring puppeteers, performance capture performers, voice-over, and interactive contract performers. Actors will need to become versed in the intricacies of green screen performances and the nuances of CGI technology—acting with and reacting to performers who aren't there. The well-trained performer will be more of an asset to a production.

CHAPTER 8

Survival Strategies

"I've been very fortunate. Since my days waiting at TGI Friday's, I've never looked back."
—Brad Garrett, Emmy-winning actor

Of the thousands of performers looking for work on a given day, almost as many thousands are spending that day working at jobs outside the industry. To make ends meet, most actors need survival jobs. We'd prefer that you think of these secondary occupations as survival strategies, even learning opportunities. These jobs provide you with a different set of life experiences that you may draw upon someday to bring depth and credibility to a role. There can be more to a "day job" for an actor than keeping the wolf from the door.

THAT'S NOT MY TABLE

Restaurant work seems to be what everyone thinks of first. We can safely assume that close to 50 percent of actors in this country are waiting tables or tending bar. There's no long-term commitment and limited responsibility, and at the end of the day a waiter can pocket a healthy amount in tips.

If you're able to get a spot at Orso or Angus McIndoe or any of the other show biz restaurants in New York or Los Angeles, you also have a chance to meet, or at least serve, some of the casting people and agents whose offices you so earnestly long to crack. Of course, you won't hand them your 8 x 10 along with the check. But you *can* be the best waiter who's ever served them. You can speak clearly as you run through the daily specials so that your professionalism shows. Nowadays, diners in Manhattan and Los Angeles almost assume that their waiters are performers anyway, so give a performance—not as Hamlet, but as the most engaging portrayal of *you*.

Sometimes restaurant work will provide the lucky break for an actor, as it did for Kevin Scullin.

> The restaurant I worked at was way out of the show business district. I got chummy with the assistant maitre d'. It turned out he was a subagent moonlighting in the evenings to make extra money, only he never mentioned it. But he was the guy who called me for my first job. I think not knowing what he was or where he worked let me sort of be myself. I was new to New York then.

What Kind of Job Should You Want?

But if you're not so lucky, and if the tables you are waiting on aren't at a "theater crowd" restaurant, or the restaurant itself is in some dreary neighborhood, ask yourself: Is this what I came to the Big City to do? We think you need more than that. You can go for alternatives that are rewarding and nourishing, that offer an outlet for your creative energy and give you a positive sense of self.

What kind of "survival job" should you want? Here's our own suggested checklist:

- Work that allows you to enjoy a sense of accomplishment and a modicum of control.
- Work that will not turn you into a drone with tunnel vision.
- Work that will add to your store of personal experience, while paying you a decent wage and not tying you down with a schedule so tight your life becomes little more than a shuttle from job to home to job. If "tied down" describes how you are spending your time and how you are feeling, you don't have a survival job—you have a job that has taken over your life.

What skills do you bring with you? For classically trained actor Mick Lauer, an instinctive understanding of what one could do with computers, coupled with his natural artistic ability, have served to make him a much sought-after designer. Because of his father's job assignments, Mick spent the first half of his life in the Far East. When he was sixteen, the family was transferred back to the United States.

I loved playing with the computer. You could have so much fun with it. I wasn't thinking about using it for anything; I was just a kid. My dad worked for Microsoft in Asia, and I went to these international schools, along with all the other kids whose parents worked for companies based in other countries. We were transferred to China, Taiwan, Malaysia, Kuala Lumpur, Japan.

High school [back in the States] was like nothing I'd ever seen. They thought I was weird! For the first year, I was this foreigner who spoke the language but didn't know what they were talking about most of the time. I spent hours playing at my computer.

Mick had always enjoyed performing in children's plays at the schools in Asia. He found it easy to get cast in plays at high school and enjoyed acting so much that he decided to major in theater at New York University. He did so well there that he went on to London's Royal Academy of Dramatic Art (RADA) and enrolled in its year-long Shakespeare Intensive course.

Mick then headed back to New York. With six other RADA alumni, he formed 7th Sign Theater company . Their mission: to present modernized versions of the classics. Their first production was *Julius Caesar*, at Theater for the New City. Here is where Mick's acting and designing skills merged.

I started designing postcards. We had no money for advertising, so we just sent out the cards. People loved the cards, but not many people came to the show. I began to amuse myself doing mock ads for advertised products. We all thought my ads were better than what those companies were using. And then people asked me to do cards for them. Which I was happy to do.

7th Sign decided next to produce a revival of Kurt Vonnegut's play *Happy Birthday, Wanda June*—a droll updating of the Odysseus legend, set at the awkward moment when the hero at last returns home. It would be the first New York production of the play since its original Broadway run in 1970.

A friend of a friend knew Mr. Vonnegut. We met him, and he loved the idea. He was going to come to the show and speak. We were really excited. Our press agent was clueless. He said nobody remembered Kurt Vonnegut. He didn't even try to get us any publicity. I did postcards like mad. We booked the Access Theatre. And, sure, hardly

anyone came, but a man who saw some of the cards offered me a job: He'd pay me twenty-five dollars an hour to design a Web site for him. I downloaded all the free stuff I could find and figured out how to do it. He liked what I gave him but felt he needed more. I knew I had to study. I took three huge design encyclopedias, my fiancée, and my computer down to Mexico, and in three months I learned all I could about designing Web sites.

It was like a whole new world! A different speed. I had to start selling myself. I called everyone. I gave out cards, and it started to roll. And people were willing to pay! They knew I was cheaper than the "going price," but I was also good.

Mick started to answer the ads in the trades, and he began to land acting jobs.

Then I auditioned for a two-person series, and got that! The company is called Traveling Lantern. We travel to schools and perform short plays illustrating particular educational themes. Doing it allows me to continue acting and get better. I've been at the Atlantic Theater Company, where David Mamet teaches. Karen Kohlhaas likes my acting as well as my art.

The thing is, now I don't have to sell myself, which I am uncomfortable doing. I am wonderful at performing, but I'm not a schmoozer. I'd rather be seen acting, having something to show. I know my art is great work.

Today Mick has his company, Human Resource Designs, www.humanresourcedesigns.com, and he is busy creating Web sites and doing design work. He is thinking of hiring an assistant to do the routine computer work while he concentrates on the art and aesthetics—while freeing up more time for his acting. 7th Sign has produced such rarely seen works as *The Just Assassins* ("Les Justes"), by Albert Camus. For the company's schedule, visit www.7thsign.info.

EXPLORING OTHER POSSIBILITIES

Some sideline careers make good use of an actor's skills. We've already mentioned the actors-as-patients programs, used by hospitals to train young doctors to cultivate a "bedside" manner (see Chapter Six, "Looking for Work"). The Actors' Fund of America recently worked with the New York City Housing Authority, which was investigating whether landlords were treating people improperly or asking for money under the table. The

Fund was able to supply "Fair Housing Testers" who posed as potential tenants to visit buildings that were under suspicion. The actors had to be people with a sense of social justice who had some social activism in their background. Perfect casting. The Fund has also helped place teaching artists at public schools in the city, where they create after-school events that introduce the students to cultural activities and also work to build literacy.

Office temp agencies that like to hire actors (who are, after all, so presentable, outgoing, charming, and disciplined) advertise in the trade papers. But why not give a thought to working somewhere within the industry? Writers need proofreaders; people who receive fan mail need an assistant to answer those letters and to keep track of engagements. Designers need assistants to check, borrow, or return fabric samples, to search for suitable props, to handle the endless details, to order the food. Do you have a terrific repertoire of fancy, down-home, kosher, Greek, Spanish, or dessert recipes? Is catering a possibility for you?

With ballroom dancing so popular once again, you might turn your dance training into paying work as a dance teacher, or even as a coach for ballroom competitions. If you've had voice training, that can open up another avenue of teaching income for you. Can you play the guitar well? Get paid for teaching others how to do it.

Make a list of your abilities and your passions. Perhaps you love dogs. In bustling Manhattan professional dog walkers earn a very respectable hourly rate. Similarly, cat sitters are a godsend to owners who must be away on business and cannot take their pet along. Your clients might be theatrical lawyers, agents, producers, or . . . why not? . . . a casting director!

ON YOUR OWN

By creating your own "survival strategy," you can also gain greater control over your life. We've all heard of personal trainers, those highly visible fitness gurus who serve a select group of affluent clients. As a personal trainer you can schedule your time so that interviews and auditions never conflict with your work.

We know an actor who is an excellent masseur. He has a license and a portable massage table. He has no trouble finding clients whenever he needs to replenish his bank account.

Are you into astrology? One actor drew up astrological charts, free of charge, for casting people he wanted to meet. He also sold his knowledge of what the future would bring to the general public on a consulting basis. What about Tarot cards as your vehicle? Your training will make your readings more dramatic. Were you a gifted gardener at home? Do you have a knack for creating beautiful floral arrangements? You might put your passion to work creating arrangements for parties given by your friends, neighbors, and colleagues—or for industry showcases produced, say, by your voice teacher or acting coach?

One actress's résumé contained the information that she was a carpenter. Anyone who's tried to hang a picture knows how welcome a skilled craftsperson is, and how hard it is to find one. When Harrison Ford grew impatient with the snail-like pace of his career, and unhappy about the quality of the roles offered him, he supported himself and his family very well by working on his own as a carpenter.

Are you fluent in more than one language? You could be an interpreter. Do you know sign language? Think of the shows you've seen that regularly employ "signers."

If you know your city well (and are willing to read up on its history and lore), you might enjoy working as a sightseeing tour guide—perhaps for groups who are especially interested in theater, film, or television. You'll get paid for speaking to audiences who will listen attentively to every word you say.

Marc Baron is "Collie" (vice president) of The Lambs, America's oldest theatrical club. . He is a man of all things theatrical: he sings, acts, directs, and has written a new screenplay. He recently combined his acting work and his knowledge of New York to create a lucrative survival job

> I've done a lot of stand-in work. So much that when the crews see me they say, "And here comes Mr. Baron, Stand-in to the Stars. I was a stand-in on the pilot of *The Sopranos,* and I worked that show for the whole season. About that time, bus companies were doing tours geared for theater and entertainment buffs, including fans of *The Sopranos.* I worked with the tour owner, and we revamped that tour so it's full of bits of inside information. As a result, I'm frequently called upon by local and out-of-town papers and talk-show hosts when they're looking for any *Sopranos* trivia.

Actress leslie Shreve (yes, she spells her name with a lowercase) tells how her know-how with her makeup led her into a rewarding fall-back career.

People so often would say to me, "Oh, you're an actress, would you help me with my makeup?" that I finally decided to learn something about it. And then I started to get calls! When I sort of fell between categories—I was no longer a young ingenue but I hadn't developed into a leading woman—doing makeup was a great fall-back. I was a replacement on the [makeup] team at *All My Children,* and would you believe it, my Emmy Award is for creating the makeup for a particular sequence on that show!

Whatever you can do that is positive will serve you in every aspect of your existence. Work that you loathe will taint your entire being. Think about it. You could be a taxi driver, going mad in traffic, never having time for lunch or a phone call, or you could take that same driving skill and become a chauffeur for a limousine company catering to celebrities. That again, would put you in a place where opportunity can find you.

Caveat: Always inform your talent reps about your job (or your business) and your weekly schedule so they know the best time to arrange auditions and interviews. And always be sure to check all the devices you use to remind yourself of your appointments for auditions and interviews—especially when you get really busy.

THE ACTORS' FUND OF AMERICA

The Actors' Fund of America (AFA) is the nation's only work-force-development program tailored to the unique needs of the performing arts and entertainment community. The fund seeks to assist all arts and entertainment professionals who are in need, in crisis, or in transition and offers a broad spectrum of programs—social services, emergency financial assistance, health services, employment and training, programs for young performers, and supportive and affordable housing. Tony Award–winning performer Brian Stokes Mitchell serves as president of AFA.

The Actors' Work Program (AWP) is one of the AFA's many programs. Lynne Hoppe, Director of Communications, describes this program as geared to helping actors find meaningful sideline work to supports themselves as they pursue their craft.

We try to give actors the tools they need to successfully pursue a life in The Business and still eat, have a roof over their heads, have health insurance, and manage financial planning. Because actors are artists and define themselves by their work, they should not sell themselves short in any work that they do. How do I adapt my skills so that I can balance the work and the pursuit of my creative projects? Young people are coming to us to take advantage of the guidance and information we offer to develop a long-range plan. That makes us happy, because it's important that actors don't wait to come to the AWP when they're desperate, when the unemployment benefits have run out, and they don't know what to do. They come here when they're doing okay, so they can have a plan in place.

Patch Schwadron, Career Counsel Supervisor, adds,

We offer career counseling tailored to the individual. Where do you want to go? What are your needs? What's your career outlook and how can we work to support that over the long haul? We have direct relationships with employers who post their jobs with us before they list them anywhere else. We will screen and refer appropriate candidates directly to the employers, given that they will pay more than fifteen dollars an hour.

We are not an agency, and we do not charge employers a fee. So this is an extremely good deal for employers. We also prep our members to get those jobs. We say to the employer, "You're going to get six résumés from people we think are perfect candidates for this position." And they say, "Fine, we will interview them." Then we work with our members in terms of cover letters and preparing for the interview.

There are lots of work issues for actors. This is a place where actors can talk to one another about these issues in an informative, creative way.

The Actors' Work Program is open to any member of an entertainment-industry union, or anyone who is getting assistance from the Actors' Fund. On Mondays, from noon to 2:30 P.M., the Actors' Work Program holds an orientation session at the Actors' Fund of America, 729 Seventh Avenue, New York, NY 10019. Orientations are also held at Actors' Fund offices in Chicago and Los Angeles.

The AFA can also provide you with the schedule of the nationwide Actors' Fund Benefit Performances, when performers donate their salaries for a given performance to support the work of the Fund. The Fund also sponsors a Career Transition Program for dancers who can no longer do those high kicks, and it administers the Conrad Cantzen Shoe

Fund. Endowed by actor Conrad Cantzen, who knew from experience how quickly actors wore out their shoes making the rounds of agents' and producers' offices looking for work, the Shoe Fund to this day provides eligible AFA members with one free pair of shoes a year.

For information on programs and activities of the Actors' Fund, visit the Web site at www.actorsfund.org.

CHAPTER 9

Understanding the Unions

"It seems to me that every problem the producer has, a union has to take into consideration. We're foolish if we don't. Because, we are bargaining partners."

—Anne Gartlan, former president, AFTRA New York

Professional actors belong to three unions: Actors' Equity Association (AEA, or just "Equity"), Screen Actors Guild (SAG), and the American Federation of Television and Radio Artists (AFTRA). These, in turn, are members of an umbrella organization, the Associated Actors and Artistes of America, known as the Four As, chartered by the AFL-CIO.

In simplest terms, Equity has jurisdiction over performers and stage managers in live theater. SAG covers appearances on film, some areas of what remains of work on tape, and some commercials. AFTRA's jurisdiction includes live and taped television shows, soap operas, cable, commercials, radio and recordings, as well as emerging areas of the new media. In addition to actors, singers, and dancers, AFTRA's membership includes announcers, disc jockeys, talk show hosts, stunt people, sportscasters, and news persons.

In an arena that prizes individuality, where a performer's personal magnetism can be so captivating that it overrides lack of technique or inspires an audience to forgive banal writing or insipid production, where the powerful chemistry between two performers can translate into a surge in ratings, the idea of performers belonging to a union may seem downright absurd. After all, what can such free-spirited, highly distinctive artists have in common with those more or less anonymous people who deliver packages, work in offices, or mine coal? Actress Roberta Reardon, AFTRA's national president, learned just how much she had in common with other professionals.

> My work here at AFTRA enabled me to earn a scholarship to the course on leadership given at Cornell University. When I walked into that class-room the first day there were twenty-four men and women and I thought, "There are no people here like me." But as the work went on, I began to realize that our difference was in how we looked and how we spoke, but basically we were coming from the same core. They are smart, coura-geous, and dedicated. Some of those men and women have become my closest pals. You should see our class graduation picture.

What unites actors and members of other professions is the fact that they all work for their living. And the work they do can be quite specifically defined and measured in terms of time and/or productivity. Moreover, the people they work for, simply by virtue of the fact that they control jobs, are powerful, and may even belong to power-enhancing organizations of their own. So, like sanitation workers, bus drivers, airline pilots, and countless others, actors (and singers, dancers, announcers, stunt people, sportscasters, and news persons) have found that by belonging to a union they gain a measure of clout.

Through the process known as collective bargaining, representa-tives of performers (unions) and employers (producers, networks, and ad-vertising agencies) arrive at agreements regarding performers' wages and working conditions. The resulting contracts establish the minimum sala-ries—or scale payments—for performances on stage, film, records, televi-sion, cable, or radio for a stated length of time; usually these agreements are for a period of three years.

Wireless, the Internet, and everything that comes under the heading of New Media has yet to be negotiated. As neither the employers nor the artists have any idea how broadcasting or narrow-casting (which implies that programming, also called *content*, may be delivered to a specific au-dience, selected for certain attributes) will deliver program material, or how they will be able to measure what anybody is looking at, both sides have agreed to freeze contracts for two years, to gain some insight as to how the pieces may fit together.

Other agreements cover what is known as nontheatrical employment, such as industrial shows, educational or documentary films, and material recorded for purposes other than commercial broadcast. These are negotiated separately.

Today's union members are the beneficiaries of all the gains their predecessors risked their careers to obtain. The high unemployment rate notwithstanding, union scale would appear to be acceptable compensation: $126 for extras, $759 for principals per day's work in film; $737 for principals on a thirty-minute soap opera; $844 for an hour-long soap; $567.10 for shooting a TV commercial; $1,465 a week for a Broadway show. With health insurance, pension coverage, and cost-of-living adjustments (COLAs)—all history-making benefits when they were first achieved—it's easy for newcomers to think that there's nothing more a union can "do" for them. After all, their representative, not a union, will negotiate any over-scale payment.

Veterans become indignant at this attitude. Upon hearing the newest young leading man boast that his slightly over-scale salary indicated that the producer valued the "pizzazz" his performance would add to the show, the matriarch of one of the long-running soaps, whose distinguished career encompassed theater and films as well as TV, raised her cultured voice so that everyone in the commissary could hear her.

> Darling, She purred: you would be working gladly for five dollars, without the efforts that all of us have put in, for years. You think they're paying you all that money because they're in love with your blue eyes and your talent? Don't be a fool. They're paying you because a lot of actors who worked for a lot less money than you, fought to get those minimums up to a decent level. You are riding on the shoulders of all those other people, and don't you forget it.

A BRIEF HISTORY

Professional theater has been a part of American culture since colonial times. European settlers brought the theatrical tradition from their homelands. President George Washington was known to enjoy the theater—*The School for Scandal* was his favorite play—and his regular attendance helped to popularize play-going. By the end of the eighteenth century, touring companies headed by actor-managers, performers who had risen through the ranks to head companies of their own, entertained theater audiences in most of the cities east of the Mississippi River. Years of tradition had defined both the way an acting company operated and the actor's place within that unit. One could sign a contract with these employers and be certain of what was expected.

In the boom following the Civil War, the development of transportation opened up the land west of the Mississippi, and the theater surged along with the rest of the nation's businesses. Hitherto independent theater owners and managers formed associations. Instead of traveling informally from one locale to the next, touring companies were now routed along circuits dominated by theater chains. Stars such as Edwin Booth, John Drew, and Sarah Bernhardt toured the country in lavish productions, receiving such great acclaim that by the end of the nineteenth century acting was recognized as a glamorous and rewarding profession.

In 1896, a booking office known as the Theatrical Syndicate was organized to supply shows, to systemize the production and financing of attractions, to eliminate wasteful competition, and to prevent booking tangles. By the turn of the century, the Syndicate could dictate which productions would play in what theaters, which actors would appear in them, and what the financial terms would be. The great actor-managers, such as Joseph Jefferson, Richard Mansfield, Fanny Davenport, Minnie Maddern Fiske, David Belasco, and James O'Neill (father of playwright Eugene O'Neill) now had to contend with a new species of theater citizen, the efficiency expert/manager, who knew nothing about theatrical tradition and couldn't care less.

To these businessmen, actors were not the backbone of the theater. They were merely one of many cost items on an income statement, to be obtained as cheaply as possible. The Syndicate had become so tyrannical and their terms so severe, that the great Sarah Bernhardt bought herself a tent and toured the country playing in it, rather than accede to their demands
.   There was no standard contract. Managers wrote different agreements for each performer, demanding concessions and inserting loopholes. There was no minimum wage for performances, and no pay for rehearsals. Plus, because rehearsals were free, there was no limit to them. Eighteen weeks' rehearsal was not unusual for a musical show; ten weeks was the average for a straight play. Actors worked seven days a week, playing as many performances as the managers wanted.

Under his contract with the Shubert organization, one unfortunate actor rehearsed twenty-two weeks and played only four nights. Incredible as it may seem, he appeared in three plays: the first ran two days, the other two ran one night apiece. According to his contract he was entitled only to payment for the four performances he played.

At the beginning of the twentieth century, it was not unusual for stock companies to play ten performances a week—seven evening shows and three matinees—while rehearsing the next week's play each morning. Salaries could be paid any day of the week, following performance, whenever the manager got around to it. Holidays then, as now, were peak attendance periods, yet managers paid half salary for Christmas week, Easter week, and Election week, even if there were no elections.

The centuries-old custom of two weeks' notice was abolished. Managers could declare actors "unsatisfactory" and fire them on the spot. Productions could be closed with no announcement to the cast. More than a few unscrupulous managers were in the habit of leaving town while a performance was in progress, taking the entire week's receipts along with them. The abandoned actors, unable to pay their hotel bills, had to sneak out of town on their own, which may explain why so many innkeepers on the theater circuit posted the warning: "We do not rent to theatricals!"

Many managers refused to pay transportation from New York, where the actors were engaged and where they rehearsed, to the opening town, or from the city where the show closed back to New York. So, if a show opened in Wilmington, Delaware, and closed in St. Joseph, Missouri, the cast had to purchase their own tickets to Wilmington and from St. Joseph back to New York.

The November 8, 1913, issue of *Billboard* reported, "The West Coast company of Victor Herbert's *The Enchantress* was stranded in Los Angeles. The production was abruptly canceled and the cast of sixty-seven performers and stage managers had to 'look otherwise than to the management for railroad tickets back to Broadway.'"

This was a decorous way to say that the performers, dragging their suitcases with them, were reduced to performing in the streets, passing their hats for donations from passersby at the end of each number.

Performers were required to supply their own wardrobes, a particular hardship for the women, as the cost of elaborate costumes, which they could use nowhere else, could be greater than their salary if the play closed early in the run. The actress Clara Morris wrote that at the start of her career in the 1870s, she was particularly proud that she was "gifted with her needle" and found ways to rework the fabric of her gowns again and again. No one in the audience realized she was, in effect, wearing the same dress she had toured in during the previous season.

Dressing rooms, usually in the cellar, or way at the top of the building, were filthy, unheated spaces. They rarely had running water or room enough to set out makeup and to change one's clothes.

A UNION OF THEATRICAL PERFORMERS

That was how things stood in May of 1913, when 112 performers, both men and women, met in a ballroom near New York's Columbus Circle and agreed to form the Actors' Equity Association (AEA). They adopted a constitution, elected officers and a council (among whose members were such stars as George Arliss and Charles Coburn), and set about trying to achieve a standard contract, which covered seven key issues:

- Free transportation from New York and back to New York
- A limit on free rehearsal time
- A two weeks' notice clause
- Protection from dismissal without pay for actors who had rehearsed for more than one week
- No increase in the number of extra performances without pay
- Full pay for all weeks played
- Adjustment of the situation regarding women's clothes

Negotiations with the managers dragged on for six years. The managers were determined not to give in on any item.

Finally, in the summer of 1919, the membership, now grown to more than 2,500, voted to strike. In this drastic action they had the support of featured players and chorus people as well as the leadership of major stars, among them Eddie Cantor, who was in rehearsal for the Ziegfeld Follies, leading ladies Ethel Barrymore, Pearl White, and Marie Dressler, and the beloved comedian, Ed Wynn, then starring in *The Gaieties of 1919*.

On August 7, the cast of *Lightnin'* informed the management of their theater that they would not perform that evening. There was more than ordinary drama in their action. *Lightnin'* was actor Frank Bacon's first Broadway success. After more than twenty years in stock companies and on the road, as star, author, and part owner of a hit show, he was looking at his first real chance to make some money and enjoy a strong career.

If the strike failed he would surely lose everything and have to go back to playing the provinces. Yet Bacon ordered his company out without hesitation, saying, "When this whole thing began, my wife said to me, 'We'll stick to our own people. I can still cook on a one-burner oil stove, if necessary.' So, we're stickin'."

Frank Bacon and the cast of *Lightnin'* led a boisterous parade of 2,000 actors, dancers, and musicians marching down Broadway from 59th Street and Columbus Circle all the way to 23rd Street and Madison Square. The stage hands brought up the rear, carrying a banner: NATIONS ARBITRATE, THOUGH MANAGERS WON'T. Remember, the year was 1919; this was the first summer of peace after World War I. It was also the summer of the Black Sox baseball scandal, and the start of Prohibition.

Sympathy and support for the performers came from unexpected places. Landladies of theater district rooming houses, where so many chorus girls lived, stopped asking for the weekly rent while the dancers were on strike. Taxi drivers pasted EQUITY FOR ACTORS banners on their cabs. Merchants on 45th Street donated 10 percent of their gross to the Actors' Equity strike fund, and Broadway area shops offered discounts to striking actors. One cigar store owner posted this sign in his window: STRIKING ACTORS GET YOUR CIGARETTES HERE. PAY ME WHEN YOU WIN. The management of Gimbel Brothers, the huge department store on 33rd Street and Sixth Avenue, telephoned Equity headquarters to offer jobs to any actors who needed them.

When a motorcade of fifteen touring cars, driven by Broadway's handsomest leading men and filled with the theater's most vivacious chorus girls (newspapers described them as the prettiest strikers in history), rode through the Financial District, the Curb Exchange (later the American Stock Exchange) declared a recess and gave them an ovation. Here was an audience well aware that Show Business was the fourth largest industry in the United States. They told passersby, "Their cause is just."

Frank Case, proprietor of the Algonquin Hotel, on 44th Street between Fifth and Sixth Avenues, offered free space to the Equity Publicity Committee and their clerical staff. For the duration of the strike he had their meals delivered to the meeting room. He not only refused to accept payment, he donated $1,000 to the Equity strike fund.

In Chicago, the nation's second-largest theater town, star Hazel Dawn and the cast of *Up in Mabel's Room*, walked off the stage.

Lillian Russell sent a telegram:

THE SHUBERTS OWE ME $100,000 ON ONE OF THEIR CONTRACTS WHICH THEY NOW CLAIM IS SACRED. IF ANY MIRACLE WORKER CAN BE FOUND TO COLLECT IT, I WILL BE GLAD TO TURN IT OVER TO THE ACTORS' EQUITY. BEST WISHES.

The managers, led by Marc Klaw, A.L. Erlanger, and E.F. Albee, still refused to recognize Actors' Equity, or the contract. Secretary of Labor William Wilson sent two assistants to New York to persuade the managers to negotiate. New York's Governor Alfred E. Smith met with both sides in an attempt to get the managers to settle. Their efforts were fruitless.

Then Samuel Gompers, president of the American Federation of Labor, returned from the Versailles Peace conference. Whisked to a special Equity meeting, he announced to the members and to the waiting reporters, that "all the power of the American Federation of Labor was lined up behind the actors."

The performers went wild. That meant there'd be no truck drivers to deliver sets or costumes, no chauffeurs, electricians, or ticket sellers. No motion picture projectionists. (A number of theater owners had kept their theaters open by showing silent films, thereby losing no money while the actors were out on strike.)

Now, the managers were willing to negotiate.

Minutes before midnight on September 6, 1919, the first Actors' Equity contract was signed. The strike was over. It had lasted thirty days, spread to eight cities, closed thirty-seven plays, prevented 167 productions from opening, and cost actors and managers about 3 million dollars. During the strike, membership in Equity increased to more than 14,000.

THE SCREEN ACTORS GUILD

Twenty years after the first Equity meeting, a handful of film stars met at the Masquers Club in Hollywood to discuss what could be done to improve their working conditions. Hollywood was turning out 600 films a year. To do this, everyone had to work six days a week, with no limit on hours. Actors could finish a day's shooting after midnight and be told to report to the set at 9 A.M., which meant arriving at the studio at 7 A.M. for makeup, hair dressing, and wardrobe. Allowing for travel time, this often meant a 5 A.M. wake-up call. Meal periods were at the producer's convenience.

There were no rules about compensating actors for travel to and from locations; no restrictions on weather-permitting calls (a practice that allowed studios to book actors then cancel at the last minute, without compensation, to keep them from working for anyone else); no arbitration machinery for handling contract disputes. Under the studio system, a handful of moguls controlled the industry. Contract players were property, to be developed, groomed, improved, and rented out to other studios at a profit.

One actress, under contract to Metro Goldwyn Mayer, recalled:

> I was only in five pictures at MGM. By being lent and sent around to other studios and independents I made two dozen pictures in five years. My hair changed color in every picture. We had nothing to say about our appearance. We weren't asked, we were told.

In March 1933, the moguls decreed that contract players would have to accept a 50 percent pay cut. Nonstars at that time earned about $75 per week. Pay for freelance actors would be cut 20 percent. With no organization to turn to for support, they had to endure the cuts. Talk of a union became louder.   Articles of incorporation were filed on June 30, 1933. The eighteen founding members named actor Ralph Morgan their president. Within a year membership rose to 2,000. Eddie Cantor, as big a star in films as he was on Broadway and radio, was then elected president.

Getting the Screen Actors Guild recognized as a labor union, and then getting the contract, took four years and many Clandestine meetings. Actors would park their cars several blocks away from the meeting place, so as not to be seen, and penalized, by the producers. Their proposals covered:

- An eight-hour day, with fifteen hours of rest between calls
- Regular one-hour meal periods
- Sundays and holidays off
- Overtime pay
- Payment for transportation expenses
- Contracts in writing, with a copy of the contract given to the actor
- Continuous employment pay (several nights might elapse between calls for the same part, during which time the actor had to be available and could not accept work from anyone else, yet was paid only for days on the set).

In May 1937 the producers finally accepted the Guild's demands. Membership, now grown to 5,000, had voted to strike the studios. President Robert Montgomery, a major film star who had been instrumental in establishing the Guild, declared "the victory of an ideal." Scale was $25 per day.

FROM AFRA TO TVA AND AFTRA

The last of the major talent unions to organize, the American Federation of Television and Radio Artists (AFTRA), came about through the merger of AFRA, the union of radio performers, which had been chartered by the Associated Actors and Artistes of America in August of 1937, and Television Authority, TvA, which had been established in 1952.

In her entertaining book, *Tune in Tomorrow*, veteran radio actress Mary Jane Higby recalled that in the early days of radio, performers received five dollars for an hour-length program that they might have rehearsed for two days. Sometimes performers were expected to work merely for the glory of doing the show. When noted radio actress Barbara Luddy asked the producer of *Hollywood Hotel* how much she'd be paid for appearing as the female lead on the show, she was told, "You're not getting paid, you're getting billing!" It took great courage for her to face a powerful producer and assert that she could not afford to work for nothing.

Veteran announcers tell similar stories. Silken-voiced movie idol Conrad Nagel was one of the many movie actors who were frequently "invited" to appear on radio shows to talk about their latest film. "Then they'd do a dramatization of the picture, with four or five us actors working for free."

In New York and Chicago, small bands of performers who were proficient at reading a script and delineating a character gained a foothold in the industry and did quite well. Extremely versatile actors played two and even three roles in the same show. As more and more radio stations were licensed, more and more performers joined the talent pool, and more and more producers realized they could always find someone who was willing to work for less money. Before long, according to the late Jackson Beck, voice of Kellogg's Tony the Tiger: "Every agency was trying to do it a little bit cheaper. We'd spend the whole day rehearsing, with no meal breaks or even time for coffee, and end up with a check for $11.88 for the show *and* the repeat" (rebroadcast of the same show three hours later for stations on the West Coast).

As James Thurber wrote in *The New Yorker*, "Before the American Federation of Radio Artists and the Writers' Guild were formed, the broadcasting industry took easy and cynical advantage of actors and authors."

Fortunately, the many stars who had been down the same road with AEA and SAG were among the earliest supporters of the idea of a union. Nominees for the board of directors were Eddie Cantor, who subsequently served as AFRA's first president, as he had at SAG, Jack Benny, Bob Hope, Bing Crosby, Dick Powell, Don Ameche, and Helen Hayes.

When performers at stations across the country learned that New York, Chicago, and Los Angeles actors were forming a radio union, they wrote to the nearest headquarters asking for help in organizing their own areas. Within the year there were AFRA locals in several cities across the country!

Management realized that AFRA's proposals for a code of fair practice would benefit employers as well as talent. With standardized payment, rehearsal rates, and times, they could, in a sense, stop worrying about whether they were getting the biggest bargains, and concentrate on getting the best work done. The first contracts were signed in July 1938.

HOW THE UNIONS WORK

Equity, SAG, and AFTRA are unique in that they are governed by the members. Their specific structures differ, but essentially they are run by councils, or boards of directors, whose elected members are performers who serve with no remuneration. Policies determined by these bodies in weekly or monthly meetings are then executed by a staff of paid, professional executives.

Contract demands are formulated by volunteer committees made up of performers active within each field. Their proposals for wages and working conditions are presented to the union's highest governing body—the convention or meeting of elected delegates and the local and national boards—where they are accepted, rejected, or modified. The executive staff then attempts to negotiate the union demands with representatives of management.

Actors' Equity, AFTRA, and SAG customarily negotiate three-year agreements. Because so many contracts are needed to cover all areas of employment, the unions inevitably have to "stagger" the contracts, so that they expire on different dates. Therefore, different contracts come up for negotiation every year. During these negotiations, the unions try to make their contract demands reflect the needs expressed to them by their members working in each job category. For the latest accurate information on what the contract codes contain—or to offer input about your needs as a performer, with an eye to the next round of contract talks—contact the union in whose jurisdiction you will be working.

The unions *cannot* get any performer a job. What unions can do is protect all performers in their relations with employers. By negotiating and then policing their contracts, the unions guarantee minimum salaries and the conditions under which performers will work. Union reps regularly visit studios, production centers, and location shoots to make certain that contract provisions are observed and that union members are being employed.

Performer safety is a new concern. As the so-called "reality" shows proliferate, even soaps search for outrageous situations and dangerous, exotic locales in which to place their main characters. Pressure to be a "good guy" and do your own stunts can be heavy, though trained persons are required to be on the set at all times to perform those feats.

Field reps also deal with member complaints about the day's work. These are handled with absolute secrecy as to the identity of the complainant. No actor who voices a legitimate complaint need ever fear reprisals.

Union contracts also guarantee that performers will be paid within a certain time after their performance; otherwise a late payment penalty is invoked. You should never have to call an employer to find out when or if your check is in the mail.

Unions have also won reuse, or residual, payments for recorded material. While this is something we take for granted today, at one time commercials were replayed endlessly without provisions for compensation for the performers. The advertisers received exposure, while the performers could only point to the screen and wail, "There I am again!" Old-time movies, such as the comedies of Abbott and Costello, were televised repeatedly on Saturday mornings, for the kiddies to watch while Mom did the laundry, yet many former stars received not one cent from those uses and were, in many instances, living in poverty. Management once argued that session fees were high enough and that performers should not expect to be paid again for work for which they'd already been compensated. The performers' point was finally won. The life of a performance in commercial or program material is now protected through a system of use and reuse fees. The unions have departments devoted to processing residual checks and monitoring reruns of recorded material.

Hardest fought for, and possibly the unions' most important achievement, are their health and retirement plans. These are plans financed by employer contributions based on a specified percentage of each performer's salary, original payments, and reuse fees. The retirement plans manage to offer a modicum of financial security to retired performers, based upon their earnings and length of employment. With group medical coverage (and life insurance), for which members qualify by earning a certain amount in the union's jurisdiction each year performers are freed from the terrible fear that unexpected medical expenses will bankrupt their families.

Members learn about union activities, triumphs, and concerns through their local's publications, through the union's local hotline, and on union Web sites: www.actorsequity.org, www.sag.org, and www.AFTRA.org.

Addressing Issues

Union concerns extend beyond money matters. It was a SAG committee that first monitored TV commercials and agitated for a change in the way women were portrayed. "We do other things besides the laundry," the report stated. Equal opportunity committees have also pressed for better minority representation in casting. Fortunately, in this they have had the support of many in management.

Another SAG committee reported on rip-offs by phony talent agents. The Attorney General of New York effected a crackdown on the offenders and, with the SAG committee, created the office's warning brochure for the industry.

At New York AFTRA, the push has been to offer seminars on many new aspects of the business. The "If It's Tuesday It Must Be AFTRA At Work" program has offered sessions on such topics as audio books, voiceovers, how to create your own recording studio at home, how to enjoy auditioning, and how to turn a nonunion offer into a union job.

AFTRA and SAG have each created indie production contracts, to make it easier for independent producers with low budgets to work under union contracts and for union actors to work with them. Independent producers who have signed with AFTRA have secured distribution rights to every production in every venue, which means that this low-budget work, which might otherwise have been nonunion, is now covered by a union contract. The performers will get whatever residuals may apply, plus contributions to their AFTRA health and retirement plans.

Proof of Citizenship

Working with immigration officials, union reps have helped modify regulations of the Immigration and Reform Act of 1986 requiring all workers, at the time they are hired, to show proof that they have the right to work in the United States. While the original intent of this legislation may have been to stem the tide of aliens who slip into the country illegally, the result has been to force actors to show proof of their citizenship every time they show up at an audition.

Instructed to bring their passports to every engagement, actors were irate: while proving their citizenship they were being forced to disclose their age. Their livelihoods were in danger if casting directors ever discovered that an actress who looked like, and was frequently cast as, the ideal young married, was really old enough to be the mother of the bride. After union intervention, actors may obey the law and still maintain privacy by showing a voter's registration card and a Social Security card.

Inquiries as to your age and national origin, as well as your marital status and sexual preference, are violations of the law. If anyone asks, "Confidentially, how old are you, really?" simply answer, "I play from twenty-seven to thirty-five," or "I'm usually cast as. . . ." Then, quickly, quietly call your union and let them know what has happened. The union will take appropriate action and protect your anonymity.

Income Tax Assistance

One of the most successful membership activities, which all three unions sponsor in concert, is a program initiated by the late Michael Enserro, an excellent character actor. He saw that people in The Business had special problems in making out their income tax forms because of the sporadic nature of their work. He set out to provide tangible help in the form of Volunteers Providing Income Tax Assistance (VITA). At first Michael was a one-man committee, working each tax season at Equity's offices. Today, a growing committee of trained volunteers, headed by actor Conard Fowkes, carries on the work he began.

A Credit Union

Forty years ago, when a young woman who was one of the leading actors in a daytime serial, and who had always paid in full for everything when she bought it, had been advised to establish credit, she was told by a bank officer that, since her show could be canceled the next day, he could not approve her request for an $800 loan. The program is still on the air; the bank no longer exists. During the same period, Actors' Equity established the Equity Federal Credit Union. Within a few years, AFTRA in New York, and AFTRA and SAG on the West Coast, followed AEA's example. The separate entities have since merged into The Actors Federal Credit Union, which now offers full banking services, its own low-rate credit card, loans, free ATMs, and other financial services. Arthur Anderson, a past credit union president, says, "Of course, actors are still interviewed for loans. We do have to know that the money can be repaid. But at least you are interviewed by someone who understands the life you lead."

Local Services

Union branches or locals may engage in whatever membership activities the members vote for and are willing to finance. For instance, AFTRA locals in Boston, Chicago, Miami, Philadelphia, and Washington/Baltimore distribute talent directories to the industry. Other locals have set up and maintained casting hotlines. SAG and AFTRA in New York have each invested in top-of-the-line audio and video equipment that, for a small annual fee, members can use to improve their skills. In addition, members volunteer to teach others the fine points of soap opera, voice-over, and commercial techniques, as well as playwriting—or whatever else they have to share.

RESPONSIBILITIES OF UNION MEMBERS

We have gone into some detail to describe what the performers' unions have been able to achieve for their members. There is a reverse side to this picture: what the members are obliged to do—not for the union, per se, but for the professionalism of the whole.

Actors must accept the same responsibilities as professionals in any industry. Actors must do their jobs to the best of their ability. Actors must be on time, must be prepared to work, and must abide by the contracts they have signed. Actors must comply with union regulations, and let the union know where they live and can be reached—so they can receive those hard-won residual checks in the mail.

It's comforting to know that an employer can be penalized for late payment of your session fee, or for failure to break for lunch within five hours of your original call. You should know that performers can be disciplined as well, and have been, by their peers. Stars have been fined for their failure to honor contracts. Actors who have jeopardized productions have been called to account for it. Like civilization as a whole, The Business is a complicated mechanism, delicately balanced. It only works when we all respect one another and do our jobs.

To do your job, you have to know what it is. Take advantage of the professional assistance your union offers. When you don't know something, ask. Got a problem? Someone will try to help you. If you feel strongly about your place in The Business, contribute. Join a committee. Volunteer.

How to Join a Union

The simplest way to join Equity, SAG, or AFTRA is to get a job in their jurisdictions. A signed contract with a legitimate producer, saying that you are engaged for such and such a role in such and such production at whatever salary, immediately confers upon you the status of professional. You will then be required to pay the initiation fee and six months' dues.

However, there are other ways to get your union cards.

American Federation of Television and Radio Artists

AFTRA is an open union. Any actor, singer, or announcer can sign the membership application and pay the initiation fee, which is $1,300 as of this writing. Basic dues of $63.90 are paid semiannually and working dues—a percentage of gross earnings from AFTRA employment—are calculated on a sliding scale, based upon the previous year's income.

Under the Taft-Hartley Act it is possible for you to do your first AFTRA job, then work in TV or radio for up to thirty days without joining the union. After that, if you continue to work, membership is mandatory. To learn more, go to www.aftra.org.

Screen Actors Guild

If you have been a member of either AFTRA or Equity for a year, and have worked as a principal in either of their jurisdictions, you may apply for membership in SAG. If you have not been a member of the other unions, and now have a commitment for a role as a principal in a film, a commercial, or a filmed television show, you will be accepted for membership.

You must bring a letter from a signatory producer, or the producer's representative, stating that you will be playing a principal part in a specific picture. SAG's current initiation fee is $1,474, plus the first semiannual basic dues payment of $50. The fee is payable in full at the time you apply, by cashier's check, money order, or (in some branches) a credit card.

Personal checks are not accepted for joining fees. In addition to the basic annual dues, members pay a percentage of SAG earnings, on a sliding scale. For more information, go to www.sag.com.

Actors' Equity Association

If you have been a member of either AFTRA or SAG for a year or more, and have performed work comparable to Equity principal work, you will be eligible to join AEA. Since 1978 it has been possible to earn a membership card by means of the Equity Membership Candidacy Program, under which nonprofessional actors are allowed to credit fifty weeks of work in participating Equity theaters toward AEA membership. This work does not have to be at one theater, nor does it have to be consecutive. The program is in effect at dinner theaters, Equity resident theaters, Chicago Off-Loop theaters, and in resident and nonresident stock companies throughout the country. One of the great benefits of this program is that by the time you have earned your union card you have acquired experience and built a résumé: You are qualified to be in the company of professionals. As many as ten weeks of the fifty may be spent doing technical work. Membership candidates at stock companies may also receive credit for weeks as production assistant to a stage manager.

A membership candidate, after securing a position at a participating theater, must register for the program by completing the nonprofessional affidavit (supplied by the theater) and sending it to Actors' Equity. Once you've accumulated your fifty weeks of work, you have five years in which to join AEA. During that period, if you get a job at an Equity theater, you will be required to join the union. Equity's 's current initiation fee is $1,100. Basic dues of $59 are paid semiannually. Members also pay working dues. The maximum amount of earnings subject to the working dues is $100,000 per year. For more information, go to www.actorsequity.org.

The Right Time to Join

We cannot overemphasize the fact that being a member of Equity, AFTRA, or SAG will not automatically get you a job. Your only guarantee is that as a union member, when you work you will enjoy the same benefits and protections as received by all other union members.

A discerning casting person will be able to tell from your résumé whether you have merely purchased that union card or have earned it. If you are really new to The Business, have not had a great deal of experience in any area, and have few contacts among professional people, you should question whether it is essential or even advisable for you to attempt to join any of the unions at this time. As a union member you will be prohibited from working with nonprofessionals, and amateur groups, community theaters, or school groups may be the very places you should be looking to for the experience you need.

Temporary Withdrawal

If you think you are not going to be active in a jurisdiction for six months or longer (for instance, you may sign to tour with a play for a year or more and thus be unable to work in film or TV) you may elect to take temporary withdrawal from AFTRA and/or SAG. At that point you will not be required to pay dues to those unions, but you will, of course, be paying full dues to Equity . If you go on location for a period to shoot a film, you may temporarily withdraw from Actors' Equity.

The important thing to remember is to apply for a temporary withdrawal card and not let unpaid dues accumulate. An oversight may lead to a fine, and may even endanger your membership status. Once you return to your home base, remember to reinstate yourself as an active member.

FOREIGN ACTORS ON THE AMERICAN SCENE

SAG and the Alliance of Canadian Cinema, Television and Radio Actors (ACTRA) have adopted an equitable exchange agreement in an effort to equalize the number of performers crossing the border to work in film and TV. Both unions have also agreed to police each other's contracts on production shooting in either country and provide help to union members with production problems on location.

Performers who are not American citizens will need to show proof that they are permitted to work in the United States. Unions can be helpful here, too, and their legal staffs will be familiar with immigration procedures and work permits. One such permit is the O Visa, which is issued to individuals who demonstrate extraordinary ability in the sciences, arts, education, business, or athletics, which has been demonstrated by sustained national or international acclaim. They are temporary visas that are available for three years and are renewable annually.

The Green Card is a lifelong visa allowing a foreigner to live and work in the United States. The card itself is a government-issued plastic ID card that serves as proof of permanent resident status. It is not citizenship, and can be revoked if a person does not maintain permanent residence in the United States, travels outside the country for too long, or breaks certain laws.

Obtaining a Green Card is a federal matter, customarily handled by the immigration departments and/or consuls of this country and the performer's native country. The application for a Green Card is available at the official U. S. Citizenship and Immigration Services Web site, www.uscis.gov. You can download forms from the site and also find answers to many of the questions you might have.

Our suggestion for an actor who does not have U.S. citizenship and is looking for work in the United States is to get expert advice. Consult with one of the unions, as well as an attorney with expertise in immigration law.

CHAPTER 10

It's About Jobs!

"Never mistake your salary for your income."   —Lillian Gish, legendary actress

In this chapter, we will give you an overview of what kinds of jobs exist for actors, what they entail, and some idea of what you can expect to earn when you land them. Whatever the job, you should be sure to check with the appropriate union (see previous chapter) regarding the fine points of your contract.

IF YOU WORK ON THE STAGE

Opportunities for stage work range from Broadway to Off-Off-Broadway and all across the country in regional theater, and in venues as varied as dinner-theater stages to cabarets. Up-to-date information on wages and working conditions in all forms of stage work is available on the Actors' Equity Web site, www.actorsequity.org.

Broadway

The minimum—*or scale*—payment for actors, singers, or dancers in a Broadway show is $1,465 per week, as of 2007. Chorus people who perform a specialty number receive $20 per week above scale. Dance captains receive $300 more per week. Understudies who are also cast members receive $33 per week additional pay for each role they under-study, plus one-eighth their weekly salary each time they perform the role. Understudies who are not cast members earn the minimum $1,465 per week, plus a one-eighth weekly salary bonus for each show they actually play. Such performers may be signed to understudy as many as three roles without additional payment.

Stage managers on a musical are paid $2,408 per week; those working a dramatic show, $2,070. Assistant stage managers earn $1,904 per week for a musical and $1,691 for a dramatic show. Scale for second assistant stage managers on a musical is $1,691. Rehearsal pay is the same as performance pay. This applies to all performers, unless their contracts have been otherwise negotiated. Dramatic productions may rehearse for up to eight weeks. Musicals may rehearse principals for nine weeks; chorus members for ten weeks. If the rehearsal period lasts longer, performers then receive whatever salary their agents have negotiated.

Remember, these are minimums. Actors and stage managers with a long list of credits negotiate higher salaries. Stars will receive many times scale, and usually a percentage of the gross receipts. Remember also that whatever a performer's salary may be, scale or higher, the producer contributes a portion of the performer's salary to the AEA's health and retirement funds—currently about 8 percent.

Touring Companies

The pay is the same for national touring companies as it is for the performers doing the show on Broadway. On the road, however, performers are required to pay for their own accommodations, so they receive a per diem living allowance.

Off-Broadway

This uniquely New York institution continues to offer opportunities to talented beginning actors, as well as to established stars.

Off-Broadway theater blossomed in New York City in the late 1940s, with productions staged in small theaters away from the famous Times Square Theater District. In these out-of-the way houses, writers could try experimental works without the commercial pressures of Broadway. At the same time, Off-Broadway offered opportunities for new performers, talented young people who had no established reputation to risk and didn't mind working for pennies more than carfare.

The late Jason Robards and the late Geraldine Page are two stars whose lives changed dramatically after they were seen Off-Broadway. Both appeared in productions staged in Greenwich Village by a company calling itself the Circle in the Square: Robards in Eugene O'Neill's *The Ice-man Cometh*; Page in *Summer and Smoke*, by Tennessee Williams. Not only did these two artists go on to notable careers, but the production company has since become highly respected both on Broadway and Off-Broadway. One of the founders, Paul Libin, is now producing director for Broadway's Jujamcyn Theaters Company.

Today, established players are just as eager as the rest of us to be seen in an Off-Broadway play that might settle in for a long run, or even make it to a Broadway house. Stars of TV series welcome the opportunity to work in front of a live audience Off-Broadway when their shows are on hiatus. From the producers' point of view, the hope is that such a highly visible star will attract more audiences to the theater.

The terms of Off-Broadway theater contracts vary with the size of the theater and its potential weekly gross. Salaries for performers working Off-Broadway range from $506 per week, for performers working in theaters seating fewer than 200 people, to $890 per week for work done in theaters with a capacity of up to 499.

The current contracts allow for a five-week rehearsal period, with rehearsal pay the same as the minimum salary. As on Broadway, stage managers working earn a bit more than performers do.

Off-Off-Broadway

Off-Off-Broadway came into existence because of the increasing costliness and commercialism of Off-Broadway. Off-Off-Broadway productions are staged in lofts, basements, and hotel function rooms, usually for a limited number of performances. Under Equity's Showcase code, actors must be reimbursed for their expenses, which often amount to no more than their carfare. Under the Funded Non-Profit Theater Code, producers may charge admission, and performers may be paid a stipend based on the size of the theater, the show's potential gross, and the number of performances. Many of the Off-Off-Broadway playhouses are on Manhattan's Theater Row—that is, 42nd Street, west of Ninth Avenue. As one subscriber to the area's theaters told us:

> Companies like the Actors Theatre and the Vineyard are remarkable. A committed group of actors, name performers. Thank the Lord for

them. They'll work for the lowest minimum and give themselves time to go out and do a special or a film or whatever, to make enough money to come back and do this. They're willing to take less money, willing to take the risk of bad reviews. They do it for the sheer love of theater.

Regional Theater and the LORT Contract

Regional theater now employs the largest number of professional actors. More than seventy theaters belong to the League of Resident Theaters (LORT), among them the Mark Taper Forum in Los Angeles, the Tyrone Guthrie Theater in Minneapolis, the Actors Theatre of Louisville, the Cleveland Playhouse, and the Indiana Repertory Theater.

Increasingly, productions originate in these theaters, away from the scrutiny of powerful metropolitan theater critics. After they've ironed out their kinks, regional productions may move to New York, with hopes of translating their regional success into greater success on Broadway. LORT theaters are classified by the unions according to their seating capacity and potential gross. Salaries for actors in a LORT production range from $536 to $816 per week.

Jenny Strassburg recently worked with Salt Lake City's Pioneer Theatre Company in a production of *Pride and Prejudice.*

> The cast included local actors as well as those cast in New York City. As New Yorkers and actors, I think we often become jaded. These audiences were wonderful. Their love of theater art was shown in their readiness to laugh, and in their heartfelt applause at the end of the show. This was a house of nine hundred thirty people. Sold out at every performance! A nice change for us New Yorkers, accustomed to small theaters and black boxes where oftentimes only a few seats are occupied. In sum, regional theater is a fantastic opportunity for change, travel, and working your process. Every experience has been distinct. I will always jump at the chance to work with a new theater in a distant part of the country.

Additional Opportunities on Stage

To encourage the development of professional theater, Equity has hundreds of contracts that cover a wide assortment of venues. These may be modified as local conditions within categories change. Here, we'll take a look at some of these alternative forums for talent.

Summer stock. This used to be the actor's best training ground, but the number of summer stock playhouses has dwindled over the years. The remaining theaters work under the Council of Resident Stock Theaters (CORST) contract. Salaries are based on theater capacity and potential gross.

Outdoor drama. Historical pageants with large casts, special effects, and stunt people have become increasingly popular. Actors who love this work say it's like a rock concert on the History Channel.

Dinner theater. The link between actors' salaries and seating capacity also applies to dinner theater. The number of dinner theaters is dwindling, and many of those that remain are located in resort areas. Under the current contract, performers must pay for their own accommodations, but not more than 20 percent of their salary. Performers should find out what their living expenses will be before they accept such bookings, keeping in mind that room rates go sky-high in vacation season in many of the places where dinner theater is still popular.

Children's theater. A national organization promoting theater for children, Theater for Young Audiences has a membership of about fifty professional companies. Some of them pay on a weekly basis; others pay per performance. Resources are sometimes limited and actors may frequently double as assistant stage managers. Rates will vary, as always, according to size of the theaters and potential gross. Rehearsal pay is the same as performance pay.

Business theater. Here you'll be cast in industrial shows, created for corporations and performed for an invited, nonpaying audience. Formats vary widely, from star-studded, high-spirited glitzy musicals, to formal presentations of educational material, to comedic routines geared to promoting products or services. Some shows travel for four to six weeks. Stage managers are paid $807 for the first day; actors are paid $536, and assistant stage managers are paid $426. Contract terms for this form of theater are unusual in that rates go down on subsequent days of work.

Cabaret theater. In this genre, you'll be cast in revues, and you'll usually be performing in restaurants, nightclubs, and hotels. *Forbidden Broadway* is the hilarious, longest-running example of cabaret. Pay scale is again based on the size and location of the venue.

IF YOU WORK IN FILM

In keeping with contracts negotiated by the Screen Actors Guild (SAG), scale is same for films made for theatrical release or prime-time TV. Above-scale payment can, of course, be negotiated by your representative.

For a principal performer, scale is $759 a day, $2,634 a week. Background players make $130 per day, while stand-ins earn $145. Scale is the same for extravaganzas and small, intimate stories. However, modified union agreements do exist for low-budget films and for independent films. To qualify for any of these categories, producers must submit the script, the shooting schedule, and a detailed budget for scrutiny by SAG executives.

SAG has also negotiated agreements to cover work intended for nontheatrical use—in workshops, training situations, limited runs, and festivals. These agreements allow producers to work with professional talent while staying within budget, and they give union members the opportunity to work and thus qualify for free health insurance each year, while adding to their retirement benefits.

The SAG Indie Low Budget program was designed to encourage members to "do your own stuff." This is exactly what the well-known actor Peter Reigert did when he found himself unable to get an audition for a script one of his friends had written. The moviemakers didn't think he was right for the part. Turning his anger into something positive, he dug up a piece that he'd written a few years earlier. He shot *By Courier* with friends, in one day, and submitted it to a small film festival, where it was well received. He then submitted it to the Motion Picture Academy and got an Oscar nomination in the short film category! "I paid everyone scale," he says. "We had a wonderful time. If the material is interesting, people will want to participate. People like to work! And you may get lucky!"

IF YOU WORK IN TV COMMERCIALS

Television commercials are covered by contracts negotiated jointly by AFTRA and SAG and the employers' representatives. Rates for performers are the same in both unions. For an on-camera principal, a person recognizable to the general public gets $567.10 per day at scale, whether he or she has lines to speak. Voice-over performers, those who are heard but not seen, are paid $426.40 per session for national spots. Payment for work performers do exclusively for use on cable will depend on the number of subscribers to the cable system.

People who do commercials can receive additional fees if the commercials get a great deal of play. Residuals, or payments for repeated uses of performers' work, are computed according to complicated systems that measure number of uses, size of market, and whether the spot is shown within a program or during station breaks. Some very fortunate performers have been known to regale their colleagues with stories of how the residuals from a couple of TV spots have allowed them to send their sons and daughters to the colleges of their choice!

It stands to reason that if you are seen on TV extolling the virtues of Toothpaste A, you can't sing the praises of Toothpaste B, or any of its other competitors. To do so is to have a "product conflict" and you run the risk being sued for damages by the first client. If Toothpaste A doesn't want you to work for any other product, you must at least be paid double scale for your work. But let your agent negotiate that.

IF YOU WORK IN TELEVISION

Television offers great variety for actors, from daytime soaps to prime-time dramas to nondramas that use actors, such as *Saturday Night Live.* Principals on a thirty-minute daytime serial (soap) get $737 per show; those on a sixty-minute soap get $844. Background actors on soaps are paid $140 a show.

AFTRA and SAG jointly negotiate the contract codes for prime-time dramatic shows. Actors working for scale get the same pay whether the job is under AFTRA's jurisdiction or SAG's: $1,386 for a sixty-minute show; $1,028 for a half-hour show. On nondramatic shows, such as *Saturday Night Live*, singers and dancers are paid $543 and $570, respectively. Background players earn $178. Thanks to the diligent work of Tom Shillue and AFTRA's Comedians Caucus, a system-wide agreement with the Comedy Central cable network has been negotiated. Stand-up comedians who appear on the network are now covered by a union contract.

IF YOU WORK IN RADIO AND RECORDINGS

Do a lot of networking within your unions to get an edge in finding radio work. There is so much happening in radio, and so much work is "publicized" by word-of-mouth, that pro-active actors are likely to hear about it first.

The fastest-growing segment of the entertainment business is interactive video games, and this means more work for voice-over artists. *The Voice Over Resource Guide* lists West Coast talent agencies that handle voice-over actors (www.voiceoverresourceguide.com/la/agencies.htm). *Ross Reports* provides similar information.

IF YOU WORK IN NONBROADCAST AUDIO

Nonbroadcast audio provides actors with another potential paycheck. As the U.S. economy expands, so does the need for training and instructional materials for the countless new products and services coming to market. This part of The Business, like regional theater, employs people all over the country, not just in the major cities. Every client company has its own needs, and the material will change according to the marketplace. The Nonbroadcast and Industrials Committees in AFTRA locals deal with such work on a per-project basis.

IF YOU WORK IN PROMOTIONAL ANNOUNCEMENTS

The local radio or TV staff announcer is being replaced by the independent promo reader, who typically works nowhere near the broadcasting station. Rather, he or she records the station's promos in a private studio—perhaps at home in a soundproof closet. According to Wendell Craig, the last remaining staff announcer at CBS:

> Many work-at home-announcers are now using their computer to record [a promo] and then sending the file to the station via Internet. You just attach it to an e-mail and send it to your client.
>
> You can have a Web site that showcases your work. Your demo is your Web site. Every announcer has some form of that. I went to an audition the other day, got there early, and chatted with the casting director, who said, "We're only seeing twelve people for this." But they're also getting or listening to voices from everybody on the Internet with a demo and a good voice.

The recognized Queen of the Promo Announcers is Anne Gartlan, a former president of AFTRA who was born in Virginia and came to New York in the 1970s.

> When I was in college my goal was to make a living in this business. I am not a star, but I am a working stiff, and that's all I've ever done. So, to me, one of the things about success is being able to define it, to know when you've achieved it. I have a niche.
>
> In New York, I was working so many secretarial jobs, I couldn't get arrested. I was a young character woman, and it was either gain twenty pounds or lose twenty pounds, depending on the show. I decided it wasn't worth it. I went to Atlanta, where I'd be warm in the winter, and

> I started making phone calls. I'd call ad agencies and say, "Hi, I'm Anne Gartlan, I just got here from New York." And they'd say, "Come on in!" I got my first radio spot that way. I was the voice of an ATM machine.

Within three years, Anne had done theater, commercials, a movie of the week, and a TV pilot. It was time to move to back to a major market. She returned to New York with a demo full of authentic spots, polished and professionally produced. She was ready. And she found an ideal agent. Anne is now said to be the busiest of all promo announcers. Her day begins at 8:00 A.M. in her basement studio and frequently lasts until 1:00 A.M. She can name a slew of high-level clients. She uses a high-speed ISBN Co-Dec digital recorder, has a second one at her mother's house, and carries a portable model when she's at conventions.

> I find the union work very stimulating. I learn a lot about The Business through it. But the AFTRA job did not get me any work of my own. That's a great misconception. You learn about job openings by nurturing all those relationships you've built up over the years. Someone you worked with at one spot gets promoted, moves to another outlet, or tells you about an upcoming opportunity.

IF YOU WORK IN AUDIO PUBLISHING

Increasingly, performers are recording material such as self-help tapes and best-selling books. Paul Ruben, an independent producer of audio books and a director of Audio Publishers Association (www.audiopub. org), a not-for-profit trade association, talks about the opportunities in this growing field.

> Recorded books are getting longer these days, and the impact of digital technology will lead to more work in more areas. The human voice is the most incredible instrument. This is an actor's medium, a performer's perfect medium: storytelling. Go to www.audible.com and you will hear Barbara Caruso, who is considered the top female narrator. There is a very subtle difference between performance and narration. The main character is the storyteller. But a compelling story is in the narration. To have the listener suspend disbelief, you connect with the listener not as an actor but as a storyteller. You have a storytelling persona.

> "Talking books" use male and female narrators, depending on the story. Sometimes the narrator switches gender. How does one do

that? You "connect" to who the characters are. Casting is everything in this field. The actor must be intuitive and able to take direction. That's another possibility [for work]: Good actors make good directors.

Paul advises actors to make their own demo containing three samples, each one about ninety seconds long. Make samples for the three main categories of "talking books": nonfiction (first-person narration); fiction (first-person narration); and fiction (third-person narration). Perhaps make a fourth sample to emphasize your strength as a narrator in a particular category. Put the whole package on a CD, an MP3, or an ID track, and label it. Include your contact information, and perhaps a photo and résumé. Send your demo to the producers, packagers and publishers whose names and addresses you will find in *Ross Reports*, at the AFTRA office, and in *Audio File* magazine, an excellent source of information about this new source of employment.

A number of major book publishers are AFTRA signatories. However, at present there is nonunion work in this area, too.

The union Web sites have the latest information on the many jobs that call upon an actor's talent and training. We also encourage you to speak to veteran actors, who will be eager to help you and encourage your work in whatever dramatic forum you choose to pursue.

CHAPTER 11

Performers with Disabilities

"I believe with all my heart and soul that PWDs can and must be seen and judged for their abilities. We are a valuable asset and a major part of the American Scene." —Robert David Hall, "Dr. Robbins" in *CSI: Crime Scene Investigation*

Performers with disabilities (PWDs) have seldom been given the opportunity to play themselves, let alone anyone else. Hearing and sighted actors who have played these roles to great acclaim include Academy Award winners Jane Wyman (*Johnny Belinda*), Patty Duke (*The Miracle Worker*), and Al Pacino (*Scent of a Woman*) and Oscar nominee Sean Penn (*I Am Sam*). As a result, there have been few role models for talented, young aspiring actors who are deaf or blind or used a wheelchair. Plus, the few roles that have been disability-specific have perpetuated stereotypes. The number of actors in the three performing unions—AEA, AFTRA, and SAG —who identify themselves as having a disability represents less than half of one percent of the membership.

Even so, there have been exceptions, and many actors with disabilities have found a hard-won presence on stage, in television, and on film, enjoying success and stardom. In this chapter we will look at some of the growing opportunities for actors with disabilities.

A LOOK AT THE PAST

In 1915, during a brilliant theatrical career, the divine Sarah Bernhardt (1844–1923) had to undergo surgery to have her right leg amputated above the knee as a result of complications from improper treatment in an earlier surgery. The rumor that she wore a wooden leg for the rest of her performing life was untrue. She categorically refused to wear a prosthesis, because it was cumbersome, and also rejected crutches and a wheelchair. Until her death, she had herself carried in public on a specially designed litter. She mastered the art of illusion on stage by appearing upright by a table or sitting in a chair or being positioned on a sofa. Contemporaries who saw her perform noted that she finessed her disability so that no one in the audience was aware of her physical challenge.

British-born movie star Herbert Marshall lost a leg in battle during World War I. He disguised the handicap successfully enough to enjoy a lengthy screen career, during which he played urbane romantic leading men opposite Katharine Hepburn (*A Woman Rebels*), Bette Davis (*The Little Foxes* and *The Letter*), Marlene Dietrich (*Blonde Venus* and *Angel*), Greta Garbo (*The Painted Veil*), Claudette Colbert (*Zaza*), and Joan Crawford (*When Ladies Meet*).

Lionel Barrymore, best known for his portrayal of the sinister bank president in the Frank Capra classic *It's A Wonderful Life*, was forced by a disabling illness to play many roles sitting in a wheelchair. Oscar winner Harold Russell (*The Best Years of Our Lives*) lost both hands during World War II.

Visually impaired stars have included Sammy Davis Jr., Peter Falk, Ray Charles, George Shearing, and Stevie Wonder. Mark Medoff's prize-winning drama, *Children of a Lesser God*, deals with the relationship between a hearing man and a deaf woman. Stage versions have helped launch the careers of many well-trained deaf actors, and the very talented Marlee Matlin won an Academy Award for her performance in the film version, which launched her successful career in such acclaimed series as *The West Wing*.

TO JOIN THE MAINSTREAM

Since 1986 the Non-Traditional Casting Project (www.ntcp.org), under the guidance of executive director Sharon Jensen, has worked to address and seek solutions to the problems of exclusion and racism in theater, film, and television. Part of the group's mission is to ensure that Deaf and hard of hearing artists and artists with other disabilities are ensured equitable professional opportunities. To assist casting directors and other industry professionals, the group publishes a series of resource guides that include *Listening with an Open Eye,* which includes information about Deaf culture and American Sign Language, as well as advice on for planning and executing a production with Deaf and hard of hearing actors. Since 1987 the group maintains Artist Files, the most extensive listings in the country of actors with disabilities and actors of color, and makes this resource available on the Internet through Artist Files Online (AFO).

VSA Arts is an international, nonprofit organization founded in 1974 by Jean Kennedy Smith, former U.S. ambassador to Ireland, to create a society where all people with disabilities learn through, participate in, and derive pleasure from the arts. VSA Arts showcases the accomplishments of artists with disabilities and promotes increased access to the arts for people with disabilities. The acronym stands for Vision of an inclusive community; Strength through shared resources; and Artistic expression that unites us all. The group sponsors a Playwright Discovery Award, promotes apprenticeships at the Williamstown Theater Festival, and publishes a VSA Arts registry, a listing of visual, performing, and literary artists with disabilities.

For information on contacting a local affiliate, call 1-800-933-8721 or 202-737-0645 (TDD) or visit www.vsarts.org.

HOW THE UNIONS ARE HELPING

Actors' Equity, the American Federation of Television and Radio Artists, and the Screen Actors Guild have established committees to increase the visibility of professional performers with disabilities among casting directors and producers and to help create job opportunities.

As a result of the dedication and passion of such performers as Catherine Gaffigan and members of Equity's PWD Committee, the three unions published *Everything You Always Wanted to Know About Working with Performers with Disabilities but Were Afraid to Ask* and *Everything Production Needs to Know When Performers with Disabilities Are Hired*. These laminated cards, published in English and Spanish, are distributed to production companies, talent agents, casting offices, and other industry-related groups. The cards provide answers to frequently asked questions as well as such details as key contact numbers for arranging necessary accommodations. They help promote understanding that actors with disabilities can and do find work. You can access these resources at www.sag.org.

SAG also publishes *The Employment of Performers with Disabilities in the Entertainment Industry*, a summary of a study that SAG commissioned to create a comprehensive profile of the employment of SAG members with disabilities. SAG members describe their experiences and views about getting an audition, disclosing their disabilities, discussing the need for accommodation to an employer, treatment in the workplace, and perceived barriers to employment.

To prepare this study, the National Arts and Disability Center at UCLA held four focus groups in New York and Los Angeles and sent a mail survey to 1,237 SAG members who had identified themselves as having a disability or using adaptive equipment. One of the key findings was that SAG members with disabilities have extensive training and education. Twenty percent have a college degree in theater and approximately half are involved in a variety of professional experiences through other entertainment industry unions. Overall, the respondents believed that their prospects for employment were very limited and identified the three greatest barriers as: only being considered for disability-specific roles; a lack of acting jobs in general; and the difficulty of getting an audition.

Alternate formats of this report are available through the SAG Affirmative Action/Diversity Department. In Los Angeles, contact them at (323) 549-6644; in New York, (212) 827-1542; or visit www.sag.org.

THEATERS THAT MAKE A DIFFERENCE

The National Theatre Workshop of the Handicapped (NTWH) aspires to be the finest theater-arts training institution in the world for persons with physical disabilities. A nonprofit educational, production, and advocacy organization founded in 1977 by Brother Rick Curry, S.J., PhD, NTWH offers workshop classes, theater and community workshops and forums for dramatic literature on themes of disability. The group's mission is to challenge the exclusion of disabled students from existing theater programs by offering both academic and practical programs; create a theatrical arena in which disabled and able-bodied actors and playwrights collaborate, train, and perform together; and provide students with communication and job-training skills that empower them to contribute to their communities and increase earning potential. Campuses are located in New York City and Belfast, Maine.

Brother Rick was born in Philadelphia without his right hand and forearm. He always wanted to be an actor. In an interview with Rita Delfiner in the *New York Post* he said, "I once tried to audition for a mouthwash commercial, but never got past a receptionist who laughed when she saw my empty sleeve." That is when he decided to help other performers with disabilities, and he is constantly thinking of new ways to reach more people.

One of those ways is the NTWH Program for Wounded Warriors, a writing workshop for wounded warriors coming back from Iraq and Afghanistan, not only to teach a skill but to help them tap into their imagination as a resource to help with life's issues. Workshops are open to all physically disabled veterans and provide them with opportunities to transform their stories into dramatic monologues for the stage and screen, to meet and interact with other disabled combat veterans, to train with professional playwrights, and to develop invaluable writing and communication skills for future growth. Selected work is given a public performance and developed for readings. Scholarships are available for qualified applicants.

According to Brother Rick, the workshop is more of a class in confidence-boosting than acting. "I'm always looking for my next Gielgud," he told the *New York Post*, "but the skills are transferable in everyday life. Jesuits believe that theater skills empower the student through a 'perfection of eloquence.'" To learn more, go to www.ntwh.org.

Theater By The Blind (TBTB) was formed in 1979 as a sighted company recording plays for closed circuit broadcast to the blind over the In Touch Networks, an international reading service. This led to an acting class at the Jewish Guild for the Blind and, in 1981, the company's first integrated production, a revival of Neil Simon's *Barefoot in the Park*. In 1985, the company began staging plays for the general public under the Equity Showcase Code. At first Theater By The Blind concentrated on traditional plays that allowed the company's core actors to develop their craft. In the fall of 1991, they began writing original material revealing the world of the blind.

Once the company's new play and touring programs were in place, Theater By The Blind returned to working on traditional material. A "talking program" that describes the characters and setting and verbalizes essential stage directions makes their productions completely accessible to visually impaired audience members. After celebrating its twenty-fifth anniversary, the theater went on Actors' Equity's Letter of Agreement contract, making it an official Off-Broadway company, a major step toward the further recognition of their professionalism by The Business.

One reviewer said that, while watching a show, he stopped wondering who was and who wasn't blind after awhile and just enjoyed the performance. This was due to the way that the company integrates visually impaired and sighted performers seamlessly and uses behind-the-scenes techniques to facilitate the staging.

On the first day of rehearsals, actors are given versions of the script specifically created for them based on their degree of visual impairment. If actors can't see printed type, they use Braille scripts and/or tape recorders to learn their lines. Others with partial sight require scripts printed in large print. The rehearsal periods are a bit longer than those for sighted theater companies. This allows the performers extra time to familiarize themselves with the script and the stage set. Designers create stage environments that are helpful to the most visually impaired actors. In one production, the scenic designer built a tiny, almost invisible rim at the front edge of the stage. When the actors felt the rim, they knew that was where the playing space ended. Color plays an important role; high contrast color schemes are easier for partially sighted actors to make out.

In addition to main-stage productions, TBTB offers a fall reading series of four plays by disabled writers and/or using disabled artists as directors and actors. For more information, go to www.tbtb.org.

SOME ROLE MODELS

A freak accident several years ago crushed Lyena Strelkoff's spinal cord, paralyzing her from the waist down.

> The accident didn't rob me of my hands or my breath, and I'm independent in a wheelchair—all very important when it comes to my quality of life. I'd studied movement for thirty years. To dance was to be perfectly myself. It was therapy, church, recreation, and a workout rolled into one and full of joy. I'm also an actor, so being paralyzed didn't mean I'd have to give up my dreams. What I didn't imagine was how much being injured would help my career, nor how much being an artist would help me heal.
>
> Life with a disability is rich and varied, yet when was the last time you saw a "wheeler" in a TV commercial for anything other than wheelchairs? If I waited for the industry to wake up to my value, I'd be eighty before anyone hired me

Lyena started telling friends the complicated truth about her new life with an injury and she wrote down spiritual insights and anecdotes about the funnier side of the catastrophe.

> I took charge by nurturing this material into a full-length play, *Caterpillar Soup,* which opened a couple of years ago and has been playing, off and on, every since. I became an artist with something to say.

When she's not touring *Caterpillar Soup,* Lyena helps others craft one-person shows and dances in her wheelchair. Her work is available on video at www.lyenastrelkoff.org.

The extraordinarily gifted Peter Dinklage (*The Station Agent*) has brought his own stamp of uniqueness, vocal presence, imagination and intelligence to every role. He is one of very few little persons to make it to star status and his contribution has created more doors to be opened.

Robert David Hall's portrayal of Dr. Robbins on *CSI: Crime Scene Investigation* is a perfect example of a role where huge audiences see the character first, not the disability. Hall's performance proves that there is a broader range of characters that people with disabilities (PWDs) can play other than just disabled-specific characters. Casting director April Webster (*Alias* and *Lost*) picked him for the role when she cast the pilot. "When it came to *CSI*, we needed a person who spoke with authority. He seemed like a natural. I saw him as a talented performer, not as a disabled actor."

According to Mr. Hall, who lost both his legs in an automobile accident and serves as the National Chair of the Screen Actors Guild's Performers with Disabilities Committee,

> If you support diversity and think shows should give a portrayal of what America truly looks like, performers with disabilities must be included in that equation. I want to see a realistic rainbow. Let us show our talent, give us a chance to be something more than the bitter 'cripple' or the amazing disabled guy, which are the extremes. We are mothers, fathers, lovers, and professors. We are part of the story. There are fifty-six million of us in America—that's a huge minority.

THINKING OUTSIDE THE BOX

The hope for the future is that the American audience will eventually view a visual landscape that includes a more complete spectrum of actors. Sometimes, though, employment opportunities for PWDs can seem bleak. The National Theatre of the Deaf in West Hartford, Connecticut, and Deaf West Theatre in North Hollywood, California, for instance, were recently hard hit when the U.S. Department of Education cut 2 million dollars in federal grants to theater companies by and for the Deaf. William Morgan, the artistic director of Cleveland's Signstage Theatre, has said the lack of funding is due in part to lessening visibility of the importance of deaf companies. Many companies are finding that soliciting the aid of private donors and foundations is preferable to waiting for months to get money from the government. The National Endowment for the Arts makes every dollar stretch as far as it can.

The good news is, many casting directors are trying to convince their employers to use performers with disabilities for roles in episodic series, features, soap operas, and commercials. Sharon Bialy, CSA, award-winning casting director (*The Unit*, *Jericho*) says, "Support from the top is crucial," and a good example of that is Stephen Herek, director of *Mr. Holland's Opus*. He insisted on hiring Deaf actors for Deaf-specific roles.

Casting director Liz Oritz-Mackes, who once worked for the Non-Traditional Casting Project, says, "I will provide the opportunity if it makes sense. I use the SAG database on PWDs and I have my own files. I have attended productions at the Theater By The Blind, and I am friendly with several of the playwrights. In *I Believe in America*, starring Jamie Harris, I had to fight to use a Hispanic PWD who has spina bifida. I had met him when I was at NTCP and knew he was a brilliant actor. What a PWD shouldn't do is play the victim card. The person who is the best actor and most appropriate for the role deserves it."

West Coast–based talent agent Melissa Berger says she always tries to think outside the box.

> We have an actress named Shoshanna Stern who is hearing impaired and who had a recurring role on *Weeds* as the girlfriend of a series regular. She wanted to be considered for hearing roles. The first thing I did was call my friends in network positions. I contacted the director of casting at Paramount TV. Shoshanna was called in to read for a hearing role in the pilot of *Jericho.* She is able to speak and we often pitch her as a younger Marlee Matlin. Shoshanna was cast in a guest starring role and is now a series regular. The producers/writers had never conceived of the part as hearing impaired. They loved the idea of it once she came into the room and they loved her as an actress. There was something so very special about her. You have hearing impaired people in regular life, why couldn't you have one in a show?

John Frank Levey, casting director for *The West Wing* and *E.R.*, describes his philosophy as an industry professional in *Listening with an Open Eye*, published by the Non-Traditional Casting Project, Inc.

> When a role is Deaf-specific, I believe I have a responsibility to the producers, to the audience, and to the Deaf community to create authenticity. Calling in Deaf and hard-of-hearing actors also creates opportunity in the Deaf community. It doesn't guarantee employment, but it creates access which is very important to me.
>
> I have found that casting Deaf actors has affected the creative and production process in profound ways: all the hearing actors involved on the set and the crew went through an experience of communicating in ways they had not previously experienced. It created an awareness of others who are both like us and not like us. This heightened experience increased our passion for the project which translated into making the show better.

Irene Lewis, the artistic director of Center Stage in Baltimore, describes a relationship with Willy Conley (Deaf actor and playwright), who is also a Pew Fellow and an artistic associate. "Willy has had great patience with all of us here at Center Stage in trying to teach us about the world of deafness and Deaf culture. When I approach Willy about being in a show, he reads the scripts and then submits ideas about how best to use a deaf actor in it."

Kenneth Albers, actor/director with the Oregon Shakespeare Festival, gives the following account:

> During my thirty-plus years in the professional theater as an actor and director, some of my most memorable and fulfilling experiences have been those involving deaf artists and American Sign Language. My work began in Cleveland in the 1970s at what was then the Fairmount Theatre of the Deaf and is now Cleveland Signstage. I directed *The Glass Menagerie* and *Waiting for Godot.* Both of these maiden voyages into deaf culture filled me with a wonder for the theatricality of sign language and an unexpected respect for the education and training of the Deaf actors, who were not only able to grasp and understand complex concepts, but also translate them into another language and medium.

GETTING OUT THERE

PWDs are extremely passionate about mainstreaming in society and seeing those reflections on stage, on television, and in film. The performers who are hired are ready for the jobs. They have the necessary training, intelligence, experience, self-knowledge, self-esteem, and confidence in their talent. If this is the journey you choose, get together your photos, résumés, DVDs, and CDs for voice-over work, and network with organizations such as the National Theatre Workshop of the Handicapped, Theater By The Blind, or the National Theatre of the Deaf. Get involved with the PWD committees at the unions. Go to open calls, have a half dozen monologues at the ready. Do not be afraid to admit you have a disability; consider it one of your many attributes as an actor.

CHAPTER 12

Regional Markets

"I wanted to work nonstop and to do big parts, and it seemed to me that the best place to do that was in regional theater."

—Jayne Houdyshell, Tony nominee, *Well*

There is a life, potentially successful and rewarding, and opportunities to act outside of New York and Los Angeles. In addition to Chicago, which has become known as the "Third Coast"—thanks to its award-winning theaters, its status as a first-class production center for features and series, and a host of superstar alumni who launched their careers there—there are other cities where work may be more available, union cards more easily obtainable, and the quality of life more attractive.

This chapter will focus on the scene in Chicago, as well as Atlanta; Miami; Dallas; Washington, D.C.; San Francisco and the Bay Area; and Philadelphia. Each of these areas offers a rich cultural environment, shaped in no small part by the theatrical and commercial climates that exist there.

CHICAGO: THE CITY THAT WORKS

If you are intimidated by the hustle of New York City, if you don't have an agent or manager to open doors for you in Los Angeles, you might explore the opportunities that exist in Chicago. Early in their careers, the city was home to Joe Mantegna, Dennis Franz, David Schwimmer, Bill Petersen, John Malkovich, Gary Sinise, Joan Allen, John Mahoney, John and Joan

Cusack, Gillian Anderson, Jim Belushi, Dennis Farina, and Vince Vaughn.

No small part of the appeal of Chicago is the cost of living. Housing costs are far more affordable in Chicago than they are in New York or Los Angeles. A good-size studio rents for $600 a month; a share in a large three-bedroom can cost less than $600 a month for each roommate. The public transportation system is efficient, which saves you the expenses of owning a car.

According to Joan Cusack, a Chicago native who still calls the city home, "There are extremes on the coasts that are tough to live with, but staying here is definitely about wanting to have a normal life."

Chicago is probably the busiest market in the country for industrials, voice-overs, and commercials. For information about theatrical features being filmed in the Chicago area, visit the Web site of the Chicago Film Office at www.cityofchicago.org/ film. A division of the Mayor's Office of Special Events, the film office leads the city's efforts to attract and facilitate the making of feature films, television shows, commercials, and all other forms of film and video production.

Since 1980, more than 750 feature films and television productions have been made in Chicago, pumping 1.3 billion dollars into the local economy. Steady growth has made Chicago one of the most important and respected production centers in the country. Chicago's independent-film community is the fastest-growing segment of the city's entertainment industry. Fed by nationally recognized talent and a creative energy hard to match elsewhere, Chicago produces many films, and many of them are created by Chicagoans.

According to casting director Jane Alderman, "There is a loyalty to Chicago from the actors who have trained, worked, and lived there. They want to come back. They all love one another. Harold Ramis, who directed *Ice Harvest* starring [fellow Chicagoan] John Cusack, insisted on shooting here. Jane Anderson came here with *Normal*, her movie for HBO, and said she wasn't doing it unless she did it in Chicago. Vince Vaughn convinced Warner Brothers that the film *Fred Claus,* also starring Paul Giamatti as Santa, had to be shot in Chicago."

From the mid-1990s, Chicago's film industry did see a decline. Hollywood returned to the Windy City—and by extension to the state of Illinois—thanks to a new tax incentive that went into effect in January 2004. Since then, films like *Oceans Twelve, The Weatherman, Batman Begins*, and a remake of *The Amityville Horror* have helped create jobs and produce revenue in both city and state.

Starting a Career in Chicago

Many in The Business say there's no place like Chicago to launch an acting career. Casting director Jane Alderman believes that "actors choose Chicago to begin their careers because even though they are very talented and have been trained by the best, they have to start at the bottom. This isn't the magic place; it is hard getting work here, too. But here you can do it and actually practice what you have been taught."

Mattie Hawkinson says she was fortunate to make her living in Chicago as an actor and was one of a small group who was able to survive without another job. "If you want to be onstage and stretch and grow by playing meaty theater roles, you can get them in Chicago."

Mattie attended the acting program at Northwestern University, just outside Chicago in Evanston. In college she played mostly ingenues such as Antigone, and Cordelia in *King Lear*. Since graduating, she has had the opportunity to do more character roles.

> While I was at Northwestern, I went to London to a summer conservatory for American students. I worked with Mary Zimmerman, who is also a member of the Lookingglass Theatre. In 2003, I went to New York City with other Northwestern grads for the New Leagues auditions [held at NYU]. These were attended by casting directors, agents, and managers. I chose to stay in Chicago and got my Equity card right away with Steppenwolf. In *I Never Sang for My Father,* I got the role of the waitress because I could do the Irish dialect. I had this sort of romantic idea of Chicago theater, and it really hasn't disappointed.

Mattie went on to win an After Dark Award for her supporting role as a maid in David Mamet's *A Boston Marriage*. In addition to her work with Steppenwolf, she has performed at the prestigious Victory Gardens, the Chicago Shakespeare Theater, and the Lookingglass Theatre. She has since relocated to New York, where she is now part of the city's large Northwestern alumni network.

> Unlike New York agents, Chicago agents do everything and cover almost all the areas, actors can list with multiple agents and a few will sign exclusively with one agent or agency. Agents will pull heavily from the training programs in the area—DePaul, Columbia College,

Northwestern, Roosevelt. I got my agent after I did a mailing. They called me for an audition. I was freelancing until I signed with them. Another way to do it is to get a referral from a friend or invite an agent to see you perform. They will probably go to see your work.

New York casting directors come to Chicago constantly to find talent for a touring company or replacements for existing Broadway shows. They contact actors who've gotten their attention through the actors' agents or Actors' Equity. If a new production has received a lot of positive reviews, they will travel to Chicago to see it. Casting directors from Los Angeles also use Chicago as a "feeder" for sitcom talent (the city is home to the renowned Second City troupe and more than 100 improv companies)—to cast in comedy series or in TV-movies. Agent Bob Schroeder finds talent by attending the theater in Chicago, normally catching at least one show a week. "We meet actors who are recommended by casting directors, local ad agencies, or agents in smaller markets with whom we've maintained a relationship," he says. "Some actors are called to our attention by other actors."

The Unions in Chicago

Mattie Hawkinson describes Non-Equity theater in Chicago as "fantastic."

You can work all the time, playing great roles, and the casting directors respect it. If there is an Equity general audition coming through town and you are an Equity member, you can call the office and make an appointment. They have nice studios for auditioning, warm-up rooms where you can practice your monologues before you go in, and really nice monitors. Non-Equity actors are welcome to crash, knowing Equity members will always be taken first. They can sit in the same room as the members—not like in New York, where they have to stand out in the hall by the elevator

According to Linda Swenson at the AFTRA/SAG office in Chicago, there are 5,000 union performers in the city. Because AFTRA is an open union, you can just walk in and apply. There are no work requirements. The city's union branches offer payment plans for the initiation fee and dues. The AFTRA-SAG Conservatory holds various training programs and special-event workshops throughout the year.

The AFTRA/SAG office has successfully created the first resource center in the country designed to support an entire metropolitan community of professional actors. Since its inception in June 2001, the Kaufherr

Members Resource Center (KMRC) has logged more than 15,000 visits by local actors eager to take advantage of everything it has to offer. The KMRC's mission is to support professional actors in marketing their talent, honing their acting skills, and sustaining their resolve to earn their living at their craft. It offers all Chicago-area AFTRA/SAG and Equity members free access to a state-of-the-art audio studio; a video digital editing suite; computers, printers, a fax machine and a copier; and high-speed Internet.

Theater Groups

Chicago is also the home of the world-renowned Second City company and the professional birthplace of some of the best improv comedians and comedy writers in the country. More than 200 theater groups (both Actors' Equity and non-Equity) manage to survive in Chicago, and the Steppenwolf Theatre Company has really put the city on the theater-arts map by premiering new plays, some of which have won enough critical acclaim to move to Broadway.

Nathan Allen was one of eight graduates of Southern Methodist University who came to Chicago in 2001 to start a company called the House Theatre, an ensemble that works together to create new works of popular theater. According to Nathan, "the theatrical community here is competitive in a healthy way." On October 31, 2001, Nathan's play *Death and Harry Houdini* opened on the seventy-fourth anniversary of Houdini's demise. It received great reviews in the underground press and sold out for its entire six-week run. Thanks to the critical buzz, the artistic director of Chicago's Lookingglass Theatre contacted Nathan, said she had seen the show, and extended a huge welcome to his company. She gave them rehearsal space and arranged an introduction to Martha Lavey, the artistic director of Steppenwolf. She was also responsible for calling the critics of the *Chicago Tribune* and the *Chicago Sun-Times* to cover the House Theatre's second show, *The Terrible Tragedy of Peter Pan*, an adaptation of the classic.

Nathan recalls: "We put up the show in a bigger space, which we had rented in the off time during the summer. "This warehouse had no air conditioning, and it turned out to be the hottest summer Chicago had seen in fifteen years. We had floor fans and gave the audience popsicles. It didn't matter. On the poster it said, 'Wear shorts.' There was a considerable amount of combat in the show, and the actors were slipping on their own sweat. We used towels to swab the stage. We were just in the right place at the right time with a show that was good and fun and appealed to a young audience. Critics hailed us as the 'next big thing' and the 'next Steppenwolf.' The show ran for five months."

The Pine Box Theatre (www.pineboxtheatre.org) is dedicated to staging modern works that are age-appropriate for the twenty-somethings who are members of the company. Jane Alderman attends every one of the shows because, she says, "I am so fascinated with their talent and commitment."

The Pine Box was conceived in August 2004, by students who had attended the summer intensive program at the School at Steppenwolf. (In its tenth year, the School at Steppenwolf auditions 700 to 800 applicants annually and selects twenty-two.) According to Jonathan Edwards, one of Pine Box's founding members:

> Eleven of us started Pine Box. We wanted an excuse to work together again and thought it would be just one show. We felt it was one thing to be a part of a school program, and quite another to form a company. We might have driven each other nuts. Our first meeting was in January 2005. In May, we picked the show *Life and Limb* by Keith Reddin, after months of readings and planning and weeding out the tag-alongs. The show opened in January of 2006, and we were so proud of the results we decided to become a company. The critics were impressed with the production's 'beguiling performances' and 'earnest staging.' We didn't know about all the minor details of starting a company. We did get help from other people including our friends at Steppenwolf, but in particular from company actor Erin Wilson, who is a founding member of Trustus Theatre in Columbia, South Carolina.
>
> If you're coming to Chicago, you need to know you're not going to get rich and you're not going to get famous, but you will become better at your art. More so than anywhere else in the world. Staying in Chicago was the smartest decision I ever made. You can work one day job and afford to pay your rent and your bills and have time to do a show. And there's such a strong sense of community and support here. We will hear about an actor who has gotten sick with a kidney problem and can't afford the medical expenses and the whole theater community will have a benefit to raise money to pay the bills. In the future we will premiere a new play and connect it to a charitable group in the city. We'll give a donation and try to work with them as

much as possible. That makes us feel better and opens our minds to what is happening in the world, not just in the theater. I think once the element of fame and fortune is taken away, it makes everything a lot less cutthroat and competitive. Everyone backs everyone here.

Ethnic Theaters

Opportunities for ethnic performers abound in Chicago, as multicultural-ism has grown stronger and stronger in America. Steppenwolf, Goodman, and Victory Gardens are the leaders of Chicago's minority theater scene, providing space for ethnic-centered theater companies and using minor-ity playwrights, actors, and directors.

Hispanic actors can work at prestigious theaters such as Teatro Vis-ta (www.teatrovista.org), founded by actor-director Henry Godinez, who is currently an artistic associate at the Goodman Theatre but still serves on Teatro Vista's advisory board. In 1989, Godinez organized a group of Eq-uity and non-Equity actors who keenly felt the need for better representa-tion of Latino actors and playwrights. The mission of Teatro Vista—whose name means Theater with a View—is to share and celebrate the riches of Latino culture with all Chicago theater audiences. The company feels the answer to breaking down prejudice and stereotyping lies in understanding cultural differences.

After the terrorist attacks of September 11, 2001, Malik Gillani and Jamil Khoury felt galvanized to respond to the anti-Arab and anti-Muslim sentiment that swept the United States. They hoped to counter negative representations of Middle Eastern and Muslim peoples with representa-tions that were authentic, multifaceted, and grounded in genuine human experience. In the summer of 2002, the Silk Road Theater Project (www.srtp.org) opened to showcase playwrights of Asian, Middle Eastern, and Mediterranean backgrounds whose works are relevant to people whose origins trace back to the ancient caravan route called the Silk Road, an expanse stretching from China to Italy. The company, which also provides mentoring and professional opportunities to artists of Silk Road back-grounds, is Chicago's first-ever theater company dedicated to represent-ing such a diverse grouping of peoples and cultures.

The Congo Square Theatre Company (www.congosquaretheatre.org) produces high-quality theater inspired by multicultural diversity. The late Pulitzer Prize– and Tony Award–winning writer August Wilson was a longtime supporter of the company. After he saw their production of his play *The Piano Lesson,* he was "immediately impressed with the company's professionalism, its passion, and its high production values." The chief theater critic for the *Chicago Tribune* was so enthralled with the company's work that Martha Lavey, the artistic director of Steppenwolf, checked them out, and the company has done several collaborations with Steppenwolf using the larger company's mainstage and studio theaters. Since Congo Square opened with *The Piano Lesson* in 2000, they have produced nine other shows, all of which have met with artistic and critical acclaim.

The eta Creative Arts Foundation (www.etacreativearts.org), incorporated in April 1971, is recognized as one of Chicago's leading African-American cultural and performing-arts institutions. The group has gained a national and international reputation for the quality of its artistic product, management, volunteer leadership, and community involvement. Led by its cofounder and CEO, Abena Joan Brown, and its artistic director, Runako Jahi, eta has produced more than 180 mainstage productions of new works by black writers, of which 98 percent of them were world premieres. They have also produced more than fifty plays for children.

For more information about all 200 theaters in the Chicago metropolitan area, visit the League of Chicago Theatres at www.Chicagoplays.com.

Surviving in Chicago

Most actors in Chicago simply *must* have a survival job/strategy. There are quite a few temp agencies in the city that cater to actors, and many restaurants simply love them. Starbucks offers flexible hours and good benefits. As in any city, actors with technical skills such as Web site design should be able to find work that supports them. Nathan Allen has worked as a tour guide on the trolley that travels down Michigan Avenue. Because of his position as the artistic director of a young, respected theater company, he also receives a modest stipend to talk to college students about the ethics of the House Theatre. What often impresses these young people most is that Nathan has a lot of control over his life—professionally and in other areas. As he puts it, "If I'm going to starve, then I might as well be my own boss."

New York–based Robert Petkoff studied theater at the University of Illinois in Normal (known for the alums who began Steppenwolf Theatre). Upon graduation he moved to Chicago and lived there for more than two years, most of the time waiting on tables. He would make the rounds of the agents and every now and then snag an audition. But he felt uneasy without solid representation. One day, he reports, the agent he was targeting came to the restaurant with a well-known client and he waited on them.

> At the end of the lunch when they wanted the check, I said, "No, lunch is on me." When I was asked why I was doing that, I replied, "You are my agent, and I don't often get to take my agent to lunch." When the agent returned to her office, she told her staff to get me something, any audition they could find. The first thing was for a voice-over. I got it. They started sending me out commercially. I got cast in a non-Equity Shakespearean production at the Absolute Theatre, and it got a nice review in the *Chicago Tribune,* which prompted her to come to the show and sign me to an exclusive contract.

PerformInk

If there is a must-read resource for actors in Chicago, it is *PerformInk,* the city's biweekly entertainment trade paper. Chicago's actors pore over the paper to find casting calls. Casting directors will post open-call notices both in the paper and online at www.performink.com. Both the paper and the Web site are the primary sources actors in Chicago use to get information about auditions.

Theater news, theater business, and Chicago's industry personalities are just a few of the areas covered in each issue, and the articles affect the careers not only of performers but also directors, producers, designers, and filmmakers. Regular columns include "Money and Taxes"; "Comedy Bites," which surveys the improv landscape in Chicago; and "Out Takes," a behind-the-scenes look at independent filmmaking in Chicago.

PerformInk also periodically publishes revised editions of *The Book: An Actor's Guide to Chicago*, which contains updated information about the art of *living* as an actor in Chicago, as well as a directory of services and products utilized by film and theater professionals.

The Illinois Theater Association (ITA) holds annual auditions for more than sixty national and Illinois-based theaters (both resident and summer stock), talent agencies, and casting offices. Among the companies that have attended these auditions are the About Face Theatre, the Bailiwick Repertory Theatre, the Goodman Theatre, the Lookingglass Theatre, the Noble Fool Theatricals, the Steppenwolf Theatre Company, and the Victory Gardens Theater.

Applications for these auditions must be received by mid-February. The auditions are open to students currently enrolled in a college in Illinois, college students intending to move to Chicago after graduation, and non-Equity performers. A letter of recommendation from a faculty member or a professional in the dramatic arts is required. Aspiring actors have three minutes to present two contrasting monologues, or four minutes if they wish to add sixteen bars of a song. (The accompanist is provided.)

Visit www.iltheassoc.org to download an application, or contact the association by e-mail at iltheassoc@aol.com.

ATLANTA: A UNIQUE MARKET

Atlanta now boasts close to a hundred theaters, eight talent agencies, seventeen production companies, fifteen advertising agencies, and one major TV and film casting office.

Shay Bentley-Griffin, founder and CEO of the Atlanta-based Chez Group, has launched the careers of many nationally recognized actors who have been featured in soaps, films, and TV series. The Southeast's preeminent casting director is always encouraging producers to consider filming in the region and to use local talent for supporting roles. She has cast more than 225 television and feature film projects, including eight seasons of *In the Heat of the Night* and the Peabody Award–winning *I'll Fly Away*. She has also worked with such directors as the late Robert Altman, Clint Eastwood, Sam Raimi, Wes Craven, Jon Avnet, and Edward Zwick. A partial list of her credits includes *Remember the Titans*, *Sweet Home Alabama*, *Drum Line*, *The Diary of a Mad Black Woman*, *Madea's Family Reunion*, the CBS miniseries *Elvis* and the feature *We Are Marshall*. She has been nominated for three Emmys for the HBO Original features *A Lesson Before Dying* and *Miss Evers' Boys*, and for the HBO miniseries *Warm Springs*.

Currently Shay has a position with the Georgia Production Partnership, an organization of film industry leaders throughout the state who work to promote Georgia locally and nationally as a shooting location. She credits the partnership and other organizations with working hard to reviving the Georgia film industry, and points to their role in the passage of a tax-incentive bill "that enabled us to market Georgia more aggressively than we had been able to do." She also applauds the influence of Reuben Cannon and Tyler Perry, coexecutive producers of Tyler Perry Productions, who bought a studio in Atlanta and transformed it into a soundstage for their series *House of Payne* and *Meet the Browns*. There are plans to construct another major studio in the future. Tyler Perry's screen adaptation of his stage play *Diary of a Mad Black Woman* won five of seven awards for which it was nominated at the 2005 BET Comedy Awards. He has since filmed his second movie, *Madea's Family Reunion* (he created the character of Madea while touring the country and performing for black audiences), and *Daddy's Little Girls* premiered nationwide in 2007.

As a casting director, Shay is constantly searching for new talent and produces workshops and seminars to help actors learn their craft.

> There are a number of actors in the Southeast who can make a living. That is why I think we became a unique market. The fine talent who stayed here make up the creative backbone of the regional talent pool, and it began to affect Wilmington, North Carolina *[Dawson's Creek* and *One Tree Hill]*, and Charlotte, Orlando, and Nashville to some degree, so that in every one of these markets there are talented people as good as the talent anywhere else. Others, like Kyle Chandler *[Early Edition* and *Friday Night Lights]* went on to Los Angeles, but they left here extraordinarily well prepared.

Since the inception of the Georgia Film, Video, and Music Office in 1973, more than 500 major motion pictures and TV-movies have filmed on location in the state. In 2005, Georgia hosted 261 productions, including movies, TV series, commercials, and music videos, all of which added 145.6 million dollars to the state's economy. In 2006, the economic impact of film and television projects increased dramatically and generated more than 300 million dollars. For more information visit www.georgia.org.

The bulk of the work actors get is in radio spots, commercials, and industrial films, along with corporate video narration, audio training programs, and nonbroadcast industrial productions. Atlanta is home to the regional or national headquarters of 400 of the Fortune 500! Corporate giants such as Coca Cola, United Parcel Service, Holiday Inn, and Home Depot have their own in-house production facilities—with virtually unlimited budgets and a flair for cutting-edge creativity.

Because Georgia is a right-to-work state, actors don't have to join a union to work in the industry. Sandy DeLonga and Mark Oliver are actors who have been working and making a living in the Atlanta market for a number of years. Sandy is a member of Actors' Equity, and both of them are SAG eligible. But if they joined SAG, they would have to turn down the nonunion jobs that pay just as well. According to Mark, "A lot of clients don't want to have to deal with the paperwork that is attached to union jobs. The downside is there are no pension or health benefits. If we were in New York or Los Angeles, no question we would become union members. I am not anti-union. But given that Georgia is still a right-to-work state, I would be shooting myself in the foot."

Sandy and Mark say that new technology has enabled them to market themselves better, using Atlanta as a base for work around the country. They estimate that, like them, about 75 percent of the actors in Atlanta do their auditions from home. Mark says,

> Some of my out-of-state clients will call and say they want me to travel to Charlotte and audition for them. Instead I can put myself on tape, edit it down into a quick-time movie, and send it to them over the Internet. I save myself hours of driving time. To sell myself for a job as an industrial spokesman, I wear a suit. I use a remote switch when I put myself on camera.
>
> Voice-over has become fifty percent of my workload, and I can do that from home. It is the only reason I can do acting fulltime. Sandy and I go to a Web site called www.Voice123.com which is more like a casting service. Depending on your demographic and your type of voice, they will alert you to ten to fifteen auditions a day. You pick the ones that are right for you. Time is of the essence. You have to be right there by the computer.

All the World's a Stage

The Atlanta Coalition of Performing Arts (www.atlantaperforms.com) has twelve Equity theaters and eighty nonunion theaters. The non-Equity theaters will often hire Equity actors under Guest Artist contracts. There are quite a few black box and progressive theaters in Atlanta, which stage more edgy, often original works and give actors opportunities to sink their teeth into unique roles.

The Alliance Theatre at the Woodruff

Since 1968, the Tony Award–winning Alliance Theatre has been Atlanta's foremost theater, and it has become one of the leading regional theaters in America. The Alliance has produced more than forty world premieres, including an adaptation of Carson McCullers's *The Heart Is a Lonely Hunter,*

Pearl Cleage's *Blues for an Alabama Sky,* and the Tony Award–winning production of Alfred Uhry's *The Last Night of Ballyhoo.*

The Alliance Children's Theatre is one of the nation's oldest and most respected programs serving young people. Throughout the school year, Alliance professionals visit more than 150 classrooms at more than thirty-five Georgia schools. For more than twenty-five years, the Alliance has offered continuing education in stage, film, and television acting through its acting program. For more information visit www.alliancetheatre.org.

The Georgia Shakespeare Festival

Georgia Shakespeare, the second-largest professional theater in Georgia, is a vibrant and dynamic theater company with an ensemble of professional artists who create bold interpretations of the world's most compelling stories. The works of Shakespeare serve as the core inspiration for both their productions and their educational programming, in addition to classic works by such playwrights as Anton Chekhov, Arthur Miller, and Tennessee Williams.

Their season kicks off each Spring in midtown Atlanta with a week of free performances in Piedmont Park. They then move indoors to the Conant Performing Arts Center, where their mainstage season runs from June through November. The company's nationally respected education program reaches out statewide with summer programs in theater arts. They are on the Web at www.gashakespeare.org.

The New American Shakespeare Tavern

Home of the Atlanta Shakespeare Company , this unique theater mounts colorful productions in a publike atmosphere. Professional Atlanta-based performers can mail their headshots and résumés: Casting Director, The Shakespeare Tavern, 499 Peachtree Street NE, Atlanta, GA 30308. It is recommended that actors see a production there first to immerse themselves in the theater's philosophy and aesthetic. Audition notices are posted in April and May at www.ShakespeareTavern.com.

The True Colors Theatre Company

When artistic director Kenny Leon and managing director Jane Bishop teamed up in 2002 to design a new theater, they envisioned a smartly managed, inclusive theater company that would achieve both local and national impact. Their inaugural three-play season was launched in 2003, featuring works by August Wilson, Robert Harling, and Langston Hughes.

The name True Colors Theatre Company reflects the founders' promise to strive for truth and clarity. True Colors puts African-American classics at its core and branches out from there, producing the works of playwrights from various times and cultures.

Prior to founding True Colors, Kenny Leon served as artistic director of the Alliance Theatre Company for more than a decade and has directed at many prestigious regional theaters. The company's Web address is www.truecolorstheatrecompany.com.

Going South

There is affordable housing in the Atlanta area, but you must own a car and be prepared to suffer through long delays on the metro area's often congested roadways. Prominent casting directors from both coasts teach workshops and do talent searches in Atlanta for movies, pilots, and Broadway shows.

MIAMI: A MELTING POT

The Governor's Office of Film and Entertainment has created an enticing slogan to lure producers to shoot their films in Florida: "A Production Paradise from Every Angle" appears on specially designed postcards. There was a decline in film production in Florida a few years ago. Very active hurricane seasons didn't help the situation. Then things began to change. Luc Besson's *Transporter 2* and National *Lampoon's Pledge This!* used Miami as a location. So did Wes Craven's *Red Eye* and Michael Mann's film version of *Miami Vice.* Susan Seidelman's drama about retirees, *The Boynton Beach Bereavement Club,* wrapped in Palm Beach County. Director John Singleton *(2 Fast 2 Furious)* reported how impressed he was with Florida's melting-pot mixture of people from South America, Europe, and the Eastern seaboard. He also liked the flat, open expressways that were perfect for his film and the topography, which he believes is unique to Miami. Michael Bay, director of *Bad Boys II,* says, "The locations, the weather, and the lights are kind of interesting. Miami's got this sexy vibe. It's a melting pot. The city just has a lot to offer."

The Florida entertainment industry scored another coup when Fox Television's *Burn Notice*, a one-hour drama about a fired CIA spy using his training to help others in trouble, was picked up and began production in

Miami in the spring of 2007. For additional information on what productions are filming in Florida, visit the Governor's Office of Film and Entertainment at www.filminflorida.com.

Actors with film or TV aspirations should find Miami an ideal place to
get their start and perhaps their union cards. The Florida Branch and South
Region Office of SAG based in Miami has approximately 3,500 members and
is the fourth largest division in the nation. There are thirteen union talent
agents. Actors who can speak Spanish fluently have additional opportunities
to work in commercials and in the *telenovelas* that are filmed in Miami.

The Actors Info Booth

The Actors Info Booth (www.actorsinfobooth.com) was launched in 2001
and continues today under the guidance of Laura and Lisa Bunbury. They
have a passion for the film industry, both behind the scenes and in front of
the camera, and want to bring information, instruction, and tools to actors
in South Florida and beyond. Their mission is to help new actors learn how
to get started, keeping them away from the most common pitfalls, and
provide training that builds their confidence. Visit their Web site and click
on "Important Resources" to see a list of union and nonunion agents and
casting directors in South Florida plus links to the best photographers,
duplicators and industry-related organizations in the state.

The Theatre League of South Florida

The Theatre League of South Florida (www.theatreleague.net) is an alliance of theatrical organizations and professionals dedicated to nurturing
and promoting the growth and prestige of the South Florida theater industry. Members receive weekly e-mail "blasts," including audition notices for
member theaters. The League has more than fifty participating theaters,
and it provides contact information and a mailing list on its Web site.

Every year in early February the League holds Unified Auditions for
all of its members. In one day, actors will have the opportunity to audition
for up to fifty theater companies at once. Registration information, actor
application sheets, and audition tips from artistic directors at participating theaters can be accessed on the League's Web site.

The League's Unified Auditions are only for Equity members and
professional non-Equity actors who are currently members of the Theatre
League of South Florida. Participants must prepare a sixty-second mono-

logue of their choice. They also have the option of singing sixteen bars of a song following their monologue. With so little time to audition, Rafael De Acha, executive artistic director of the New Theatre in Coral Gables, advises actors "to jump on it like onto a moving train."

DALLAS: A STRONG TALENT POOL

Dallas is an extremely good market for a young person just getting out of school who needs to build a résumé. Independent films offer actors with a range of experience a chance to stretch their creative muscles and start building their DVD reels. The largest sources of income are commercials, voice-overs, and industrials, and the amount of television and film work generally enables newcomers to get their union cards. There is a growing volume of Spanish language work and Texas is becoming a major player in the worlds of animation and video game production, providing recording and motion picture work for talent. Many local performers dub Japanese anime at production companies in Houston and Dallas.

There are fifteen franchised agents and a dozen casting offices in the state of Texas, and the Governor's Office for Film and Television has always made an aggressive effort to encourage studio heads to use the state's talent and technical resources. The Texas Motion Picture Alliance is working to pass incentive legislation that should make the state more competitive regionally and nationally, and the Fox series *Prison Break* and the NBC series *Friday Night Lights* are shot in Texas, in Dallas/Fort Worth and Austin, respectively.

Linda Dowell, executive director of the Screen Actors Guild for Dallas/Forth Worth and Houston, says, "Performers often stay in Texas for quality-of-life reasons. Some performers grow their chops before taking the leap to New York or Hollywood. Others return here seeking a more peaceful lifestyle."

The theater market really depends on your type, experience and how you promote yourself. The boldness of the Dallas theater scene is remarkable. Artistic directors will tackle the most difficult and controversial plays. You can volunteer at the midrange union houses and possibly end up on their stage at a later date.

Actors' Equity maintains an actors' hotline for its members; all actors can contact the Society for Theatrical Artists' Guidance and Enhancement (S.T.A.G.E). Founded in 1981, S.T.A.G.E is a nonprofit organization that provides service and support to the theatrical and film communities of the north central Texas region, offering classes, studio space, and updates on the local acting scene. For more information visit www.stage-online.org.

AustinActors.net is run by actors helping actors. The site lists resources for theaters, agents, coaches, and industry-related organizations in the Austin area. *The Biz Directory* and *The Biz Interviews* are two widely respected and critically praised resources produced by Mona Lee. *The Biz Directory* lists phone numbers, street addresses, e-mail addresses, and Web sites vital to those who want to pursue an acting career in Texas. The *Biz Interviews* contains revealing discussions with top casting directors and talent agents who offer career and marketing advice.

WASHINGTON, D.C.: A THEATRICAL CAPITAL

There are more than fifty active theaters in the D.C. region, not only in the capital proper but in suburban communities such as Arlington, Fairfax, and Alexandria in Virginia; and Columbia, Bethesda, and Olney in Maryland. In 1984, when the Helen Hayes Awards were created to increase an awareness of the D.C. theater community and celebrate the excellence of its productions, fewer than half that number of theaters were open for business. Washington has a large community of actors who live and work in the city or nearby suburbs. Altogether, theaters and theater artists have contributed to the economic vitality of the Washington metropolitan area, and to the enhancement of the region's quality of life.

Four times a year *Curtain Up: The Guide to What's Playing in Washington Theaters* publishes current production schedules. The periodical is also responsible for announcing the Helen Hayes Award nominees for achievements in local theater. The Helen Hayes Web site, www.helenhayes.org, is a valuable reference source for actors as well as the theater-going public. The site provides information on theaters and their schedules, which you can navigate by week, month, or specific date, as well as a directory of Washington theater companies, with direct links to each theater's Web site.

Looking at the evolution of theater in Washington, Zelda Fichandler, founder of Arena Stage, maintains that "Washington has become one large company that works in a number of theaters instead of a [small] company that works in one theater."

You might want to subscribe, for a nominal annual charge, to *Washington Theater Review* (www.washingtontheater.com). Published by Betsy

Karmin and Manny Strauss, this quarterly includes well-written features on the movers and shakers in the Washington theater scene—actors, directors, playwrights, artistic directors—and interviews with the likes of Robert Prosky, Avery Brooks, Christine Baranski, and Zelda Fichandler, who have contributed their talents to the vibrant theatrical scene in Washington, D.C..

The League of Washington Theatres

The League of Washington Theatres (www.lowt.org) is an association of non-profit professional theaters and related organizations in the greater Washington metro area. (The word "professional" connotes that actors and principal staff members are compensated on a regular basis.) The League was established in 1982 to create greater public awareness of, and appreciation for, theater in the Washington, D.C., area. Prior to becoming a League member, a theater must have produced and/or presented a minimum of sixteen public performances annually in the Washington area for three consecutive years and have achieved sufficient organizational ability, staffing consistency, and size to ensure full participation in League activities.

One of the League's major ongoing activities is its annual area-wide auditions, held over a five-day period each June or July. For information contact info@lowt.org.

One Actor's Odyssey

Broadway actor Joey Sorge earned a B.A from the University of Maryland in College Park, which is just north of the nation's capital. He started his acting career in the D.C. area and got cast in *Spiele 36,* about the 1936 Olympics in Berlin, at the First Amendment, a small professional theater based at George Mason University in Fairfax, Virginia.

> That is how I started earning my AEA points: through a TV show called *In Our Lives,* fifteen-minute stories that dealt with teenage issues. It aired Saturdays on the local CBS affiliate, and I got my AFTRA card. I then started doing jobs that were performance-related. I worked at the National Portrait Gallery at the Smithsonian in an outreach program that went to nursing homes. We would perform forty-five-minute musicals about the portraits, which could be George Gershwin, Irving Berlin, or Lerner and Loewe. I kept doing performance-related temp jobs and didn't have to wait on tables. I got my AEA card at Ford's Theatre appearing in *Christmas Carol.*

I realized that as an AEA actor in the D.C. market, why would they hire me when they could hire the college kid for half the price? I was always haunted by New York. Everyone comes down here from there. The joke was that to get a job in New York you had to go to New York to get a job in D.C. I started taking the train up to New York for specific auditions I found in *Back Stage.* Finally I auditioned for a production of *Forever Plaid,* got a callback with sixty other guys, figured I didn't have a chance, and returned to D.C. The director called me at home, gave me some tips, and I got the role. Once I finished the run I had finally gotten "in the loop.

As we've said more than once, actors who work in theater need to find a day job to survive. Joey Sorge was savvy enough to find performance-related temp gigs that kept his skills finely tuned. As Joey's breakthrough strategy—riding Amtrak to Broadway—suggests, a big upside to living in the D.C. area is that it's easy and affordable to get to and from New York for auditions in a day.

SAN FRANCISCO AND THE BAY AREA

The San Francisco Bay Area is the third-largest theater center in the country, with more than 400 companies in eleven counties. It is also home to the third-largest community of Equity actors, trailing only New York City and Chicago. Some 200 plays are premiered in the region each year. Theatre Bay Area (TBA) was founded in 1976 to serve this vital artistic community (www.theatrebayarea.org). Its current membership consists of more than 365 Bay Area theater and dance companies, from multimillion-dollar organizations to grass-roots community groups. Some 3,000 individuals, including actors, directors, designers, playwrights, and technicians, call these companies their professional home.

Theatre Bay Area, a monthly magazine, is the region's central source for information on the theater community, while TBA's Web site (www.theatrebayarea.org) contains one of the most comprehensive local theater listings anywhere. It also lists numerous grant programs for emerging theater companies and local theater artists, and it is a voice of advocacy for the theater and dance communities on the local, state, and national levels.

When you become a member of TBA, you can access the latest audition and job notices and post your headshot and résumé in their online Talent Bank. You'll learn about discounted ticket offers and get a subscription to the magazine, as well as the opportunity to apply for the annual Theatre Bay Area General Auditions, where actors can be seen by more than eighty theaters and numerous casting directors. Other membership benefits include discounts to monthly workshops, seminars, and professional networking events.

Bayareacasting.com has been creating a connection between actors and filmmakers since 1993. Actor and teacher Hester Schell bought The Business from the founder in 1996, and by 2000 her decision to get rid of the old owner's hard-copy publication led to the creation of the first online audition resource in the Bay Area. She sees San Francisco as a stepping stone where actors can make mistakes, learn their chops on the set, and build a reel, necessary if actors are going to Los Angeles. In her own words,

> San Francisco has always been home to great artists, and there is a huge creative energy driving the city forward. If I were a budding director or producer, I'd come here for the wealth of talent willing to work for "copy, credit, meals, festival exposure." If I were a budding actor, I'd come here for experience, to build a reel from actual film projects, to get into some film festivals with all these low-budget indies, and to get all my marketing tools ready for prime time.

Comedy clubs are very big in the area as are sketch groups and one-person shows. The Marsh Theatre supports solo work. Brian Copeland's *Not a Genuine Black Man*, which concerns racism in the '70s when he was growing up in Oakland and San Leandro, was a huge hit for a couple of years at The Marsh, and it went to New York for a run Off-Broadway. After seeing a tape of the show, Carl Reiner forwarded it to his son Rob Reiner, who was so taken by the material he agreed to back it as a potential television series. There are tax incentives in place to bring more film production to San Francisco. The Film Commission Web site has more information about recent tax breaks.

As a base of operations, San Francisco is only a short flight from Los Angeles. It is also a welcoming community for anyone who wants to start a career. According to Hester Schell, "Being an actor in San Francisco is a lifestyle choice." You won't find as much work or compensation as you would in the major markets but even so, many extraordinarily talented singer-actors in San Francisco are happy to work for the sheer joy of it. The energy is similar to that in New York, and young actors will gladly work on new plays in lofts, small black box theaters, or a friend's apartment, because they need to release and stretch their creative muscles. This type of theatrical fervor "in the air" enables the talent pool in the Bay Area to grow and stretch and get ready for the bigger ponds down the road.

PHILADELPHIA ON THE RISE

In a *Variety* article titled "Pa. Has Got a Brand New Bag," writer Carole Horst reported that Pennsylvania saw an opportunity a few years ago to stand out from the crowd of states lining up to attract TV and film production. Sharon Pinkenson, executive director of the Greater Philadephia Film Office, was frustrated that "we were losing Philadelphia stories to Toronto." With the help of the mayor, the governor, and key lawmakers, the state legislature passed a tax-incentive package for film producers in 2004.

The fact that M. Night Shaymalan always shoots in Pennsylvania was the initiative's best advertisement. Director Jonathan Demme is also a fan of the state. Hitting major film festivals and making connections with filmmakers is standard operating procedure for state and city film offices, but there was a new, upbeat, almost evangelical attitude about how Pennsylvania started selling itself. How do Philadelphia and Pennsylvania make good on their pitch? Pinkenson says, "The answer is to provide services on a level that no one else can provide. If you come to Philadelphia, you're getting access to a free government-owned soundstage, free police service, free production office . . . you can't beat the service, and this is all about repeat business."

Since 1992, the Greater Philadelphia Film Office has facilitated the production of more than 200 films and TV shows, so that Philly is now considered a "movie town." Some of the feature films produced in the city in recent years include *Rocky Balboa*, *The Book of Caleb*, and *Charlotte's Web*. New York ad agencies have discovered that it is cheaper to shoot in the Philadelphia area. And local independent filmmakers are making more low-budget films now than ever before. The train to New York (for headshots or auditions) takes about ninety minutes. Meanwhile, Philadelphia's theater community continues to attract playwrights, directors, and trained actors to its own turf.

Michael Lemon has been casting in the Philadelphia area for more than twenty years. A former actor, he clearly admires and respects talent and empathizes with any performer's bumpy ride through the ups and downs of The Business. As he says, "Discovering new talent, finding the right actor for every role, helping hardworking actors get breaks they've earned, and helping filmmakers tell their stories through the talent I've submitted, are some of the real joys of this work." Michael is committed to providing his clients with the best talent in the most effective way, which for him means using the Agency Pro online software program in which actors enter all of their information and scan in a current head shot. Lemon charges no registration fee but he does charge actors an *activation* fee.

If talent is interested in principal work, staffers from Mike Lemon's office will evaluate them at the monthly open call held the first Wednesday of every month from 2:00 P.M. to 4:00 P.M. For this audition, they have to prepare a one-to-two-minute monologue from a published play or screenplay. Actors with professional representation can ask their agents to arrange an appointment time on another day. For more information visit www.mikelemoncasting.com.

Participants in the Theatre Alliance of Greater Philadelphia's annual auditions must live within a 50-mile radius of Philadelphia's city center. Actors who qualify are given three minutes to showcase themselves for more than 100 theater professionals, including local agents, casting directors, and representatives from Alliance members, including 1812 Productions, the Arden Theatre Company, the Delaware Theatre Company, the Philadelphia Theatre Company, the Prince Music Theater, the Walnut Street Theatre, and the Wilma Theater.

The Theatre Alliance also hosts an audition workshop, where applicants meet with area casting directors, and its Web site features the Philly Talent Database, containing the résumés of actors and behind-the-scenes personnel from throughout the Philadelphia area. Check www.theatrealliance.org/auditions for updates on auditions as well as an excellent list of audition tips.

FILM COMMISSIONS

As you must surely realize by now, feature films, made-for-TV movies, television series, industrial films, and even ten-second commercials are being produced all over the country. These productions can mean a huge revenue stream for the locations in which they're shot. To alert producers to the scenic, atmospheric, and financial advantages of choosing their area as a location for a film or TV series, every state government has at least one and sometimes a few film commission offices. The Association of Film Commissions International (AFCI) has more than 180 members. Go to their Web site, www.afci.org, click on a state or a country, and discover how each place promotes its locales, crews, talent pools, and the advantages for filming there. While there are many other factors you'll be weighing when you decide where to start your career, it can't hurt to know which states and cities are selling themselves more effectively than others—it may translate to more work for *you*.

We have profiled key markets in this country you might consider living in to build your résumé, connect with movers and shakers, establish your professional network, and get yourself prepared for moving to the major leagues in New York and Los Angeles. Wherever you decide to set up housekeeping, dedicate yourself first to forging a productive career in that regional market, and to joining the ever-growing, ever-changing population of working actors who create the vibrant theater and film communities that exist there. Remember that talent does not come from any specific region—talent simply *is*.

PART TWO

THE BREAKS

CHAPTER 13

Finding a Vehicle to Showcase Your Talent

"We wanted to do something where we could create our own work. We cast ourselves in roles that would challenge us."

—Randi Berry, co-artistic director, Wreckio Ensemble

Whether you're doing a showcase, performing a one-person show, or creating your own theater company, as an actor you can find just the right vehicle in which you can express your creativity.

THE SHOWCASE

"Call me or send me a postcard when you're in something. I need to see your work!" Actors hear this mantra from agents and casting directors every day. Then comes the warning, "But, please don't invite me to a turkey."

Makes you stop and think, doesn't it? It's supposed to. No matter how wonderful you think you are going to be in a showcase, keep in mind that the casting directors and agents you invite to see your work will also be watching the possibly mediocre-to-dreadful performances of your fellow cast members. If you stand out because you have no competition, reconsider inviting anyone to see you.

A showcase can be a great opportunity, giving you a chance to do a short, two-to-three minute monologue or other scene for an invited audience that can help your career. But if your instincts tell you in the first days of rehearsal that a showcase is not going to be a rewarding experience, do yourself a favor: Get out of it. There is no stigma, no blot on your record, no punishment for trusting yourself and making the right career move—all the more so since you're not getting any financial compensation for a showcase. In fact, appearing in a showcase can cost you money: Somebody—and that's often you, as a performer who wants to show off your talent—has to pay for the theater rental, the rehearsal space, possibly for the director, and certainly for the publicity and program materials.

On the other hand, when your fellow performers seem as energetic and talented as you, and the material has obvious entertainment value, don't hesitate. Give it your best. The rehearsal period and limited number of performances of a showcase (usually ten to twelve should be an enjoyable, challenging growth process that opens doors to opportunities for paying jobs in the future. You want all aspects to be of professional quality.

For starters, make sure that the producer and director guarantee advance publicity, and that invitations or flyers are available at least four weeks prior to opening night. The program should contain your brief biography and contact information (a number for your agent or your business phone number or Web site or e-mail address). If the cast prefers not to have numbers printed in a program that's given to the public, management should see to it that casting directors and agents receive a contact sheet containing this information. Some showcases provide packets of pictures and résumés for industry VIPs; some have sign-in books for these guests, so cast members can follow up by sending them a note along with their pictures and résumés.

- To ensure a good impression, pay attention to packaging and direction.
- Be sure you appear confident.
- Select a scene to which you feel connected. You might even write your own material.
- Select roles to play that are age-appropriate and realistic for your physical type.
- If your director is inept, reblock the scene and enlist the aid of a "third eye" you respect.
- Choose your wardrobe carefully. It should suit the character you are playing.
- Wear clothing that flatters your shape and fits well.
- Wear actor-friendly colors and wardrobe components (see Chapter Two, "Getting Your Act Together").

- Don't run the gamut of emotions in your ten minutes. It's not truthful.
- Be sure your scene partner is as good as you are.
- If you have a gift for comedy, use it.
- Avoid scenes by Gorky, Chekhov, Strindberg, Ibsen ("Oh, no, not another *Hedda Gabler*!") and the popular American playwrights whose works have been overexposed.

Actors as Showcase Entrepreneurs

The better showcase theaters are listed in the Arts and Entertainment sections of your Sunday papers, and in *New York* and Los Angeles magazines and on their Web sites. *Time Out New York* lists showcases and, if the entertainment calendar isn't full that week, sometimes carries a brief review. You'll also find showcases listed on the theater Web site www.playbill. com. Attend performances at theaters whose choice of material strikes a responsive chord. You may be able to open some doors by volunteering to work as an usher, in the office, or behind the scenes.

A number of groups, such as the New York Musical Theatre Festival, sponsor staged readings of new works, which do not require a lot of rehearsal time. They are performed only once, possibly for potential backers. The playwright gets a chance to hear his or her words and discover where revisions are necessary. If the play moves from there to a production, you may have a chance of reprising your role. The hit of the 2005 NYMT Festival was *[title of show]*, by Hunter Bell and Jeff Bowen. The ninety-minute musical went on to a run at the Vineyard Theatre, with the original cast, and won an Obie Award.

Actors on both coasts have discovered that if they raise the money to rent a space and finance publicity and refreshments, they can be their own "Angels" for a showcase evening of scenes. Having control of the casting process ensures that the players will share a similar level of experience and professionalism. You lessen the possibility of being placed on the program after three boring scenes and losing any member of that valuable industry audience.

The format practically guarantees industry attendance: in a ninety-minute program, talent seekers can view the work of twenty actors. A bit of wine and cheese before the show will let them feel at ease. The advantage to the actors is that everyone is in the spotlight, doing a well-chosen scene, for about the same amount of time—there are no bit parts.

Having discovered that the excitement and the challenge of producing a sparkling evening of scenes were more creatively fulfilling than performing in them, a number of actors have gone on to become i showcase producers.

JOINING A COMPANY

Actors who move to a new location find that, after they've settled themselves, what they need next is a theater home, a place where people speak the same "language." As actress Suzanne Friedline says, "For me, finding a home was the most important thing. A place where I could work my craft, do fully produced, quality theater, and be seen by industry professionals. I went to see a production at Actors Co-op."

Actors Co-op

Founded in 1987 by a dozen actors in Los Angeles, Actors Co-op is a dues-paying membership company. The company now numbers about seventy professional performers. The company is primarily interested in classic American theater and has been the recipient of 125 DramaLogue Awards, five Drama Critics Circle Awards, an *LA Weekly* Award, and an award for sustained achievement in a smaller theater. Actors Co-op holds auditions for admittance to the ensemble. Photos and résumés are accepted year round. For more information, contact Actors Co-op, 1760 North Gower Street, Hollywood, CA 90028; www.actorsco-op.org.

The Road Theatre Company

Taylor Gilbert had done a great deal of work in San Francisco, to much acclaim, and then realized she wasn't interested in fame. In 1991 she became one of the founders of the Road Theatre Company in Los Angeles, of which she is now artistic director.

> I felt it was more important to create a company, where we could work as an ensemble and produce whatever we wanted to produce," she says. "We are interested in the plays, the theater, new works. Part of our mission is to create future American classics.

The Road Theatre is known for presenting cutting-edge work, such as a recent play, *Bunbury*, by Tom Jacobson. Bunbury, the nonexistent, but much talked-about character in Oscar Wilde's *The Importance of Being Earnest*, finds out he's an off-stage character and can't believe it. He joins up with Rosaline, of *Romeo and Juliet*, also a nonexistent character, and they travel through time on a quest to bring all off-stage characters to life. *Bunbury* has won a slew of awards: for best production, best author, best original play, best ensemble cast, and best direction, as well as best sound, lighting, sets, and costumes.

Actors talk about the "wow" factor at the Road, which in a relatively short time has earned a reputation as a solid company that consistently produces excellent shows. The company accepts photos and résumés from actors year round and holds open auditions twice a year, listed in *Back Stage West*. "Part of our mission," according to Taylor Gilbert, "is to create future American classics," and the theater accepts submissions from writers. For more information, go to the Web site www.roadtheatre.org.

New York Theatre Workshop

This innovative company recently celebrated its twenty-fifth anniversary, a rare event for an Off-Broadway theater company. This longevity is all the more noteworthy given the fact that the company survived the after-effects of 9/11, which were financially devastating to the Lower Manhattan neighborhood where the theater is located.

NYTW's Associate Artistic Director Linda S. Chapman, a former member of the Wooster Group, and Artistic Director James C. Nicola, the longtime casting director at New York's Public Theater and artistic associate at Washington's Arena Stage, put the emphasis on ensemble work and development. "No deadlines, more process time to develop a work," says Linda.

> Rent was four years in development. *El Conquistador* was in germination for six years, and our Pirandello piece, which we called *Kaos,* was in progress for ten years. We work on a lot of projects on an ongoing basis and when the 'cream rises to the top,' we produce as much of it as we can. Our subscribers know that we do unpredictable work. I think that's what they like about the Workshop. You may not like everything, but the variety of work is wide and they appreciate it for one reason or another.

NYTW goes to Vassar College in Poughkeepsie, New York, for two weeks every summer to work on projects that are in early development. The company then goes to Dartmouth College in Hanover, New Hampshire, for three weeks in August, where they put on performances.

> We look for ways to encourage actors to use themselves as material."
>
> "Lisa Kron is a good example. *Well* was originally a one-person piece. She developed it into a full-character play that went to Broadway,

where it was nominated for many awards. I think actors too often take what comes. I think universities should be more demanding that actors create their own vehicles. That gets them to read, to explore, to find interesting things to work on. And a part they can play for years.

Works developed at New York Theatre Workshop are seen on stages throughout the city and around the world. For more information, go to www.nytw.org. By the way, volunteer ushers get to see NYTW's challenging work for free.

Rep Stage

Less than a year after Michael Stebbins took over as artistic director of Rep Stage, a small, professional theater in Columbia, Maryland, his productions were making it into the "best" lists on the Baltimore and Washington, D.C. theater scenes. Shakespeare's *Hamlet,* the musical *Tintypes,* the one-person comedy *Fully Committed,* and the comedy *Stones in His Pockets*—all produced by Rep Stage in the same season—were among the top ten money makers in the theater's fourteen-year history.

Michael Stebbins never had the desire to do anything but be in the theater. "I was an actor first. Only after graduate school did I delve into other aspects of theater. While working with Walt Witcover and his Masterworks Laboratory Theatre in New York I acted, then stage managed and also directed. Then I started my own not-for-profit company, Stage Door Acting Ensemble of New York."

Rep Stage's revenue depends on subscriptions, contributions, and grants. The company is on an aggressive campaign to increase all three.

A new artistic director brings a certain taste to the table. I also consider the tastes of our demographic, the variety of people who I'd like to get into our seats as well as the people we currently have in our seats. I look at programming a season as a recipe. We want to have a great menu to offer. Not all trendy foods. Not all exotic dishes. Longtime subscribers thanked me for putting on a musical. I want to give our audiences a chance to see something here which they might have little chance of seeing unless they get up to New York. And always, I am considering the budgetary parameters.

Rep Stage is a "professional school in residence," on the campus of Howard Community College. There are three theaters: the Smith Theatre seats 400, the black box can seat 200, and the recital hall, which is used for play readings, holds 125. The season runs from September to May. The Rep Stage Summer Institute, for teens and pre-teens, runs from June through August. For more information, visit www.repstage.org.

STARTING YOUR OWN THEATER COMPANY

When theater is their great passion, some artists need to do more than perform on stage in other people's plays. They need to do it all. The vehicle for them is a theater of their own, to communicate their philosophy, their feelings, as only theater can.

Rachel Reiner says she wanted to do theater from the day she was born. "I know that sounds strange, but it's true," she says. She acted in plays in elementary school, but found working behind the scenes more enjoyable. In high school she directed plays—*and* did the publicity and programs *and* sold tickets. "That was fun. Besides, no one else wanted to do that. I was very valuable. I carved out a niche for myself."

Rachel went to Brandeis University, where she walked into the theater and never left for three and a half years. She produced eleven shows— plays, musicals. She loved it! While other students went abroad between their junior and senior years, Rachel applied for and was awarded two internships on Broadway.

> I can tell you that an internship is the best way to get your foot in the door, whether you're an actor or on the production side. You learn The Business from the inside out and make connections. Even if you're not interested in being a general manager or a company manager or a producer, you'll understand when you talk to those people what their business is, what they do all day.

While in New York, Rachel worked two days a week at Pace Theatricals (now Live Nation). Her boss was the executive in charge of mounting *Jekyll and Hyde*.

> I was able to read all the contracts, sit in on the general manager's meeting, and attend auditions. The other three days I worked at Richard Frankel Productions as an intern on *Smokey Joe's Café*. They were launching the London and Australia companies, so there was a lot to do and learn. The experiences during those internships and the recommendations I received led me to my first position at the League of American Producers.

In addition to her position as director of development programs at the League, Rachel is the founding producer of Rachel Reiner Productions and the managing director of a nonprofit company, Resonance Ensemble, which has a unique mission. "We do new plays that are inspired by classic plays," Rachel explains. "We run them in repertory. You can watch both of them and see the universality of the plays. We're doing a world premiere of a new play by Charles Mee, *The Mail Order Bride*, in repertory with Molière's *The Imaginary Invalid*. We also do workshops and readings, and are always searching for new playwrights and actors. I love it. We are all passionate about our work. You have to feed your creativity."

Rachel says that there is a lot someone interested in starting a small theater company in New York City can do: Join ART/NY. Visit the Foundation Center (on Fifth Avenue and 16th Street in Manhattan). Apply for the Nancy Quinn Grant. Apply for New York State Council On The Arts (NYSCA) funding. Take the CTI (Commercial Theater Institute) course, which was created by a working actor, the late Frederic Vogel. Read the programs of nonprofit shows you attend and see who is giving grants to these companies.

Looking back, Rachel recalls:

> "I was very tall, and the boys laughed at me. My mother said, 'People come in all shapes and sizes and do all kinds of things and you can do and be whatever you want.' I feel tremendously fortunate that I had such moral support." She has one regret. "For years I never read *Variety, BackStage,* the *New York Times.* That was foolish, I could have learned so much more about The Business and how things happened!"

The Looking Glass Theatre

"Reflecting life on the stage with truth and theatricality while exploring a female vision." That is the mission statement of Looking Glass Theatre, ensconced in a cheery space a few steps below street level on Manhattan's far West Side at 422 West 57th Street. It's a school by day, a theater in the evening. "That was the solution to our money problem," says artistic director and founder, Justine Lambert. "It's a multiple-use space."

> All of our plays are by women, or directed by women, and they deliver what I call a woman's sensibility. I have long felt that women in theater needed to find their voices. They are exciting, the search is exciting.

A graduate of the Neighborhood Playhouse, Justine studied with the legendary Sanford Meisner.

> He was failing, a little bit, but he was passionate and didn't let you

get away with anything! A wonderful teacher. Before the Playhouse, I attended Edward R. Murrow High School in Brooklyn, which had a great theater and language department. I did lots of acting there, and I enjoyed it. My stepfather was an actor, and whenever he was in a show he took us to the theater, and backstage, which I loved. So, early on, I felt very comfortable in the theater.

Justine got a job as assistant to a director at the East 13th Street Theatre, sitting next to him at rehearsals and taking his notes. "I did that for two years. It gave me a new way of looking at acting. I realized I was thinking his notes before he whispered them to me. I was becoming very detail-oriented."

That experience led to more opportunities on the directing/teaching side, at a time when women weren't doing such things. With her husband, Justine produced summer programs of children's classics outdoors in Central Park. "We didn't have to pay for the space. We were creating our own work. I felt liberated."

Her career evolved into directing and producing original work.

> I also mentor directors. We analyze what works, what doesn't, and why. Everyone needs an outside eye. That we offer a women's perspective I think comes from the sexism I have seen throughout my career and about which I had to be silent. An example: A crew was building a set. I saw something that needed to be changed. I spoke to them. They nodded, "yeah, yeah," and went on with what they were doing. I asked my second husband, Ken Nowell, who is a director, to make the same suggestion. They quickly did exactly what he told them.

Justine admits it's been a struggle, but the theater moves forward. "Receiving an award from the League of Professional Theater Women has done a great deal to raise our stature," she says. "Our next show is a female view of *Hamlet*. A woman meets her father's ghost . . . and what does she do?" The Looking Glass Theatre, www.lookingglasstheatrenyc.com, accepts manuscripts, photos, and résumés.

Urban Stages

> When Frances Hill was acting in California, she never dreamed that she'd be an artistic director and the founder of a theater in New York.
>
> "I must tell you that I just fell into it. "I decided that as an actress, I was never in control of my work. After each job it was like

starting all over again. So, like many actresses, I decided to write. Someone who had a theater in Boston wanted to produce a play that I wrote. And I said, 'Let's start one in New York.' It was that simple. I loved using both sides of my brain. After the first year or so we took a play by Jim Lehrer that I had directed to the Kennedy Center. Suddenly, we were launched and had a following."

In addition to mounting plays at its Manhattan theater, Urban Stages runs Adopt-a-Library, which conducts theater arts programs in libraries throughout New York City. Adopt-a-Library recently taught more than 200 hours of theater arts classes at the Harlem Day Charter School. At Urban Stages' Summer Theatre Camp, children from ages nine to fourteen spend five weeks with professional theater artists, learning dance, acting, and improvisation, which enables them to create their own shows. The children have produced musical fairy tales and their own interpretations of historic events. Urban Stages' New Play Development Program presents readings at the Mercantile Library

"Doing what I love to do is a great victory," says Frances. "It's exciting to see each play come alive on the stage with the combined talents of all the artists involved. I've enjoyed working with various playwrights, seeing them develop their work to greater heights, and have it move to larger stages. I believe theater does have the power to change people's lives." Urban Stages, www.urbanstages.org, has an open submission policy; they read about 500 plays a year. Their theater is at 259 West 30th Street in Manhattan.

The Cherry Lane Theatre and the Mentor Project

The Cherry Lane is New York's oldest, continuously running Off-Broadway theater. It is located in a red brick building at 38 Commerce Street in Greenwich Village, and has been a landmark on the city's cultural landscape since it was established in 1924. The late 1940s, the golden age of theater in New York, saw a production of *The Dog Beneath the Skin*, by W. H. Auden and Christopher Isherwood. In the cast were the gifted actor Gene Saks, who later became one of the theater's most successful directors, and Bea Arthur, making her stage debut in a career that would include award-winning performances in *Mame* and *Golden Girls.* Cherry Lane's production of *No Exit,* by Jean-Paul Sartre, was possibly the first presentation of the play in America.

New owner and producing artistic director Angelina Fiordellisi has reorganized the Cherry Lane as a not-for-profit theater company that focuses on the playwright as central to theatrical excellence and innovation. "I had been working with the New Harmony Project and the Carnegie Mellon Showcase of New Plays," she explains, "developing new plays in two-week workshops. I loved it. I was more interested in that work than in acting, which is where I started."

When a local zoning board wouldn't allow Angelina to build a barn that would serve as a theater next to the family house in upstate New York, she went to look at the Cherry Lane, which was then for sale.

> I did something really crazy. I bought it. I felt there were spirits calling me to do my work here. It's where I was meant to be. We practically rebuilt it, and then I created a resident nonprofit theater company. I took the best of New Harmony and Carnegie Mellon programs and expanded our development program into our Mentor Project. We had to start out very small. We couldn't have open submissions with only three or four people to read thousands of scripts. I formed a nominating committee of theater professionals from around the country—directors of regional theaters, literary managers, artistic directors—who would submit three new plays every year. Pamela Perrell, program director for the Mentor Project, and I read through the submissions, pick the best fifteen to twenty plays, and send them to the mentors. They make the final selection.

Mentors include such award-winning playwrights as Lynn Nottage, Jules Feiffer, and Michael Weller. The process begins with a private reading of the play. Then the mentor and playwright go off to discuss the play and how they might improve it. Each January, the theater does readings before the public, to get audience reaction and input, then in the spring stages a full production. According to Angelina, "By the time we are done, the playwright either has a finished play or a much stronger draft to send out to potential agents and/or producers."

Other successful programs at the Cherry Lane celebrate women playwrights and black playwrights. A late-night program presents unique pieces on Thursday, Friday, and Saturday evenings.

"Between our Mentor Project and our late-night programming, I think I have the youngest audiences in New York," Angelina says. "None of this would be happening if it wasn't for my managing director, James King. I have none of his skills. He has made a world of difference."

To learn more about Cherry Lane programs, go to www.cherrylanetheatre.org.

The Wreckio Ensemble

"For our first venture, all we could afford was a tiny room in the lobby of the Gershwin Hotel, which sat thirty-five, maybe forty people. We packed it!"

—Randi Berry, co-artistic director, Wreckio Ensemble

Randi Berry began thinking about starting a theater company when she was training at New World School of the Arts in Miami. The ability to create your own one-person show in senior year has motivated several grads to start their own companies. Patrice Bailey, Dean of Theater at New World School of the Arts, strongly believes that assigning seniors to create their own one-person shows encourages their writing, directing, acting, and producing abilities and gives them a vehicle they can use during their professional careers.

Randi is now co-artistic director of Wreckio Ensemble in New York. Their first production was an adoptation of Peer Oynt. "We continue to find inspiration in the movement training that we got at New World," she says. "At New World they really nurture the rehearsal process. So when we can afford it, we have a really long rehearsal, a good experimental process at the table and in the room before we produce anything."

Randi and her co-artistic directors and writers hope for a grant or a large donation, so the company can one day pay them. "We are all very driven and excited and passionate. "There are days that are tough. When you do eighteen-hour days, you get tired. But you hope that the drive and the passion that we share in performing will help us do the work each day."

THE ONE-PERSON SHOW

Over the years, on stage and on television, we have seen famous players perform one-person shows: Hal Holbrook as Mark Twain (which he reportedly created as his senior class project at Northwestern University), Jean Stapleton as Eleanor Roosevelt, Laurence Luckinbill as Lyndon Johnson, Billy Dee Williams as Paul Robeson, Tovah Feldshuh as Golda Meir.

Lynn Redgrave wrote her one-person play, *Shakespeare for My Father*, as a tribute to her father, Sir Michael Redgrave (and also to resolve her intricate, often frustrating relationship with the renowned British actor). The show, originally presented for a limited run at the Helen Hayes

Theatre in New York, garnered ecstatic reviews, played 272 performances, and earned Ms. Redgrave a Tony Award nomination, a Drama Desk nomination, and the Elliott Norton Award.

Why do top-level performers venture onto a stage to work alone? For the same reason we encourage you to do it: They want a vehicle that will exhibit their talent. And for well-known players the reward is frequently the same one that you yearn for: They attract lots of favorable attention to themselves, people come to see their work, talk about how good it is, and the phone starts to ring.

Christopher Plummer's solo performance as John Barrymore relaunched his career as one of Broadway's matinee idols. A generation of new young casting people who probably had never seen him perform was exposed to his magnetism on stage.

Jefferson Mays's performance in *I Am My Own Wife*, for which he won a Tony Award, vaulted him to stardom. In *At Liberty*, Elaine Stritch rejuvenated her career by telling the story of her life, in ninety minutes, first at the Public Theater and then, by popular demand, in a Broadway house.

The list of possible subjects is endless. At Primary Stages in New York, Casey Childs presented Amy Irving in *Safe Harbor for Elizabeth*, playwright Marta Góes's exploration of the life of Pulitzer Prize–winning poet Elizabeth Bishop. The story is set against the background of Brazilian politics in the mid-twentieth century. Production values—including authentic costumes and memorabilia that had belonged to Elizabeth Bishop—made this a very successful solo piece.

Actor, playwright, director, author, agent, and producer James Brochu and his partner Steve Schalchin won an Ovation award for the musical they cowrote and starred in, *The Big Voice: God or Merman?* Now, Brochu has written and performs in *Zero Hour*, a two-hour-long solo play about an actor considered by many to have been among the greatest of the twentieth century, Zero Mostel.

Luke Yankee has performed his one-man show *Diva Dish!* on tour and around the country for the past several years. The son of award-winning Broadway and film actress Eileen Heckart, he tells of growing up amid Hollywood legends. Marilyn Monroe was sometime his babysitter, Paul Newman gave acting tips in his parents' living room, and Ethel Merman taught him how to make martinis. *Diva Dish!* inspired his book, *Just Outside the Spotlight: Growing up with Eileen Heckart*.

Susan Claassen, artistic director of the Invisible Theatre in Tucson, found her subject on the History Channel. She had done one-person shows, including *Shirley Valentine,* and assisted other people creating one-person shows. She was watching *Biography* one night and saw the story of Edith Head.

I had known of Edith Head from the movies, and I love clothes and I love style, but I never knew about her. She was tenacious. She spent forty-four years at Paramount, then when the studios were breaking up, she navigated her way to Universal, and stayed there for the last fourteen years of her life. No other woman, no other designer had such longevity. The story had never been done. She'd left her estate to the Motion Picture and TV Fund. I contacted them. They loved the idea.

Then I found Paddy Calistro, who wrote the book *Edith Head's Hollywood.* She was living in Santa Monica. I said, 'I run a little theater in Arizona, I'm thinking of doing a piece on Ms. Head. Can we talk?' She said, "Sure." I flew over. When we met, she said it was like déjà vu, because I do look just like Edith Head. Collaborating was great. Paddy is loved in the film community, so all these doors opened. The Motion Picture Academy loved it because Edith left all of her papers and her eight Oscars there. Bob Mackie had been her sketch artist, so he was wonderful, and Art Linkletter did his own voice-over for the show!

It took close to two years before Susan was ready for the first reading. The challenge was to come up with the format. How to portray the story? How to inject conflict? How to keep the narration from becoming a list? Susan and Paddy managed to solve all the scenario problems, Carol Calkins was called in to direct, and *Sketches: Edith Head's Hollywood,* was launched. Bookings followed almost immediately. They had a smash hit. Then, an amazing thing happened: Susan and Edith Head were invited to appear at the International Theatre Festival in Georgia—Russia, that is, in the town of Tbilisi. "It was the grandest experience," she recalls. "The festival was so supportive. I taught three master classes at the university. The Georgian people are so passionate about their art. There were two other Americans, plus companies from Spain, Italy, Azerbaijan, all over. Each night we'd all go out and toast each other. All these different countries. See what the arts can do? We are that bridge."

You may not open on Broadway or Off-Broadway, or in Tbilisi, Georgia, but there are many outlets for one-person vehicles. Lecture bureaus and agents for concert attractions book such programs for universities, community organizations, and corporate events. Getting your program together may take time, but the effort is worth it if you achieve creative freedom.

CHAPTER 14

Interview and Follow-up

"I prefer people to be at peace with themselves, comfortable and personable. A good disposition helps in this business."

—Marilynn Scott Murphy, talent agent, Professional Artists, New York City

Before you get a chance to work on a stage or in a studio, you will need to succeed at two other kinds of performances: the interview, which we'll discuss in this chapter, and the audition, which we'll discuss in Chapter Fifteen. Interviews and auditions are inescapable realities of the industry. Or at least they will be until you become so well known that the mere mention of your name as a candidate for a role triggers an instant "Oh yes, just the one we were thinking of." And even at *that* level you may still be invited to "take a meeting."

The interview gives you a chance to be seen by agents, casting directors, and managers, all of whom can help you. Remember that these people aren't sitting at the entryway to the industry, like Roman emperors in the arena, waiting to give you an immediate thumbs-up or thumbs-down. They won't throw you to the lions. They may well want you to be their next big star, someone whom they can guide, develop, and nurture on the way to that first big break. They are on your side, and they will respond positively to actors who have a strong sense of self, an inner warmth, and an engaging, appealing personality that makes it easy for them to establish rapport.

This is why "good" interviews are critical to building a career as a performer, and why you must learn to think of them in the proper light—in a way that reduces your stress level at the very moment when you most need to be "on" and impressive. You also have to learn practical techniques that will help you interview well. For a few rare performers, good interviews just seem to happen naturally; but most actors need to learn a solid set of interview skills.

REDUCING STRESS

But not everyone sees interviews as opportunities. Many actors are so nervous and insecure about being "judged" by the buyers and sellers of talent that when they sit down with, say, a potential agent or a network casting executive, they perspire; they don't focus attentively on the agent's questions; and they answer in monosyllables—none of which inspires confidence for the interviewer. With time and enough interviews, such extreme displays of nerves may disappear—but how many opportunities will you have lost by then? If you are going to be unsure with an agent, who is trying to make you feel comfortable, odds are you'll be at least as nervous— probably more nervous—when you meet with auditioners.

PREPARING FOR YOUR INTERVIEW

Do you remember how, as a teenager, you would prepare for a party where you expected to meet Mr. or Miss McDreamy? How you went about getting that unsuspecting person to ask you for a first date? Remember the determination, the research? Was he interested in football? You learned who Joe Montana was, and reminded yourself not to call him Joe Mantegna. Or vice versa. Did she like classical music? You happened to have tickets for a Yo-Yo Ma concert. And before the grand occasion, all the time spent planning what to wear, how to look—which earrings, lipstick, nail polish; aftershave, cologne, the right shirt and tie. Recall the excitement, the pent-up energy, the expectation. The electricity! The adrenaline rush! Bring that concentration, that fervor and anticipation, to your preparation for your interview.

Find out as much as you can about the person you are going to meet. Your scene partner, your roommates, or an acting teacher may be able to give you a clue. You can go to the Internet and research the person on such sites as www.imdb.com. Many talent agents have their own Web sites. Interviews in *Back Stage* often feature prime-time, soap opera, theater, and commercial casting directors. The actors' unions will often have seminars or panel discussions featuring casting directors and agents.

Organizations like New York Women in Film and Television (NYWIFT) or Women in Film (WIF) also sponsor special events featuring agents and casting directors who represent or cast actors working in films.

For example, a few years ago, the talent agent Margaret Emory was on a NYWIFT panel at Marymount College in New York City that featured guests who developed and promoted actors' careers. She said that to her, "Talent is the primary aphrodisiac in the romance between agent and actor." How inspiring it was for the actors in that audience to hear her say those words. The way she delivered them, her personality, her wit, her intelligence, revealed her credibility and integrity and gave her listeners genuine insight about her as a person.

It's always useful to take a positive approach in your interview. If your research reveals that an agent has a preference for Yale grads, you might turn it to your advantage by saying, "I think Yale has produced some superb actors, writers, and directors. I wish I'd had the chance to go there."

Rehearse what you are going to say about yourself, but keep it relevant. Don't launch into a speech about everything you've done since you were in your sixth-grade play or your kindergarten pageant. Don't go on about how well you work with children and animals. Practice will put you at ease when interviewers pose routine questions like "Well, what have you been doing?" or "Tell me about yourself" or "How did you enjoy working with the director at the Such-and-Such Theater?" or "What is your favorite role?" Since such questions invariably come up in an interview, being able to answer them well will give you a big edge in making a good impression.

A Tool for Self-Knowledge

We've created this questionnaire to help you think on your feet at an interview or audition. Do this exercise, and you won't freeze when the most basic questions are hurled at you.

Name: _____

Age Range :_____**Height:** _____ **Hair:** _____ **Eyes:** _____
Training(Acting,Singing,Dancing):_____
_____
_____
_____
Education : _____

_____

_____

_____

Skills: _____

_____

_____

Sports: _____

_____

_____

Hobbies: _____

_____

_____

Favorite Color: _____ **Least Favorite Color:** _____

Favorite Actor: _____

_____

Favorite Actress: _____

_____

Your Favorite Role: _____

_____

Type of role you'd like to play (villain, bitch, hero, heroine, lawyer, blue collar worker, etc.) _____

_____

_____

Name a fictional character on prime-time or daytime TV you identify with and why: _____

_____

_____

What screen role would you like to play and why?

_____

_____

_____

_____

After completing the questionnaire, practice talking it through as if you were delivering a monologue about yourself. Try to do it in sixty seconds. Even in this compressed time frame, try to squeeze in some humor. Watch the speed of your delivery, and don't let the sixty-second time limit make you swallow your words. Ar-tic-u-late! Watch your vocal inflections. End your sentences with periods, not with question marks. (You know, like this?) Avoid fillers such as *uh, like, y'know.* And don't forget to breathe.

Make yourself credible. Show passion and commitment. You'll sound wishy-washy if you lard sentences with "I think," or "I guess," or "I'm not sure but. . . " Look at your face in the mirror when you mention your least favorite color. What you're seeing is how passionately your face reacts to something you do not like. (Orange, yellow, and puke green are the most likely to get unfavorable reactions.)

Know your age range. And know what the term means: It's about the ages of the characters you're able to play believably (as in, "I am still believable from late teens to early twenties"). You will be asked over and over in this business how old you are. Remember that the U.S. Department of Labor and the talent unions have strict rules about age discrimination. Know your age range, and keep it realistic—within no more than five years, in either direction, of your chronological age.

Don't stray from the subject at hand. Actors have a tendency to share more of their life stories than asked for. We call that TMI Syndrome, for "Too Much Information." Stick to answering the questions, be concise, and have a definite point of view. Don't come across as being defensive about your opinions. They are yours and unique to you, so be proud of them. You are an actor, and you should have opinions about who thrills you as an actor or actress. You should also be familiar with the mediums that you want to work in, and have a feeling for the roles you could realistically play.

With all this information about your background on the tip of your tongue you'll be able to listen and to answer the basic questions intelligently, and let your interviewers see your engaging personality.

Dressing for the Interview

We have discussed the professional closet for men and women in Chapter Two, "Getting Your Act Together." Clothing for your interviews should always flatter you and be appropriate for The Business. Have a checklist that tells you at a glance whether your clothing needs to be cleaned, buttons need to be changed or sewn, spots removed, or creases pressed. What you wear, as an ensemble or as coordinated separates, will say something about how you see yourself: upscale; sophisticated and stylish; middle-

American; down home; outdoorsy; suburban; unpretentious; comfortable with yourself and others. Pay attention to programs and commercials. See where you fit into the array of types portrayed on TV. Remember that you're packaging the real you. What you present to your interviewers is your essential self and how you want them to remember you.

What Not to Wear to the Interview: Ladies

- Sheer or shiny clothing
- Slip dresses, lace camisoles, or anything that looks like it came out of the bedroom
- Skirts higher than two inches about the knee
- Distracting prints like gaudy florals, polka dots, leopard prints and other animal motifs
- A plunging neckline
- Excessive or noisy jewelry
- Stiletto heels (no heel over two inches) or thick, clunky heels
- Sandals, or ankle-strap or open-toe shoes
- Brightly colored or patterned hosiery
- Heavy makeup, wild hairstyles, unnatural hair colors
- Long or chipped nails, dark nail colors, patterned nails; invest in a manicure
- Tops that expose the midriff

What Not to Wear at the Interview: Ladies and Gents

- Caps or hats of any kind
- T-shirts or sweatshirts, with or without logos
- Worn-down heels, scuffed shoes
- Tattoos or body piercings that are visible
- Overflowing bags, backpacks
- Neon or extremely bright, upstaging colors near the face
- Excessive perfume, cologne, or aftershave

In addition, men should not appear at the interview with facial stubble or unkempt hair.

What to Keep in Mind Before Your Interview

Practice shaking hands. A handshake is the very first thing that happens when you're making that critical first impression—and this commonplace gesture can be problematic. We've all shaken hands with a vibrant, healthy person whose handshake felt a dying fish, and we've all had to stifle a wince while shaking hands with a bone-crusher.

If your hands tend to be cold when you're under stress, go to the restroom and put them under warm water before you're introduced. If nervousness makes them moist, carry a handkerchief and dry them before you go into the agent's or casting director's office.

Plan your day so you have plenty of time to arrive for your interview and, once you're there, to relax, comb your hair, check your face, and so forth. Factor in transportation delays and leave early. In New York or Chicago, always allow for the possibility that your train will get stuck between stations. Allow for crowded, slow-moving buses and gridlock. In Los Angeles, you'll almost surely be driving to your appointment—and we don't need to caution you about the city's slow-moving traffic.

If you are fortunate enough to have several appointments on the same day, make every effort to allow sufficient time between them. You may end up waiting for an agent who is on a conference call, or a casting director might ask you to stay longer than you expected to read or meet the executive producer of the show. You cannot concentrate on an interview if you are worried about being late for your next appointment.

Finally, even though we have the Internet to thank for electronic submissions and sending photos by e-mail, always bring a supply of hard-copy photos with your résumé attached. And always have a couple of your voice-over CDs and DVD reels with you in case the interviewer wants to listen to your voice work or look at samples of what you have done after you've gone. Be prepared to perform a dramatic or comedic monologue and perhaps sing a song, and always have several choices ready that you can offer the interviewer. Talent agent Marilyn Scott Murphy prefers to see a monologue that lasts about two minutes, and she believes that you should choose characters you would realistically play, "to give me an indication of what you are right for. Stretching is for the classroom, not for an audition."

WHEN YOU GET THERE

Actress and teacher Caryn West conducts classes in interview skills. She is most emphatic about your entrance into the office.

Every door has a threshold. You have to be very cautious crossing it.

A lot of people hold their breath walking into the room, and when you hold your breath, your fears build. So first let's breathe, and second let's have a mantra that says, "I am here to be a great collaborator," or, "I am here to meet new people and have a joyful experience." Whatever you bring in is what you are going to attract. If you are coming in with "It is such a hassle today," that is what you will attract.

I advise people, when they're in the waiting room, to breathe and concentrate on what they want to happen in the office. A lot of us practice our fear, worrying about what will happen—"I'll forget my lines" or "She won't like me." You have to project what you want to happen. Thoughts make things [happen].

You have crossed the threshold in a relaxed, confident manner. Look around. Notice the paintings, photographs, posters, framed prints, collectibles, the color scheme in the office. Get a feel for the atmosphere. Is it muted and dusty or full of light and verve? Are the phones ringing? How are they answered? Do you sense an attitude of respect? Civility? Are the people there happy? Pressured, intense, exhausted? Would you want these people to represent you? That decision is always mutual.

During the interview, the agent will explain his or her areas of activity and where he or she sees your greatest potential. A big question is always "How do you see yourself?"

Filling out our questionnaire earlier in this chapter, and rehearsing your responses, should prepare you to answer that question without missing a beat. Actress Roberta Reardon once met with an agent who asked her that very question, and she realized she hadn't really thought about it. But Roberta is blessed with an ability to think fast on her feet.

I said, "Well, actually let's say there is a Tide commercial and there are two women. I'm the one who knows how to get the stain out. I'm never confused." And he started laughing and said, "You're right." I was never an ingenue. I had a lot of authority. He began to work with me, and that was the beginning of my career.

Know which "you" is walking in the door. I know that when you're young, it really is about having twenty people inside of you: Which one is going to come out today? But you have to figure that out if you are meeting a commercial agent.

Then one part of your preparation should be to watch television and find five commercials that you know you are right for. If you list some types you saw on commercials, it tells the agent two things: that you are paying attention to your career and that you know yourself.

The very best thing that can happen, and what everyone hopes for, is the equivalent of love at first sight. Your originality, dynamism, and talent will wow the first agent you meet, who will introduce you to everyone in the office and immediately telephone a casting director, who will agree to see you right way. That's possible, but it rarely happens.

If the agent can't visualize you in any of the projects he or she is working on, you will be ushered out with the standard line, "Keep in touch."

Between those extremes are lines such as "Let me know when you are doing something. I want to see your work," or "It's been nice meeting you, give my regards to so-and-so" (the person who suggested you contact this colleague). That adds up to keeping in touch, which is exactly what you must do. No one will say to you, "Are you out of your mind? Go back to Allentown, you don't belong in this business!"

Don't give up. You may discover that an actor you knew in college is now a casting assistant at an ad agency or a soap opera or a network office. At the end of the day, note all of this in your journal, record book, or the organizational software that helps keep your career on track.

Meeting a Casting Director

If good fortune shines on you, your interview with an agent will lead to a meeting with a casting director. Do your homework before any meeting you have with a casting director. If you are meeting with a CBS casting executive, be familiar with the shows on that network. A feature casting director will be impressed if you are aware of the films he or she has cast. A major faux pas occurs when the actor auditioning for an ABC soap opera tells the casting director her favorite soap is *The Young and the Restless,* which airs on CBS. There is no excuse for not knowing who casts the programs you feel a connection with. We've already mentioned the resources that give a listing of the shows and who casts them, but they're worth repeating: *Ross Reports Television* and *Henderson's Casting Directors Guide.*

It's doubtful that any casting director will ask you to audition using your prepared material. They will want to see how you handle the scripts they are currently working on. For commercials, a generic piece of copy will be given to you, and you'll have little preparation time—which you shouldn't need anyway. A product pitch is usually copy that doesn't take more than sixty seconds to say, usually in a natural, energetic manner. For soaps, the casting director may hand you a two- or three-page scene and schedule you to come back a couple of days later. Or, rather than give you copy, a casting director may put you on tape and ask you questions about yourself. The questionnaire on page 273–274 will help you "nail" this on-camera interview.

If you're meeting with the casting director of a prime-time series, be sure you've watched at least one or two episodes so that you are familiar with the narrative and the types who are cast in the show.

Get into the habit of paying attention to the opening and final credits of films and dramatic shows. Movies, episodic series, and TV-movies always credit casting directors as well as writers and directors. Go to www.imdb.com to find out more about casting directors' other credits and their backgrounds. Then, when you meet someone like Matthew Barry, you can congratulate him on the fabulous casting job he did for *The Notebook*. You might say, "Ryan Gosling and Rachel McAdams had such great chemistry!" Which they did.

Try not to shoot yourself in the foot, like the actor who wanted to make an impression on a well-known director and went on at length about how much he had enjoyed a particular film that the fellow had directed. Then he added, "I'm so sorry that I was one of the few people who saw it." That director's interest in the actor quickly faded.

Handling Your Exit

Most interviews last no more than ten or fifteen minutes. Don't overstay your welcome. Make a graceful exit. And when you say thank you, say it with sincerity and feeling. You really should be grateful for getting a chance to advance your career. Just like your entrance, your exit is pivotal. You can greatly dilute—or even destroy—the positive impression you've made during the interview by making an awkward exit. Just as you did when you walked in, show confidence when you leave. Make eye contact. Smile. Sometimes the casting director may ask you to send in the next actor. Let them him or her know that you are only too happy to oblige. A simple "Sure thing . . . and thanks again," spoken with confidence and in an upbeat tone, will do the trick. You have had a "joyful experience." You want to be invited back for another visit.

Handling Emergencies

Despite all your careful preparations, the unexpected can happen. Emergencies occur: Your wallet may be lost or stolen; a pipe bursts in your bathroom, you sprain an ankle, you've got strep throat or the flu. You may get a flat tire and find yourself stranded on the highway. You forgot to charge your cell phone, and can't call for help or contact the talent agency or casting office to say you will be late. Don't panic. You are not missing the only opportunity of a lifetime. Do the best you can. As soon as you are able to, call to reschedule your appointment. Stuff happens. That is part of the human condition. Remember that casting directors and talent agents and managers also suffer through temporary crises.

What makes no sense is to get up from your sickbed and head for the office with your box of tissues, or hobble in on crutches. A casting director can't tell anything about you, let alone your work, when you're unable to move gracefully, when your eyes keep tearing, or when you're sneezing and spraying the office with your germs.

Emergencies occur on the other side as well. The interviewer's baby may be sick, there may be a casting crisis requiring that an actor be replaced immediately, an agent's incoming flight may be canceled due to severe weather, or the agent may be called out of town unexpectedly. It's a disappointment to the actor, of course, but such is life in The Business. When either you or the agent is under the weather or under duress, meeting at a future date would surely be more productive—and you'll be able to make a better impression.

THE FOLLOW-UP

Shortly after the meeting, a brief nice-to-have-met-you note is in order. Mention whether you've followed any suggestions or advice the agent or casting director may have offered. Thank them for being so generous with their time and attention, and say you look forward to seeing them again.

Be sure that if you do get involved in a showcase, or an Off-Off-Broadway production, or a musical revue, or a staged reading, you send them an invitation. Always let them know when you are "in something." Put together an imaginative flier. Nowadays, you can create such a promotional piece on your own computer.

Every few weeks, send the agent or casting director a photo postcard with news about what you are doing to grow as an actor and generate work for yourself: taking a class; attending a seminar; getting better headshots; learning a language or how to play the piano; improving your voice; or taking a course in sign language. And, of course, let them know when you get a paying job in The Business, when they can see you "in something."

Your assignment as a working actor is to keep in touch, regularly, pleasantly, respectfully, and with the understanding that establishing yourself in anyone's mind is going to require a bit of time. You are building a relationship. Be patient and persevere.

"TOM JONES" ADAPTED BY JOHN MORRISON STARS SCHUYLER YANCEY AS TOM AND JENNY STRASSBURG AS SOPHIA FROM JULY 20 - AUGUST 5.

FOR DETAILS CONTACT info@dorsettheatrefestival.com

Dorset's very own John Morrison brings the lustful, rollicking romance of Fielding's novel to the stage. Join Tom, Sophia, Squire Western, Molly, Lady Bellaston and all the rest. A theatrical experience you will never forget!

Henry Downey Talent Management: 212-459-4545

Auditions and Screen Tests

Auditions are performances. They are your chance to show, in however many minutes you may be allotted, what you can do with a particular piece of material. Directors want to see where your basic instincts will take you, that you are prepared, and that you can show them an original and inventive interpretation that is organic to the character.

As we've noted before, the vast majority of directors *want* you to be good and to succeed. They also want you to be yourself. Rob Marshall, the director of the features *Memoirs of a Geisha* and *Chicago*, looks for "someone who is passionate about what they do and lets themselves out. They don't try to be something else because they're enough." That is a great reminder about the type of mantra you should be repeating before every interview or audition: "I am enough. I have enough. I want to share it." Be secure within yourself.

Lynn Redgrave recalls her audition to get into the London Academy of Music and Dramatic Arts (LAMDA) as a teenager.

> Nobody had helped me work on audition things. I didn't know about an audition. And I didn't want to ask them. Really stupid, isn't it? I

had all this help at home. I remember my LAMDA audition. Somebody had said to me, "Remember right before you do the speech, take a moment to yourself. Turn away and take a moment." But nobody told me what to do in that moment. I did Perdita in *Winter's Tale.* You could see their faces fall. [It was] the most terrible audition piece. She just talks about some flowers. What now am I supposed to do while I speak? I was dreadful. They thought I was dreadful. The principal knew my mother [Rachel Kempson] and wrote a note saying, "At this time she shows no sign of talent." I was so pissed off that I went and auditioned for the Central School of Speech and Drama. By that time I had figured out [what] to do, and I got in.

Lynn's story illustrates that the right preparation before any audition is essential to your success. She could have approached members of her illustrious theatrical family to gain some insight but instead chose to listen to bad advice. After failing to get into one drama school, she vowed she would do better the next time, chose better material, improved her technique, gained confidence, and began working professionally upon her graduation. A successful audition hinges on such basics as the selection of good material, rich with interpretive possibilities; advance research (which can simply mean talking to experienced actors) about what to expect in the audition room; and confidence.

In this chapter, we focus on these basics—the general guidelines for auditions and screen tests. In Chapters Eighteen through Twenty Two, we show you how to do an in-depth analysis of the actual material you will be assigned for the audition.

GENERAL RULES FOR AUDITIONING: MONOLOGUES AND SCENES

Every audition will have its own special conditions. However, the following do's and don'ts will help you avoid the most frequently made mistakes.

- **Do** remember that industry professionals want to get to know you through your audition. The process begins when you enter, cross, come down, and introduce yourself. That introduction reveals your sense of self and presence and contributes to a positive first impression.
- **Do** pay attention to what you wear. (See the professional closet guidelines in Chapter Two, "Getting Your Act Together.") Your attire should not be distracting nor should it be a costume. Think about your shoes:

jogging soles squeak on floors and rugless surfaces, and they do not give you any grace of movement; thin stiletto heels or backless slides make *clickety-clackety* noises. Any clothing, like a tight skirt, that inhibits your movement or calls attention to itself is inappropriate.

- **Do** choose material with which you can connect—emotionally, physically, and intellectually. Just as we all have our favorite musicians, composers, and novelists, we have playwrights with whom we feel really comfortable. Understand your limitations. A classically trained actor feels a strong affinity for Shakespeare's characters and knows that characters like Falstaff (*Merry Wives of Windsor*), Sir Toby Belch (*Twelfth Night*), and the porter in *MacBeth* are more suited to him than Romeo, Lysander (*Midsummer Night's Dream*), or Orsino (*Twelfth Night*). Other actors might feel no connection to Shakespeare and would rather do the edgy, complicated characters living in a Sam Shepard play like *True West* or *Curse of the Starving Class*.

- **Do** pick a selection that answers the five Ws (who, what, where, when, and why). Climactic scenes don't do this; setup scenes do. Such scenes create a specific sense of time and place, and reveal your character. Picture the character you are addressing and achieve an objective.

- **Do** be aware of what your body is doing. Keep hands off the hips, don't slouch or slump, stand with your feet firmly planted, hip width apart. You body, voice, and mind must work together. Learn more about the Alexander Technique or take a class in the Linklater Method (see a discussion of both in Chapter Five, "Training Is Everything"). Just one terrific physical choice can make the whole monologue or scene come together.

- **Do** start the scene or monologue with the knowledge of what has happened the moment before the action begins. If you don't know what will happen the moment after the scene ends, an in-depth study of the characters may provide clues. Use your imagination.

- **Do** allow a transitional "beat" between two audition pieces. This can be accomplished by using an accessory: a scarf can become a shawl, a cane can be morphed into a rifle, a scrunchie on the wrist can create a pony tail, varying the hairstyle. Roll up your sleeves, take them down. Rehearse these transitions from one selection to the next so that they unify your audition.

- **Do** choose a scene partner who is as strong or stronger than you, and whose energy will motivate a powerful reaction. You will be challenged to do your best work.

- **Do** bring sexual confidence to your performance. Sensuality and a visible connection with the body come from within the character. Characters are driven by desire and the need to be loved. What Marilyn Monroe, James Dean, Marlon Brando, and Elvis Presley brought to every role they played was enhanced by their organic sexuality.

- **Do** embrace your nerves. How many times do you admit how nervous you are? Use the nervous energy at your audition in a positive way. Too much emphasis on yourself instead of reaching out to the audience increases the risk of shaky knees, moist hands, and a tight throat. Your emotional connections are the springboards from which everything flows and opens up your mind and body to your character's pulse and dynamic and truth.

- **Do** investigate plays that were written before 1970! Know the whole play, and bring a sense of the whole to the excerpt you are doing. Continually search for ways to keep the material fresh. Once you get bored with it, it no longer serves its purpose. You should be constantly looking for new and challenging monologues and scenes.

- **Don't** choose heavy, climactic scenes. Excerpts that allow you to be truthful and sincere involve us more than "over the top" ranting and hysteria. A temper tantrum out of context reduces the development of the depth of a relationship with another character.

- **Don't** choose a scene from a play or a film that has been inextricably linked to a major star, unless you are certain that you can do it much, much better. Examples of memorable, award-winning, transcendent portrayals are: Jodie Foster as Sarah Tobias in *The Accused*; Nicole Kidman as Virginia Woolf in *The Hours*; Judy Holliday as Billie Dawn in *Born Yesterday*, Marlon Brando as Stanley Kowalski in *Streetcar Named Desire*; Mary-Louise Parker as Catherine in *Proof*.

- **Don't** show the audience how hard you are working. Noticeable signs of tension are strained neck muscles, a tight throat, a furrowed forehead, vocal problems, forced laughter, and false emotion. When you are pushing for effect, your timing is off and you are not relating to your partner.

- **Don't** choose to do a British character, in a British play, by a British author, unless you do a British dialect with integrity and skill. Avoid plays by Oscar Wilde, George Bernard Shaw, and Noel Coward unless you have a thorough understanding of the period, the style, the wit, and the use of language. The same is true of any play requiring a dialect; do it well or do something else.

- **Don't** confuse a comedic monologue with a stand-up act. The forms are different. This type of monologue requires you to speak to another character in a full-length play without knowing how funny you are; the stand-up comedian is talking directly to the audience to get laughs.
- **Don't** choose a scene partner whose performance is weak or dull. Your performance will not look better by comparison. The other actor will only pull you down and ruin your timing.
- **Don't** use nonspecific physical behavior or emotional choices. Irrelevant unmotivated gestures or speaking tentatively with eyes cast down to express sorrow or self-deprecation telegraphs to us that you have lost your way in the scene/monologue and you will forfeit your audience' s attention.
- **Don't** play "mood." It is *doom* spelled backwards. Actors will often interpret a character as depressed, angry, sad, suicidal, or desperate and get trapped by those feelings. These self-indulgent emotional choices destroy the other dimensions of a multifaceted character. Playing only the dark side of a human being results in a boring, one-note performance.

Smart Choices for Monologues and Scenes

To be prepared for any audition situation, all actors should have at the ready at least ten monologues that contain a range of characters from contemporary comedy, farce, drama, melodrama, and the classics. Karen Kohlhaas, senior teacher at the Atlantic Acting School in New York City, and Charles Tuthill, a working actor and monologue coach who conducts classes at the Atlantic and also teaches a grad school prep class at the Actors Center in New York, believe that finding the right monologue is essential to your success. A major concern most actors have is trying to avoid choosing a monologue that has been done too often. Kohlhaas and Tuthill contacted ten industry professionals and theater educators and asked them to grade more than 100 monologues on the following scale:

    1: I have not seen it.

    2: I have seen it but am fine seeing it again.

3: I have seen it so often that it doesn't matter how well an actor does it. I'm completely sick of it!

There was no monologue in their survey that didn't get at least one 3. The "winner" in the overdone monologues category for both men and women was the "tunafish" story in Christopher Durang's *Laughing Wild*. For all of the results visit Karen Kohlhaas's Web site, www.monologueaudition.com, and click on "Overdone Monologues!" in the right margin.

These experts believe that actors are best served by contemporary material—written or produced in the last few years—and that their pieces should be edgy, perhaps about sexual issues or relationships. To find contemporary work, read and attend the plays being produced Off-Broadway, on Broadway, in regional theaters, and new play festivals like the New York International Fringe Festival. There are new writers' works constantly being showcased in universities, repertory companies, and playwriting intensives in regional theaters throughout the country.

Many resident theaters, graduate theater training programs, and regional Shakespearean Festivals will also need to know if you have any training or experience in classical plays. But how many Romeos, Juliets, Hamlets, Violas, and Rosalinds have the casting offices heard over and over again? To save you worrying about overdone Shakespearean monologues, a list has been compiled by Walton Wilson, head of voice and speech and associate chair of the Yale School of Drama, and Charles Tuthill, who says, "Like most overdone monologues, they are some of the best and most accessible." So why not investigate Cymbeline, Coriolanus, or Henry VIII? This list will also be found at www.monologueaudition.com.

You can access a Shakespearean monologue at www.shakespeare-monologues.org/womensmonos.htm or type "menmonos.htm" after the slash. According to Tuthill, "You will see that there are many monologues that are not overdone." The pages list women's and men's monologues, with the play, character, verse/prose, act, scene, line number, and first line, which, when you click on it, will instantly download you a .pdf file of that monologue. Then go to www.absoluteshakespeare.com, where you can read plot summary, learn more about the character, and read the play in its entirety (which you *must* do, says Charles Tuthill). You'll also find facts that will enrich your understanding of the play and enhance your performance.

Found Monologues

In addition to the aforementioned resources, you can adapt material from books, magazine articles, newspaper columns, and Internet sites. Also check out diaries, journals, collections of letters, or first-person memoirs as potential sources. Resourceful actors can even find true-to-life monologues in, for example, a blog about a date or in a collection of humor pieces by the late Erma Bombeck. Do a Google search for the work of playwrights you admire and read the reviews in such sources as www.nytimes.com or www.variety.com to see what the critics liked about the production, and how the actors played their parts to win the critics' approval. Use that information as "coaching input" for your own monologue, should you pull one from the play. At such places as New Dramatists in New York City, which supports new works and writers, you'll find a library where you can read the entire play. While there, find out how you can get involved in a staged reading of the work.

AUDITIONING FOR THE THEATER

Confidence, empowerment, and being in control are essential for every live audition. Having a pleasant face, wearing the right outfit, making eye contact, being able to take direction, and possessing an overall agreeable behavior are all significant to the success of your audition. Readers for theatrical auditions have told us what it is like to be on the other side of the desk when actors are not prepared.

When Hunter Bell and Jeff Bowen, cocreators of [title of show] held an open call for understudies in their musical, they were looking for one male and one female. Out of hundreds and hundreds of people who showed up, there were very few callbacks. According to Hunter:

> Some people looked like hell. To me this speaks to issues in their personal lives. I thought, "They have talent but are they going to show up for rehearsal?" Some were short with the accompanist. The people who found a way to be themselves and center themselves were the ones who impressed us. Take a yoga class the morning before an audition, some deep breaths outside the door or when you get in, or just being honest in assessing how you feel. Say, "Let me get together for a second, because I am nervous." Nobody expects you to be perfect or a superhero, they want you to have your stuff together, to be prepared, to be normal.

We observed the behavior outside the audition room when we would take a break. How people behave out there speaks to where they are emotionally with their lives in The Business. Would we want to go on a second date with them? With the actor we chose, there was no flurry of activity, no noise caused by nervous energy. He was an amazing actor, completely comfortable in his skin, confident, present, and relaxed. He knew the material and he had selected an incredibly funny and appropriate song. He had not yet seen the show, but had done the research and checked out the Web site and the blog.

Casting directors for theater companies planning several productions per season will want to see prepared material—usually a contemporary selection and a contrasting piece from a classic. Artistic directors who are producing new plays will want to see how you deal with a segment, or "sides," of the script.

When Robert Petkoff auditioned for director Sir Peter Hall and writer John Barton for *Tantalus*, a ten-hour-plus epic about the Trojan War, he helped his own cause by asking one simple question:

I felt they were less than impressed and I left. I asked the casting director what they were looking for. She said they wanted an actor who could play very young and old. I offered to do a Romeo monologue. She asked them if I could, and I went back into the room.

I did the Romeo and they worked with me on it a bit, and they liked what I did. Later I got a call from my agent saying Sir Peter wanted to see me the next day and to prepare as many as ten monologues so he could see a variety of my work. The opportunity presented itself and I was ready. I got the job.

Don't be afraid to do the same, if something's not clear to you at an audition.

Rob Ruggiero, co-artistic director of Hartford's TheaterWorks, advises actors to do the best audition possible—and to accept the fact that they simply cannot control what goes on in a director's head: "You can have an amazing audition and be someone who can totally do the role, but if you are not how the director sees it, it's a losing battle. Still, I have seen people I loved whom I called back at another time."

Directors look for actors who make strong choices, rather than those who give a safe, generic, indecisive reading. If the actor takes chances, the director can always ask them to make adjustments and see if they can make a change.

Taylor Gilbert, the artistic director of the Los Angeles–based Road Theatre, says the audition is all about the truth. "I am always interested in someone who comes in and gives me something that I have never heard, It is unusual that people will go to that depth."

The Role of the Reader

Actress Suzanne Friedline believes that every actor should be a reader—that is, the person who reads the role of the "other actor" in the scene with the auditioner. Actress Donna Lynne Champlin urges actors to work as readers because it provides a priceless education.

> To be on the other side of the table is the best way to learn about auditioning techniques. You start to see how a casting director sees things. You realize how impersonal it can be. They are looking for something, and even if they don't know what that something is, if you don't have it, you're out of the running. There are simple things like how an actor walks into a room. I got my first offer for a Broadway audition from being a reader.

Donna Lynne has noticed that how an actor enters the room can have either a positive or negative effect on the casting director. Robert Petkoff was once called to be a reader for a casting session. He offers the following advice:

> Contact every casting director in the city if you are just starting out and ask if you can be a reader. The minute I sat on the other side of the table, I watched six actresses come in the room, four of whom were unprepared and the other two—it was like night and day. I thought, "I see myself now. I am the actor who walks in, does the cold reading, can put things together pretty well, but there is nothing going on in my head, no intentions being played." An actress walked in and changed my career. She was prepared, memorized, making choices. She was interesting. I knew right away that anyone else who came in that room had no chance. She walked in and took the role.

Hunter Bell is a big proponent of being a reader as well.

> I was a reader for casting director Pat McCorkle for about a year. I encourage people to do that because it opens your business eyes. I learned so much from that office, probably as much as you do from an acting class. It is like a master class for learning how to have your act together: being on time, being a person, being yourself, how much

you talk in the room, how much you don't talk. It shows you the reality of the casting process. You may be the best person that day and still not get the job. Like they love her, but she has curly hair and so does the other girl, whom they've already cast. To know that kind of information takes a backpack of stress off you. You were the best person and didn't get it, but welcome to The Business. Figure out who you are so that when you go into that crazy arena called an audition, no matter what they throw at you, you have to have a strong sense of self.

AUDITIONING FOR COMMERCIALS

Commercial casting directors say that an actor's believability is the most important quality they look for at an audition. An actor's sense of spontaneity is also critical. You must be able to analyze a commercial script like a monologue.

If you've studied improvisation or taken a commercial class, you will come to the commercial audition equipped to take different approaches to the material. Casting director Donald Case, of Donald Case Casting in New York, selects actors for commercials that pitch a wide range of products, including toys, pharmaceuticals, and retail items. He says, "Have an idea of what you want to do. Even if it's the wrong idea, it's always good to bring something to the party. And *listen*."

Be selective in choosing the directions you might want to take the copy. Your choices should not upstage the material, or interfere with its integrity or message. If you are clever and imaginative enough to take a creative risk that impresses the casting director—you deserve the job!

Your audition may take place in the casting director's office, at the ad agency casting director's office, or in a studio that has been rented for the session. If it is a voice-over job, you may be able to do it at home in your own studio and send your audition to the client or your agent via the Internet.

Arrive early, sign in, get the copy. Isolate yourself so that you can work privately on the script. Some actors retreat to the nearest restroom to practice without interruptions!

Constant auditioning can affect actors' readings—so much so that the readings begin to sound impersonal. Remind yourself, always, to treat the copy as a scene: Who are you talking to? What's the relationship? What was the moment before? Why are you saying these words? All of us do commercials every day—whenever we tell a friend about a book we absolutely couldn't put down, or the fabulous food we enjoyed at a terrific restaurant across the street, or that new lipstick that feels so good and stays on so long. Nothing gets the adrenaline going as fast as discovering a sale or bargain. Bring that positive energy and enthusiasm to the audition.

Treat the script you are given as your own property. Mark it, make notes to yourself—whatever helps you to do your best. Like any other material, commercial copy can be brilliantly or poorly written, with most of what we see falling between those two extremes. You may think the copy is poorly executed; the concept may strike you as pure corn. If you do that, you've already broken the First Rule: Don't judge the material! You must believe in it 100 percent, and never for one second let on that you don't. You must motivate and justify every word that you say. If you have no spoken lines, you must make every action and reaction believable. As a trained actor you should be able to adapt to sudden changes in direction. Your job is to create a credible glimpse of a character's life in anywhere from ten to sixty seconds. The audition begins the moment you meet the casting director, who will explain (if there is time) what the client is looking for. If there is anything that isn't clear, ask. When you are ready to begin, you will be instructed to "slate" yourself. Smiling, tell your name to the camera or the microphone. As far as casting directors are concerned, your short intro is an integral part of the audition. It establishes your strong sense of self.

Another challenge actors must contend with at commercial auditions is the Polaroid snapshot. The agency and the client want to see you as you look at the time of the audition. If that is the procedure at the casting office, have a roommate take a photo of you at home in the outfit you're going to wear to the audition and bring it with you. You will feel more relaxed and look better. Some clients want to see your headshot and résumé. Casting director Terry Berland is amazed at the number of auditioners who hand in a photo without a résumé, even when they are in the office on a callback:

> That is a mistake. I look at the résumé as I am bringing someone in the callback room to see what the actor has been up to. Almost every producer and director wants to look at a résumé. I feel that not bringing one shows a lack of respect for them and the casting director.

She also reports that more actors are working in commercials than in the past:

> Now, on average, as many as twenty-five actors are up for one role. Years ago, there might have been five or ten. Unfortunately there is

very little personal contact with actors; very little time to sit down and have general interviews. Basically, the actor at a commercial audition must know how to expand the small space they are working in and reveal dimensions of their personality very quickly. It's all about personality, not sell.

According to David Elliott, commercial agent, Don Buchwald Associates, New York:

There used to be a very small group of actors that did all the commercials. Now it is larger and much more competitive for the actors as well as the agents. If they don't have on-camera training, I recommend a commercial class for several reasons: They will learn how to do act on camera, first of all. And the people teaching them are good people to know, because often they are commercial casting directors. You can establish a contact with them right there in class. Finally, you will meet other actors like yourself who can lead you to other contacts.

Bear in mind that casting directors, directors, and writers are constantly watching commercials to find exciting, undiscovered talent. Recently a West Coast casting office released a notice on Breakdowns that they were searching for the agent or manager representing the actress in the "Ford Fusion Bold Moves" commercial. She is the one who drives up in a black Fusion at the end of the commercial. She looks like Jennifer Garner. We hope her representative called that casting director, and that the actress is now a series regular.

Hosting

Commercials aren't always about selling something in a minute or less. Almost every commercial talent agency has a hosting division—which places actors in so-called infomercials and product-information DVDs that run much longer than the typical thirty- or sixty-second ad. Actors should have some knowledge of the subjects they'll be presenting—such as home entertaining, fitness, or the culinary arts—and they also need good improv skills, a strong personality, the ability to convince audiences they know what they are talking about, and, of course, physical attractiveness. They have to know how to make the script their own, communicate to the audience with great authority, make the situations real, and be totally engaging. Actress Kim Shively cut her commercial chops when she was the spokeswoman for Toyota in the Northeast. When she relocated to

California, she put together a DVD that showed her engaged in a variety of lifestyle-related activities such as gift wrapping and food preparation. After she met with the hosting agent at her commercial agency and gave him the DVD, he signed her.

AUDITIONING FOR A SOAP OPERA

Daytime dramas offer actors challenging work and the opportunity to play a wide range of emotions, while working with some of the sharpest professionals in the industry. We're not exaggerating when we say soaps may provide actors with more of a chance to show off their range than any other theatrical form.

Soaps are for actors who love to work. They are the electronic equivalent of being in a repertory company. Rather than playing different roles in a series of plays, the actors have to stretch by playing the same character thrust into a range of emotional situations.

Working on a soap opera is a great training ground for how to behave in front of a camera, how to learn lines fast, how to have self-esteem, and how to get along with your fellow actors. Mary Clay Boland, Emmy-winning casting director of *As the World Turns*, believes that soaps are so difficult she won't hire day players (actors whose characters have limited runs or make sporadic appearances in the soap) unless they've listed some soap opera work on their résumés. So how do you build the door to soap opera opportunities? Well, you can write a cover letter to the assistant casting director listed in *The Ross Reports*, which contains information about your training, your theater credits, and any on-camera experience you have acquired and then request an interview. The assistant casting directors at soap operas cast extras and the associate casting directors are responsible for under-five roles (with less than five lines of dialogue) as well as input on day player roles. Have realistic expectations. You can't expect an audition for a contract role without any soap opera experience. Actors chosen for principal roles must be attractive; the camera must love their faces. Because so much of daytime drama is a close-up medium, you must be aware of your physical strengths.

Daytime casting directors will notice you in plays they attend or from commercials in which you appear. John Martin got his role on *One Life to Live* when a casting executive spotted him on a gum commercial. She called the ad agency and learned his name and that he was on the West

Coast and she contacted him directly. His background included day-player work on several soaps. He screen tested for the show and was hired.

There are also opportunities for novices who begin as under-fives to graduate to principal contract roles. This happened to Jennifer Landon (Emmy winner for her role as Gwen on *As the World Turns*). Her talent so impressed the writers and the producer that a larger story was created for her. Daytime Emmy winner Tom Pelphrey (ex-Jonathan) got a contract role on *Guiding Light* almost immediately after graduating from the theater training program at Rutgers University in New Jersey. As Rob Decina, casting director of *Guiding Light*, says, "Even if you don't get a contract role right away, you have to realize that where you are today at this moment does not mean that's where you'll be tomorrow. You can either be sitting at home dreaming about being on TV or you can make it happen."

Hillary Bailey Smith has been playing Nora on *One Life to Live* for more than fourteen years. She knows from experience that the better you take care of yourself, eating right and staying fit; the better you prepare; and the more disciplined you are about your craft, the longer you'll be around. She also knows that the actors who excel at soap auditions know who they are. She explains:

> I have taught improv and some audition classes. It is really about teaching actors what to expect when they walk into a room, and what they need to bring with them, not just the picture and résumé. They need to bring their personality. Be the whole person when you walk in and read the script and transform yourself. In order to bring a character to life, you have to begin with yourself.

Judy Blye Wilson is the award-winning casting director of *All My Children*. Based on her experience, her do's and don'ts for soap auditions include:

- **Do** endow the lines with your individuality.
- **Do** the job you came in to do and exit gracefully.
- **Don't** make judgments and jump to conclusions about the other actors in the waiting room.
- **Don't** be rude to the assistant. Today's assistant could be tomorrow's power player.
- **Don't** bring props.
- **Don't** ask a lot of unnecessary questions.
- **Don't** attempt to score points with the casting director by dropping

names, or by trying to convince them that you are "just like this character because . . . "

- **Don't** make excuses.

> In my opinion, a successful audition is one in which the actor is on time, prepared, and professional, If he or she is physically right for the part, nails the reading, and lands the job—well, that's the icing on the cake.

Judy tapes every actor who auditions for a principal role, and in preparation she recommends:

> Make sure you can work within the restrictions of the camera lens. You have to remember to keep the performance smaller for the camera, different from the projection that is needed for the stage. Rehearse in front of a camcorder or DVD recorder at home or in a class. Get accustomed to working with the lights. Don't upstage yourself with gestures that are too broad or facial expressions that are too big. Don't be shy about asking what your parameters are, or how tight the shot is. Control your nerves. The camera never lies. It picks up every nuance.

Auditions for day players usually take place in the casting director's office. Most likely you will be reading with the casting director and an assistant or a reader who is hired so that the casting director can watch you. A brief character description is provided in the script or by the casting director. When you're handed the script, analyze the scene; understand the relationship; play the intentions. Flesh out a history for the character if it is hard to find one just from reading the scene. Endow the lines with your own individuality.

Some day players, after several days of solid work, are delighted to learn that the writers like them enough to expand their part into a contract role. That possibility always exists, so attack the scene in the audition as if the role is already yours—and could be enlarged into a steady job.

Actors auditioning for contract roles usually have two to three days to get themselves ready. The scene is e-mailed to them by their agents or managers. They have time to hire a coach or work with their acting teacher, who can rehearse the scene with them. Memorize the material so you have more control over it. Although a character description (often called a backstory) is provided in the script, the more you enhance it using your own imagination, creating a rich personal history for the character, the more substance you can bring to the audition. (See "The Character's Background: A Resource for the Character Profile" in Chapter 18.)

Mark Teschner, the winner of three Artio Awards for excellence in daytime casting, and the winner of two Daytime Emmys, has been the casting director of *General Hospital* for more than seventeen years. He loves daytime and gets a thrill when he discovers new faces. He understands how important it is for an actor to turn in a good audition—and he does his best to help.

> If I don't create a "safe place" for the actor to do good work, it's not helping me to do my job. There's no question auditioning is tension-filled and highly pressured for an actor. I know that, and I don't need to make it more pressurized than it already is. When they come in they know they're going to read with me, and that I will be in the moment with them in the scene, giving as much as I possibly can to connect with them, so they can do the kind of work they need to get the job. If I am not there for the actor, how can I expect the actor to be there for me?

Don't count on all casting directors to be as sensitive to the actor's needs as Mark. If you sense an impersonal vibe at your audition, lean on your very best resource and supporter: yourself. You walked in strong and confident. Stay that way. Play your scene to perfection. Are you ready for your close-up?

Dressing for the Part

Fran Bascom, former casting director for *Days of Our Lives,* advises actors not to go overboard with looking the part at the audition. "Maybe hint at it with the hair and makeup," she says, "but don't come in dressed as a cowboy or police officer. You want us to be able to consider you for other roles."

If the actor gets the job, the producer and the costume designer will decide which type or style is best for the character. If the actor walks into the audition room wearing a costume that is too far out, he upstages his audition. Too much attention on the wardrobe choice will take time away from preparing the script, which should always be the first priority.

The use of the imagination separates brilliance from mediocrity. The most illuminating example of the marriage of preparation and dressing for the part was in the early 1980s when Dorothy Lyman created the role of Opal Gardner on *All My Children*. Dorothy was no stranger to soap opera; she had been a contract player on *Another World*. But it wasn't until she tried out for Opal that her comedic talents got their chance. She wore spandex tights, a bathing suit bra exposing her midriff, a cropped denim jacket, and huge dangling earrings. Her blonde hair was piled up and pulled to one side and her mouth was a vivid shade of red. She also found the voice, accent, rhythm, physical behavior, and "key" to her relationship with her daughter Jenny. The scene took place on a hot dusty bus somewhere between Nebraska and Pine Valley. The bigger-than-life Opal was urging her overwhelmed daughter to put on some lipstick and comb her hair so that she could make a good impression on the "folks" in PV and become a much sought-after model so they could be on "easy street." Talk about a fantasy! Opal had it all figured out. And the actress's interpretation of the character had just the right amount of openness, confidence, brassiness, and naïveté, which was obviously covering a heart of gold.

Well, there was no one else for this role. The decision was unanimous. Dorothy Lyman launched a new kind of character in daytime drama. She took what the writers had created into a place they had never envisioned.

The point of this story is that this process is only successful when there is a real and deep synergy between the actor and the role. Anyone could have dressed up in a slightly trashy flamboyant way, but without the instincts, the timing, and the talent, the attempt would have been deemed superficial and ridiculous. We don't advise extremes in dress for soap auditions. But certain colors relate to the emotional and psychological makeup of each character. We advise a color that connects to that character, or an accessory like a piece of jewelry that can serve as a trigger in the character's life. Visualize the character's closet.

Common sense is the rule. If a juvenile is described as a mechanic who owns a "hog" and loves the open road, then a jacket and tie would be totally inappropriate. If an ingenue role is an inexperienced, sheltered, sweet, and extremely introverted heiress, then a tight skirt and sweater combo would never be in her closet. Most important, once you have taken the time to select a color, an accessory, or an ensemble for your character, you have used your imagination and intuition for the audition, and this may give you the competitive edge.

The Screen Test

Here is your ultimate chance to convince the producer, the writing team, and the network executives that you can do the job better than anybody else. Given the hard work you'll be doing, this may be a difficult time for you to hold on to the thought that they already love you. They want to scrutinize your work under the lights and see what kind of chemistry exists between you and the contract player who will be playing opposite you.

For your on-camera audition, you'll be asked to arrive about three hours early, for makeup, hair, and wardrobe. This will be followed by the director or the assistant director "blocking" the action of the scene. Now you're getting a taste of real-life working conditions on the set. You'll rehearse a run-through of the scene, and then it's time for: Lights, camera, action! It is difficult to relax under these conditions. Added to the stress is the fact that screen tests are sandwiched between the run-through and dress rehearsal of the day's regular episode or tacked onto the schedule at the end of a long day. Before the cameras stop rolling, the producer of the show may interview you to get a better handle on your personality and intelligence—things that the scene itself may not have revealed.

Being Ready for the Big Break

With increasing frequency, actors from all parts of the country are being put on tape at the request of a soap's casting director. What a fabulous opportunity for someone who is prepared!

Years ago, a network casting consultant conducting a regional talent hunt visited Seattle and put a twenty-year-old actress in training on camera. She never imagined she would have the opportunity to become a leading player on a soap opera. She had performed in local theaters and had taken many acting classes, but New York seemed to her like a dream, not a reality. All that would change. When the producer of *One Life to Live* reviewed the tape, she was wowed by the girl's beauty, presence, and special quality. A role was created for her. After she had relocated to New York City, the girl signed up for more classes and started working with a coach the show had hired to help her understand the new medium of television. She found the cast extremely supportive and welcoming. Her theatrical training already provided her with a strong foundation and an understanding of how to be part of an ensemble.

That actress would find a very different work environment on soap operas today. Hillary Bailey Smith, who worked with this ingenue on *One Life to Live*, would tell her there is very little time to rehearse. Because everything is shot out of sequence, soaps are no longer compared to live theater.

With the advent of digital editing, they can change the ending of a scene—for example, when two actors can't look at each other in the scene because it is too painful for their characters, and the scene just isn't working, the producer can find a place where the two did seem to look at each other earlier and edit the scene so it looks like they are facing each other.

When I started, the medium was kinder to the director. You would have a blocking rehearsal with the director and get notes. After a break, you'd rehearse for the cameras. After lunch you'd come back, get into hair and makeup and wardrobe, and have a full rehearsal, then tape. You could ask questions. You knew where the arcs were and you had read the whole script—and you were doing only one show that day.

That is all changed now. Now we block and tape and do it set by set. Every scene that is set in the mansion or in the library gets done during that session. So everything is out of order. All the scenes that take place that week in the diner are done on Monday, and all the library scenes are done on Tuesday. You are doing scenes from scripts you haven't read yet. You are forced to ask "actor questions," like "Am I coming or going?" These young kids who are coming in are overwhelmed.

Because they are going with younger and less experienced actors, soaps are losing the quality they used to have. These days a lot of the young actors get their training on a soap set. There used to be a coach, but that doesn't exist anymore. Actors used to get guidance from the directors [but directors don't have time to give notes any more]. Today, if they choose, they can learn from watching other actors at work. Award-winning actors like Erika Slezak [Viki on *One Life to Live*]. She comes in every day prepared, knows her lines, where her mark is, and has asked her questions well in advance.

Hillary is right. Much has changed in the production of soaps. But one thing remains a constant: The genre provides actors with perhaps the richest opportunity in The Business to play an endless range of emotions and situations, to grow in their craft every day, and to get paid for doing what they love—at a high professional level.

AUDITIONING FOR A TV SERIES

In prime-time TV, everyone auditions—whether for three-line parts or costarring roles. The only difference is that walk-on bits don't usually require a callback, while principal roles always do.

It is imperative that you watch and know the show for which you are auditioning. Carol Goldwasser, casting director for such series as *The Hughleys*, *American Dad!*, and *Hannah Montana*, says,

> I love it when an actor is well prepared and they've seen the show, so they understand the tone of the show, because that's going to make their audition so much better. Particularly with comedy, the tone is so variable between multicamera sitcom and single-camera that it can range from realistic to wacky. If you are going to fit into the ensemble that week, it's great if you understand the style of that particular show.

How actors get leading roles in prime-time series can be as simple as being in the right place at the right time. David Krumholz had been cast as nerds and geeks for many years in Los Angeles-based series until the day his agent got him an unforgettable audition. When coexecutive producer Cheryl Heuton was looking for the character of Charlie Eppes in the CBS series *Numb3rs*, she began to think she had written an uncastable part—until David Krumholtz walked in one morning. The role, described by one reviewer as "Sherlock Holmes for the slide-rule set," required an actor who could tackle monologues with a lot of math language and make it sound natural. Krumholtz readily admitted that he is no mathematician. "I think it's more important that I learn who a mathematician is and how he sees the world than it is to actually learn the math." It is a matter of great pride to the actor that he won acceptance for his role after being stuck for years in a Hollywood niche he found frustrating. He was known for playing mostly nerds.

After ten failed pilots, Kathryn Morris (Lilly Rush on *Cold Case*) finally landed a role that is as good as she is. Her success proves that as an actor you need to keep refining your craft and—no matter if a pilot doesn't become a series, or if a series suddenly gets pulled from the schedule—you have to keep your focus, believe in your talent, and be confident that the right part will come along.

> I feel really great that I get to play Lilly, when so many girls would never have a crack at playing a role that is so complicated, especially blondes. I always felt I'd have a long, interesting road—I'm really glad it evolved this way. You should do the horror movie, you should do the low-budget sci-fi stuff. You should do all those crazy things in your friends' backyards, because it really teaches you to be a good actor.

Most often, episodic series cast ten days ahead of the shoot. There isn't much time to pre-screen or pre-read actors for the smaller roles. The casting directors keep extensive files and a database that will give them the reliable actors they need—and who they feel will be approved by the producer. As Rob Decina, who worked for Warner Brothers, casting on series like the New York–based *Third Watch*, reports, "When you are in an East Coast office working for a Los Angeles–based production studio, most of what you are doing is putting actors on tape and sending the tape to the producer, director, and writers. As the associate casting director, I would bring in five to seven actors for each role in the episode—and forward them to the people involved in the decision. The ownership is with the creative people."

It is important to remember that no matter how wonderful your audition for a series has been, the decision rests with the producer and the writers. Their vision of what the physical, emotional, and intellectual qualities of the character must be will decide whether you are going to get the role. Never take rejection personally, and keep moving forward. Kathryn Morris and David Krumholz have earned their success because they kept studying, stretching, auditioning, and working.

The Casting Process in Prime Time

We think you should understand how casting directors are able to find the right "marriage" of talent and role in episodic series. There is so little time for pre-reads or meetings, the casting office relies on its extensive files as well as a producer's preferences. If you want to work in this medium, it's important to study it: Watch prime-time television and discover what kind of actors are hired for leading, supporting, and minor parts.

Linda Lowy and John Brace were approached to cast the first season of *Grey's Anatomy* and when they read the script they couldn't put it down. Shonda Rhimes, the show's creator/executive producer, gave them freedom to put together a remarkable ethnically diverse cast. Linda recalls,

> We knew we wanted a diverse cast to reflect reality, but we didn't have any specific criteria in mind. It was very liberating to not be limited by any color scheme or pre-set agenda and it opened up our minds and the talent pool.
>
> Often casting directors are asked to come up with a list of names or to fill in the blanks with a name actor off a list that everyone is excited about but you know is stereotypical. But Shonda empowers her department and gives us free range.

What's so amazing about our regular cast is that they are all so talented that they can all stand alone. But they've set such a high acting bar that the challenge is meeting that standard with our guest cast.

With only eight days to cast an episode, the process begins with a meeting at which the entire creative team discusses the characters in the upcoming show. Key to their success is the amount of time they spend auditioning unknowns to find a fresh face. Casting the small part of an anesthesiologist is as exciting as selecting a guest star.

The Pilot

A pilot is the first episode of what could become a hit one-hour drama, half-hour sitcom, or (nowadays) a reality show. Pilot season traditionally runs from February to early April. In January, actors in New York and other cities sublet their apartments and head west, hoping to get auditions for roles in the next *West Wing* or *Everybody Loves Raymond*. Before you book a flight, you must understand the hard business realities of breaking into episodic TV and you must have representation.

Every year dozens of pilots are submitted, reviewed, scrutinized, compared, and assessed in terms of what it will cost to produce, which A list star or stars might be interested, what backup list to turn to when they are not available, and what the target demographic (viewers who are eighteen to forty-nine) is. Then, if the pilot is given the green light, or go ahead, it is produced and screened for the network executives who will determine if it will become a series. Then it will get a "pick up" order for either six, thirteen, or twenty-four episodes. So many chiefs are involved that it is miraculous when we see the first episode aired in the fall. Along the way, there will be cast replacements or cast additions, and ultimately the fate lies in the hands of us, the audience.

There is great pressure every pilot season to find the ideal cast, that magical ensemble on view in hit series such as *24* and *NCIS*. Casting directors have extensive files of actors they already know, most of whom have established their careers, and who they know to be dependable, professional, and respected by the producers. Casting directors are also in tune with the tastes of the networks and the cable channels. Moreover, writers also have favorites they want to see cast for the roles they have created. New York–based casting directors who work for the networks, studios, and cable channels are well acquainted with the local talent pool. They cover theater from Broadway to industry showcases. They meet actors at general interviews and in classes they teach. When pilot frenzy begins in mid-January, they will audition the actors whose work they know.

If you decide to stay put in New York (or Chicago, or Atlanta, or Dallas), your agent can tape your audition and send it to a casting office on the West Coast. A casting director who thinks you are a possibility for the role will show the tape to the executive producer and to network executives. Sometimes, even if rarely, your tape will be such a hit that you'll be flown to Los Angeles to test and audition for the network brass in the entertainment division.

Once your agent has arranged an audition time, probably for a pre-read, he or she will e-mail you the script and sides. Working with a teacher can help you feel more prepared and less anxious in the waiting room, where the atmosphere of competition is palpable. Focus on the material. Always remember that the casting director wants you to nail it. In his book *Acting Is a Job: Real-Life Lessons About the Acting Business*, actor Jason Pugatch advises working actors on how to generate "heat" before pilot season:

> A great review in a big New York show that people are hearing about in Los Angeles may be enough to get you out there. Some great New York theater credits and a guest lead or two, and you could be good meat for the MGM lion. No credits and no heat mean that you're going up against other actors who have it. You might be better off sticking in the home court and continuing to build where you've laid the foundation.

We couldn't agree more.

The "Plus" Factor

Landing a leading role in a prime-time series entails interviews, auditions, callbacks, screen tests—*plus* an elusive quality having little to do with your talent, yet may be the very thing that gets you the job. Actress and acting teacher Catherine Gaffigan describes the "plus factor": "There is a light on inside, a tremendous appetite for the work, a love of the work, and a personality characteristic called persistence. The greatest actors of all have the "plus factor." Playwright Tennessee Williams sensed that the brilliant Laurette Taylor's interpretation of Amanda Wingfield in the original Broadway production of *The Glass Menagerie* had "hints of something that lies outside the flesh and its mortality—there was a radiance about her art which I can compare only to the greatest lines of poetry and which gave me the same shock of revelation as if the air about us had been momentarily broken through by light from some clear space beyond us."

Casting director Mali Finn has defined a good actor as somebody who "takes risks, who really knows himself, who will reveal something personal and unique. It is someone who has great humor and charisma, someone whom the camera loves, someone who can peel the layers of the onion away to get right down to the core of communicating on a very intimate level."

Most actors we know strive to bring these qualities of self to their work. But the elusive quality—the plus factor—may not be so easily attained. Combined life experience, the powers of observation, a love of the work, persistence, and risk taking can all contribute to achieving the internal "divine spark." When you can hold the audience in the palm of your hand, when they are mesmerized by your performance and the critics finally acknowledge that you have "arrived"—then all the sacrifices and the hard work will be worth it.

AUDITIONING FOR A FILM

An audition for a film, whether it is a major feature, a SAG modified-low-budget, an ultra-low-budget indie, a student thesis, a sci-fi thriller, or a straight-to-DVD production, will most likely start out with the independent casting director hired by the producer. If you can get advance info on the casting director you'll be seeing, that can be invaluable. However, as Tony Award–winning actress Patricia Elliott points out, "There are also general differences in style between casting directors on the two coasts.

> In Los Angeles, they want to see what they are going to get. They don't want to chat. My manager in Los Angeles said I had to be the character, and that was hard for me. In New York I was used to schmoozing with the casting directors, who knew me, and then going into the character. I was up for a movie role. The character was a real bitch type, cold as ice. I was playing a scene on a witness stand. So I thought, "Okay, I am going to try this." I walked into the audition and decided I was going to be who I was during the whole audition. I was the bitch woman—cold. The other people auditioning tried to make conversation, and I was very matter-of-fact with them. I learned the casting directors don't want any conversation at all. Their side glances to each other indicated to me they thought I was interesting. After I read one of the sides, they were very responsive. And one of

them asked me where I was from and I immediately lost the "cool" and said, "Oh, I am from New York and I am a stage actress." And I went right into the personality of Patricia Elliott, cheerleader from Denver, whose boyfriend was the captain of the team. [And she lost the part.]

If the part is small, you may be hired from that first audition. No call-back necessary. Actors trying out for pivotal roles will be called back for a screen test. The late Ruth Warrick, known to millions of daytime fans as Phoebe Tyler Wallingford on *All My Children*, remembers her first screen test for *Citizen Kane*, starring and written and directed by Orson Welles. Her reminiscence carries a lesson for young actors about the value of on-camera training—before you ever dare to go for a screen test.

I will never forget the screen test at RKO. When I arrived, Orson was waiting for me in makeup and costume. He was going to do the test with me. This was the first time Orson would see himself on film. Well, all of a sudden, five men in hats and coats walked in and stood in the back looking very stern. They had an attitude, and Orson had cold beads of sweat on his face and brow. I also was nervous, but I per-suaded him to go behind the set and I dabbed his face with a hand-kerchief, which calmed him down and, by focusing my attention on him, calmed me, too. My nurturing instinct created a bond between us from that day.

Orson told us to remember how big we are going to be on that screen, so we can't do what we do on the stage. It has to be smaller, and for that reason, more intense. It is all in the thinking. Don't say, "How am I going to read this line?" Don't rehearse thinking that, but think of the whole picture, the whole scene. Remember, your eyes are going to tell more than any other part of you. I have been told that they remember my eyes because that is where the intelligence comes through. Think about Spencer Tracy. He almost never did anything, but you knew what he was thinking.

Casting director Ellen Parks (*Sideways*, *Secretary*, *Songcatcher*) has some no-nonsense advice for actors who audition for her:

Really use your brain in preparing material. Anybody can do a generic version of the role. It's your particular psychology, emotional life, and instinct that can make your audition special and distinctive and that will distinguish it from the crowd.

The actor Patrick Boll recalled an amazing audition he had for the film *United 93*. It just goes to show that an actor can stretch and grow anywhere—even under the pressure of competing for a job.

> It was all improvisation, completely in the moment. The casting director took her time. The instruction was not to act like the real passengers on the plane did, but to try to act like what you think happened. Feel what the experience of getting on the plane as a normal person is all about, because you have no idea about the outcome. You have to portray a normal person. You walked out of the audition feeling like you had a soulful experience.

Joe Mantegna believes that the actor should go into the film audition with a clear idea of what he wants to do with the role. But he has to keep himself totally open and flexible.

> You may run into a director like David Mamet, who is usually very specific on how he wants something done, the way his words are spoken. His dialogue is usually written in stone. On the other hand, you can have somebody like Woody Allen, who very often will only give you those couple of pages of the entire script that he wants to see you do. If you go afield of what he may want and he throws out some suggestions, you have to be instantaneous and go with the flow.
>
> For a film audition, the actor has to leave some ego at the door and be able to ask questions—"Where do you see this going?" "What do you have in mind?" But don't go in like you have no ideas at all. The actor has to be prepared to say, "If you see this in a different way, give me some clues and I will try and do that for you.

FACTS OF LIFE

We cannot ignore the fact that some producers and directors are rude, ungracious, and into "power trips." If you are not what they are looking for, on sight, they may ignore you as if you were not there.

Take your place on the stage and hold your ground. Never let rudeness get you down! You must rise above it and keep your sense of humor.

At most auditions, however, you will be treated with respect and courtesy. Remember, the casting director and the other decision-makers are much more likely to be rooting for you. They need good actors as much as you need them.

How, then, to sum up what auditioning means to a working actor?

Here, from actress and teacher Roberta Reardon, is as good a definition as we know:

> Your job as an actor is to fall in love with auditioning. Because you will do that much more than you will ever get paid for work. But you have to understand, that's the door to everything. I've heard so many students say, "Oh, I'd love to work but I can't bear auditioning." Fall in love with it. When you walk in—and I don't care what the gig is, a recorded book, a commercial, a play, an episode of *Law & Order,* any kind of acting—you walk into that room and you stand in front of the microphone or the camera or that X on the floor or in front of the table, and you start working. That's your opportunity. That's the door to everything you want. And if you can't fall in love with that, you're in big trouble. Because that is the door everybody goes through. And you have to do it over and over and over again.

CHAPTER 16

Congratulations! You've Got a Job!

"Once I take a role, I become the character and I say 'I.' I never say 'he.' That's an act of separation."

—Martin Landau, Oscar-winning actor

"Dear, they want you to do it."

Seven one-syllable words and it's hallelujah time. You are going to be a working actor. You are going to create a definable character on a soap, in a sitcom, in a movie, or on the stage. Or, maybe you'll be appearing in a commercial. You will be paid a salary, perhaps every week, for as long as the project lasts. And one thing to understand deep in your soul is that once you join any company, on screen or on stage, you are become part of a business family. Respect this alliance. Avoid the childish temptation to test the rest of this family's love for you by behaving foolishly—forgetting to learn your lines, losing your script, being late for rehearsal, or not showing up at all. You are considered too grown up for that. Remember how hard you have worked for this reward. Love your business and love yourself, and have fun with it.

"You have to understand. We couldn't do any of this without all the other people who make it possible every day. The crew. We're all just journeymen, working together. There are no prima donnas here."

—Don Hastings, "Dr. Bob Hughes" in *As the World Turns*

WHAT ABOUT MY CONTRACT?

Actors whom the casting director has called directly—usually the extras and under fives—will generally confirm with the assistant the date, time, and place of the call (the industry term for day of employment). If you have been submitted by an agent, the agent's office will give you your call and will then confirm your acceptance of the call with the casting director. In either case, your script will be sent to you via the Internet.

If you are doing TV, commercial, and film work, the standard contract will be presented to you after your arrival on the set on the day of shooting. At some point in the day the production assistant will collect the signed forms, and your copy will be mailed to you or given to you at the end of the shoot. If you have been selected for a part in a stage play, you will be signing an individual contract.

If you have managed to win your role without an agent, this may be a good time to get an agent or a theatrical attorney to represent you. Some performers scoff at hiring an agent, considering it tantamount to "giving away" 10 percent of their salaries. But actors are often not as knowledgeable as they can be about the subtle business aspects of their jobs. Try to look at it as an investment. The agent will try to get as much for you as you are worth. Moreover, the agent may start scouting for other projects for you—work that does not conflict with the demands or restrictions of your current job. With so many things happening so quickly in The Business nowadays, it should be to your advantage to have someone who really knows the territory looking out for you.

An actor we know couldn't believe how clever his agent turned out to be in dealing with a prospective employer. "I would've taken their offer gladly. But by the time he finished talking to them about the clauses and the possibilities and the guarantees and all that, I knew I was going to be making a helluva lot more money!"

Once you're working steadily, it invariably follows that other people will want to hire you. Be sure you understand the terms of your contract. Are you precluded from doing commercials or any other jobs? If you happen to be presented with a better opportunity, what are your options? For example, on soaps, actors generally need to give six weeks' notice for four weeks out, after their first year or more on the show. These matters should be negotiated before you sign. In the words of movie mogul Samuel Goldwyn, "A word of mouth agreement isn't worth the paper it's written on."

A DAY ON THE SET

You will begin preparing for your scene long before you arrive on the set. If you have words to say, learn them. If you interact with any of the regular characters, watch the show so you will recognize the actor you will be talking to.

When Ron Raines learned that he had been chosen to play Alan Spaulding on *Guiding Light*, he took this a step further.

> For two weeks I went every day and stood around the set. I asked the stage manager questions about everything I observed that I didn't understand. I watched the actors. I was stepping into a new arena. It is another language. If you don't ask a question, they will assume you know it. But if you have a question, they are there for you.

If you have any questions about the character, the scene, or the words that were not answered at the audition, make notes to yourself to ask the director during rehearsal of your scene. Wait until the director tells you what he or she wants: The director may have anticipated your query.

Pack everything that you will need, including personal items such as shoes, mirror, comb, brush, or whatever you use to do your hair. Remember to include a copy of the script, plus a pen or sharpened pencil. You will need to write down any line changes that may be made during rehearsal, as well as to mark your entrances, exits, and whatever moves or bits of business the director gives you.

If you are bringing a wardrobe to the set (see below), check the day before the shoot to make sure everything you have selected is clean and in wearable condition. Try the outfit on, just to make sure all the buttons are where they should be. Pack the garments in a wardrobe carryall or in a lightweight suitcase.

Prepare a "care package" of healthful food to get you through the day. Yes, there is a lunch break, but you might need some nourishment before that time, and the craft table may have nothing left but sugary Danishes. Some actors put everything they intend to take with them right at the front door. They don't want to think about where anything is. They just want to open the door, and go.

Check the weather report. If you're driving, make sure there's enough gas in the tank. If you're taking public transport, make sure you have fare for the bus or subway. In New York, you'll want to make sure that have you have enough money on your MetroCard to cover your trip—you never want to stand in line at the vending-card machines or the change booth during morning rush hour. Try to anticipate every emergency. Set your alarm early enough to go about your morning ablutions calmly.

If you feel a cold or a sore throat coming on, take care of yourself! Nothing prevents a professional actor from appearing at a job. Bring your vitamins, cold remedies, tissues, and nose drops with you, and be as un-stressed as possible.

Women would be wise to wash, set, or blow-dry their hair, either the night before or on the morning of the call, so that it will be shiny and healthy looking. Yes, there is a stylist on the set, but the stylist's first responsibility is to the principal players. Every project has one or more makeup artists, but be ready to do your own face in case they are very busy.

Finally, set your radio alarm, and your alarm clock, and perhaps a back-up alarm if yours has ever been known to fail. Get a good night's sleep. We'll see you on the set.

YOUR WORKING WARDROBE

Costumes are created or rented for special events, such as historical series or fantasy or sci-fi sequences. For "normal life" as depicted in commercials, soap operas, and most nighttime shows, designers are pleased when a performer's personal wardrobe is suitable for the scene; that saves the production company shopping time and rental expense. The wardrobe person will ask you to describe your clothing and tell you to bring the outfits that seem most appropriate at the time of your call. You are paid a wardrobe fee for each garment that is used and you will also enjoy the comfort and confidence of wearing something that fits well.

Try to find out what the scene is about, where it takes place, or something else that will give you a clue about which clothes will work best. Bring choices. Some colors will look better in the set than others. Women might bring a number of blouses in a medium tone (no whites) so you'll have variations on the housewife look. Definitely bring a dark skirt if you have to play a waitress (everybody on a soap is always going to the local restaurant). If it's a party scene, bring an evening dress that's pretty but not glittery, and not too revealing. Don't wear anything that rustles when you walk.

The color of your outfit can be important in films, where setting up group shots for the big screen means that actors will be positioned so that the composition of the shot will (a) look beautiful, and (b) support a narrative point in the story. An actress we know was seated next to the leading man, whose character was about to receive some sort of honor, because her ball gown was just the right cranberry shade. She and her dress were beautifully noticeable in the final cut. But of course, the actor has no control over such matters, which are all in the eye of the designer.

If you're a man, it's easy. A blazer jacket and slacks will take you almost everywhere. And if the scene is particularly sporty or grungy, you'll probably be given those details.

As we said, color choices are made for reasons that frequently have nothing to do with you. But while you are in the wardrobe area, notice the colors and fabrics that predominate and how accessories are used. You may glimpse an ensemble that would be perfect for an upcoming showcase. The wardrobe person may even tell you where it's from.

It is essential to be on time—by which we mean early. It's also important to be polite. When the person in charge of wardrobe says, "Wear this," just do it.

IF YOU'RE WORKING IN A SOAP OPERA

Digital has invaded the world of soap opera, transforming the way shows proceed from script to the television screen.

Originally, the scenes of each day's episode were rehearsed more or less in sequence. Actors loved working this way because it was the closest thing to being in live theater. By the end of each day, they would have run through the material five times; an entire show would have been taped, to be edited into the prologue and acts one through six that the audience sees each day.

Today, there is very little rehearsal. Single sets are put up at the beginning of the week, and all the scenes that take place in that set—say it's the diner—are recorded. Then the next set—call it the library—is put up, and whatever action goes on in that set is recorded. This continues until all scenes have been shot, all to be edited, digitally, at the end of the week.

It's a challenge for the actor to keep a tight grasp on the continuity of the storyline and the emotional arcs.

"Everything is out of order. You're doing scenes from scripts you haven't read yet. I truly believe you have to be familiar with the whole script. You're forced to ask actor questions, like 'am I coming or am I going?'"

—Hillary B. Smith, Nora, *One Life To Live*

Dry Rehearsal

Day players and extras are advised to arrive fifteen minutes before their calls. They show their IDs at the desk (or the gate) and proceed to the rehearsal room, where they check in with the production assistant (P.A.).

In the rehearsal room folding chairs have been placed to represent sofas, desks, tables, and other furniture. The director gives the actors their pre-planned blocking, and at the same time manages to pay attention to performance, giving acting notes. First run-through is inevitably a stop-and-go process. Lines may be changed. Actors may need to ask questions: Can I move when he says that? Do I have to interrupt him? Do I have to say the line? Can't I just look at him?

After a short break they return for a second run-through, where the scenes begin to flow and they see how everything really works. With their staging set, the actors can try to explore the nuances of their performance. After the second run-through, the actors are released to go to makeup and wardrobe, and go over lines with one another. And the next group comes in to block their scene.

> **"For a young actor, soap is more than a great training ground in how to be in front of a camera. It is a great training ground in how to learn lines fast, how to have self-esteem, and how to get along with your fellow actors."**
>
> —Patricia Elliott, Tony Award–winning actress

Makeup, Hair, and Wardrobe

Each show employs a staff of makeup artists, hairstylists, and wardrobe mistresses. Makeup artists are expert in adjusting actors' makeup to the particular demands of the new cameras and lighting. Hairstylists do cuts, colors, perms, and wigs if necessary, so that on camera, everyone's hair is perfect and the color is always consistent.

Wardrobe is a space unto itself, a gigantic closet in which clothing is arranged by character. On a show like *All My Children*, assistants take care of everything: hems up or down; seams released or ripped; creases steamed or pressed. There's a washing machine, in case clothes that are needed in the next day's set of scenes are soiled. Every principal character has a rack. They say that leading lady Susan Lucci, who plays Erica Kane on *All My Children*, has seven.

Tech Rehearsal

The cast, now in full makeup and costume, is called to the studio, one group at a time. This is the first time the camera crew sees the action, although they will have a list of the director's pre-planned shots. The sound crew wheels in the overhead mike boom. Standing at a movable lectern, the director can view the action on his or her monitor and talk to the technical director (T.D.) in the control room if it's necessary to adjust a shot. This part of the process is known as Block and Tape. Once this blocking run-through is done, there is a short break, then the scene goes right to taping. A performer may have thirty such segments in a day.

> **"We start at seven A.M. and try to finish before dinner. There are times when we go later. Pacing is essential for your day—when you eat, when you put up your feet and rest, when you run the lines. I got a pullout couch for my dressing room. There was no way I could make it home at night and come back in the morning and have time to learn lines. I finally got an apartment in the city."**
>
> —Hillary B. Smith, "Nora," *One Life To Live*

IF YOU'RE WORKING ON A SITCOM

> **"I've been performing in front of three hundred people every Tuesday for eight years. We have a studio audience. They're listening and laughing—or not laughing."**
>
> —Eric McCormack, Emmy Award winner, *Will and Grace*

Acting on a sitcom is the equivalent of doing a half-hour play each week. The morning after taping in front of a live audience, a sitcom cast begins again with a new script. Every one assembles for the "table read." They read for most of the morning, then the cast goes to lunch while the producers, writers, and director confer about possible changes in the script.

Some shows will attempt a run-through on the first day. This is when guest actors have to show their best and demonstrate that they're in sync with the chemistry of the principals on the show. Doing a guest shot is the hardest job. They come in cold, to a group of actors who have been working together for a long time. It's like being a stranger in an established community, in this case a cast and crew of about 120 people.

The next day is given over to run-throughs for the producers and writers. There they learn whether or not the re-writes made after the first day's read-through work.

> **"With Will I wasn't saying the same thing for five days in a row, be-cause we'd change our scripts every day. Things get rewritten and thrown out."**
>
> —Eric McCormack

The third day is far more pressured, because that's when the network executives in charge of comedy, the studio casting people, and the network casting people all come to look at the run-through. The cast digs in to find the humor that's not apparent on the written page—with tone of voice, gestures, glances, and the characteristic bits of "business" the audience has come to expect.

During these rehearsals, the executives pay close attention to the wall of monitors. An actress we know spoke from experience:

> I was in the little room with all the producers when they were taping a new show. They have a phone, and if one thing they don't like happens on the set, they pick up the phone and say, "Who was that actor? I want him off the set, now! I don't like his style, his attitude." Gone. Boom. And if you make a mistake, you cannot stop yourself, and say "I'm sorry, can we do that again?" Just keep going. Make it work. If you have a two-line part, or a guest shot, do your job and don't take charge. Because people will yank you off the set, and you'll never know why.

Next comes camera-blocking day, which can be very long. The cast gets to do their scenes many times. This is where stand-ins are used. After the original camera blocking, stand-ins do the onstage work with cameras and lighting, while the cast repairs to the green room, with the script supervisor, who listens to the scenes. Actors are without their scripts now. They continue rehearsing until they are released.

On performance day, the call is at noon for makeup. The company does one more run-through for the cameras, and another rehearsal. They tape a matinee performance in front of an audience, after which the cast goes to dinner, and gets director's notes. They have just a little time before their second performance that day, the final taping in front of a live audience.

Tomorrow, they start all over again.

IF YOU'RE WORKING IN A COMMERCIAL

Doing commercials well can be as challenging as making a feature film. And like features, commercials have a variety of roles for an actor to play. The actor might be a spokesperson delivering the sales pitch directly to the audience; a character in a dramatization involving husband and wife, sister and brother, mother and child. He or she can be part of an "ensemble" cast portraying a group of people at a resort, at a Christmas dinner, or at a business meeting. The actor may even work as an off-camera announcer delivering the message as we watch the action. Some commercials are meant to be funny, some are low-key or soft-sell, some use a forceful, hard-sell approach. Making a commercial demands sense memory, improvisation, mime, characterization, voice production, concentration, and timing from the actor—just as theater, film, or episodic TV would.

At a commercial shoot, the number of people and the noise will equal that of a prime-time crime drama set. Everyone moves with careful speed, spraying down the shine on a doorknob, masking the light behind a window. The director decides to put a table on blocks, so then the lights must be repositioned. The product is the star, and the star must look perfect. A full day's shooting is not uncommon.

Even on a thirty-second commercial, the director will break the script down into short shots. Each of these moments will be filmed again and again, from different angles and at different distances. For each change, the lights will need adjusting. These changes may reveal other details that need attention. If the camera wobbles on the dolly, the director will need another take. If an actor sneezes, or perspires visibly. . . .

Now that shot will be perfect! But a light blows. Take it again.

Technical problems. Human error. On location, the sun disappears behind a cloud, a passing plane ruins the sound track, someone forgets the bug spray. Saying the lines is the easy part. Synchronizing words, pictures, and product can take a whole day. And it does.

IF YOU'RE WORKING IN A FILM

"They must pay us for the waiting, because we would gladly do the acting for free."

—Orson Welles, Oscar-winning writer, actor, and director

To actors accustomed to completing hour-long shows in one day, the idea of spending an entire day of shooting to complete one scene of a film is, well, kind of like sleepwalking. "How can it take a whole day to do a two-page scene?" they ask. It can, and does, primarily because the motion picture camera sees and magnifies everything. On one-camera film shoots, every detail must be flawless. With time and reshooting, such perfection becomes an attainable goal. Actors called to arrive at 8:00 A.M. or 9:00 A.M. know that they may not be called to the set until after lunchtime. Technical matters will hold up their work. Yet, they must be ready.

ON THE FILM SET, WITH JOE MANTEGNA

Joe Mantegna is an actor's actor. Everyone who has worked with him always speaks of him with the utmost respect and admiration. He has remained loyal to the Chicago acting community with whom he bonded at the beginning of his career. When he got the opportunity to remove his actor's hat, he was given the challenge to transfer David Mamet's play *Lakeboat* to the screen. Because he had a production schedule of five weeks, there was very little rehearsal time available. He had directed the play several years earlier in Los Angeles, yet he felt that production had to be forgotten when working with his new ensemble cast. Because they were pros, he wanted them to make the roles their own.

If you've got the racehorses, let them run. My job as a director is to make sure the track's in good shape, they know the direction to go, and make everything around them work.

As an actor you can get spoiled. You do your part and then you go back to your trailer and let the director worry about everything else. Well, now I had to be that guy who has to worry about everything else. And this is where the buck stops. When the questions come, you better have an answer. I had to have a clear idea of what I wanted. Yet I have to keep a strong sense of myself open to whatever they were going to bring me.

Even typical days can be untypical because film is a director-driven medium. A typical day on the set with Woody Allen is going to be different from a typical day with Francis Ford Coppola or David Mamet. Each director set his own parameters, depending upon how he works. A typical day on a Woody Allen set will have less communication between actor and director, because he felt you were the right person for the role, so there really isn't much to talk about. His whole process is based on camera angles. He shoots "in master" a lot—no rehearsals. You go out, he'll say, "Roll 'em," and you do it. It is like life, and that is the way he is.

Mamet may want to sit down and spend the first couple of days just reading the script. It will be two weeks before you even get to the set. He will listen and maybe make some changes and then put some of it on its feet. I have found that rehearsing for film is a whole different ball game from rehearsing for theater. Its benefits are not as great as one would imagine. There is a limit to its value. What you find out in film is that nine times out of ten, when you are ultimately shooting a scene it is going to be in an environment that is totally alien to however you may have rehearsed it, because you are going to be adding a million other elements. For example, let us say the scene is going to be outside on a bridge, and it is going to be thirty degrees, and then there are the cameras and the lights and you have to deal with all those conditions. So the rehearsal hall system doesn't apply anymore. If you rehearse too much, then it is difficult to be flexible.

Some directors love to shoot sequentially, but it proves to be very costly. Mamet tried in *House of Games.* There is a reason to shoot out of sequence: logistics. If the writer wrote it that way, then you can do it. But let's say you have a scene that takes place in a house three different times in the movie. You shouldn't have to break down the set three times. You shoot them all at once.

What is really difficult is when you shoot the last scene of the movie on the first day. You might be a victim of the location or the weather. The movie might span a three-month period. It is supposed to end in the dead of winter and start sometime in the early fall. Your shooting schedule might start in late February, and then you will have to shoot the end first because of the snow on the ground. If you are fairly new at this game, and you have come primarily from the theater, you might panic at the thought of shooting the last scene first. You are not sure what the character has been through—where he has been, what he has done, all the motivation questions. You start to realize that unless you want to make yourself crazy, you have to trust that what you shoot on Monday is going to match up with what you shoot on Tuesday, which might be the first scene of the movie. I would certainly know the whole script and the structure.

What works for me is to take each day's scene, or work, as a film unto itself. You give each day a beginning, a middle, and an end, and play for the reality of that scene. If it has been written correctly, you won't have to worry about it. You play the reality of that scene. You do every scene that way and then it is the editor's problem to put it all together, and it will mesh.

319

From the first moment they say "Action!" you have to make your choice. You have to be whoever you are going to be, and that is disconcerting, especially the first couple of days. You are making a commitment with little or no rehearsal time, and no history of relating to the other characters or actors. Most actors would say, after two weeks of shooting, "Great, now I feel comfortable, so let's throw this film away and start over." Woody Allen can and will do that. Few directors will, because after the film is put together, no one in the audience is going to know that that scene was shot on the first day.

When they say "Roll 'em" it doesn't matter where you are. I learned that in the theater. When I was opening on Broadway *[in Glengarry Glen Ross]* the anticipation was awesome. The first moment you step out you realize it is just people in seats, and it is no different than when you did it in high school. It is the same thing filming at different locations.

There is not a lot of difference between directors outside of their personalities. There is no one magic way of doing things. The bottom line is that they all have to say, "Roll camera," and you have to act, and they have to say, "Cut."

I have been lucky, because some of the great directors I have worked with also write—Coppola, Mamet, Allen, Barry Levinson, Steven Zallien. The advantage is that the director is more in tune with the creative process. Coppola is very big, very expansive in his descriptions. He paints pictures with everything at his disposal.

There has to be trust between the director and the actors. On stage, when the play starts, the actor is steering the car. It is like the gun goes off for the race: I have to run it now—there is no stopping until the finish line. In a film there are a million finish lines. The director can totally orchestrate how you run to that finish line. If he doesn't like it, he can stop it and say, "No, run it this way." So there has to be tremendous trust. Because even if you run it ten different times, and you think number nine was the one, it may not be the one he liked. You are at the mercy of the director's talent and decisions. Mamet is terrific with actors. He is patient, knowledgeable, and smart. But no director will give the final editing approval to any actor.

ACTING ON THE STAGE

"Theater, to me, is the only place left where you can't fake it. You can turn in a lousy performance in movies, and a good editor can make you look decent. But theater! You gotta get up there and give, for two, two and a half hours, however long it takes."

—Anthony LaPaglia, award-winning actor, "Jack Malone," *Without A Trace*

We are assuming that our readers have some familiarity with theatrical production—the relatively long rehearsal period and the hoped-for long run of performances. In this medium the challenge is to keep the performance fresh, to retain the illusion of the first time. You may be doing your hundredth performance, but the audience may have never seen the show before.

Joe Mantegna's remark about having his actors in *Lakeboat* make their roles their own ("If you've got the racehorses, let them run") reminds us of a story about the great actor Alfred Lunt. He was also a sought-after director, and he once directed the London company of Terence Rattigan's play, *O Mistress Mine*.

Leading lady Ann Lee (who was quite tall) was leaving the company. Her understudy, Bessie Love (who was not tall), was to play the part the next evening. At the understudy rehearsal, Ms. Love started to do the same "business" as Ms. Lee. Mr. Lunt stopped her. "No, Bessie dear, you can't do Ann. You have to do yourself."

The consummate professional, Mr. Lunt continued to grow in performance. Just before the matinee before the final performance of a comedy he was doing, Mr. Lunt told Dick Van Patten, who was playing his son, "I think if you say this line at this particular point, we can get another laugh." Van Patten did so, and they got the laugh. This was after a two-year run. That's acting. That's commitment to excellent acting.

COPING WITH SUCCESS

"I think one of the big problems is that no one walks anywhere. The car goes to the restaurant and the valet parks it. There is none of that brush with humanity, and after a while people start to feel entitled to a Mercedes, to live in a nice place, to be treated a certain way. 'I am wearing these wonderful clothes. How dare you not give me the respect I deserve?' Then when you have an actor who gets a little bit of success and they have a chair with their name on it, assistants on headsets catering to their every wish, it can become

ridiculous. As soon as you start believing your own press they need to throw you an inner tube because you are lost at sea."

— Ms. Sam Downey, personal manager, Henry Downey Talent Management

When you decided to become an actor, did you visualize an Oscar, an Emmy, or a Tony in your future? Did you watch the Oscars every year, fantasizing that one year they would be calling your name? Did you practice an acceptance speech, just in case? But if that dream comes true, how do you deal with all that comes with it?

Some actors have a hard time coping. For instance, it seems strange to us that, after working so hard and so long, anyone would flee from success. But that is precisely what one young woman chose to do. She had a contract role on a highly rated daytime soap. It was, she said, a dream come true. But as her story line progressed, she began to dislike the work. Doing the show two, three, or four times a week was too tough. She didn't like her story line. She hadn't made any new friends. She wanted to be with her boyfriend, and she missed her family.

And so, without consulting anyone—her agent, her producer, or her union, all of whom had helped in some way to ensure her respectable status in her chosen career—she announced, "I don't want to be here." And she quit the show.

There was no way she could be persuaded to stay until the end of her story line, or until a replacement could be found. She refused to consider the other actors whose careers were linked to hers. She just wanted out. Her story line was accelerated, and out is what she was.

We tell this story to alert you to the natural anxieties that can suddenly overtake you when everything seems to be going almost too well.

Let's look at another scenario. Let's assume that you have become highly successful and very visible. You've been able to buy an old movie star's mansion, you show up at the most photographed parties. You park your Mercedes in a space that has your name on it.

You have an entourage: a business manager to handle your finances, a publicist to handle requests for interviews, a secretary to handle the deluge of fan mail. Then there's the fashion consultant, the tailor, the on-call hairstylist, the masseuse, the personal trainer, the chef, the housekeeper, and, most important, the bodyguard. Not to mention your top-echelon agents and personal manager, who work so hard for you. Your phone number is unlisted. You've got what you've always dreamed about.

But what's missing in this picture? Where's the support system you relied upon as you were climbing up the ladder? The trustworthy friends and family members? The agent who got you your first big breaks? Think of all the sacrifices you have made. And for what? To lose your privacy, to be trailed by greedy paparazzi, to succumb to a dependence on drugs and alcohol? Who is that drawn, anorexic, burnt-out, unhappy actor you see in the mirror? The dream has become a nightmare.

This short scenario is not an exaggeration. You frequently read about a celebrity's cocaine habit, drunk-driving arrest, barroom brawl, or overdose, and then the predictable visits to detox centers, clinics, and courtrooms.

Coping with the pressures of staying on top must be very difficult for those who are catapulted to stardom in today's celebrity culture without training or experience, because they haven't paid their dues. Actors with extensive stage credits, who've studied with the likes of Frank Langella or Alice Spivak, are able to accept the accolades of an adoring public without going off the deep end. But the very young—whether they are exceptionally beautiful, handsome, or off-beat types—who have been lucky enough to be selected, say, from an open call and relocated to New York or Los Angeles to assume contract roles in soaps or features, may have difficulty keeping their feet firmly on the ground. They are vulnerable to the temptations of living it up, listening to the wrong people, and believing their own publicity.

When, or if, you start to wonder "What's it all about?" and "What am I doing here?" turn to the people whose job it is to help you. Talk it out. Calm down. Give yourself, and the people you work with, a chance.

> **"You really have to think about your career as a life. It's so different now. You used to get your experience coming up through the ranks. Now there are lots of theater-training programs, but nothing to tell young people about The Business, or their future in it. I try to encourage people to really get down to the finite details. Just imagine what they want their life to look like . . . when they get that dream job."**
>
> —Amy Dolan Fletcher, Actors' Equity Outreach executive

THE IMPORTANCE OF A SUPPORT SYSTEM

Actors become commodities associated with dollar signs. They lack a solid support system—family, teacher, mentor, close friends, or sweetheart who can exert a positive influence and give them a reality check. Here's how some successful actors have put a foundation in place:

"No career is more important than the way you are as a human being. That philosophy has enabled me to go through just about everything. Nobody stays a star. A long-range goal, or a series of goals, is important for a long-term career. You have to have a foundation, be a person of integrity."

—Judith Light, Emmy Award–winning actress

"Our relationship comes first. Obviously, there are times when we have to be apart. We also have not taken work so that we could be together. When we talk to young people who are just getting into The Business, we tell them, 'It will never make you happy, it's a business of highs and lows. There are many wonderful moments, but you always want more. And you always have to find another job.' I feel blessed that I have found my life partner. That is my focus. Jason is truly what makes me happy."

—Tony–nominated actress Marin Mazzie, who met her husband,
Jason Danieley (Curtains), when they were cast in the same musical

"I think you have to have somebody as a partner who shares what you value in life. I've always loved raising a family, and Don always gets that it's a big important job and a hard job. And it never ends."

—Meryl Streep, Academy Award–winning actress

Let us offer some suggestions to help you realize your worth as a successful human being and artist:

- **Keep in touch with who you were before success came along.** This is your "reality base." This connection is easy if you have a family. Your kids don't treat you like a star, just as a parent.

- **Live well, but not beyond your means.** Do not attempt to create an image of a lifestyle for yourself that is exaggerated and dishonest.

- **Invest in yourself.** Continue going to classes, rehearsing plays, reading, participating in creative projects such as writing or producing. Gain a sense of control over your own life.

- **Love yourself.** Value your psychological and physical well-being. Do nothing to harm your body or alter your consciousness, otherwise it will show, not only on camera but in life, and will continuously jeopardize your personal life.

"I went through a personal and emotional crisis in the mid-seventies when I was living here in Los Angeles. I sort of reached my wits' end. I saw that my life was running downhill. So I started a whole series of new habits. **When I made that conscious decision to change direction, it was like that hand of fate came down and said, 'Okay, you want to change direction, we'll help you.' It was a peculiar change of destiny. I can't describe it exactly, but ever since that day my life has taken on a whole new color and hue of brightness. My life has been blessed ever since."**

—Sir Anthony Hopkins, Academy Award–winning actor

Keep your sense of humor, and continue to enjoy the process.

CHAPTER 17

Child Performers

"The thing that makes most child actors wonderful is that they don't do a lot of head work because they are too young to know anything about craft. The inspiration comes from their inner selves. I think that is something that all child actors have contributed to this industry. The purity of instinct."

—Darryl Hickman, former child actor

Today's gifted children have more opportunities than ever before to work in commercials, soap operas, films, and theater. Commercials probably use more children than any other medium. Stage musicals, such as *Oliver, The Music Man, Annie, Gypsy, The King and I, The Sound of Music, Mary Poppins, Billy Elliot, High School Musical,* and *The Lion King* have for years continued to give children the opportunity to demonstrate their acting, singing, and dancing talents.

There has also been a noticeable increase of young people getting leads in films. Who doesn't remember Tatum O'Neal, who at ten was the youngest person to win an Oscar for her "old soul" portrayal in *Paper Moon?* Anna Paquin won the best supporting actress Oscar at age eleven for her role in *The Piano;* Keisha Castle-Hughes was nominated for best leading actress for her first feature, *Whale Rider;* Abigail Breslin was nominated for best supporting actress for *Little Miss Sunshine;* and Haley Joel Osment was nominated for best supporting actor in *Sixth Sense.* Reese Witherspoon made her debut at fourteen in *Man in the Moon;* and at the age of six, the phenomenal Dakota Fanning held her own with Sean Penn in *I Am Sam* and became a bona fide star opposite Denzel Washington in *Man on Fire*. Her agent has said that "Dakota has a one-hundred-year-old soul. There's something magical about her."

Television shows such as *7th Heaven*, *Everybody Hates Chris*, *The Medium*, *Six Feet Under, Weeds*, and *According to Jim*, require children, often as family members. Young performers are also often seen as guest stars in emotionally draining roles on episodic series such as *Law & Order*; *CSI: Crime Scene Investigation*; *Without A Trace*; and *Cold Case*. Daytime dramas hire toddlers to tweens to portray the children of the principal characters.

Child actors were given starring roles on Nickelodeon and the Disney Channel, founded in 1979 and 1983 respectively for a younger audience. *Lizzy McGuire* made Hilary Duff a star, and *All That* featured a young Kenan Thompson, who became a regular on *Saturday Night Live*. In casting the *New Mickey Mouse Club* (1988–94) Matt Casella gave Ryan Gosling, Keri Russell, and Justin Timberlake their starts.

CHILD STARS OF YESTERYEAR

Adult stars of the vaudeville circuits used to refuse to appear on the same bill with children and animals, because they knew they would be upstaged by them. W.C. Fields always sneered at Baby Leroy in his films, and while his sarcasm was hilarious, there was true fury behind it.

In movies of the 1930s and 1940s, appealing moppets like Shirley Temple, Freddie Bartholomew, Dickie Moore, Dean Stockwell, Natalie Wood, and a wide-eyed sweet-voiced Margaret O'Brien could steal the focus from any adult in the picture. Can anyone forget Miss O'Brien's Tootie in *Meet Me in St. Louis*? And then there were the irresistible musical comedy talents of such teen stars as Judy Garland, Mickey Rooney, and Jane Powell.

Recently Shirley Temple received the SAG Life Achievement Award. When she accepted it, she advised the audience and the viewers who wanted longevity in The Business to "Start early!" Shirley was the third child of a mother who had wanted to be a performer. During the pregnancy, she would attend dance recitals and listen to music on the radio and the record player, hoping for a daughter who would be artistically inclined. Her strategy must have worked because little Shirley could walk at thirteen months, start keeping time tapping her feet to music at age two, and began dancing school at age three. She was discovered at the school and signed for $10 a day to star in a series of one-reel films.

Although rejected by Hal Roach, along with thousands of other hopefuls, for the *Our Gang* comedies, Shirley got work in a series of two-reelers at the whopping salary of $50 each. After bit parts in feature films, her singing and dancing talents and natural acting ability got her noticed and she got cast in her star-making turn as *Little Miss Marker*. Her costar, character actor Adolphe Menjou, declared that "if she were forty years old and on stage all her life, she wouldn't have had the time to learn all she knew about acting." He called her an "Ethel Barrymore" at age four.

Shirley's approach to acting was considered unique. "When you start anything at age three, you don't realize it's work," she said. Her costars and directors referred to her as "One-Take Temple" because her memorization of scripts—including everyone else's parts—was photographic and her movements usually perfect the first time before the camera. Even the great tap dancer Bill "Bojangles" Robinson who taught her how to tap felt she was the best living tap dancer for her age. He taught her strenuous routines without letting her know it was work or allowing her to become tired, a technique her mother had taught her.

Behind every child performer there seems to be a very strong or aggressive parent. The "pushy stage mother" has been immortalized on stage and screen in *Gypsy*, the saga of Mama Rose and her daughters June (June Havoc) and Louise (Gypsy Rose Lee), whom she pushed, dragged, and forced into show business. June Havoc spoke to cast members of the *Gypsy* revival starring Tyne Daly. While she certainly enjoyed the musical, many of the details of life with her mother and sister were actually fantasy.

> I didn't earn a penny until I was two years old. At eighteen months, I stood up, although I didn't talk yet, and I danced around the sugar bowl. Mother was in an unhappy marriage and I think that she did what almost any other woman would have done. I became her "escape clause." We boarded a train for Hollywood when I was two. I never really got work until mother got over the fact that fluffing my hair out and making me look as pretty as she could didn't work. When I started playing waifs and orphans in rags we cleaned up and did well. I was also able to appear in comedies with Mary Astor, Bebe Daniels, and Harold Lloyd. When I finally started appearing in Vaudeville I was billed as the "Hollywood Baby." Louise never wanted to work in Vaudeville. She kept wanting to go back to Seattle.

INITIAL CONCERNS

Both parent and child need to know the right ways to seek stardom or simply good, honest work opportunities for a child. The most important rule is: *The child must want to do it!* We think it is appalling that a parent will sometimes force a young person into a life of commercial auditions and tap, singing, and acting classes when the child would prefer to be playing with the neighbors' children. It is dangerous to attempt to live vicariously through children. Let the choice be theirs.

There are two types of parents: those that influence children in a good way and those that influence the kids in a bad way. The parents who have a good influence on their kids are primarily looking out for their child's welfare. Those who aren't manifest their bad behavior in many telltale ways. Sometimes parents who fall into the "bad" category will program a child to compliment the casting director, as in, "You're the prettiest casting director I've seen" or "My last casting director said I was *so* good." Sometimes these parents coach their kids inappropriately—to do a specific hand gesture for each line, for example, so the kid might repeat the gesture over and over. With this sort of ill-conceived coaching, kids get stuck, can't change, and can't take direction. Meanwhile, 80 percent of the reason to cast certain kids over others is their ability to take direction.

If a casting director takes the time to tell the parent the child is not strong enough, the parent should not argue the point. One desperate mother wrote a casting director after her son had been turned down, begging her to hire him because, among other things, she was disabled. "Please," she wrote, "give him a chance."

Another example of a turnoff from parents is playing petty games of one-upmanship, letting everyone know a child is especially gifted and successful. Some parents will lie about their child's age and then blame the agent who told them to do that. Some parents feel entitled to make outrageous demands once their child is cast, and this behavior often results in the young performer losing the role. Some parents arrive at auditions bragging about their child's shoot in New Zealand; others try to "psych out" kids by making sure to slip in offhand references to hotshot agents and big-time auditions.

When children work, one parent is required to be on the set at all times, which means that job hours must be flexible and take a back seat to the child's career. Agents and managers prefer families with no financial limits as well as the commitment of one parent to treat the child's career as a full-time job. A typical scenario is that of a mother who relocated to southern California and started a new business with her husband to help their teenage daughter pursue her dream. In the beginning it was difficult to break even, much less make a profit, when they were paying for acting classes, manager's commissions, and a private coach. They soon discovered that it takes from forty to fifty auditions for every job the young performer lands, which translates into many hours on the road.

Lola Love, President and CEO of LHB Entertainment in Los Angeles, has more than twenty years of experience in the entertainment industry and specializes in guiding the careers of a very select group of young and up-and-coming talent.

> I love working with kids and when I find that combination of a parent who cares about the child and the child who cares about the parent, it is magic. When you have the right pieces that fit together so well you create a wonderful synergy. You can't help but have success.

> I am more productive if I am in synch with the entire family, not just the child. If anything is out of whack, it is going to affect the child. I tell the parents all the time to be careful about what they say in the car, because the child will walk into that casting office and repeat what they said.

> Parents have to be calm and patient, nurturing, and encouraging. If they are not, the child will adopt other qualities that are the opposite. You need a calm kid on the set. It is the parent's responsibility to see that their child is welcomed. That can mean more scenes, a creation of stories for them, because they are a delight to be around. Child and parent—it's a package deal.

Melissa Berger, talent agent at CESD in Santa Monica, is a former actress who now handles young performers under age twenty-one for television and commercials.

> We interview the parents, too. We have a family now where one sister is taking off, but it used to be the other sister who was getting all the work. The parents do a really good job of treating all the kids equally. They are still making their beds in the morning and cleaning their rooms.

Jaynie Jackson represents Chayil Entertainment in Los Angeles, an artist development and management company for singers, producers, writers, and actors. Some of her young clients have appeared on *Every-body Hates Chris* and Nickelodeon's *Ned's Declassified School Survival Kit*. She believes:

> It would be a good idea to give the parents of potential clients a ques-
> tionnaire regarding the family history, marital status, custody deci-
> sions, occupations, educational backgrounds, credit rating, character
> references, and medical history, including illnesses caused by sub-
> stance abuse. Too often I have loved the child and found the parents to
> be only interested in their paychecks and what it could do for them.

Parents of young performers should keep the following in mind:

- Young people are extremely impressionable and, like adults, sensitive to rejection. They can become hard, as well. One casting director was stunned by the level of talent and competitiveness that
exists among young performers today. They need constant encour-
agement and a solid support system at home. Parents who disagree
about the wisdom of a show business career for their children often
become so combative over the subject that their marriage is jeopardized. We hope such cases are rare.

- Good stage mothers need to follow through on instructions, be
pleasant and professional and, despite the L.A. traffic, always deliver the talent to wherever they need to be on time. A veteran's car
is stocked for the sudden audition or callback: snacks, water, headshots, demo reels, hair products, and several sets of clothes.

- Casting directors want young performers to be kids. Kids who have
no personality or are cold fish are turnoffs. Some mothers have
been known to dress their daughters to look like dolls in a toy store
instead of real people. The child should be permitted to wear something comfortable and should have a choice in the outfit. A casting
director, director, or producer may be completely won over by the
individuality and personality expressed in the child's selection. They
don't want to see young girls in high heels and short skirts. It's difficult
to watch them squirming and wobbling. Young boys can get away
with wearing baseball caps, T-shirts, or football jerseys. That is appropriate. Avoid baggy pants. If the casting director wants to see a specific wardrobe for the audition, the parent will be told in advance. Children arriving in costume get mostly negative reviews. Photos should
accurately reflect what the child looks like now, not a year ago.

- Casting directors want to see that the kids have something going on in their lives besides being actors. They are more interesting if they do karate, play sports, have life experience. Personality and confidence are essential and they have to be comfortable with rejection. The parents have to take some responsibility.

GETTING A START IN SHOW BUSINESS

School plays, choir and instrumental recitals, and dance festivals offer opportunities to perform in front of an audience and acquire a sense of discipline. Participation in the high school drama club, in speech contests or forensic events such as debating, original oratory, humorous, dramatic, or oral interpretation are all invaluable for developing good speech, projection, poise, timing, and appearance, as well as acting and writing skills.

Cherry Jones, two-time Tony Award–winning actress (*Doubt* and *The Heiress*), says, "I had a couple of childhood teachers growing up; Miss Ruby Krider, who taught creative dramatics to little children in my hometown, and her protégé, Linda Wilson at the high school, who spent hours taking us to speech tournaments and directing us in school plays."

If a child wants to be in musical theater, training in tap, ballet, baton twirling, and singing should start at an early age. If the parents can't afford lessons, singing in the school or church choir will suffice. In fact, the majority of kids who audition for *The Lion King* have no training beyond singing in choir and school productions.

PLACES FOR YOUNG PERFORMERS TO TRAIN AND LEARN

Wherever you live and work, you can find community theaters, children's theaters, and even university theaters where there are productions that need children, such as the annual presentations of *A Christmas Carol*.

Growing and learning should be encouraged, of course, but parents should keep in mind that there are a lot of get-rich-quick entrepreneurs preying on naive parents (some have been wanted in six states!). If you are in doubt about a teacher's qualifications, or if you find that certain schools are interested only in financial profits or make false promises, contact the local Attorney General's office, the Department of Consumer Affairs, or local office of actors' unions in your area.

Here are some of the many excellent places where young performers are challenged, nurtured, inspired and constantly preparing for their big break.

Summer Camps for Performing Artists

Every year the *New York Times* Sunday magazine will advertise a number of summer programs for child performers. Usually they are coeducational, welcome ages six through eighteen and hire trained teachers for the singing, dancing, and acting classes and choreographers and directors for a number of well-rehearsed productions. Do a Google search for performing arts camps and an extensive list of sites will appear.

For thirty years, Stagedoor Manor (www.stagedoormanor.com), located in Loch Sheldrake, New York, has offered total theater immersion for young performers ages ten through eighteen. Projects the camp has originated include a development workshop of *Rent* for high schools and the world-premiere production of Disney's *High School Musical*. Every summer, working alumni—directors, agents, producers, and managers— visit the camp to share their insights in The Business with the young performers. "I was born at Stagedoor Manor," says writer/director Todd Graff. "The camp is like Oz. Your real life is in black and white, but the minute you step off the bus, everything is in color." Other renowned alums include actors Natalie Portman, Zach Braff, Jon Cryer, Mandy Moore, Robert Downey Jr., and Jennifer Jason Leigh.

Children's Theaters

Many children's theaters offer conservatory training to child performers ages five to eighteen as well as producing a full season of plays to entertain young audiences. Some also stage productions featuring the students.

The Walden Theatre

The Walden Theatre (www.waldentheatre.org), a private, nonprofit conservatory in Louisville, Kentucky, provides young performers with a solid foundation in the performing arts and has been producing prize-winning student playwrights and actors since 1976. Each season, the theater presents plays that run the gamut from classic comedy to cutting-edge contemporary drama, all with important themes that are socially relevant to the times we live in. Artistic director Charlie Sexton is a firm believer that "seeing a play at Walden will help ensure that the community continues to have a positive place for young people to find themselves and follow their dreams." A typical schedule of plays would include *The Hotel Baltimore,* by Lanford Wilson; *Playing for Time,* by Arthur Miller (in partnership with the Louisville Youth Orchestra); *Tartuffe,* by Molière; a Young Playwrights Festival featuring the work of the young writers at Walden; and the Young American Shakespeare Festival, featuring productions of *King Lear, As You Like It, and Troilus and Cressida.*

The Walden Theatre Young Playwrights Program has been in existence since 1981. A sample of a monologue and an excerpt from a short play written by Walden's young playwrights appear in the Script Analysis sections of Chapters 18 and 22.

Dallas Children's Theater Academy

According to director of education Nancy Schaeffer, the Dallas Children's Theater (www.dct.org), is firmly grounded in the belief that theater is a great art form for children of all ages to explore. The approach is developmentally age-appropriate: Pre-K students work with classic stories and create characters; students aged five through eleven work on drama techniques by creating, rehearsing, and presenting an original show; students ten through twelve have options in scene work or movie-making classes; students twelve and up work with professional actors, directors and teachers to improve and enhance their acting skills. Students twelve and older are also members of the Teen Conservatory and can join The Improv Troupe, which performs for the public every year. Those who qualify after an audition for the Crescent Players, in addition to attending advanced classes, have the opportunities to audition for mainstage shows and work with experienced theater professionals. The sessions are twelve weeks in length and include a final showcase. There is also a Showbiz summer and Teen Conservatory.

Children's Musical Theater San Jose

The mission of Children's Musical Theater San Jose (CMT; www.cmt.com) is to use musical theater to nurture and to educate the youth of today to become the artists, patrons, and leaders of tomorrow. Its goals are to provide a healthy environment where young people are empowered and instilled with universal life skills; a supportive and creative experience for children and young adults to develop self esteem; an opportunity for children and teachers to integrate the arts into the learning experience; an instrument for children to learn communication skills; and a place where any child with an interest in the performing arts can practice live theater fundamentals and experience the pride of accomplishment.

Founded in 1968 to meet the need for a community-based youth theater, CMT has grown from a grassroots, volunteer organization run by parents to the largest theatrical and performing and training organization of its kind in the nation. Each year, CMT mounts eight productions at the 500-seat Montgomery Theater in downtown San Jose. Nearly 800 young performers are featured in the four Rising Stars productions (ages six to thirteen) and four mainstage productions (ages fourteen to twenty). Because every child who auditions is cast, directors are faced with the challenge of using more than 100 performers whose talent and experience vary widely. Consequently shows are double cast and works selected in part because they offer options to augment casts by including multiple featured and ensemble roles. Kevin Hauge, CMT Artistic Director since 1996, says,

> We have an opportunity to work with kids whose caliber of performing varies greatly. It's easy to make talented people look great. The challenge is being able to take the kids that have all the heart and soul and energy, and harness that into something that will stretch them to be the best that they can be. I believe that children's theater is an art form unto itself. It is not just about children's shows or diluted versions of Broadway classics. It is about taking a fresh approach, stimulating kids, fostering an appreciation of the arts, and teaching the interpersonal skills and self-confidence to help them succeed in their education and adult lives.

CMT's Theater As Digital Activity (TADA) division is an online theater program that allows young people everywhere—including those isolated by illness, disability, or geographic distance—to share in the excitement of creating a theatrical production from concept to stage. The program uses Internet technology (including live chats, electronic bulletin boards, e-mail, and an interactive Web site) to bring kids together with theater professionals who help turn their idea into a production. TADA's debut musical, *PULSE: The Rhythm of Life*, inspired by kids' experiences of growing up with a disability or serious illness, was the subject of an Emmy-nominated PBS documentary, narrated by Annette Bening.

CMT has received a recent string of honors, including a National Endowment for the Arts Access to Artistic Excellence grant. The company is the first non-Equity theater group in the nation to produce *Miss Saigon* and *Aida*, and has been granted West Coast premiere rights to Radio City Music Hall's *A Christmas Carol*.

A Network of Performing Arts Schools

The popular movie Fame brought international attention and recognition to New York's La Guardia High School of the Performing Arts. The school's alumni comprise a Who's Who of the worlds of theater and music. Some 350 other arts-focused secondary schools, as well as colleges and universities, are members of the International Network of Performing and Visual Arts Schools, which inspires and promotes excellence in arts education. Most of the schools require an audition and a degree of academic achievement as entrance criteria. According to former executive director Rod Daniel, "It is inspiring to know the true successes that go on every day in our schools. They are a playing field where we demonstrate the qualities of sportsmanship, tenacity, competitive spirit, and teamwork."

To find out about a school near you, visit www.artsschoolsnetwork.org.

youngARTS Program®

youngARTS, a program of the National Foundation for Advancement in the Arts (NFAA), is based on the belief that the arts sustain their power only if they are continually renewed and refreshed by the vigor and perspective of young artists. Every year, youngARTS Recognition and Talent Search identifies the nation's 160 most talented high school seniors in the performing, visual, and literary arts, and makes scholarships and awards available to them.

youngARTS receives 6,000 to 8,000 applications annually, and each January the national ARTS awardees are flown to Miami for a week of master classes and seminars to compete for cash prizes. Twenty are named Presidential Scholars in the Arts for excellence in theater, voice, dance, film and video, jazz, music, visual arts, and writing.

Theater awardees have enjoyed careers as working actors on Broadway and Off-Broadway, in touring companies and in regional theaters. They have appeared in many major films and television shows. Brandon Victor Dixon (awardee in Theater, 1999) was nominated for a Tony award for outstanding featured actor in a musical in *The Color Purple*; Sean McCourt (Musical Theater and Presidential Scholar in the Arts, 1989) has been in a string of musicals that include *Mary Poppins*, *Bat Boy: The Musical*, *It Ain't*

Nothin But the Blues, *A Woman of No Importance*, and *Wicked*; Raul Es-
parza (Musical Theater, 1988) has starred on Broadway in *Cabaret, Chitty
Chitty Bang Bang*, and the revival of *Company*; Michael James Scott (Musi-
cal Theater, 2001) was a cast member in *The Pirate Queen*; Tony Yazbeck
(Musical Theater, 1997) is featured as Al in the revival of *A Chorus Line* on
Broadway; Cricket Leigh (Theater, 1991) is the voice of Mai in Nickelodeon's
hit animated series, *Avatar*; Alison Lohman (Theater, 1997) has appeared in
the features *White Oleander*, *Big Fish*, and *Matchstick Men*, and she won the
ShoWest Female Star of Tomorrow award. Donna Lynne Champlin (Musical
Theater and Presidential Scholar in the Arts, 1989) has several Broadway
musicals to her credit, including the 2005 revival of the Tony Award–winning *Sweeney Todd*, starring Patti Lupone. Donna Lynn remembers:

> ARTS week in Miami was at once both marvelous and terrifying. It
> was marvelous because I'd always felt very isolated socially in my age
> group and all of a sudden I was with a bunch of kids I could communi-
> cate with and really understand.
>
> Ironically, ARTS gave us a feeling of kinship with each other
> and there was none of the jealousy that seemed to be so prevalent in
> my own school surroundings back home. I knew my talent, and I knew
> my direction, but ARTS helped me to realize that I didn't have to be
> alone my whole life to pursue it. I went home more socially confident.
>
> On the flip side, ARTS week made me realize that the pond
> back home was nothing compared to the ocean I was now in at NFAA.
> This epiphany was a necessary "ego blow" for me and I learned that
> while I was a young artist worthy of recognition by ARTS, I was also
> one of many artists worthy of that recognition. That was a big step
> towards letting the fear go and the art in.
>
> The scholarships from both NFAA and the Presidential Schol-
> arship in the Arts were helpful in financially surviving Carnegie Mellon
> University. The fact that at the age of seventeen I performed at the
> Kennedy Center and met the President of the United States and shook
> his hand is still mind-boggling to me decades later.

For more information, visit www.youngARTS.org.

Rita Litton's ACTeen®

Acting schools throughout the country specialize in classes for children and
teens. In New York, ACTeen teaches teens and young adults (ages thirteen to

twenty) acting skills for on camera work (film, television, and commercials). ACTeen's students are offered acting training in theater and on camera acting fundamentals, as well as electives that strengthen the "total actor."

Rita Litton, who founded ACTeen in 1978, began her career at UCLA and San Francisco's American Conservatory Theater and has appeared in more than a hundred roles in theaters in New York and regionally. Her background has prepared her to help her students develop a professional attitude toward their work.

> There are requirements, exercises to complete, homework preparation. An ACTeen graduate learns to take responsibility for the work. Remember you have a scene partner who is depending on you. You don't come to class and not know your lines. You never talk while a director is talking. Responsibility for the work means you are looking for a career with longevity. Personality is not enough, great looks are not enough, being oneself is not enough. Well-trained actors know how to find solutions to problems; they are flexible, directable, yet not afraid to make choices; they are well spoken, have ensemble skills, confidence, and physical grace. Youth can open doors; but the door stays open for the wise actor with training.

ACTeen alumni get the opportunity to appear in Talent Agent Showcases twice a year in September and May, by audition only. Graduates include Daniella Alonso (*As the World Turns*), Jordana Brewster (*Annapolis*), Jamie-Lynn Sigler (*The Sopranos*, *Beauty and the Beast*), Jon Seda (*Close to Home*, *Third Watch*), Kimberly Williams (*According to Jim*), and Jordana Spiro (*My Boys*, *Cold Case*).

For more information about the ACTeen programs, check out the Web site at www.acteen.com.

LEARNING ESSENTIAL SKILLS

Children who grow up in the metropolitan New York area have the advantage of plentiful theater and television job possibilities, but they are frequently disqualified from major roles because they talk with a regional accent. Their intonation and pronunciation are peculiar to Brooklyn, the Bronx, Queens, Yonkers, Long Island, and New Jersey.

Any regional speech is limiting, whether it's Southern, Midwestern, Northeastern, or Texan. Children whose speech shows signs of becoming so accented should go to authorized speech teachers or voice coaches who specialize in nonregional speech. The earlier they start (dialect coach Amy Stoller believes it's preferable to begin before the age of nine) the easier it will be to develop good speech habits and a good ear, so they will be able to assume whatever dialect a role demands. Amy tells the story of Dylan, a nine-year-old:

> He came to work with me on losing his Alabama accent. I told him I didn't want him to lose his accent completely so he worked very hard acquiring an additional speech pattern (Non-Regional American speech). His new speech pattern eliminated specific regional markers in his natural speech. He was then prepared to audition for young Tarzan in the Broadway musical and he got the role.

Reading ability is also important. It is shocking nowadays to discover that a great many high school graduates cannot read properly. Reading skills should be practiced on a daily basis. Children should be encouraged to read aloud, and parents should set aside time to listen to poetry, a story, a fairy tale, a nursery rhyme, or an essay, perhaps even one that the child has written.

Too often an unqualified parent will coach a child with commercial copy or a scripted scene. The child will try to imitate the parents' amateurish line readings. Parental pressure to get a script line-perfect can produce so much panic for the young actor that he will forget any or all of the over-rehearsed script. We cannot overstate the need for proper training with a respected teacher. Better study habits will help the young performer avoid a memory loss and give him the confidence to win the part. Young performers should also be familiar with stage vocabulary, so that if the director says, "Use a head voice, not a chest voice," the child knows what that means.

Talent agent Melissa Berger offers sage advice about the skills a beginner must acquire for a successful career.

> I tell young actors to read out loud every day, five, ten minutes a day. Make that your homework. Don't just go from pages five to twenty. Go back over the same page two more times. Play with your voice. Learn how to internalize the text, make it so the words come off the page and out of your mouth so that it is natural. Open your imagination with that. You can do a lot on your own. You should be in class. You should have that other eye.

BREAKING INTO THE BUSINESS

Kids enter The Business by various routes. Letters from eager parents seeking breaks for their beautiful babies, talented dancers, or child prodigies pour into the offices of casting directors and agents. Sometimes a mother will read in the local papers about a beauty pageant or a modeling and talent talent competition. Judges at those events might be casting directors, agents, or managers who specialize in young talent. Elijah Wood (*Lord of the Rings* trilogy) was discovered by a manager at a modeling competition; Mitch Holleman who played Reba McIntyre's son on her popular sitcom, was discovered at another competition.

New York, Chicago, and Los Angeles offer the greatest number of opportunities for child actors. They also have the best photographers and the largest reservoir of teachers and coaches who specialize in working with young performers. In New York alone there are approximately forty-five talent agencies and more than forty managers who represent kids. On the Internet you can access a number of their Web sites and discover how they go about finding their clients. Across the country there are hundreds of union and nonunion (in right to work states) agents who submit talented children and teens for features, prime-time series, and commercials.

Talent agent Melissa Berger estimates that on any given weekend:

> One or two of our agents are out on the road, looking for people. We travel all over the country. A lot of the kids who come to Los Angeles for pilot season are from our travels. They are from New York, Chicago, Florida. There is an excellent acting teacher in Dallas and one of our clients was in her class. She's six, going on thirty-five. She booked a role on the pilot of *Jericho* and plays the daughter of *The Rock* in a feature. Her mother is fabulous and very supportive.

Sharon Chazin Leiblein, vice president of talent and casting for Nickelodeon, auditions approximately thirty kids for each role in every pilot the network is casting. She and her staff try to throw as wide a net as possible to include young performers they have seen in theater and acting classes. They contact acting teachers for recommendations and release breakdowns on Web sites so the information is accessible to anyone who is interested. They will occasionally hold open calls in cities around the country and she and her staff claim to look at every picture and tape that comes in the mail. Most of the children that Nickelodeon eventually hires are trained, though Sharon feels they don't have to be; sometimes training gets in the way of the kid's personality.

BEING CAST IN A PILOT

Every year an increasing number of families uproot themselves from their lives to come to Los Angeles because they think their children should have an opportunity to pursue their dream by being cast in a pilot (the first episode of a proposed television series). In the past, parents rarely came out for pilot season without a basic understanding of how The Business worked. These days casting directors and agents are seeing an upsurge of novice parents who are committing to staying for the entire four months. The flood of green arrivals may be influenced by the exposure to celebrity news shows, teenage entertainment magazines, and behind-the-scenes TV programs that give parents a misleading sense of confidence about the way show business works. With the popularity of *American Idol* and the Internet, everyone seems to think they are savvy about what's going on in the industry.

Here are some facts that we have gleaned from those who are in the know.

- Parents must make a huge investment of time and money. The stakes are very high.
- The child has to really want to do it. It cannot be the parent's dream; it is the child's.
- Parents must continue to ensure their children are being educated; young performers have to keep their grades up in order to keep their work permits current.
- If a mother or father quits a job to bring the child to Los Angeles, it is assumed the child is supposed to be the breadwinner. This pressure can force the child to deal with very mature issues.
- To be in Los Angeles for four months, you should expect to pay a minimum of $15,000 on rent, maintenance, car, materials, fees and emergencies.
- Some managers will help families find affordable housing on a month-to-month rental agreement basis.

Talent agent Melissa Berger is puzzled by the parents' lack of reality about the way The Business works:

> I don't understand how parents think they can come out for pilot season and then try to find an agent. I think you have to have your team in place. As an agent it is hard to get the clients I have signed with me working as well as the people from other places who I am welcoming into the fold. To get interested in someone I don't know, who comes

to me with the "Oh hi, I am out here shopping" idea, is very hard when my shelves are stocked.

Nickelodeon casting director Harriet Greenspan has these words of advice for parents who bring their kids to Los Angeles for pilot season.

- Try to come to Los Angeles earlier in the year to secure representation before pilot or episodic season begins.
- Don't come to Los Angeles unless you can afford additional rent. You will be paying rent and/or mortgage payments back home as well as a high rent in Los Angeles. A one-bedroom at a short-term rental could be $2,300, a two-bedroom $2,800. It would be ideal to share an apartment with another family.
- Do your research on short-term rentals. Choices include the Oakwood Apartments in Toluca Hills; the Royal Equestrian in Burbank; the Ramada Inn in Burbank; Extended Stay in Burbank; the Holiday Inn at the Media Center; the Premiere in Sherman Oaks; Studio Colony in Studio City: the Villas and the Palazzo at Park LeBrea.
- If you don't bring your car to Los Angeles, you will have to rent one. Payless Car Rental has monthly deals that are less expensive than those offered my most companies. Enterprise also has deals if you are renting for more than one month.
- Don't get into conversations with other parents regarding auditions. Try to keep your business and your kid's business your own. Otherwise you start comparing who is going out on what and it becomes a competitive race rather than a unique and wonderful experience.
- Don't get new pictures taken until you get an agent or manager. L.A. photographers have a style that differs from those in any other part of the country.
- The more jobs you book, the more the casting director wants to see you.
- Never walk into a casting office with excuses, i.e. "I just got the sides!" You are actually admitting you're not prepared. In that case, you shouldn't be there. Always make sure you have the right sides. If you received them by fax, make sure they are in the right order. Most of the time memorization isn't necessary. You should be familiar enough with the sides so that you just need to glance down once in a while to retrieve a word. Be comfortable and familiar with the character.
- Get your child in acting class as soon as possible. Commercial and voice-over classes are especially helpful because that might be the

work your child books more often.

- Casting directors rarely run on time. However, out of respect and consideration, notify them if you will be late. Usually auditions run as late as 8:00 P.M. during pilot season and can also extend to weekends to accommodate kids that are in school during the week. Episodically, auditions are usually in the afternoon between 3:30 P.M. and 6:00 P.M.

- Memorize the lines for a callback. Try and do the same performance you did at the casting office. If the producer or director redirects you, make those changes. Sometimes they just want to see if you can follow directions.

DOING VOICE-OVERS

The Walt Disney Company has used children's voices in its animated features since 1942's *Bambi,* and now children find many opportunities in voice-over work. Young performers communicate a sense of the child that adults can only approximate, and audiences won't accept imitations.

Young actors enjoy voice-over work because it's creative and fun. They love not having to fuss with makeup, hair, and wardrobe. Parents find recording studios far more kid-friendly than the average high-pressure movie set. Voice-over work is quick and can be extremely lucrative.

No one in the industry expects children to have the full tool kit of voices and accents that adult voice actors possess. Kids win roles when their normal voices suit the characters they are asked to play. But acting chops are also essential: Voice-over artists need emotional range and the ability to bring scenes to life. They also should be focused and flexible, because changes often arise during recording sessions. The ability to speak fluent Spanish is a plus. But above all, they should love to experiment. Talent agent Melissa Berger explains that the "performers who do well are the ones who are fearless. They don't care what they look like when they're voicing a crazy character. They just go with the moment."

Normally, dialogue is recorded before animation is complete. But young actors must summon technical skills when adding their voices via ADR (Automated Dialogue Replacement, also known as Looping) to pre-existing footage. This can happen when foreign films, such as Hayao Miyazaki's anime classics, are released in English-language versions. Child actors also are faced with voice changes at a certain age. Haley Joel Osment was hired to play Mowgli in *The Jungle Book 2*. During the lengthy production period, his voice changed, necessitating major rerecording. The onset of puberty is a challenge for every young male voice actor. Casting directors love scratchy prepubescent voices, but a teenage boy can't sustain that sound indefinitely.

For talented youngsters, voice-over work can be a stepping-stone to on-camera roles. But some are reluctant to leave a field in which looks and ethnicity don't count. That's the beauty of animation. It's colorblind. It comes down to who's best for the role. Zachary Tyler Eisen is the voice of Aang in Nickelodeon's *Avatar: The Last Airbender*. He doesn't mind the anonymity that goes along with voice-over work. The twelve-year-old New Yorker, who stars in the Nickelodeon telemovie *The Fury of Aang*, says most people in his life don't know about his career. A teacher turned on the TV, heard his voice, and asked him about it. "I don't mind sharing if other people are talking about it, but I don't bring it up. It would just seem kind of obnoxious . . . like I'm full of myself."

SEIZING THEIR DESTINY

Claire Danes knew she wanted to be an actress when she was five. Then at seven or eight she realized that most actors don't make a lot of money and she amended her plan. But at age nine, she says, "I seized my destiny. I made a formal announcement to my parents that I had to be true to my art. Money or no money, acting is my calling."

We know two young performers who are on their way to a life in The Business because they love it.

Ele Gilliland

We will start with a nine-year-old from the Atlanta area who traveled to New York City to audition for the role of Jane Banks in *Mary Poppins* before it opened on Broadway. At age eight Ele Gilliland was spotted at the finals of a talent competition wearing an appropriate costume and singing "I Love to Laugh." Her stage presence, energy, enthusiasm, sparkle, and vocal talent attracted the attention of a manager from New York City. Her parents were very excited about the relationship and, of course, Ele desired more than anything to get a chance to audition for the role of Jane Banks. Her folks produced CDs with her Mary Poppins photo on the label and three songs, including "I Love to Laugh," plus an edited DVD of her stage performance singing the song. They also had better headshots taken. The manager was then

able to send a packet of these materials to the casting director and to the head honcho at Disney Theatricals. After persistent phone call to the casting office, a time for Ele's audition was finally set. Since there was not enough time to find reasonable airfares, the Gillilands decided to drive to New York, where they spent a couple of days seeing the sights as well.

Ele worked on the scripted material with her manager and the songs with a well-respected voice coach. Being prepared helped her at the audition. The family then went to Alabama to spend Easter with relatives and on their return to the Atlanta area, a week later, the casting office notified the manager that Ele had a callback. Once more Ele's parents packed the SUV and drove her back to New York. While Ele didn't get any further than the callback it was a wonderful adventure and she was encouraged to write a journal about her experiences. What follows is an excerpt:

The Audition

My first sight of New York City was truly awesome! The room number in our hotel was 1707. My audition was scheduled at Ripley Grier Studios in Studio 17C and Jane Banks lived at 17 Cherry Tree Lane. I thought it was pretty neat.

We met with my manager on Saturday so she could work with me on my lines and listen to my songs. She helped me to find a voice coach to help me prepare for my audition on Monday. Ms. Shirley Callaway helped me warm up and rehearse all my songs.

When we got to the studio, a nice lady with a British accent checked me in and said "break a leg!" After a short wait, a man appeared and said "you must be Ele Gilliland" and I said yes. "I am Eric Woodall." He asked me if I wanted to say the lines or sing a song. Sing first, I said. I had three songs prepared and began with "I Enjoy Being a Girl." Mr. Eric thought I did a good job. Then he asked what other songs do you have. I have "Shy" and "I Love to Laugh." He told me to sing "Shy," because it was a fun song. He asked me to start over and sing it without all the motions. Then he wanted to read the script with me.

After we were finished, he wanted to talk to my parents. He told them I had done a good job and was well prepared. He also said it would probably be awhile before they decided on the children for the musical. I had a great time at the audition and felt that I had done my best.

After the audition, Ele got to see some of the city, including the Crystal Room at Tavern on the Green, where a photographer took the family's picture. Ele told her she was in town auditioning for a Broadway musical and she asked her to sing something. The diners heard "I Enjoy Being a Girl" and applauded. The photographer asked Ele for her autograph. The next day they boarded the double-decker bus for the city tour. Sitting on the upper level, "the tour guide kept talking to me and found out that I could sing," "She gave me the microphone and again I sang 'I Enjoy Being a Girl.' I felt so happy singing on top of that bus."

Strolling down Fifth Avenue, visiting Rockefeller Center and the ice-skating rink, and looking at the flowers in Macy's windows, were highlights of the first trip.

The Callback

Ele returned to New York for her callback less than two weeks later.

We headed back to New York City and stayed at the Edison Hotel. It was the first hotel in New York City to have electricity. On the morning of the callback, my manager met us at the hotel and we went to the Little Shubert Theatre. After we got inside she gave me a beautiful gold angel pin. I sat down on the sofa to wait. In a few minutes, Mr. Eric Woodall came out with a list of all the boys and girls who had callbacks. We then left our parents and went into the theater. A man helped us warm up with dance moves and singing at the same time. They wanted to hear "Let's Go Fly a Kite." We got to sing—well, not even ten words. I got to sing the very last phrase, "Let's go . . . fly a kite." Everyone else who sang that phrase held the last note for a long time. I stuck to the way the music was written and cut if off. We learned hand motions and dance moves to "Supercalifragilisticexpialidocious." We had to sing and dance and do the hand motions faster and faster. After a short break we went back into the theater and they lined us up by height and paired us with the "Michaels." So by height and not because we favored each other, I was paired with an Italian boy who had slick black hair, brown eyes, and olive skin. Then we did the scene from "Temper, Temper."

After about two hours, we all left the stage and everyone, including the parents, went to a small room. Eric had a list of the people they wanted to keep working with. He thanked everyone for coming and then he began to call names. My name was not called but I felt okay because I did not understand at that point that I did not make it. We got our things and left the theater. I told Mom that the names he called were the ones that needed improvement. No, she said, they were the ones chosen for the musical. I was shocked and sad . . . and well, a tiny bit mad. But I am okay about it now.

The Gillilands did not go back to Georgia until they had seen a Broadway musical and visited the Toys "R" Us Store, where they rode the Ferris wheel and played in the giant Barbie house.

Both of my trips to New York City were so much fun. Although I did not make it this time, I will keep on trying. Just going up there and doing it was awesome. I will always remember that moment of happiness and joy. It was an experience of a lifetime.

Ele had some very stiff competition. So many talented children live in and around New York City and have been in Broadway shows, commercials, and TV series. Ele's parents, very special people, made two round-trips and their routines were completely interrupted. They learned an invaluable lesson and so did Ele. She will continue her training and get better and better, because this is what she wants, this is her destiny.

Gina Mantegna

Gina Mantegna, youngest daughter of actor Joe Mantegna, believes that it is becoming very common for children to pick up their parents' professions. In her case, Joe has always gone out of his way to ensure that his family accompanied him on locations around the world. As Gina remembers:

We'd always joke that we never went on vacation, but we were always traveling. I'd watch him and think that looks like fun.

Music has been a part of my life for a really long time. I was put in front of a piano at the age of three. I tried every other instrument and that love of music led to theater when I was about ten. I did lots of theater at my school. The plays at the school were written by students. I decided to branch out and go to summer school at my sister's middle school and did my first real audition. I got the lead role in *Annie.* It was so much fun and it was that experience that made me just fall in love with being in front of an audience. I had grown up with the film version and knew all the songs.

Her dad recalls: "We go to see the play and it was like a revelation. It was like, 'My God, where did this kid learn to sing and dance like that?'"

Gina continues:

It was after a performance of *Annie* that I went into the hallway and my dad's agent was there. He has always been a close friend. His face was beet red and he was smiling and laughing. He just grabbed me by the shoulders and said "Gina, I need to represent you." We all have dreams of being on film and seeing what it's like. Before I knew it I was signing papers. And I just took off from there.

My first audition ever was for a guest appearance as a girl from a very religious family and I was stealing a dog. I was terrible. I grew from that one.

I was thrown into auditions to learn instead of going to classes. I am the kind of person that would rather rehearse, rehearse, and I am better at improvisation, spur of the moment, last-minute everything. As I continued to learn every year, I would get more and more callbacks and eventually I got a few parts. It was like one big rehearsal for me until something really serious came along.

Now I have a three-picture deal with Warner Brothers. The first feature, *Unaccompanied Minors* (starring Lewis Black and Wilmer Valderrama), concerns five teens from divorced families who are trapped in an airport on Christmas day. I play Grace Conrad, a jet-setting mean girl who is misunderstood in the beginning, but eventually you hear her side of the story. I remember going in for the audition. The character was hard to cast. They were looking in New York, Connecticut, Texas, Australia, and other countries to find her. They had to make sure the group was very diverse and the actor who plays opposite me is Dyllan Christopher. As soon as he was cast my character couldn't be a blonde and it became complicated. After several auditions, they decided I fell into place with everybody else, who include Tyler James Christopher *(Everybody Hates Chris)* and Brett Kelly *(Bad Santa)*.

My mother was with me in Salt Lake City for three months. The altitude gave me headaches every day and the filming was intense. Usually films don't shoot this long, but being on location in Utah in winter weather, it couldn't be helped. Nonetheless, by the time we were going to leave, it had become almost a second home to me.

I think we've heard in the past that actors try to steer their children away from The Business. But my father has had so many good experiences, he never wants to take that away from me. My first experience in front of the camera was playing his daughter in *Uncle Nino.* He showed me around, and taught me what certain things meant.

If I need help with my acting, I will go to my father. He is the master teacher. I would advise young actors that they have to be committed to the profession, love it, have fun, and really want to do this more than anything else.

GROWING UP

When kids reach puberty, their bodies begin to change and they become so aware of themselves that their performances can become inhibited. Girls frequently wear too much makeup, elaborate hairstyles, and clothing that's too sophisticated, so their genuine appeal is hidden. This, too, is sometimes engineered by a pushy parent who thinks the thirteen-year-old will have more job opportunities if she looks eighteen. The teen years are so important in the development of self that to deprive anyone of them is truly unforgivable.

ACTeen founder and director Rita Litton works with teens constantly and sees evidence of anxiety.

They obsess about their hair, figures, facial features. Most students wince the first time they see themselves on camera, either hiding their eyes or giving their image incredible scrutiny. Half of them will find something they dislike. Fortunately, only about five percent will "angst" about it. I advise all my students to try to stay objective, to even laugh about that camera persona; to remember that it is just one of many images they project. I encourage them to value their uniqueness, while enhancing their personal style.

Unfortunately, the teens who get cast in soaps and features are sometimes expected to behave as if they have the emotional experience and sexual confidence of their older siblings. If they lack the strong support of healthy parents or a strong spiritual foundation, they may experience traumas that will take years to resolve.

Kids' agents have to deal with boys growing four and a half inches during a lengthy film shoot. This happened to Liam Aiken during the filming of *Lemony Snicket*. A cute eight- or nine-year-old can grow one summer into an eleven- or twelve-year-old. Sometimes the success they achieved as a precocious kid doesn't last.

There are some teens who we call the "old souls." They come into the world with a history. Kids like Dakota Fanning and Margaret O'Brien and Shirley Temple have poise, maturity, sensuality, emotional range, concentration, the ability to cry on cue, and extraordinary artistic instincts. They are the ones who clearly knew what they wanted to do and how to go about it.

SAFEGUARDS FOR CHILD PERFORMERS

State laws protect working children, and states require work permits for minors under certain ages, which vary from about fifteen to eighteen, depending on the state. Most states require that the first time a child applies for a permit, he or she must appear in person at the labor board office, and usually, the work permit application must be signed by a qualified employer, by a doctor who has examined the child within six weeks prior to applying for the permit, and by the principal or teacher at the school the child attends. Many labor boards will also require that you produce the child's latest report card or progress report. Permits are either free or issued for a minimal fee. They must be kept up to date, and usually will not be renewed if a child's grades slip below a C average.

The Screen Actors Guild has assembled an information packet that defines the rules about obtaining work permits in the entertainment industry for children under eighteen years of age. The SAG packet also contains rules about schooling; advice on getting homework from the child's school for the on-set teacher; general information about preparation for the interview; a checklist for the workday; safety rules concerning stunts and other potential health hazard and Do's and Don'ts for behavior on the set. For the most recent information visit www.sag.org.

Paul Petersen, who played Jeff on *The Donna Reed Show*, founded the nonprofit group A Minor Consideration to protect child actors—mainly from their parents. He counts the recent strengthening of the Coogan Law—which requires parents to set aside 15 percent of their children's earnings in a trust fund—among its lobbying successes. The law is named for Jackie Coogan, who appeared in Charlie Chaplin's films as a boy and whose parents squandered millions of his dollars.

The SAG Foundation, in cooperation with SAG's Young Performers Committee, the Actors' Fund, and BizParentz, are alerting parents to be vigilant about inappropriate behavior from managers, coaches, and photographers and to guard against suggestive poses and age-inappropriate clothing. Parents must control every photo shoot and listen to their inner voices as to what is and isn't appropriate. Boys, for instance, should avoid posing without a shirt, whether for still photos or in a production. A suggestive photo, even one captured by a cell phone camera, can appear on more than 100, 000 Web sites within just a few days.

All photos—whether suggestive or not—are protected by such laws as California's right of publicity statute and common law right of publicity. Individuals (or their parent/guardian) have the right to control commercial use of their image and may be able to take legal action if an image has been taken without consent and is being used for commercial purposes. SAG has worked with eBay to develop the Verified Rights Owner (VeRo) programs, which helps ensure that photos do not infringe on copyright, trademark, or other individual property rights.

Finally, parents should advise young performers to never, under any circumstances, give out their name, age, address, phone number, color of hair, school they attend, and other personal information on Web sites, in chat rooms, or on a blog—all places where cyberstalkers meet young victims.

A SENSE OF PURPOSE

The young performers who have become part of the acting family on soap operas, prime-time series, and features have not always been prepared for the pressure that accompanies rigorous production schedules, long hours, sudden attention from hordes of fans, public scrutiny, and a lack of job security. It is difficult not to let fame go to your head and start believing your own publicity. A supportive family and discipline based on the work ethic can keep you firmly grounded.

Parents whose children have become successful in any or all phases of the entertainment industry know the hard road it took to get there: the hours spent driving the child to classes and auditions, the waits, the baby-sitter fees, the meals out, the clothing expenses, the costs for coaching, photos and résumés, the personal sacrifices just so these efforts could be made. The rewards are obvious: a trust fund for college, working with celebrities from the stage and screen, travel to exotic places, first-class treatment, help with the family finances, and most gratifying of all, the pride in talent being recognized.

PART THREE

HOW TO ANALYZE A SCRIPT

CHAPTER 18

Suggestions for Script Analysis

"Acting is half shame, half glory. Shame at exhibiting yourself, glory when you can forget yourelf."
—Sir John Gielgud, award-winning actor

In the next several chapters, we concentrate on analyzing the material you will be assigned at the time of the audition or on the set for soap operas, pilots, primetime series (sitcoms and episodics), and films. We will show you how to investigate the depth of a character and in so doing, we share the wisdom of those who have been principals—writers and actors—in all of these media. One lesson we learn from all of them is that your material must come from your heart—you must tap into that special place and create something meaningful.

Whatever the medium, a script makes the same demands on the actor: careful investigation of the circumstances, exploration of the possibilities, consideration of the character's objectives, and realization of the moments before the scene begins and after it ends. Most important, script analysis requires a soaring imagination. The great theater actress Ellen Terry wrote about the "Three I's"—Intelligence, Imagination, and Industry. Of these she felt imagination was the most vital and potent. Imagination asks actors to visualize, daydream, take a chance, and step into the shoes, situation, and desires of another person. Imaginative actors are far more interesting to direct because they offer ideas and are risk-takers.

Here are guidelines for analyzing a script. :

- Before you audition with any kind of material, try to relax so you can concentrate on the circumstances leading up to the monologue or scene. One suggestion is to play some very soothing, not distracting, music and focus on the character's life, experiences, behavior, choices, the relationship with the other character you are talking to, and what decisions are made that lead to a discovery. When you go into the waiting room, sit, do not become intimidated by the competition. Empowerment is necessary at a time like this. Don't let anything throw you. You have a right to be there. If the other actors in the room don't look like you, think about yourself as "the other way to go." Sometimes casting sessions are about exploring options, so stay confident and show the people for whom you're auditioning how you would do the role.

- Read the scene over at least five times silently. Sense the rhythm, observe the structure, examine the character relationships, note the emotional changes.

- Read other parts. Understand where the other characters in the scene are coming from. Not only is this awareness essential to the give-and-take nature of acting, but you may be asked to switch roles at the audition and you want to be prepared.

- Decide where the character has been the moment before the scene starts and where the character is going the moment after the scene has ended.

- In most scenes there is a central conflict that creates the tension that is essential to the situation, whether it is dramatic or comedic. Discover the cause: sexual frustration, opposing value systems, mixed signals, greed, double standard, mistaken identity, role reversal, cowardice, fear, and so on.

- Look for emotional "buttons" or beats in the scene. Mark each of these, breaking it down into moments. Clues exist in stage directions, pauses, interrupted lines. Find the attack, the build, and the resolution.

- Work on understanding the structure of the scene to learn how to play it with truthfulness and integrity. Forced emotion is shallow and will jeopardize the truth of the situation.

- Discover the "third person." The third person is a presence, not physically in the scene but someone who is talked about or who has influenced the character's behavior and philosophy, such as parent, teacher, spouse, or psychiatrist. The third person can be living or dead, historical or fictional.

- Discover the secrets each character is keeping from the other.
- Always find the sense of humor, even if it isn't obvious.
- Whether you'll be performing in an office or on a bare stage, gain a sense of place by sketching a simple set design. For example, if your scene takes place in a living room, choose the furniture, the wall colors, carpets, and floral arrangements. By putting the design on paper or seeing it in a magazine or remembering someone's living room that could substitute for it, you are creating a strong sense of place.

THE CHARACTER'S BACKGROUND: A RESOURCE FOR THE CHARACTER PROFILE

Often you will be provided with a limited description and "backstory." Write a minibiography to flesh out the character, focusing on the following. You can also use this information to compile a straightforward character profile, such as the ones on pages 377–379.

Roots: What is the character's ancestry, ethnicity, family tree? For example, if there is aristocracy in the character's background, he or she may be influenced by this knowledge.

Parents: Who raised the character is key to that person's development, behavior, and physicality.

Childhood memories: Happy and sad events in the early years through grade school may impact on decisions and relationships in later life.

Environment: Where the character was raised will affect the way he or she speaks, fits in socially, intellectually, and emotionally, and influence the lifestyle, goals, and the ability to succeed.

Education: Analyzing the language of the scene will tell you about the character's schooling and how the character communicates and articulates thoughts and feelings. Notice grammar, use of metaphor, imagery, slang, idioms, wit, and regional expressions.

Religion: What is the character's spiritual connection? An organized religion or Eastern religion? Nondenominational? Buddhist? Southern Baptist? Christian Scientist? The information can come from examining heritage, parental beliefs, and occupation.

Health: What's your character's medical history? Consider childhood diseases, accidents, addictions, disability, skin disorders, inherited or genetic conditions. Mental illness can be passed down.

Love story: An active romantic agenda will determine if the character is interested in a long-term commitment or not and how active he or she is sexually.

Marital status: How many marriages or divorces have there been, or is there a resolve not to marry? Belief in the institution of marriage can be found in your analysis of the relationship.

Spouse: If the character is not married in the scene, focus on the ideal spouse. Define the match made in heaven. Perhaps your character is seeking a mate on an Internet site.

Children: Some characters will have at least one, some won't. Some may be unable to or are deliberately using birth control, perhaps secretly. The presence of children can be a source of tension and conflict in the relationship.

Work history: What is the character's current occupation? Prepare a job résumé the character might give to a personnel director.

Career goals: Those will depend upon your knowledge of the educational background, parental influence pressuring the son to join his dad's firm, and, of course, the environment. For example, if the character resides in Silicon Valley, chances are the job would be computer-centered.

Fame: How does the character feel about notoriety, celebrity, and power? Watch how Erica Kane deals with it on *All My Children*.

Fortune: Financial status will depend upon inherited wealth, present job, marital partner, and career goals.

Favorite actors: Who the character connects with indicates the cultural background and selection of role-models. A young man who idolizes James Dean might copy the way he dresses, talks, and moves. Some characters may only come alive when they are at the movies or seeing a play. For the character of Bella in Neil Simon's *Lost in Yonkers*, a love relationship at the movies makes her real life with a tyrannical mother bearable. Curley's Wife in John Steinbeck's *Of Mice and Men* constantly dreams about leaving her husband and going to Hollywood to be in "movin' pictures."

Fantasies: Investigate the character's fantasy life. With whom would he or she want to be stranded on a desert island? Is there another character who he/she daydreams about being with in the bedroom? It is human to yearn for a better way of life, social position, and marrying the rich guy to get out of the slum.

Favorite books: Your choices will affect the character's imagination, thoughts, and feelings. What books are in the character's bookcase? Deepak Chopra or Ernest Hemingway? Danielle Steel or Edith Wharton? Autobiographies? History? How-to, self-help, cookbooks, Idiots Guides? Chick-Lit? Shakespeare's plays and sonnets?

Favorite foods: Spaghetti, mac and cheese, roast duck, sushi, pizza, apple pie, sundaes?

Restaurants: Where would the character choose to eat? The local diner or a five-star restaurant? The choice will depend in part on income and occupation.

Sounds: Find the character's favorite music. You might want to put it on your iPod to put yourself in the character's place and be more present (see below).

Colors: Choose the character's favorite color by analyzing the personality (muted or loud colors), emotional state (depressed, in mourning, ecstatically happy), temperament (cold, bitter, warm, engaging), and humor.

Wardrobe: This depends on the budget and the lifestyle, style sense or poor taste. Consider favorite shops, boutiques, shopping malls, Internet shopping sites, and whether or not the character is sales savvy.

Favorite games: The character might love to play chess, videogames, Monopoly, pool, charades, backgammon, bridge, poker, or Balderdash.

Sports: Is the character athletic? Outdoor or indoor sports? Would he or she most enjoy swimming, tennis, horseback riding, hockey playing, football, basketball, Olympic contender, boxing, or inline skating?

Hobbies: Pleasurable pastimes might include stamp collecting, playing the saxophone or the bongos, wine tasting, Italian cooking, or gardening.

Other Ways to Find the Character

Filling the character's closet is another good background exercise. The closet is a metaphor for the mind—and there are infinite possibilities. The closet need not contain just clothing. It may be filled with sporting gear, safe-deposit boxes, old trunks filled with family stuff or souvenirs from foreign countries that the character has visited, stuffed animals, collections of love letters perhaps never mailed, collectibles—a vast arena of everything that can create a clear picture of the individual and give that life its shape and uniqueness. Always list at least ten items in the character's closet.

Discover one prop, something personal such as a clothing accessory, or something practical, such as a clipboard, a cell phone, a book, or a newspaper article about someone in the family—whatever you think is appropriate for the character in the scene. Choose an object that helps you to define the character. Sometimes all it takes is one visual clue to create a whole life. The article should be subtle—an engagement ring, an antique pendant or brooch, a designer scarf, an unusual belt buckle, a favorite shirt, an expressive tie, perhaps a handkerchief a beloved relative has given to your character. Or wear a fragrance that the other person in the scene might have given to you.

Transport yourself into the rhythm of the character. Realize that the character's vocal quality, physical mannerisms, and habits should not be identical to yours. From your analysis of the material, find an activity that is appropriate to the character, which helps you with the character's physical behavior, such as hair combing, makeup application, self scrutiny in the mirror, putting on a sweater, exercising, walking, running, sitting, kneeling, and so on. Experiment with the sound of the character by using an accent, a change in tone, pitch, and projection.

Find the Music

Each of us has specific music that gives us great pleasure. Find the music choice for the character. Put it in your iPod or portable CD player. Let it help you to create an emotional connection to the character's environment or a loved one or a sweet memory from childhood. It can help you determine what has happened before the scene begins and bring more specificity and reality to your scene.

Helen Hayes, the first lady of the American theater, was having trouble finding the character of the Duchess in the Broadway play *Time Remembered*. One morning she heard eighteenth-century harpsichord music on the radio and later told a prominent critic that she had "found the Duchess."

When the marvelous Lynn Redgrave selects music to enrich her characters' lives, she opts to use "music that provokes in me a way that I can make the scene more connected to the reality of my role."

For *Baby Jane* there is a scene where I am feeling very jealous and upset about the fact that in the video store they are all Blanche's movies and none of Jane's. I found the theme from the movie *The Mission*.

Go figure. I heard it one day on the radio and it linked with that scene, something so terrifyingly weird to me. At the time I wouldn't be able to tell anybody that. Once you've told the secret it's no longer magic. I am terribly superstitious about that stuff. Whatever works, I guess. For Hannah in *Gods* and *Monsters,* in a scene with Brendan Fraser where Whale (Ian McKellan) is in the swimming pool, I chose a piece from the *Gypsy Kings Live CD.*

CHAPTER 19

The Theater Audition: Creating Characters for a Monologue

"I come from the stage. It is where you can have longevity and not fret. On the stage, because of the art of illusion and the distance, you can have a longer career as long as you can persuade the audience to join hands with you and believe you and learn the lines and move."

—Lynn Redgrave, award-winning actress

In her revered book for the actor, *Respect for Acting,* the late teacher and actress Uta Hagen defines the monologue as "an actor talking to himself out loud, or to absent characters, or to objects surrounding him at a given time in a given place for a specific reason at a moment of crisis." Even though the words must be heard in the last row of the balcony, the monologue "will always be words that represent the character's thoughts or a part of his thoughts" when talking alone. In Shakespeare's day, this was called a soliloquy; in our day, it is simply people talking to themselves.

When someone else is in the same setting and can respond with a look, a snort, a wink, a yawn, a smirk, a frown, a smile, or the activity of turning away, starting to leave, or coming toward you—that is a dialogue. In Strindberg's play *The Stranger,* a dialogue exists in one actress's long speech because it is punctuated by the reactions of the person she is talking to, who remains mute. In a dialogue you are pouring your heart out to, sharing a personal experience with, confronting head-on with, or confessing a secret to another human being, and it will demand a response.

According to Ms. Hagen's definitions, when the audience becomes your partner you have delivered a duologue. There is no one specific person you wish to impress. You are sharing your memoirs with the whole assembly. Lynn Redgrave does exactly this when she describes her life with her celebrated actor-father Sir Michael Redgrave in the award-winning piece *Shakespeare for My Father*. She invited us to join her on her journey, relive her spectrum of experiences, and we were transported.

Lynn Redgrave made an equally strong impression several years ago when *Talking Heads*, by the prolific Alan Bennett, premiered in the United States at the Minetta Lane Theatre in New York. Reviewers were ecstatic about the six actors, who each portrayed complicated, intriguing, emotionally rich, and somewhat eccentric characters in thirty-minute solo pieces. In "Miss Fozzard Finds Her Feet," Lynn Redgrave played a demure spinster who oversees a soft furnishings store in Leeds.

In building the monologue, Lynn relied heavily on sense memories of her early days in the theater touring in northern England when kitchen-sink dramas, which depicted the harsh realities of everyday life, were in vogue.

> I became familiar with what the looks and smells of Miss Fozzard's rooms would be like. I was sure she kept a very neat house. In the kitchen there would be the smell of disinfectant and cabbage that's been boiled within an inch of its life.

> I have a thing about shoes being the key to a character. If I've got the shoes right, everything falls into place. I found the shoes at Payless Shoe Source for twenty dollars. Once I began rehearsing in them, the character began to move in a certain way.

> Creating a monologue involved a whole different relationship with the fourth wall. Because you're addressing the audience, you can't pretend as you do in plays that you're not absolutely aware of every single thing. Because the audience sees the comedy of Miss Fozzard's relationship before the character does, I had to determine through trial and error the degree to which her character would acknowledge the humor in a situation that the audience is already laughing about.

Whatever the subject of your selected material happens to be, the qualities that will impress the audience most are your truthfulness in telling the story, the energy with which you approach it, and the humor that must be present to make it interesting. Karen Kohlhaas, an expert in monologue technique who cofounded New York's Atlantic Theater Company, defines an effective monologue as a story in the pursuit of an immediate objective.

NEWS TO ME, A MONOLOGUE BY ELE GILLILAND

We are very proud to include in this chapter the work of Ele Gilliland, a child performer from Georgia who experienced a callback for the role of Jane Banks in *Mary Poppins* (see Chapter Seventeen, "Child Performers"). She teaches us that even at an early age in this business we can learn how to cope with rejection by writing about it and allowing it to become one of life's lessons. Being able to bounce back and move on is invaluable to the actor's journey and longevity on the stage.

> There I sat waiting for the news and dressed perfectly for the occasion. A bright blue leotard to match my blue eyes and my hair pulled back so they could see each expression on my face. I had just experienced one of the most exciting moments of my eight short years. That was to be on a stage in New York City for an audition to be in the original cast of a Broadway musical. I listened carefully as the casting director called the names of those that he said needed to be worked with further. That made sense to me because I agreed that they did need additional help. Now what about the rest of us? Mom, why do you have tears in your eyes . . . and . . . where are we going? Oh no, how could I have totally misunderstood? The audition went great. I hit every note and nailed every line. What is wrong with them? Can't they see that I would be perfect? (beat) I guess not this time but it will be okay. I will keep trying. One day not long from now, they will realize that I can act and I will become all that I was born to be.

A Lesson Learned

How many young actors in America could relate to Ele's audition experience? How many adults remember when they were children trying out for the local community theater or children's theater play or the school mainstage production? Listen to the heartbeat of a young girl who was so obviously crushed by not hearing her name for the next round of auditions. She felt so comfortable with what she had accomplished, she had worked so hard to "nail" it. What could possibly go wrong? Something that every actor has to realize is that there are so many good talented young artists looking for work. For *Mary Poppins* there were hundreds of them from all over the country who went to open calls and only a few were selected to come to New York and work with a director and a choreographer with a long list of Broadway credits.

This is an example of what former child actor Darryl Hickman refers to as "purity of instinct," inspiration that comes from a child's inner self. The innocent child lives for contact with an audience and enjoys giving and reaching out and entertaining and making a difference. The reward for all of these efforts should be having your name called to be "worked with further." And when it isn't, feel with Ele the inexplicable sadness, profound disappointment, hurt, confusion, rejection, and finality. Don't fight those tears. Just let them come down your cheeks. You have to release what you are feeling. Breathe. Exhale. Inhale a new moment, a new chapter, a new resolve that you will return to Georgia and work harder and build your résumé and appear in local theaters and make something happen. Because you were born to do this—this is your destiny. There will be another chance. That is the definition of hope that keeps the path open and always moving forward.

FLOOD, A DUOLOGUE BY JOHN WHITNEY

John Whitney went to the Kentucky Center's Governor's School for the Arts in Louisville, where he concentrated on creative writing. His work was often featured in the Young Playwrights Festival at Louisville's Walden Theatre. The following monologue begins his short play *Flood,* which he says was "inspired by my own difficulties empathizing with the people of New Orleans in the immediate aftermath of Hurricane Katrina."

> The piece was prompted by a workshop I attended the November after it happened. It was a week-long session led by Judi-Ann Mason, who asked us to draw inspiration from the catastrophe. Not wanting to write another "rising water" play, I decided to base it more off my own experiences and reactions.

When asked who he would cast as Allen, he responded "Really, I'd prefer a no-name to perform it. I wanted it to be kind of an average Joe performance."

> (At lights up, a lone actor onstage. We hear the slight patter of rain, which he listens to for a moment before he speaks.)

ALLEN

My first thought—my first thought on hearing about it was, "Thank god it'll finally cool off around here." The next day was a Monday, so I was stuck in school no matter what the weather was doing outside. I was bored and listless most of the day; then Byron showed me this picture. I think it's one of those rescue photos, I haven't seen it since, but it looked like New Orleans to me. It showed a window with plywood over it and the water partway up the wall—you know the kind—on it was painted the words "Go Away."

There was something. I knew there was something. Something said something to me through that photo. I think—thought, maybe, MAYBE it was the human condition, or enlightenment, or just a glimpse of wisdom—like a white hare disappearing into the snow. I wanted to see it again, feel that thing in my head, understand it, but it had already left the photo. I had to find more, piece it all together; build the truth for myself from these images. I gave chase.

I turned to the Internet first. It is large, powerful, choking on its own information overflow. Here I thought I might locate more images, and the same image, tiny mosaic tiles that I could piece together myself on my desk. After hours spent hunting, printing and cutting out, I was looking at the words "Go Away" spelled out in suffering faces. I had hunted most of the night for this elusive thing, but the Internet was useless for what I needed. At 3:47 A.M. I had a vision of inspiration. For the third, maybe fourth time in my life, I watched the news on television.

A day came and went. I watched CNN, I watched NBC, I watched ABC, I glanced at FOX, once. It was in there somewhere: I could smell it. I don't know if I ate anything that day, or even left the room. I only drank water—water—something—

Carol came by after school, guess she was worried.

ENTER CAROL

Analysis of Allen's Opening Speech in *Flood*

The character is rather impassive in the opening paragraph. The impact of the news he has heard is slight and he appears to be rather self-involved. It will cool off, but he is resigned to being stuck in school, no matter what the weather's doing. He admits his boredom and lethargy (listless) during the day. So far he shows no emotion or interest or sense of empathy. The actor playing him would downplay emotion during this section. We don't know what he wants or what he is going to do about it. He is closed.

Then a friend happens to show him a picture. The prop that is necessary to the character's push into action is that picture. Always be aware of the catalyst that causes a tonal shift in the writing. Now it is in his face. A photo of the scene that he describes for us who aren't looking at it with him. "A window with plywood over it and the water partway up the wall" and unexpectedly the two haunting words—"Go Away!"

A new thought creeps in to the conscious mind. "Something said something to me through that photo." How observant to remember that one picture can say a thousand words. In this case it may have spoken volumes yet to be written. What began as a listless bored state of mind has been injected with a Vitamin B shot. "Maybe it was the human condition, or enlightenment, or just a glimpse of wisdom," and then he compares that ever so fleeting glimpse to the disappearance of white on white, "a white hare disappearing into the snow." Passion is being added to the mix. Compassion. Feeling something, anything, being alive. "I wanted to see it again, feel that thing in my head, understand it. . . . I had to find more, piece it all together; build the truth for myself from these images. I gave chase."

He is the hunter on a mission. He works feverishly, sleuthlike, to piece together the image of what has stirred him into action. Where does he go first? Ah, the Internet, the omnipotent, omnipresent, ubiquitous, all encompassing, vessel of the super-information highway. Clicking on site after site, link after link, spending hours seeking the mosaic of images that would ultimately shout out "GO AWAY!" But this time, the image of one boarded up house has merged with so many suffering faces. He still feels that he hasn't found the answer.

Then the final "vision of inspiration." The "Aha" moment. Watch the networks, look at the news coverage on CNN. Clearly he is not impressed by FOX. He lost a day, he lost his appetite, he stayed in his room, he only drank . . . water.

His small, comfortable, safe boring existence has been turned upside down. For the actor working on this monologue, it is important to be utterly truthful and let the events build to the moment when he has his vision about watching TV news coverage. And then quiet desperation.

The writer has achieved a wonderful seesaw effect in the piece and his sense of metaphor, movement, and rhythm helps the actor build the momentum, establish the transitions, and understand the emotional changes throughout.

VOICES IN THE DARK, BY JOHN PIELMEIER

We are very pleased to include the work of the gifted playwright John Pielmeier. Most of you know his name in connection with the Broadway hit *Agnes of God,* which was later made into a film. Perhaps what you don't know is that he began his career as an actor, working as a company member at Actors Theatre of Louisville, the Guthrie Theater, Milwaukee Rep, Baltimore's Center Stage, and the Eugene O'Neill National Playwrights Conference in Waterford, Connecticut. *Agnes of God* was first staged at the O'Neill.

Since then he has written extensively for theater, film, and television, winning the Humanitas Award, the Christopher Award, the Edgar Award, and several nominations for Best Screenplay and Teleplay from the Writers Guild of America. His TV film, a new adaptation of *Sybil* starring Jessica Lange and Tammy Blanchard, aired on CBS/Lifetime in 2007. We have been given permission to use a scene from *Sybil*, which you will read in Chapter Twenty-one.

Voices in the Dark opened on Broadway in the fall of 1999. One reviewer praised John Pielmeier for crafting an "intelligent, masterfully plotted, and superbly engrossing tale of obsession, psychological tension, and consequences." Judith Ivey played Lil, a radio therapist, who reels from surprise to shock to terror, barely managing to control her life.

> Place: a cabin in the mountains. Time: Night
>
> Lil has gone to the mountain retreat to meet her husband. She is being terrorized by a mystery caller who threatens to kill her. (Reviewers and those who attended the play were asked not to reveal the ending to anyone.)
>
> Lil's speech is a plea for her life.
>
> I'm a coward. I'm an emotional coward. I listen to most of the people who call me and I realize how brave they are to say, in front of millions of listeners, that their lives are screwed up. Not me, other people tune in because they like to know they're not alone. The boat's going down, yeah, but dozens of others have made the same mistakes as they have, so it's all right, except for me. I'm the normal

one, I'm the sailor on the shore throwing out the life jackets. And the punchline is—are you ready for this?—I SUNK YEARS AGO!

I'm not a savior, I'm a ghost. I went through an alcohol abuse program once—big news story, right? Everybody thinks I'm a champion. I failed. I've no life to speak of. I choose the wrong men for the wrong reasons and they always leave. I can't blame them. Who wants a coward like me? I'm single-minded, self-centered, I hate my body. I won't go on television because I don't want people to see me. I'm a VOICE to them. I'm good at that. It's the one thing I can do. I try to be strong and caring, a great role model. I try to listen, and the truth is I've gone through life more TERRIFIED than anybody I know. I'm desperate. I'm too proud to ask for help.

And here I am finally on my knees begging for my life and it's too late, isn't it? I want to give people hope. That's my goal on the damn show. But when push comes to shove I don't have any left for myself.

Analysis of Lil's Plight

Because this is a woman who is trying to grasp at any straw to bail her out of her dilemma, it would be easy for an actress to become ensnared in emotional traps. One of the biggest no-no's in the interpretation of any dramatic literature is to play into the mood, which spelled backwards is doom. Lil already thinks she is doomed and therefore you can't play into that. Be more objective. Look outside of her troubles and find her core. You are able to do so in this speech because she tells you enough about her past and her present.

Note: If you were going to do this speech, it would behoove you to read the whole play. There are some extremely eccentric characters in the rural environment where the action takes place. Reading the play in its entirety will help you discover what circumstances have motivated the speech and what occurs after this monologue.

The actress playing this role is approximately in her late thirties to mid forties. She has to have a soothing vocal quality. Being a radio therapist is a voice role. Callers wouldn't be listening to her if she sounded shrill, whiny, high-pitched, breathy, or overly nasal.

Why did she choose to be a radio therapist? Give it some thought. Consider her options, since we know the following from this speech:

(1) She is good at it; it's the one thing she can do; (2) She wants to be a strong and caring role model; (3) She hates her body and won't go on television.

What is her home life like? She says she has no life. She chooses the wrong men for the wrong reasons and they always leave.

What is her medical history? She is a recovering alcoholic. Why did she drink so much? Could there have been any instances of parental abuse when she was a child? Physical abuse? Sexual abuse? Lack of communication? Neglect? Was she a latch-key child? Was she the responsible one or was she dominated by someone else?

Could her problems with men not staying be directly related to her own parents' separation, divorce, infidelity? She never knew a normal family life. Is that why she became a therapist?

Notice how many questions it takes to figure out an answer. Listening to other people's troubles and giving them hope is what makes Lil feel alive. And she has erected a glass shield around herself for protection from anyone who could hurt her, take away her control, or cause her physical pain.

Now she and her safe world are being threatened by a psychopath. The problem is, it could be someone she knows. Therein lies the mystery and what will be that surprise ending.

So actresses should play this as if they were speaking through a microphone to that black hole of an audience listening in the dark. *Mea culpa*, confession, telling it like it is, letting go completely of any safeguards—as these elements come into play, we meet the real Lil for the first time in the play.

Consider the following keywords to describe her. *Nouns:* Coward. Sailor on the Shore. Savior. Ghost. Champion. Voice. Role Model. *Adjectives:* Emotional. Normal. Single-minded. Self-centered. Strong. Caring. Proud. Terrified. Desperate. Isolated.

Now, mix these terms up and put them into phrases. Emotional savior. Normal sailor on the shore. Single-minded savior. Self-centered ghost. Strong champion. Caring voice. Terrified role model. Desperate coward. Play with all of these phrases.

Practice reading on a microphone with a caring voice. Try to find some copy that makes sense. Think about a self-centered ghost. There are films about ghosts. Watch one. Picture in your mind a sailor on the shore doing something that is a normal function. Getting ready to sail. Throwing out the life jackets. Think about an emotional savior. This is a religious reference. Think perhaps of a saint who has performed a miracle. A single-minded savior might be a crusader on the quest for the Holy Grail. Finally, think about the strong champion, the athlete. A role model who is terrified seems to describe her best and she has become a desperate coward.

It is fun to play with words and phrases in a monologue especially when you have so many juicy ones in this short speech. Study how the speech begins and how it ends. Has she spent anything from start to finish? Would she be emotionally drained? If you don't feel any change at all, then you have failed to dig deep enough into the character's life crisis.

This is a very good selection to stretch your emotional memory and muscle.

RESEARCH FOR YOUR PERFORMANCE

You can make use of many resources, some on the Internet, to give your performance more depth. For instance, www.americantheaterweb.com, contains every review and article on every play produced, not only in New York but nationwide. From the reviews you can learn how different directors work, and the site also has forums where you can talk to other actors.

You will also want to see shows by directors with whom who might be auditioning and working. As actress Susan Wands advises, if you are going to audition for Robert Wilson, you should know you can't approach his material like a soap opera. "Basically he wants actors to intone like robots," she says. "It is hard to know what directors Jerry Zaks or Mark Lamos like unless you get to know their work." In New York, play-going organizations such as Theatre Development Fund (TDF), www.play-by-play.com, www.theatermania.com, www.broadway.com, and www.play-bill.com make it possible to see performances at reduced prices.

If you are in a quandary about finding the right monologue, do a Google search—just type in "monologues" to start. You will find a number of Web sites that will be able to assist you. Who knows? Maybe one day another actor will find your original monologue online for help at an audition.

CHAPTER 20

The Soap Opera Audition: Creating Characters for Daytime Dramas

"I respond to confidence and skill, an actor who makes strong choices, who commits to the material, and makes the effort to bring it alive. What separates the people who get the job from those who don't is the degree of commitment to the craft. —Mark Teschner, casting director, *General Hospital*

Although a character description (often called a backstory) is provided in the soap-opera script, the more you enhance it using your own imagination, creating a rich personal history for the character, the more substance you can bring to the audition and to a role.

Corbin Bernsen made a definite impression on viewers when he debuted as Carly's conflicted father, John Durant on *General Hospital.* From the beginning he was involved with his character's conception—from his motivation to his wardrobe.

> When the executive producer invited me aboard, she told me what the story was. I learned about the history of Carly and Sonny and I knew that it was an important story. I wanted to create a character that has this void. Then you add, "Oh, my God, she's got a husband who has been a target of mine. It would be great for my career!" That makes it powerful.
>
> The whole story of a man who's discovering he has a daughter at fifty and reaching a point where there's a hole in his life and this seems to fill a void . . . that was really intriguing to me. I really invested

myself in that. It was important to me that Durant's daughter really meant something to the character. I had to make the hole in his life so big and make Carly out to be something big enough to him to fill it that the choice of what he does becomes that much stronger.

Although Corbin didn't choose the sets, he had input as to how they were furnished. "Durant's completely compartmentalized. When I looked at him I went, "Wow, John Durant comes to town and not only does he have a fully furnished apartment, but he's even got a tea kettle on the stove. He moves in and everything is together right away."

He is happy to report he got a good deal with Brooks' Brothers. "I wanted the character to have a conservative history, but be sort of hip, so they gave me a great wardrobe that accomplished that."

Alicia Minshew had big shoes to fill when she stepped into the role of *All My Children*'s Kendall Hart. First, there was the challenge of having to emerge from the shadow of *Buffy the Vampire Slayer*'s Sarah Michelle Gellar, who won an Emmy for her portrayal of the hell-on-wheels daughter of Erica Kane. Then, the intimidating job of working with a cast filled with daytime legends. With instinct and determination, Alicia tackled the role with relish. She chose to play her with a dash of grit and sensitivity.

Before Alicia screen-tested for the role of Kendall, she had been close to getting a role on *One Life to Live* and had already tested twice for *All My Children* and *Passions*. She didn't get the roles.

"I thought it was a blessing in disguise. I wasn't ready," she says.

I wanted to finish a two-year training program. I felt I would be ready when the time was right. I learned so much from all of the previous tests that by the time Kendall came around, I had a certain comfort level. I knew how to make sure I was in the light, stand the right way and hold the tag line.

I screen-tested with Josh (Duhamel, ex-Leo). I think they wanted to see how Kendall was going to interact with him. They weren't sure who they were going to pair Kendall with. I think it was to see if we had chemistry together. I had such a good time with Josh, because he is so natural. I really feel that he brought out the best in me. He makes everything look so effortless.

I competed with seven other actresses. Because Judy (Blye Wilson, Casting Director) knew me so well, I didn't have to go to a call-back. After the screen tests, they said they couldn't decide on anybody so they brought me back to test with five new actresses. I had mixed feelings. I thought this was a good sign, because I knew they liked me but I figured they didn't know what they wanted.

When Alicia started the role she had never seen Sarah Michelle Gellar as Kendall. She didn't want to compare herself with her. She had never done a soap before and it took her awhile to relax into the role and to understand who she was playing. It took a month before she knew about the character's background.

I worked a lot from instinct and did as much homework as I could. In time I have been able to put my qualities into the role.

As Corbin Bernstein and Alicia Minshew testify, your challenge is to put your imagination and instincts to work in creating a character.

SCENES IN SECONDS

We are extremely grateful to Jeanne Davis Glynn, nominated five times for a Daytime Emmy for writing excellence, for giving us permission to use a generic soap scene she wrote for her series of seminars entitled "What Every Actor Should Know About Soaps." In analyzing this scene, she said it's necessary to play with words. You can "play it young, play it old, play it shy, play it bold. The attitude and action are yours." Build on the words, she advises, by asking questions. Character: Who are you? Time and Place: Where are you and where are you going? Relationship and Backstory: What connection do you have to the other person? Subtext: What do you want?

FADE IN:

HE	This is the last place I expected to meet anyone.
SHE	Life is full of surprises.
HE	I don't like surprises.
SHE	I don't like life without them.
HE	Obviously, we don't agree.
SHE	Who says we have to?
HE	It might make life easier.
SHE	And boring. But why debate the issue? Since we're here is there anything else you want to say?
HE	What's to say? We don't really know one another.
SHE	Some people might say we haven't given it a chance.
HE	This is all so crazy.
SHE	Some people say, "You can't go back again."

HE	What do you say?
SHE	It might be better to move on.
HE	Or forward.
SHE	If we did that we could fall all over one another.
HE	That could be fun.
SHE	I have to go.
HE	Will you come back here?
SHE	Your guess is as good as mine.
HE	Then, again, life is full of surprises.

FADE OUT

Let's review the topics we covered in the Character's Background on pages 357–359 and decide how you'd fill in the blanks for this scene.

Roots: While we don't know who the ancestors or immediate family members might be, just think what we can do with ethnicity. The couple could be African American, Jewish, Asian, Italian, French, Irish, British, Southern. Let us say the man is Southern from a prominent family in Atlanta, Georgia. She is a New Yorker, born and bred. The dynamic of the laid-back Southern gentleman with the brash, forward-thinking, urban, sophisticated female could be a lot of fun. Of course, we could also play one younger than the other.

Education: Give the man a college education, with an advanced degree from an Ivy League school. The woman may have skipped college and headed straight for a fashion training program at a place like Fashion Institute of Technology (F.I.T.).

Marital status: One is divorced, the other is a widow/widower. Even more fun, this is their first meeting. They found each other on an Internet dating site.

Work history: How successful are they at their jobs? Who makes more money? Are they both currently employed?

Favorite books: One is a romantic, a reader of love stories; the other could be a mystery fan.

Restaurants: Since this is the last place he would expect to meet anyone, imagine an out of the way, smallish vegetarian café on the Lower East Side of Manhattan. Or a park bench. An oceanfront fish joint. A sports bar. Try different restaurants in different locales. Places you know, places you have read about.

You might write a whole new scene or several variations of this one. Can you make the characters two women or two men or a mother and daughter or a university professor and a student; a director and an aspiring actress; a stockbroker and his secretary having a rendezvous? It can be invigorating to exercise your creative instincts and discover what it is they want from each other. As you change the circumstances and the relationship, there will always be new objectives, fresh intentions. Try another historical period or decade.

CREATING THE CHARACTER PROFILE

Write a character profile for the man and woman in this sample scene. These profiles will provide you with a launching pad you can use to open up other ideas and take your characters on different journeys. It is your tool to create, to re-create, and to discover more about the characters than perhaps even the writers thought possible. It will paint a mental picture for you that will accompany you into the audition. Get a definite image for each character. Be specific!

NAME:	David O'Malley
AGE RANGE:	30–35
ANCESTRY:	Irish/Italian
RELIGION:	Raised Catholic
PARENTS:	Eleanor and Kevin O'Malley
CHILDHOOD MEMORY:	Coming in second at the National Spelling Bee
ENVIRONMENT:	Milwaukee, Wisconsin
EDUCATION:	Political Science major, Notre Dame
CAREER GOALS	Justice in the Supreme Court
ROMANTIC INTEREST:	Been playing the field
MARITAL STATUS:	Waiting for the right girl
CHILDREN:	Loves them, as long as they are somebody else's
OCCUPATION:	Junior partner in law firm
SALARY RANGE:	$75,000 and climbing
FANTASY:	Playing golf with Tiger Woods
MEDICAL HISTORY:	Appendectomy, broken leg skiing, carpal problems, mumps, measles, chicken pox
FAVORITES BOOK:	*The Firm* by John Grisham

FOOD:	Sushi and Veal Scallopine
RESTAURANT:	Four Seasons
CD:	*Duets*, Tony Bennett
MOVIE STAR:	George Clooney
MOVIE:	*Good Night and Good Luck*
COLOR(s):	Blue
CLOTHING STYLE:	Sporty/traditional, casual on the weekends; corporate attire on the job
GAME:	Pictionary
SPORT:	Skiing, in spite of the broken leg
HOBBY:	eBay auctions
PET:	Tropical fish

NAME:	Sarah Petersen
AGE RANGE:	25–30
ANCESTRY:	Not quite sure, she was adopted.
RELIGION:	Presbyterian
PARENTS:	Norm and Fran Petersen
CHILDHOOD MEMORY:	10th birthday, a surprise party
ENVIRONMENT :	Bronxville, New York
EDUCATION:	Honors in high school; Journalism major at University of Missouri
CAREER GOALS:	*New York Times* culture reporter
ROMANTIC INTEREST:	None at present. Last one killed in plane crash.
MARITAL STATUS:	Actively seeking the right guy
CHILDREN:	Oh yes, some day
OCCUPATION:	Proofreader for a major publisher
SALARY RANGE:	$55,000 with an annual bonus
FANTASY:	Live in Paris for a year
MEDICAL HISTORY:	Not sure because of the adoption but has had typical childhood diseases. Prone to colds
FAVORITES BOOK:	*Bridget Jones's Diary*
FOOD:	Grilled salmon with steamed veggies
RESTAURANT:	L'Entrecote

CD:	*Chicago*, the movie cast album
MOVIE STAR:	Annette Bening
MOVIE:	*Being Julia*
COLOR(s):	Purple and aqua
CLOTHING STYLES:	Feminine and sexy
GAME:	Poker
SPORT:	Horseback riding
HOBBY:	Photography
PET:	Harley, a Persian cat

HILLARY B. SMITH SHARES HER SPICE THEORY

Hillary B. Smith ("Nora" on *One Life to Live)* advises young people who she coaches to set their sights on their passions and develop a strong sense of self. She encourages actors to learn, to work hard, and if they get a role on a soap, to enjoy coming to work.

> I always look at the scripts as life, but a script is nothing more than a two-dimensional piece of paper. In order to bring a character to life, you must bring the third dimension to it, and that is yourself. In order to understand the character and bring it together, think of the script and life as a recipe for a cake. You need to go into your spice cabinet, which is yourself, and take an inventory. Understand your spices, your good spices as well as your bad spices, the weak ones, and learn how to improve them. When you come across a recipe that calls for a spice you may not have in your inventory, you can mix a couple of spices that you do have to get the same flavor. Understand who you are, know your strengths and your weaknesses. Understand your passion. Be able to say that is not a recipe for me or that is a recipe for me, because it is going to challenge me to work on my spice cabinet. As time goes on, your spice cabinet changes, too. I keep taking inventory of mine. I keep allowing myself to change and evolve, to grow.

CHAPTER 21

The Prime-Time Series Audition: Creating Characters for Episodic Television

> "In a TV series, what you're selling more than acting is confidence. If I'm going to hire somebody for five years, I want to know that person's not going to be nutty. If there are two actors, and one's obviously the better actor but he's a nut, and the other is really good and I know he'll show up and do his job. . . . Life's too short. I'm going to get the guy that instills confidence."
>
> —George Clooney, Oscar winner, in *Back Stage*

While a soap opera affords the actor a significant amount of time to develop the life of the character, a prime-time series demands that the characters establish an immediate love affair with the audience on the first episode.

We have witnessed the cancellation of *several* prime-time series early in the season. Mid-season backup programs may have the same fate. Therefore, it is critical that you, the actor, bring to the audition enough personality, charisma, chemistry, uniqueness, physicality, vulnerability, and talent to convince the producers, writers, directors, and network executives to take the very costly chance of using you.

In this chapter we will discuss ways to develop characters in the sitcom, the pilot, and the prime-time episodic series. Refer to the suggestions for script analysis and the character's background as you review the scenes we present.

THE SITCOM

Only a handful of sitcoms have made it past their first season. None has achieved the popularity of *Everybody Loves Raymond,* which in its prime attracted 28 million viewers a week. Phil Rosenthal, writer and producer of the hit for its entire nine-year run and author of *You're Lucky You're Funny: How Life Becomes a Sitcom* (Viking) has declared that the key is specificity.

Phil believes that "What made *Raymond* work was not simply a great cast led by Ray Romano, or a strong staff of experienced comedy writers. What really made the show stand out was the faithful reliance on truly specific, sometimes minutely so, details of married life." The details were that specific because they were based on the lives of Mr. Rosenthal, Ray Romano, and the writers. His role models were *The Honeymooners* and *The Dick Van Dyke Show*. Writing the hit series *Coach* opened the door to *Raymond* for him. "The concept of bickering families in a comedy is nothing new but few current comedies seem to get it right. A major reason might be that writers keep looking to get the next laugh instead of telling a great story."

Prime-time Emmy winner Brad Garrett, who played Ray's brother on the show, insists that the key to a great sitcom is the ensemble. He came to the show after years of doing stand-up comedy.

> Even though I did stand-up, I look at myself as an actor first. I think that's my strength. For a stand-up to go to the transition as an actor, it takes a lot of trust. The one thing I really had to learn when I took acting after doing stand-up was to listen. Stand-ups are afraid to listen. We don't want to hear silence. We're always talking.
>
> This is a business where you have to be able to re-create yourself. You can never stop training; you have to keep growing. I still train to this day with Larry Moss, who's just a genius of our time. He got me where I needed to be to play Jackie Gleason.

Unlike Brad Garrett, Emmy-winning actress Holland Taylor who plays the "hated-but-tolerated mother" in *Two and a Half Men*, came to the world of sitcom from the theater and film, where she has excelled at playing strong, intimidating women. She is familiar with the value of the ensemble and the value of playing a supporting role in a sitcom.

> Stylistically this show is about two-and-a-half men, not about two-and-a-half men and their narcissistic mother. The writers give me the motivation for my character. As my teacher and mentor Stella Adler would have said, you bring yourself to it because you can't not bring

yourself to it. It's not that I'm not imposing me on this part. It's that I am playing it. It [the part] can't help but use me—my responses, my sense of humor, the things that matter to me. I come to the party because I'm the only one invited.

Two and a Half Men is filmed before a live audience after a short rehearsal period. You've got an audience that you are instinctively trying to play for, which often takes your focus away from the camera that you should be thinking about. Your volume should not be projected to that live audience; you're on a mike. Charlie Sheen can roll with technical difficulties and barriers between him and the audience. He can feel a laugh coming, he can wait for that little artificial mechanical delay that happens for them to see him on the monitor, he can time laughs to come in at the crest of a laugh and still be heard. I marvel at him, and we all do.

The writing teams on both of these sitcoms have created fully dimensional, flawed, and witty characters. Discover the points at which a character exposes his or her inner child. Notice how the actors pause, listen, react, and respond to each other. Mute the sound and just watch the physical behaviors, notice their timing.

An interesting assignment would be to look at an episode of Everybody Loves Raymond or Two and a Half Men and profile one of the characters. Figure out how some of these characters feel about children, marriage, divorce, religion, food, relatives, family background, playing games, reading books, hobbies. List ten items in their closets. What are their favorite activities (how often did you see Ray watching a sports event on the television with his brother and father?).

Actress and teacher Caryn West conducts weekend comedy intensive workshops on both coasts several times a year. They are designed to help actors understand the tools they need to "get" what's funny. She feels strongly that the best job in Hollywood is the sitcom, the half-hour single camera comedy.

It requires you to know the comic idea of the scene. Straightforward dramatic training isn't going to help you with this. Stand-ups and sketch people (ex-Saturday Night Live comedians) are getting the jobs over actors who are classically trained. They know how to be funny. They really don't know anything about emotional truth, but nobody's asking them for it.

Somebody asked Jim Carrey in his early career whether he could act. Now he can, in a naturalistic way, and he has worked very hard at it. He is a great commedia actor. Every sitcom is really based on commedia. You have the same stock characters. Study commedia, mask work, and clown work. Commedia has been around since the Greeks. Aristotle had profound things to say about comedy. [In my comedy intensive workshops] I make people look at that history.

ANALYZING CHARACTERS IN COMIC WRITING SAMPLES

Instead of going after scenes from recognizable sitcoms, we decided to showcase the work of two writers, one very established and one who is still a student in high school. Neither sample is structured like a family-centered comedy; they concern relationships between men and women. The authors didn't write them for the medium. They were written to be performed on stage. Having said that, most of the ensemble companies of sitcoms started on the stage. We will explore and analyze the characters and how they come to life off the page. In both cases, the characters are not the same at the end of these pieces as they were at the opening.

Let's Just Be Bricks, A Tragiromantidramedy by Caitlin Willenbrink

Caitlin Willenbrink wrote this piece when she was a junior at Manual High School in Louisville, Kentucky, and a third-year student at Walden Theatre. As a student she acted in plays by Shakespeare and Arthur Miller, stage managed *Blithe Spirit* by Noel Coward, and wrote for Walden Theatre's Young Playwrights Festivals.

Caitlin says her inspiration for writing this short play came from observing complete strangers sitting in coffee shops. She found herself filling in their life stories. *Let's Just Be Bricks* is one of those stories. When asked who she would want to play her two characters, she said she loved the idea of Jason Schwartzman playing Will and Scarlett Johannson playing Gina.

The play is written in reverse chronological order (the first scene takes place after the second scene and so on). Throughout the play, Will and Gina's relationship changes. We have chosen the final scene.

(A coffee shop. WILL sits alone at a table, reading *The Sun Also Rises* by Ernest Hemingway. He is drinking his first cup of coffee ever, a soy latte with whipped cream and two shots of caramel (recommended by a friend of his). GINA also sits alone at another table, drinking the same, staring out the window instead of writing her term paper. Obviously, they don't know each other yet. The only sound is WILL turning pages in his book. After a while, WILL closes his book and gets up to leave, taking his coffee cup with him. As he walks to the door, he trips as he passes GINA's table, spilling coffee all over her pink polo shirt.

GINA   It's hot! Oh my god, it burns! What's your problem?! AAAAHH, coffee hurts! Watch where you're going! This shirt is new! Ow—(She smells the coffee on her shirt and immediately calms down). Is this a soy latte with whipped cream and two shots of caramel?

WILL   (Tries to protect himself from what GINA may do to him) I'm so sorry! Really, I am! I'll do anything for you. I'll buy you coffee for a year, and a new shirt! I'll do anything, just don't hurt me, please! (He eyes her extremely pointy-looking heels).

GINA   Was that a soy latte with whipped cream and two shots of caramel? (WILL just stares at her, an extremely confused look on his face, unable to speak.) And is that Hemingway you're reading? (She points to his book. WILL gives her an even more confused look, if that were at all possible.) Hi, I'm Gina. (She holds out her hand.)

WILL   (Instead of shaking her hand, he simply looks at it, then looks back at her.) I'm Will . . . but aren't you going to kick me or blackmail me or hit me with your purse for spilling my coffee on you?

GINA   Do you live around here?

WILL   (Not listening to her) Because, isn't that what women do? Kick you in the balls and ruin your life?

GINA   How old are you?

WILL   (Still not listening) Please don't ruin my life. Or kick me in the balls. I have a good job, and a good apartment, and I've never missed a month's rent.

GINA   (WILL and GINA's next lines overlap each other. As WILL speaks his lines, GINA speaks hers at the same time.

	Neither are really listening to what the other is saying.) Do you want to have dinner with me tonight?
WILL	—and my friends say I'm really a good guy, and I don't drink more than once a week-
GINA	At that place on 5th Street?
WILL	—and I've never stolen anything from anyone . . . well, except that one time in high school when I stole a stapler from my teacher's desk but—
GINA	I've been wanting to go there for a while now—well, actually, hoping someone would take me there. . . .
WILL	—that was just one time, and I'm sure she got a new one—
GINA	What's a good time for you? Seven? Seven-thirty? Either works for me.
WILL	—it was just a stapler anyway, it's not like it was a million dollars that I stole or something—
GINA	(Thinking to herself) So it's set then. Seven o'clock tonight at that place on 5th.
WILL	(There is a silence as he stares perplexedly at her for a very long time, trying to figure out what the hell is going on.) What?
GINA	Our date, silly! (She giggles flirtatiously) You're funny. I'm already beginning to like you! So I'll see you tonight. (And with that, she exits, leaving WILL alone onstage [yet again!] staring at the spot where GINA was just standing.)
WILL	(He speaks to GINA although he very well knows that she has gone.) So you're not going to ruin my life? (He stands onstage, pondering this, not moving. We expect him to say something else—he doesn't. All he does is stand there, hands in pockets, looking quite bewildered. "This is Our Emergency" by Pretty Girls Make Graves begins to play as WILL continues to stand onstage. Lights dim very slowly, until we are left in complete darkness. The song continues to play quietly in the dark, leading us to believe that an other scene will come . . . it doesn't.

What begins as a possible catastrophe morphs into a budding romance. One-sided, of course. Gina attempts to bond with Will, who is drinking what she is (even though she doesn't know that is his first-ever cup of coffee) and that he is reading Hemingway, which impresses her. Will is sure his life is ruined. He has become rather melodramatic in a "poor me" way. Gina has moved on. She arranges a date to get to know him better. Could this whole thing be Kismet? There are no accidents. Everything happens for a purpose. Why don't you try the Character Profile on these two strangers (see page 357)?

(see page 357)

You know where they are and what time of day. Figure out what has happened before they walk into the coffee shop. We are not quite sure how long they have been there. How often do they come there? What does Will do for a living? What does Gina do? Start thinking about their hobbies, sports interests, educational background. Who is in control of the scene? Will they exchange e-mail addresses and start to build a deeper relationship? What is the significance of the song played as the lights dim? Flesh out these details. The rhythm in the scene is dictated by the writer. She has them overlap their dialogue so that we see each of them has their own agenda. What is Gina's attitude toward men? What is Will's feeling about women? He seems to be very clear about that in one of his speeches. Dress them. What's in their closets? Do they have a future together?

Think about these things. That is your assignment.

Goober's Descent, by John Pielmeier

John Pielmeier's collection of monologues and short plays entitled *Impassioned Embraces* was published in 1989. In this potpourri of interesting pieces, one stands out for us. *Goober's Descent* occurs in a simple but attractive office. The principal characters are Stella Birdock Whipple and George "Goober" Whirmer. Both of the characters are dressed in business attire. Throughout most of the piece, both are very jovial, flirting, frequently laughing or smiling. The entire play occurs sometime in the late 1980s.

HE enters. SHE is seated behind or beside a desk, but rises to greet him.

HE	Hi there.
SHE	Hi.
HE	George Whirmer.
SHE	Mr. Whirmer.
HE	Whirmer, with a "Wh".
SHE	Whirmer.

HE	You got it.
SHE	How do you do, Mr. Whirmer. (She over-pronounces his last name whenever possible.) Please be seated.
HE	I'm super, just super. Nice to meet you, Miss . . . uh.
SHE	Birdock.
HE	Birdock. That's a nice name. You can really wrap your tongue around that one. (They laugh.) Well, you know what they say.
SHE	What's that?
HE	The early birdock . . .
BOTH	. . . catches the whirmer.
SHE	Oh, that's very funny.
HE	I'm a funny man.
SHE	You certainly are, Mr. Whirmer.
HE	Is your boss in?
SHE	I beg your pardon?
HE	Mr. . . . uh . . . (HE consults a card) Rosetti.
SHE	(Laughing) Oh.
HE	What's so funny?
SHE	I'll be interviewing you, Mr. Whirmer.
HE	Oh.
SHE	Does that bother you?
HE	Hmmm?
SHE	My interviewing you. Does that bother you?
HE	Not at all, not at all.
SHE	You seem upset.
HE	Why should I be upset?
SHE	Well, I just thought . . .
HE	With a beautiful woman like you asking me questions?
SHE	Why, thank you. Now. . .
HE	I just thought I might be seeing the boss, that's all.
SHE	He's very busy.
HE	I see. I see.
SHE	Are you all right?
HE	Yes, I'm perfectly fine.
SHE	Now, it says here on your résumé . . .
HE	Are you married?

SHE	I beg your pardon?
HE	Just thought I'd ask.
SHE	Well, I . . .
HE	I'm a happily married man myself.
SHE	Yes, it says right here . . . "Happily Married." (They laugh.) Now let's not beat around the bush . . .
HE	To coin a phrase. (They laugh.)
SHE	Exactly why were you fired from your last position?
HE	I wasn't fired.
SHE	I see.
HE	I was . . .
BOTH	. . . let go. (They laugh.)
SHE	Why?
HE	Ethics.
SHE	Oh.
HE	The boss's daughter, moving up.
SHE	Uh-huh.
HE	I wouldn't stand for it. I spoke my mind.
SHE	Good for you.
HE	I always speak my mind.
SHE	So do I.
HE	Don't get me wrong. I admire a good businesswoman more than you do.
SHE	I'm sure you do. (They laugh.)
HE	. . . but this girl was a nincompoop.
SHE	You have very nice eyes.
HE	Thank you.
SHE	Now, Mr. Whirmer. . .
HE	George.
SHE	George. There are so many eager young businessmen out on their ears in this day and age, men who have been groomed for corporate positions, and who suddenly find that they have to wait tables to eat.
HE	My good friends call me Georgie.
SHE	Georgie. That's cute. So what qualifies you . . .
HE	My very good friends call me Goober.
SHE	Goober?

HE	Think about it. (She does, but smilingly gives up.)
SHE	I give. (He quietly whispers something to her. She blushes, but laughs in spite of herself.) You're terrible. What qualifies you, Goober, above anyone else for this job?
HE	Well . . . I'm . . . uh . . . (Silence) I'm sexy. (They laugh.)
SHE	And very funny.
HE	And funny, and bright.
SHE	Uh-huh.
HE	And eager.
SHE	Oh my.
HE	And . . . uh . . . hungry.
SHE	I'll bet. (They laugh.)
HE	You're funny, too.
SHE	I try. (They laugh.)
HE	We'd make a good team.
SHE	Oh Goober . . .
HE	What are you doing tonight?
SHE	You're married.
HE	We all make mistakes. (She laughs.)
SHE	Oh I don't know.
HE	How about seven o'clock?
SHE	Is this ethical?
HE	Seven thirty?
SHE	Six.
HE	Fine. (Silence. They smile at each other.) You look very familiar.
SHE	What do you feel about working for a woman, Goober?
HE	I beg your pardon?
SHE	Woman. W . . . O . . . M . . .
HE	Rosetti's a woman?
SHE	I'm a woman.
HE	Who's Rosetti?
SHE	A nineteenth-century poetess.
HE	Ah, it's just a . . .
BOTH	. . . company name.
SHE	You got it. (She laughs.)
HE	Fine. I feel fine about working for a woman. You?

SHE	You got it. (They laugh)
HE	And I thought you were only. . .
SHE	You did, didn't you?
HE	Yes. (They laugh. Silence. They laugh.)
SHE	Stand up, Goober. (HE does) Walk away from me. (HE does so hesitatingly) Now turn around. (HE faces her) All the way. And take off your coat and tie. (As he does, he speaks.)
HE	What is this?
SHE	Do you type?
HE	Uh . . . yes . . .
SHE	What's your speed?
HE	Forty words a minute. But I'm improving.
SHE	Do you take dictation?
HE	I thought this was a . . . uh . . . more of a corporate position.
SHE	It can be. Not at first. We like to start all of our employees off in the secretarial pool. Give them a look at life on the bottom.
HE	I see.
SHE	You don't agree.
HE	Well, it's not for me to tell you how to run your business.
SHE	But you're not interested.
HE	Well . . . uh . . .
SHE	And your salary would be six hundred a week.
HE	(Whistling.) That's not bad for a secretary.
SHE	Four hundred of that is tax free.
HE	How . . .
SHE	Under the table.
HE	AH . . .
SHE	For services rendered . . .
HE	I beg your pardon?
SHE	Come over and sit down. (HE does.) Now cross your legs. (HE does.) Uncross them.
HE	I don't understand the point of . . .
SHE	You're a very attractive man.
HE	Thank you.

SHE	Would you mind taking off your shirt? (Silence.)
HE	I . . . why?
SHE	Let's say I'm curious.
HE	Yes, I would mind.
SHE	Seven hundred a week. (Silence.)
HE	Under the table?
SHE	Under the table.
HE	(Stands and begins to unbutton his shirt.) Boy, are you in for a sight.
SHE	I'll bet.
HE	I graduated Phi Beta Kappa, you know. I was doing very well for someone my age. The amount of sales I accumulated in my first years with my old company is still unbeaten.
SHE	Please don't sell yourself. Just take off your shirt. (HE hesitates, then removes his shirt.)
HE	There. I'm not getting as much exercise as I should, but uh . . . Still interested?
SHE	Very, but not sold. For eight hundred a week, let's see your legs.
HE	Isn't there a law against this?
SHE	I'm not forcing you, Goober. You can stop any time you want. (Silence. HE undoes his belt and drops his trousers.) Now what will you do for a thousand?
HE	Who the hell do you think you are?
SHE	You don't remember me, do you Goober?
HE	No.
SHE	Stella Whipple. (Silence.) I was your secretary for two weeks in 1975.
HE	Oh yes, you were the one who wouldn't . . .
SHE just	Yes, I was the one who wouldn't. You can get dressed. I wanted to see what you'd sell out for. (Silence.) You're hired, Goober. You can start work at . . . what did we say . . . six? (Silence.) Unless you're ready to begin now? (HE begins to dress.) What's the matter? Did you suddenly remember Mrs. Goober?
HE	If you think you've won, you're wrong. I've still got my . . .
BOTH	Pride.

SHE	Yes, but pride won't feed you, Goober. I know about pride. Pride is an empty cupboard.
HE	I wouldn't work for two thousand.
SHE	How about three?
HE	No.
SHE	Ah, but you hesitated. That's the difference between you and me. I didn't hesitate. I just walked. So how about it, huh? Six o'clock? (HE finishes dressing.) No one will know what's going on. I'll slip you money under the table. I'll even pretend you're the boss. (HE exits. SHE calls after him.) Not that you're worth it, Goober! Not three, not two, not even two hundred! People like you are worth nothing! Zero! Zip! Do you hear me? NOTHING! (Silence.) She returns to the desk, settles herself, then crosses a name off a list). That takes care of '75. (She speaks into her intercom.) Zilla, you can start sending in the next year. (She fluffs her hair, checks her makeup.)

Lights fade.

There are two well-defined characters in this playlet. What is delightful about the situation is that at the beginning we truly have no idea where it is going. They seem to be enjoying each other's company. There is laughter and a slight flirtation going on. George Whirmer becomes Georgie and then Goober. Very informal and cozy. She never becomes anything but the woman interviewing him with a HUGE agenda. There is a great deal of subtext in these characters. It is up to you to figure out what is going on between the lines.

Try to verbalize the subtext. For example, when the pair is exchanging names and making small talk, George is saying, "This gal is really attractive and she seems to be responding to my charm and my wit. I will have no problem convincing her I am the man for this job." She could be thinking, "I can't believe I am finally seeing this guy. He is still the conceited bore he was when I knew him. I mustn't let him know what I have in mind for him. Let me just keep smiling and laughing at him for a while."

Now you have set them up with different points of view. You can see that George is intent on getting the job. Remember the marital status? He considers himself to be a womanizer, sexy, irresistible. What must Mrs.

Whirmer have to put up with? Also, this play was written at the height of the feminist movement. Women were leaving the secretarial positions and being upgraded to executives. George is the perfect chauvinist pig! Follow their journey in this scene. Again, as with the first scene, there is a twist at the end. The woman's revenge is sweet. The characters have revealed their true selves. The author has crafted a meticulous unraveling, employing short punched speeches with longer self-revealing narrative.

Use the character profiles (see page 359) and fill in the blanks. You have much more information about these characters than you do for the characters in the previous piece. So the challenge is determining the style in which you think the roles should be played. It occurred to us while we were reading it aloud that in the so-called Golden Days of television (which are also known as the 1950s), a pair of skillful comedians named Sid Caesar and Imogene Coca would have been doing this skit on their hit TV series *Your Show of Shows*. If you don't know who these geniuses are, Google them. Watch their sketches on DVD. Their timing, their comedic instincts, their bickering antics, and over-the-top behavior would have wrapped around this sketch and made it purr!

THE PILOT

If you get the opportunity to be seen for a principal character in a pilot, you will have very little lead time to study the script and side pages. The script analysis guidelines and character profile are especially helpful when time is of the essence. As you will see, in analyzing this scene from *Building 116*, Dan Ramm's pilot for a dramatic series, imagination will help you flesh out the story and develop the characters.

Building 116

Dan Ramm explains the background of this scene from a pilot.

New Directions is a real organization located in Building 116 on the grounds of the Veterans Administration in Los Angeles. Each year New Directions successfully rehabilitates hundreds of men and women veterans, all of whom are homeless and more often than not addicted to drugs or alcohol or both. On any given night there are 30,000 homeless veterans on the streets in Los Angeles.

Most of the staff members are graduates of the program. So, it's easy to see that the staff members have their own demons to deal with. Joe Mantegna and I have worked very closely with New Directions for many years, doing fundraisers and public service announcements. I wanted to write about something that had hope, redemption, and the human condition. I have always been very humbled by the thankless work they do at Building 116 and thought that in some way developing a show about this place would bring attention to this overwhelming problem.

The characters of Jack and Sharon are loosely based on some of the remarkable people who founded New Directions. Jack is a Vietnam vet who still has a very dark side that he battles every day. Sharon is his ex-wife. Although they are still very much in love, Jack's "baggage" keeps them from being together. Sharon is the daughter of "Doc," the founder of New Directions and works there daily with Jack, who is the executive director.

When I wrote the piece I always imagined Joe Mantegna as "Jack" and I thought Dana Delany was right for "Sharon."

Scene: Doc's House at night. Kitchen

Sharon, an attractive woman in her 40s. Light red hair and fair skin. Jack Orazio, dark hair, with wisps of gray, goatee. Smokes, has tattoo on left arm.

Army sergeant.

SHARON	**Coffee?**
JACK	**(Looks at his watch.)**
SHARON	**It's your favorite kind, that one that tastes burnt. (Pours coffee into cups.)**
JACK	**He's really gotta stop, you know.**
SHARON	**I'll talk to him.**
JACK	**We both know how that will go.**
SHARON	**So what's the new secretary like?**
JACK	**He's okay I guess. He cares, that's the important thing.**
SHARON	**Well, if anyone can get through to him, it's you.**
JACK	**I just get frustrated every time I have to start over with someone new. It means more explaining, more trips, I don't know.**
SHARON	**I remember a time when you liked going to D.C.**
JACK	**When was that?**
SHARON	**Like that time we went together. I think it was for a Senate hearing or something. Anyway we were out walking and it**

	started to rain and we ducked into the first place we saw. A little Spanish place where we sat and drank sangria, ate paella, and watched the rain for hours.
JACK	Latasca.
SHARON	Oh right, Latasca.
JACK	The waiter looked like Kevin Bacon.
SHARON	Oh right. Do you remember that couple that sat next to us?
JACK	No.
SHARON	You know, they had just come from the Vietnam Wall and asked us if we'd been.
JACK	Yes, I think so.
SHARON	What would you say if they asked you now?
JACK	I'd say I'd got close. (Looks at this watch.) It's late. I should go. (He stands and walk to the front door.) Thanks for the coffee.
SHARON	You're welcome.
JACK	(Turns to the door and opens it. Before he walks out he turns back to Sharon.) I'm just not ready.
SHARON	It's okay. You'll know when the time is right.
JACK	See you tomorrow.
SHARON	(Kisses him on the cheek.) Good night.

Jack exits. Sharon closes the door behind him. She still very much loves this man.

Dan's script has a real pulse, constantly pumping with the actions of the caretakers and the inhabitants of Building 116. Short, tight scenes concern the political scene, the need to get the government to allot some appropriations for the VA center, and the tension created because the program is always on the verge of having to close down. Flashbacks are used to show Jack serving in Vietnam and suffering a serious knee injury. In scenes of the present, Jack has to bail out Doc, his eighty-year-old, outspoken father-in-law, and the staff dutifully rounds up the homeless and addicted vets and gives them shelter in Building 116.

Fleshing Out the Characters

In this touching scene between Jack and Sharon you can sense the bond that is still very strong between them. Always look in scenes like these for what isn't said. Jack obviously can't commit to more than sharing a cup of coffee and talking "shop." When he looks at Sharon, he sees her beauty and spirit and love. She looks at him and remembers happier times—dinner at Latasca, watching the rainfall, the waiter who looked like Kevin Bacon. She knows how he likes his coffee and wants him to be part of her life forever. As with a soap opera, there isn't a lot of character backstory, except what you can deduce from the dialogue and the action. It is up to you to flesh out their early married years.

An effective exercise is to write letters they might have exchanged during his time in Vietnam. When Sharon got the letter that he was wounded in battle, how did she express her grief, her love, her need to be with him? When Jack responded to that letter, was he determined not to feel self-pity, or frustration at not being able to carry out his mission, or perhaps he felt he had failed. These letters could be in a trunk in the characters' closet. Jack could have written a daily diary about what it was like to be facing death every day. He carries that "baggage" with him in the present. You could also write your own flashback scene about their first meeting. Picture them in happier times like Sharon does in this scene.

Use your imagination to find a childhood memory for each of them. You know something about Sharon's father but what about how Jack was raised? His Italian family could have been strict disciplinarians or loving, doting parents. Some of his relatives might have served in World War II or the Korean conflict. What factors in his background have made him so dedicated to helping others? What are those demons he deals with? Describe Jack's feelings when he finally gets the strength to visit the Vietnam Wall. He might be inclined to write an article for a VA paper. It would definitely be helpful to research Building 116 and understand the passionate commitment of the characters who support this cause.

THE SERIES

Working on a prime-time series enables actors to get the opportunity to create a memorable character in a well-cast ensemble that could work in hospitals, law firms, police precincts, forensic labs, or counter terrorist units. Former *New York Times* entertainment critic Elvis Mitchell defined series television as "a craft laboratory and a last chance for stardom." He cited Michael Chiklis as an example of an actor who had been cast as the lead in short-lived shows until the lead in *The Shield* came along and got him out of his "career doldrums." Acting teacher Howard Fine remembers that no one wanted to see Chiklis for this role. "They thought he was just a funny guy. He wanted to quit acting. We worked on the audition for *The Shield.* He went in (and this is a great example of finding yourself in the character) and scared the 'bejesus' out of everybody in the room."

Finding Your Character

Actors need to have the tools to find the characters within themselves and here are a few examples of working actors who did.

New York Times television critic Virginia Heffernan has praised Golden Globe–winning actress Kyra Sedgwick for the creation of a "re-markable character" in *The Closer.* How did she do it? She took risks. If you want to start a character profile on her portrayal of a police inspector, her favorite food is See's Chocolates, she was raised in the South, her essential accessory is her purse, and her love life is always in transition. She is a workaholic and tenaciously pursues the bad guys.

Gregory Itzen and Jean Smart, who portrayed President Charles Logan and First Lady Martha Logan on *24* were forced to find a backstory for their characters. In so doing, they provide a great example of how to investigate their characters' backgrounds. They tried to figure out if there were children, how Charles and Martha met, and what their marriage had been like up to the time when the audience is first introduced to them. In spite of some initial skepticism, the actors were allowed to create their own personal history. Could they have watched interviews with Bill and Hillary Clinton? Charles Logan was loosely based on Richard Nixon, whose facial expressions, shifting eyes and gestures could be studied from televised interviews and press conferences. What is it like being a politician's wife? What qualities of self helped Jean find Martha? Intelligence, social grace, conversational ease. What are her flaws? Once the good idealistic senator's wife, she sought release from the pressures of the White House in alcohol. Has her look changed because of her addiction?

You can go further when you have complex characters by writing their obituary. Imagine the cause of death, backgrounds, survivors, and what others thought of them.

When Annie Parisse was hired to play a lawyer on *Law & Order*, she was given the opportunity to create her character's personality and behavior. She was unsure about her political preference. However, she did intuit that she liked to win. *Marital status:* single. *Environment:* an apartment in Brooklyn; *Pet:* a cat; *Parents:*hoity-toity and she had removed herself from their influence. She had become a loner who was "socially defensive" and "not trusting."

> Doing a show like this is all about subtext. I have watched fellow cast members fill out their roles with their own imaginations, creating people with lives that are ongoing. It doesn't matter that the audience never sees it, those things are always there.

JOAN OF ARCADIA

Joan of Arcadia was an American television fantasy/family drama that aired on CBS from 2003 until 2005. The show was a favorite with the critics and won the prestigious Humanitas Prize and the People's Choice Award, and was one of the few television shows to be nominated for an Emmy Award in the first season, for Best Dramatic Series.

Joan of Arcadia concerns a teenage girl, Joan Girardi (played by Amber Tamblyn), who sees and speaks with God in the form of various people, such as small children, teenage boys, elderly ladies, transients, passers by. She is asked by God to perform tasks that often appear to be trivial or contrary, but the result of the action is a positive solution to a problem.

The opening credits were accompanied by Joan Osborne's song "One of Us," a hit single that begins "What if God was one of us?" The drama starred Joe Mantegna and Mary Steenburgen as Joan's parents, Jason Ritter as her paraplegic older brother, and Michael Welch as her younger brother, the science geek.

We want to thank Barbara Hall, the creator and executive producer of *Joan of Arcadia,* CBS Paramount television, and Barbara's assistant, Joe Henderson, for support and permission to use two scenes selected from several scripts. We watched the two seasons of this show and were always struck by the originality of the characters and the writing.

When asked what made her want to do this show, Ms. Hall replied:

> My longtime interest in Joan of Arc is really the jumping-off point, but I've always been interested in metaphysics and physics. I wanted to create a show in which I use the fact that I spend all my free time reading about this stuff. I thought, 'Wouldn't it be great if that were just homework, research?' From there it grew into this show about a family recovering from a tragedy and how it affects their spiritual lives,

and this girl who is a modern-day Joan of Arc, who hears from God in a time when that's the most unacceptable thing, when it can be used in court as evidence of insanity. I wanted to update the dilemma.

Scene One from "Fire and Wood"

Before the scene begins, Joan has met her brother Kevin in the park. Kevin is confined to a wheelchair due to a car accident. She is scolding him for feeling sorry for himself, sitting in the park and smoking, not attempting to get a job and turn his life around. Kevin has become embittered by his physical disability. Joan is trying to help him. When he wheels away in anger, the tears begin to fall.

Just then, a ball rolls into Joan's legs. She turns to see a LITTLE GIRL, wearing thick glasses and bobbing eyeballs on antennae, a rather startling effect.

LITTLE GIRL	**Why are you crying?**
JOAN	**I had a fight with my brother.**
LITTLE GIRL	**Because he doesn't try hard enough?**
JOAN	**You heard that, huh?**
LITTLE GIRL	**I hear everything, Joan. You know that.**
JOAN	**(AHA)**

She realizes to whom she's speaking.

Let him walk. Please? One favor and I'll never ask for another. For you, it's nothing. Snap your fingers. Blink your eyes. Just let Kevin stand up and walk.

The bobbing eyeballs bob and the LITTLE GIRL'S eyes gaze at Joan from behind her thick glasses, then

LITTLE GIRL	**People ask me to do things. Big things. Little things. Billions of times every day.**
JOAN	**What do you expect? You're God!**
LITTLE GIRL	**I put a lot of thought into the universe. Came up with the rules. It sets a bad example if I break them. Not to mention it shows favoritism—why should one person get a miracle and not everybody else? Can you imagine the confusion? It's better when we all abide by the rules.**
JOAN	**So, no miracles?**
LITTLE GIRL	**You're an instrument of God, bound by the limits of time and space. Perfect. Can I have my ball?**

JOAN gives the LITTLE GIRL her ball.

LITTLE GIRL   You'd like to give me a slap, wouldn't you?

JOAN   Yeah, except you're so cute.

LITTLE GIRL   By the way, as an instrument of Me, you should not black-mail your little brother into doing your work for you. Have some pride. (As she leaves) Do better. Do your best.

JOAN   Now, I'd like to slap you.

The LITTLE GIRL smiles and melts away amongst the other children. Joan sighs and heads for home.

Scene Two from "Jump"

The scene is the Girardi home in the den. Will Girardi is writing things down. Helen, his wife, enters.

HELEN   What are you doing?

WILL   Making a list of demands.

HELEN   Who are we taking hostage?

WILL   I've been offered a job. UnderSheriff, Arcadia Division.

HELEN   (Delighted, hugs Will) Will, that's incredible! Apparently the world hasn't gone completely insane.

WILL   Honey . . . I don't want the job.

HELEN   Oh.

WILL   Mike all but said that it's a political appointment.

HELEN   Aren't all appointments political?

WILL   It's the same job with a different title.

HELEN   Which means you're completely qualified.

WILL   I hated every minute of being a Police Chief.

HELEN   I know. We all know.

WILL   I didn't become a cop to make policy. I became a cop to put bad guys in jail.

HELEN   You are sending a large number of big, powerful bad guys to jail.

WILL   Yeah. And lost my entire police department doing it. (Off her silence) I'd like to turn down the job.

HELEN   And do what?

WILL   Get back to what I'm good at.

HELEN   Will, I want you to be happy. If it were just me, you could be a crossing guard and we'd live in a cardboard box.

WILL	But . . . ?
HELEN	Kevin. (off his look) He's got a job, today he joined a wheel-chair basketball team. He's coming into his own. And unless I'm nuts, there's a girl.
WILL	A girl?
HELEN	He's starting to be a little vain. That means a girl. For the first time since the accident, he's chasing after a life. It's harder for him than the rest of us, that's all.
WILL	(Considers) You're right.
HELEN	I'm sorry, Will.

(He takes her in his arms, nuzzles her neck)

WILL	Never be sorry. Family first.

(She kisses him. The good man. The phone rings.)

HELEN	If it's any consolation, I still hear bells when we kiss.

(Will laughs and answers the phone).

There is no need to do an in-depth analysis of the relationships in these scenes. When the writing is like butter, it is easy and uncomplicated to find the key points that are being made in the dialogue. Understand there were several months between scenes. In the first one Joan is clearly upset by Kevin's rebellion and anger. In the second scene, Kevin has started to turn his life around. He may even have a girlfriend. How human of his mother to notice his sudden "vanity." He is obviously paying more attention to how he looks to impress a female. Will's dilemma regarding his new assignment at the bureau will eventually get resolved. But in an episodic series all developments occur in their own time. There will be plenty of obstacles in day-to-day living whether in school, relationships with classmates, first love, irreversible situations. Joan's gift was the anchor in every episode. She will be missed.

CHAPTER 22

The Film Audition: Creating Characters for Movies

"The great movie stars in the studio days had this wonderful thing about listening. Forget all the big method actors of today—if you look at people like Mickey Rooney and Elizabeth Taylor they have an extraordinary charisma, an extraordinary personality. They made it all look very real, whatever their method was."
                            —Anthony Hopkins, Academy Award–winning actor

In the best situations, when you have an audition for a made-for-TV movie, a miniseries, or a feature film, you will be given the entire script to read. But there will be times when you are handed only a couple of scenes. You have to look at the nature of the relationship and make quick decisions based upon what the characters' objectives are. Making a strong choice based on your understanding of the emotional nature of the scene will put you in control.

In Chapter Five, "Training Is Everything," we have mentioned how Charlize Theron, with the help of her coach Ivana Chubbuck, was able to win the leading role in *The Devil's Advocate*, in spite of the fact that she was too pretty and too young. What Charlize discovered was that the character wasn't about where she had been born or her age but that she was trying to find her purpose in life. After five auditions the producer and director couldn't forget how she had made the part about her personal journey and life experience. The truthfulness of her choices made an indelible unforgettable impression on them.

Donald Sutherland tells a fabulous story about his early career, which demonstrates the inexplicable way in which final decisions are made when casting a film. As a twenty-something actor, he auditioned for a film in front of the writer, producer, and director, all of whom were very impressed.

> I thought I had gotten to where I wanted to get to, in the truth of the character. The next day the phone rang, and it was all three of them in the room. They said my performance had been definitive; it had informed them so much they changed the script afterward. I was thrilled. And they said, "All of us are phoning to tell you what it meant to us for you to do this and for us to explain to you why we *aren't* giving you the part. We're not giving you the part, because, for us, this character has always been a guy next door. To be absolutely truthful, you don't look like you've ever lived next door to anyone." They were telling me this like they thought they were being nice. I sat in a closet for three days.

However, he also reports that once, when he was standing in line to see a film, a producer of the remake of *Invasion of the Body Snatchers* happened to see him and said "You look good. Come and see us tomorrow." He did and got the role. The lesson here is that so much of getting cast is left to chance. Throughout this book we have talked about ongoing preparation through taking classes, working with a coach, and constantly improving your audition techniques. We must add that, psychologically, you have to muster tremendous confidence and convince the powers that be that you are the one for the role.

We think it is important to understand the casting process for a film so that you will know what is expected of you. Casting will always be complicated and to illustrate what is involved in the search for actors who will please everyone, Nancy Green-Keyes and her partner Matthew Barry discussed how they found the appealing costars of *The Notebook*.

According to Nancy:

> We love to go through numerous sessions to find those untapped talents that nobody's ever seen before, and give them the kind of exposure they deserve.
>
> The studio had gone through the A-list actors based on their popularity. The casting directors knew that Ryan Gosling, a superb young actor who had been mesmerizing in *Murder By Numbers* and *The Believer,* could give the character of Noah the right edge and sen-

sitivity. They sent him the script and arranged for a meeting with director Nick Cassavetes. Nick was sold. The movie studio executives agreed to cast Ryan for the part only if they could find a female star to play his love interest in less than a week! What followed was a journey across America, taping actresses on locations. A talent agent heard about the auditions and convinced them to see his client who had just completed a movie with Rob Schneider. So Rachel McAdams, who was relatively unknown at the time, was given an appointment. Rachel connected with the character of Ally.

Matthew Barry remembers, "When she began reading, she wound up reducing myself, my partner, Ryan Gosling, the director, and the producer into blubbering fools. It was the best audition in my ten-year history as a casting director."

What kind of roles do you connect with? Could you have made grown men cry if you had auditioned for the role of Ally? Maybe you aren't the guy next door but that doesn't mean you can't fit into a horror film or science fiction thriller. On the questionnaire for self-knowledge in Chapter Fourteen on page 273, we ask you to list screen roles you would like to play and why. Make a list of roles you feel you could have auditioned for had you been given the opportunity.

AUDITION SCENE FROM *SYBIL,* A TELEPLAY BY JOHN PIELMEIER

We wish to thank John Pielmeier, Warner Brothers, and Executive Producer Norman Stephens for allowing us to use a scene from *Sybil,* starring Jessica Lange and Tammy Blanchard. It is published with the understanding that it may not be reprinted or broadcast. An analysis of this scene will show you how complex the characters are, and what challenges they present to actors who play them.

INT. DOCTOR WILBUR'S CONSULTING ROOM—DAY

In a new session with Doctor Wilbur, a red-eyed Sybil opens her eyes and looks around.

She's in Doctor Wilbur's office. The charcoal sketch signed Peggy Lou Baldwin is pinned to the wall. The Doctor sits poised, as if waiting for Sybil to continue to speak. She hesitates, then:

SYBIL (AS SYBIL)   He - he doesn't want to see me anymore. I know it's my fault but still it hurts.

DOCTOR WILBUR   What are you talking about?

SYBIL (AS SYBIL)   Stan. He let me down in as nice a way as possible. He's such a wonderful man.

DOCTOR WILBUR   You've completely changed the subject from what we were talking about a moment ago. Are you aware of that?

SYBIL'S lost, completely confused. Trying to avoid the doctor's question, she digs in her purse—

SYBIL (AS SYBIL)   He - he left me this letter and—

—and pulls out the letter, now taped together. But she freezes—someone has scribbled all over the letter in black magic marker the word "Stupid."

SYBIL (AS SYBIL)   Oh god.

DOCTOR WILBUR   What?

SYBIL (AS SYBIL)   It's done it again. Time runs away. It doesn't do that to everybody, does it?

DOCTOR WILBUR   What do you mean "runs away?" What just happened?

SYBIL (AS SYBIL)   I don't know. I don't know what happened. I'm here and then I'm not and then I'm here again and everything is different. Things are different and people are different and—

Suddenly SYBIL rises in a fury, rips up the letter, and tosses it in the wastebasket.

She now stands very still, clenching her fists and face in anger. She seems to have shrunk in her clothes, acting all of a sudden like a little girl mid-tantrum.

SYBIL (AS PEGGY)   (CONT'D) You just can't trust 'em. You can't, you really can't. You really really really really—

Then she turns and heads for the Doctor's windows, pounding on the glass and screaming.

SYBIL (AS PEGGY)   (CONT'D) Let me out! I want out!

The Doctor rises and moves quickly toward her.

DOCTOR WILBUR   Sybil—

but before she can get there SYBIL has smashed her fists through the pane of glass.

Doctor Wilbur grabs her forearm, then gently pulls her hands back through the broken window, avoiding the broken glass.

DOCTOR WILBUR   Careful, careful. Let me see your hands.

The Doctor examines SYBIL's hands—luckily, there's no cut—while SYBIL watches her wide-eyed.

SYBIL (AS PEGGY)   What about the window? You don't care about the window?

DOCTOR WILBUR   Of course not. Windows can be fixed a lot more easily than people.

SYBIL (AS PEGGY)   There's blood.

DOCTOR WILBUR   No blood. You didn't cut yourself.

SYBIL (AS PEGGY)   In Grandma's bed. Just before she died. And in the hayloft. When Tommy Ewald was killed.

Doctor Wilbur, unsure what's happening, is very alert.

SYBIL is disturbed, chattering like a little girl.

SYBIL (AS PEGGY)   He fell on the fork he was dead I stayed with him til the doctor came because I didn't want to leave him lyin' there like I did my Grandma she was bleeding I called for help they took me away and wouldn't let me see her she was dead oh dear God Grandma Grandma don't leave me!

Doctor Wilbur is very concerned, sympathetic. She's not sure what's going on, but she's playing along anyway. After a long beat, she speaks.

DOCTOR WILBUR   Go on, Sybil. Tell me about your Grandma. What did you feel (when you were with her?)

SYBIL (AS PEGGY)   (accusing) What do you care? You don't care how I feel.

DOCTOR WILBUR   Yes I do. I care very much.

SYBIL (AS PEGGY)   You're just trying to trick me. Lots of people trick me, just like they trick Sybil. (A quick correction) Me. Like they trick me.

The Doctor studies her patient. Something's wrong, different.

DOCTOR WILBUR   Who are you?

SYBIL (AS PEGGY)   Sybil.

DOCTOR WILBUR   No. No you're not.

SYBIL stares back. Another beat. Should she tell the truth?

SYBIL (AS PEGGY)   You can tell the difference?

DOCTOR WILBUR   You bet. What's your name?

A beat. From now on we will refer to the personality who is present.

PEGGY   Peggy. Peggy Lou Baldwin. We don't look alike, me and her, but most people can't tell.

DOCTOR WILBUR   (nodding to the sketch) Is that yours, Peggy?

PEGGY   Uh-huh. I like to draw in black and white 'cause I don't paint as good as her.

DOCTOR WILBUR   Oh, I think it's very good. Tell me something—if you and

	Sybil don't look alike, are you still related? Do you have the same mother and—
PEGGY	No, no, she's not my mother! Don't say that!
DOCTOR WILBUR	Okay. I'm sorry. I just wanted to know. Can you let me talk to Sybil? Do you control that?

Peggy takes a breath and for a moment seems to grow larger. Then she looks around, blinking, like someone waking up—and we realize it is now Sybil who is present, taking in the room and broken window.

SYBIL	What happened? Did I do that? I'll pay for it. I'm sorry. I'm sorry.

Doctor Wilbur is almost too astonished for words.

DOCTOR WILBUR	No, that's all right, Sybil. Have you broken glass before?
SYBIL	(near tears) I do it all the time. But I don't remember how or why—
DOCTOR WILBUR	You blacked out. It's what we call a fugue. How long has this been going on?
SYBIL	For as long as I can remember. Oh god—you know. Now everyone will know.

Sybil is becoming more and more upset, edging toward hysteria as her wall of defense finally crumbles.

DOCTOR WILBUR	Don't worry. I won't tell. When do the blackouts happen? Are you aware of a pattern that—
SYBIL	No, no, what's wrong, what's wrong with me?
DOCTOR WILBUR	I don't know, Sybil, but you and I are going to (figure this out together).
SYBIL	(fearful) You won't hypnotize me, will you? You won't use drugs or put me in a hospital?
DOCTOR WILBUR	No, no of course not. I need you conscious and (alert to—)
SYBIL	I don't want to go to a hospital—
DOCTOR WILBUR	You won't—I promise. We're gonna meet three times a week, more if we have to. Don't worry about money, we'll work that (out later—)

Sybil holds herself close and starts rocking backwards and forwards like a traumatized child.

SYBIL	Oh god, oh dear god. I'm losing my mind.

Doctor Wilbur grabs her arms, stopping the rocking, speaking simply and directly:

DOCTOR WILBUR   No. You're not. Listen to me. You're not losing your mind. This is a beginning. We've begun.

> Sybil meets the Doctor's gaze. For the first time, tears spill from Sybil's eyes and run down her cheeks.

ANALYZING COMPLEX CHARACTERS

The original miniseries of *Sybil* starred Sally Field as the title character. It launched her career as a serious dramatic actress. She was mesmerizing and totally focused on the creation of the several personalities that Sybil possessed.

Judging from this beautifully crafted scene between the doctor and Sybil, the actresses must have worked very hard to create living, breathing, thinking human beings. This is a lengthy scene when you consider that so many films consist of mostly action with spurts of dialogue. This scene is more theatrical in nature and is filled with rapid emotional changes. Both actresses need to be in touch with their emotional lives. These are demanding roles and need to be thoroughly analyzed.

Exercise: Take the scene apart moment by moment to figure out the structure, tonal shifts, and where every change the actress playing Sybil has to play when she switches between herself and Peggy. Count the silences; there are many, especially when the doctor is trying to decide what to do next. Why are Sybil's eyes red when the scene begins? What has happened before the scene starts? She mentions Stan and that he has let her down and pulls out a letter with the word "stupid" scrawled on it in black magic marker. The doctor is trying to understand her but she changes the subject so often, it becomes more and more difficult. The mood in the room is changing from subdued to emotionally charged until Sybil stands up, tears up the letter, and hurls it into the wastebasket. There is a major shift from the red-eyed adult Sybil to a child throwing a tantrum and putting her fists through a pane of glass. All of this behavior happens in less than a page of dialogue.

A number of other exercises will help you develop a deeper understanding of this complex character.

- Write in a narrative form all of the actions, reactions, and other physical and emotional changes that occur.
- The actress playing Sybil has to work with the vocal differences for each of her personalities. Practice the different voices that suit her.
- Write up character profiles to flesh out the different sides of Sybil and the doctor.

- Write a journal of the encounters with Sybil from the doctor's point of view.
- If you are auditioning for the doctor do some research on multiple personality disorders.
- Sybil/Peggy likes to draw with charcoal. Practice drawing the black-and-white sketches that come out of her imagination.

Assignment: Rent *The Three Faces of Eve* and study Joanne Woodward's Oscar-winning performance as a young woman with multiple personalities and their three separate lives.

We shall close this chapter with the method employed by Lynn Redgrave when she is working on a film.

> You have to do a lot of work on your own for a film. You have to be ready to show up and if the light is right (particularly on lower budget films where there always seems to be too short a schedule and no budget) you must be ready. You might not get another chance. How many takes will you get?
>
> I usually make myself a little notebook, start putting pictures in, things, whatever is useful about that character. I can then, on the set, between times go to it just to give myself something to ground myself. I almost always, though I didn't for *Kinsey,* find music that means something to me for the character, because the hardest thing is the hurry up and wait. Maybe the difficult dramatic emotional scene suddenly will get delayed. You're exhausted, it's six P.M., and you are losing the light. But if you've found the music that is your secret, that for some reason brings up that moment that you've got to enter into on ACTION, you're there and so I find these things often by trial and error. It is what turns me on and makes me instantly there. I can also cut out any of that other film stuff that is going on which isn't my business but can be distracting. I have my disk player and listen to it and with certain films I can hang around and chat with people and some I just can't.
>
> With Hannah *(Gods and Monsters)* I couldn't stand around and chat. I would just sort of walk way and just be Hannah. I know when I finished her character, I couldn't get out of my costume for about an hour. I didn't like the idea that I wasn't going to meet her anymore. I didn't want to lose her.

BELIEVE IN YOURSELF

How To Succeed in Business Without Really Trying (music and lyrics by Frank Loesser) ran on Broadway for more than 1,400 performances in the 1960s. The eleven o'clock spot was "I Believe in You," sung by the lead character J. Pierrepont Finch, to his reflection in the restroom mirror. We can remember the thrill of hearing Robert Morse's distinctive phrasing as he proclaimed his belief in himself. As he gazed at his reflection, the "face that somehow I trust," he took stock of his "cool, clear eyes," which indicated a "seeker of wisdom and truth." He knew he was blessed with the "sound of good, solid judgment" whenever he spoke. When his "faith in his fellow man"—substitute "talent rep" here—"all but falls apart, I've but to feel your hand grasping mine and I take heart." Finch possessed what most actors need to embrace: a sense of self, an honest arrogance, and the determination to beat the odds.

A young actress who was also a certified yoga instructor recently overheard a conversation about actors experienced in kung fu, martial arts, and yoga who were auditioning for the ensemble in a major feature. She found out who was casting and called everyone she knew to try to get an audition. She called her commercial agent, who was out of town, then asked the legit agent in the same office to submit her. She e-mailed her qualifications to the agent, who in turn contacted the casting director. The actor had several callbacks, competing against professional dancers and stunt people. Her professional movement experience secured her a place in the ensemble and steady work for seventeen weeks. She believes you have to push to get seen for a part you know you can do and convince the agent to follow up.

Years ago a very gifted young actor auditioned at the Public Theater in New York City for the premiere of Jason Miller's play *That Championship Season* and was told he wasn't old enough for the role. He returned later with makeup, a wig, glasses, and a different name, and read again for the part. He was hired.

An actor felt frustrated that she had no auditions or meetings scheduled and was feeling blue. A fabulous cook, she decided to bake bread, put on her game face, and visit her commercial agents. They were delighted to see her, complained it was a slow period, and introduced her to the hosting agent, who eventually signed her. "Sometimes," the actress said, "you've just got to bake the bread."

Take heart, trust your talent, turn things around, love what you are doing, and go for it.

Adler, Stella. *The Technique of Acting.* New York: Bantam, 1988.

———. *Stella Adler on Ibsen, Strindberg and Chekhov.* Edited by Barry Paris. New York: Knopf, 1999.

Alterman, Glenn. *An Actor's Guide—Making It in New York City.* New York: All worth Press, 2002.

———. *Creating Your Own Monologue.* Second edition. New York: Allworth Press, 2005.

Ball, William. *A Sense of Direction: Some Observations on the Art of Directing.* New York: Drama Book Publishers, 1984.

Belli, Mary Lou, and Dinah Lenney. *Acting for Young Actors: The Ultimate Teen Guide.* New York: Back Stage Books, 2006.

Belli, Mary Lou, and Phil Ramuno. *The Sitcom Career Book.* New York: Back Stage Books, 2004.

Berland, Terry, and Deborah Ouellette. *Breaking Into Commercials: The Complete Guide to Marketing Yourself, Auditioning to Win, and Getting the Job.* Second edition. Los Angeles: Silman-James Press, 2006.

Blumenfeld, Robert. *Accents: A Manual for Actors.* New York: Limelight Editions, 1998. Includes CD.

Caine, Michael. *What's It All About?* New York: Random House, 1992.

Carson, Nancy, with Jacqueline Shannon. *Raising a Star: The Parents' Guide to Helping Kids Break into Theater, Film, Television or Music.* New York: St. Martin's Griffin, 2005.

Chekhov, Michael. *To the Actor.* New York: Routledge, 2002.

Chubbuck, Ivana. *The Power of the Actor.* New York: Gotham Books, 2005.

Clurman, Harold. *The Fervent Years.* Cambridge, MA: Da Capo Press, 1983.

Decina, Rob. *Art of Auditioning for TV.* New York: Allworth Press, 2004.

DeKoven, Lenore. *Changing Direction: A Practical Approach to Directing Actors in Film and Theatre.* Amsterdam: Focal Press (Elsevier), 2006.

Emory, Margaret. *Ask An Agent.* New York: Back Stage Books, 2005.

Gielgud, John. *An Actor and His Time.* New York: Applause Books, 2000.

Hagen, Uta. *A Challenge for the Actor.* New York: Charles Scribner's Sons, 1991.

Hagen, Uta, with Haskel Frankel. *Respect for Acting.* New York: Wiley, 1973.

Hickman, Darryl. *The Unconscious Actor: Out of Control, In Full Command.*

Montecito, California: Small Mountain Press, 2007.

Kondazian, Karen, with Eddie Shapiro. *The Actor's Encyclopedia of Casting Directors, L.A.* Los Angeles: Lone Eagle Press, 2000.

Kerr, Judy. *Acting Is Everything: An Actor's Guidebook for a Successful Career in L.A.* Eleventh edition. Los Angeles: September Publishing, 2006.

Kohlhaas, Karen. *The Monologue Audition.* A Practical Guide for Actors. New York: Limelight Editions, 2002.

Lewis, M. K., and Rosemary R. Lewis. *Your Film Acting Career: How to Break into the Movies & TV & Survive in Hollywood.* Los Angeles: Gorham House, 1997.

Lewis, Robert. *Advice to the Players.* New York: Stein and Day, 1980.

_____. *Slings and Arrows.* New York: Stein and Day, 1984.

_____. *Method or Madness?* New York: Samuel French, 1958.

Meisner, Sanford, and Dennis Longwell. *On Acting.* New York: Random House, 1987.

Merlin, Joanna and Harold Prince. *Auditioning: An Actor-Friendly Guide.* *Vintage New York;* Vintage Edition, 2001.

Morrison, Malcolm. *Classical Acting.* Portsmouth, New Hampshire: Heinemann, 1995.

Moss, Larry. *The Intent to Live: Achieving Your True Potential As an Actor.* New York: Bantam, 2005.

Olivier, Laurence. *Confessions of an Actor.* New York: Simon and Schuster, 1982.

Peterson, Lenka, and Dan O'Connor. *Kids Take the Stage.* Second edition. New York: Back Stage Books, 2006.

Pielmeier, John. *Impassioned Embraces: Pieces of Love and Theatre.* New York: Dramatists Play Service, 1989.

Pugatch, Jason. *Acting Is a Job.* New York: Allworth Press, 2006.

Seff, Richard. *Supporting Player: My Life Upon the Wicked Stage.* New York, Xlibris Corporation, 2006.

Seldes, Marian. *The Bright Lights.* Boston: Houghton Mifflin, 1978.

Schreiber, Terry. *Advanced Techniques for the Actor, Director and Teacher.* Foreword by Edward Norton. New York: Allworth Press, 2005.

Spivak, Alice, with Robert Blumenfeld. *How to Rehearse When There Is No Rehearsal: Acting and the Media.* New York: Limelight Editions, 2007.

Shurtleff, Michael. *Audition!* New York: Walker and Company, New York, 1978.

Tappert, Annette. *The Power of Glamour.* New York: Crown Publishers, 1998.

Witcover, Walt. *Living On Stage. Acting From the Inside Out. A Practical Process.* New York: Back Stage Books, 2004.

Working Actors Guide, L.A. Los Angeles: Aaron Blake Publishers, annual editions.